Sumantra Ghoshal on Management

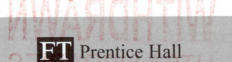

FT Prentice Hall
FINANCIAL TIMES

In an increasingly competitive world, we believe it's quality of thinking that gives you the edge – an idea that opens new doors, a technique that solves a problem, or an insight that simply makes sense of it all. The more you know, the smarter and faster you can go.

That's why we work with the best minds in business and finance to bring cutting-edge thinking and best learning practice to a global market.

Under a range of leading imprints, including *Financial Times Prentice Hall*, we create world-class print publications and electronic products bringing our readers knowledge, skills and understanding, which can be applied whether studying or at work.

To find out more about Pearson Education publications, or tell us about the books you'd like to find, you can visit us at www.pearsoned.co.uk

PEARSON
Education

Sumantra Ghoshal on Management

A force for good

Edited by
Julian Birkinshaw and Gita Piramal

FT Prentice Hall
FINANCIAL TIMES

An imprint of **Pearson Education**

Harlow, England • London • New York • Boston • San Francisco • Toronto
Sydney • Tokyo • Singapore • Hong Kong • Seoul • Taipei • New Delhi
Cape Town • Madrid • Mexico City • Amsterdam • Munich • Paris • Milan

PEARSON EDUCATION LIMITED

Edinburgh Gate
Harlow CM20 2JE
Tel: +44 (0)1279 623623
Fax: +44 (0)1279 431059
Website: www.pearsoned.co.uk

First published in Great Britain in 2005

ISBN-10: 0 273 70183 5
ISBN-13: 978 0 273 70183 5

British Library Cataloguing-in-Publication Data
A catalogue record for this book is available from the British Library

Library of Congress Cataloging-In-Publication Data
Ghoshal, Sumantra.
    Sumantra Ghoshal on management : a force for good / edited by Julian Birkinshaw and
Gita Piramal.
        p. cm.
    Includes bibliographical references and index.
    ISBN 0–273–70183–5
    1. Management. 2. International business enterprises—Management. 3. Organization. 4.
Organizational behavior. I. Birkinshaw, Julian M. II. Piramal, Gita. III. Title.

HD30.5.G55 2005
658—dc22

                                                                              2004060214

10 9 8 7 6 5 4 3
09 08 07 06 05

Typeset in 10.5/13.5pt Sabon by 35
Printed and bound in Great Britain by Biddles Ltd, King's Lynn

The publisher's policy is to use paper manufactured from sustainable forests.

This book is dedicated to Sumantra's family:
Susmita, Ananda and Siddhartha Ghoshal.

Contents

Foreword

We compiled this book in honor of our close friend and colleague, Sumantra Ghoshal, who died suddenly in March 2004. In the months after his death, those close to him at London Business School (LBS), and at many other institutions, thought about the things we could do to remember his life and his ideas. We held memorial events at LBS and at academic conferences, we dedicated a special issue of *The Smart Manager* to Sumantra, and at the time of writing we are in the process of establishing a Chair and a number of scholarships and fellowships in Sumantra's name.

We also wanted to create – through this book – a permanent record of Sumantra's academic work, because we feel strongly that his ideas and insights have the potential to make a lasting impression on the entire field of management research. Of course, his work can already be found in every library and through every electronic database, but as with the work of any prolific writer, it is easy to lose sight of the broader agenda he or she was pursuing when individual papers or books are read in isolation.

By putting this book together, we would like to show that the whole is greater than the sum of the parts. Sumantra did not spend his career obsessed with a single phenomenon; neither did he jump from issue to issue. Rather, his research evolved, with every major project building on insights gained from the previous one, and with certain consistent themes recurring and developing over time. Concepts such as the *differentiated network, the organizational advantage,* and *cooking sweet and sour* formed the backbone of what he and Chris Bartlett called a "Managerial Theory of the Firm." And with careful reading, it is possible to trace these and other ideas back to Sumantra's earliest publications.

One obvious challenge faced by any editor attempting to synthesize the total output of a productive career is choosing what to include and what to leave out. Sumantra's writing was aimed at professionals and academics – two very different audiences. Academics would read his tightly-argued and densely-referenced prose in journals such as the *Academy of*

Management Review. Executives would enjoy his more free-flowing style of writing, packed with illustrations and examples from companies, in journals such as *Harvard Business Review* and *Sloan Management Review*. We considered focusing the book on one or other of these two types of publications, but eventually we decided that both should be included. Why? Because that was the essence of Sumantra's work. He was equally at home with both audiences, and he wanted to make a lasting impact on both theory *and* practice. This does not make the entire book an easy read, but it is an authentic representation of his output.

Our final task in this foreword is to thank those involved in the project. Chris Bartlett, Heike Bruch, Lynda Gratton, Henry Mintzberg and Gita Piramal wrote personal reflections, which are reproduced in the final section of the book. Peter Moran, Janine Nahapiet, Nitin Nohria, and Eleanor Westney all offered their thoughts and help at various stages. Colleagues at LBS, including Costas Markides, Yiorgos Mylonadis, Bjorn Lovas, Don Sull, Michael Jacobides, Freek Vermeulen, Dominic Houlder, Phanish Puranam, and George Yip, were involved in the initial discussions about how best to create a lasting memorial to Sumantra's thinking. Judith O'Connor provided excellent administrative assistance in the preparation of the manuscript. Finally, Jaime Marshall at FT Prentice Hall did a superb job of bringing the whole project together and creating the cover photo.

Julian Birkinshaw
Gita Piramal
January 2005

A force for good: the life and work of Sumantra Ghoshal

Julian Birkinshaw

In the first few years of the twenty-first century, the world of business was in good shape. Most companies had recovered from the collapse of the dotcom sector, and were moving into a new cycle of growth. Consumer confidence had returned, and economic growth was solid. The business press was once again focusing its attention on stories of growth and turnaround, rather than on scandals and bankruptcies.

But for Sumantra Ghoshal, Professor of Strategic and International Management at London Business School, these superficial signs of good health hid an underlying malaise and creeping sclerosis in the world of business. Addressing 500 business leaders gathered at the school's annual Summit in June 2003, he put forward a compelling and heretical point of view. Big business, he argued, has lost its way. Business leaders were rated lower than lawyers in rankings of professional integrity. National governments were passing new regulations to curb the greed of top executives and the opportunistic behavior of individual managers. And economic growth had come at great cost to society through the increasing inequality of rewards and the short-term thinking of corporations. As he observed:

> "Does this loss of legitimacy matter? Yes it does. History teaches a profound lesson. Institutions, no matter what role they actually play in society, lose their influence as well as their effectiveness when they lose their social legitimacy. This is what happened to the institutions of monarchy and aristocracy in nineteenth century Europe. This is what happened to the Church and the State. This is precisely what would happen to companies and management unless the tide of suspicion and distrust is turned."
>
> (Chapter 1, this volume)

Business, Ghoshal argued, should be a force for good in society, but this potential was being squandered.

Perhaps even more surprising, Ghoshal went on to argue that a large part of the fault for this state of affairs lay in the theories and the teachings of business schools. Business schools, he observed, are often faulted for being out of touch with the real world in their reductionist and sterile approach to academic research. But in fact their influence is far greater than they themselves have realized, in their "amoral and pessimistic world view" of the practice of management. Management theories, he argued, have been highly influential, but in ways that have exacerbated the problem, rather than remedy it. Or in his own pithy words: "Bad management theory is destroying good management practice." For the executives and academics listening to Ghoshal's address, the argument was provocative, even heretical. But it was impossible to ignore.

Ghoshal's controversial pronouncements were part of a broader agenda – some might say crusade – to challenge the underpinnings of management thought; to expose, rework and replace the foundation stones on which the entire edifice had been built. The opening chapter in this book, "Towards a good theory of management," spelled out the challenge to business leaders and business schools. Other working papers began to develop important parts of the agenda in more detail. But his untimely death in March 2004 meant that much of the work remained undone. Some parts of the agenda continue to take shape through the work of his co-authors and others who shared his vision. Other parts remain unexplored.

Hence this book, the first collection of Ghoshal's most influential works. In it we aim to highlight the main currents of his thinking, and show how they took shape over the course of his career as an academic and practitioner. Our hope is that by bringing his ideas to a wider audience we will spur their continued development.

We also hope to demonstrate how good ideas and a passion for collaboration can have a profound impact on both academic and business thinking. Ghoshal was fond of arguing that business needs to become a force for good. In this book, we hope to show how *he* had become a force for good in the arena of management thought, and, by extension, a force for good in management practice. We recognize that many do not buy his arguments, and that parts of his agenda will not take shape as he thought; but his challenging and contrarian point of view must not be forgotten.

The problem with management theory

This book begins at the end: with one of Ghoshal's final pieces of work, "Towards a good theory of management" (Chapter 1). In this chapter, Ghoshal took on two sacred cows: the nature of business school research, and the substance of management theory.

Business school research, he argued, should not focus on causal relationships as its mode of inquiry. Such an approach works in the natural sciences, where the behaviour of the particles or organisms under scrutiny is not affected by the ideas of the researcher. What separates social science from other disciplines is *human intentionality* – the ability of the subjects of the research to learn from the past, to adapt their behaviour, and to act in ways they perceive as beneficial to themselves. Conversely, if intentionality is not part of our theorising, then we have misunderstood the nature of the phenomena we are studying.

As for management theory, Ghoshal argued that theories as influential and wide-ranging as transaction cost economics agency theory, population ecology and Michael Porter's "five forces" have influenced management practice for the *worse*. Far from being irrelevant or obscure, such theories have profoundly influenced the behaviour and beliefs of an entire generation of managers. And while these theories have undoubtedly been valuable in many contexts, their overall impact has been debilitating to the practice of management.

Ghoshal ends this paper with statements of exhortation and intention, rather than with actual answers. We need positive theories that address human intentionality, he states, and we need to start with building blocks that have stronger moral foundations. If in fact most people come to work looking for ways to help their customers and their colleagues, rather than shirk or steal, our management theories should reflect such predispositions.

While this paper was the end point of Ghoshal's intellectual journey, its full meaning can only be understood by looking at the entire journey. The bulk of this book, then, describes Ghoshal's 20-year academic odyssey, picking up on his key works, and providing reflections from those close to him along the way.

Part I Managing across borders

After a successful but brief business career in Indian Oil, in 1982 Ghoshal won a scholarship to study at MIT. On completing the requirements for a masters degree, he enrolled in MIT's PhD programme, and subsequently signed up to do a second doctorate at Harvard Business School. He followed the two programs in parallel, and graduated with two doctorates – one on environmental scanning in Korean multinationals (from MIT), the other working on the strategic, organizational, and managerial challenges facing multinational corporations, working with an Associate Professor at Harvard, Chris Bartlett.

It was of course this latter stream of work that launched Ghoshal's career – first the bestselling *Managing Across Borders* (1989) and a stream of articles with Bartlett; and subsequently a number of papers with Nitin Nohria that culminated in their book *The Differentiated Network* (1994). In the current volume, we have reproduced four of these articles. Chapters 2 and 3 are reprinted from two editions of *Sloan Management Review* in 1987, and are essentially a synopsis of the core strategic and organizational arguments in *Managing Across Borders*. Chapter 4 is a theoretical treatment of the multinational corporation as an "inter-organizational network" (all co-authored with Chris Bartlett). Chapter 5 is a co-authored paper with Nitin Nohria that examined some of the alternative organizational forms taken by multinational corporations, depending on their strategic context.

At its heart, *Managing Across Borders* offered a very rich sense of the strategic challenges facing multinational corporation (MNC) managers in an increasingly competitive world. Where competitive success once was possible through a focus on local responsiveness, global integration *or* worldwide learning, the reality for MNCs in the 1980s was that they had to become adept at managing all three forces simultaneously.

But more importantly, and of great relevance given the subsequent direction their work took them, Ghoshal and Bartlett recognized that the formulation of strategy was the easy part. The challenge was not in the analytical process: it lay in the development of an organizational infrastructure, and a management capability, to support that chosen strategy. As they liked to say, MNCs were implementing "third generation strategies through second generation organisations run by first generation managers."

The shift in emphasis from strategy to organization, which took place during the *Managing Across Borders* research, led to the formulation of a stylized model of the large multinational – the Differentiated Network – that formed the centrepiece of their subsequent work. This model had three elements: a decentralized network of affiliate operations (subsidiaries) with sufficient autonomy to pursue their own entrepreneurial initiatives; a linked set of activities and processes in these subsidiaries that created interdependence between them; and an approach to coordination and control that built on the development of social capital and normative integration, rather than on formal rules or top-down decision-making.

None of this appears unusual today, 25 years on, but the enormous success achieved by *Managing Across Borders* is testament to its originality and timeliness as a way of thinking about the MNC. Informed as it was by the practical insights of the executives closest to the action, it offered a powerful way for companies to think through their organizational challenges, and to formulate their strategic priorities.

Moreover, the research also offered new insights for the academic community. As Ghoshal and Bartlett's paper "The multinational corporation as an interorganizational network" (Chapter 4) showed, it was possible to make sense of the MNC from a number of different theoretical points of view. This particular paper adopted the network perspective to model the relationships between operating units in the MNC. But Ghoshal also saw the opportunity to reconcile other bodies of organization theory with contemporary research on MNCs, a project that resulted in an influential book, *Organization Theory and the Multinational Corporation* (Ghoshal and Westney, 1994).

Part II The individualized corporation

The success of *Managing Across Borders* led Ghoshal and Bartlett to embark on an equally ambitious study that resulted in their book *The Individualized Corporation* (1997). Like *Managing Across Borders*, this work built on a series of case studies of highly successful global companies, out of which emerged a set of important insights into the nature of high-performing organizations. Chapters 7 and 8 of the current volume are articles published at the same time as the book, which pick up on some of its major ideas.

The core theme of the individualized corporation was an extension of their observation about third-generation strategies, second-generation organizations, and first-generation managers. Taking the strategic context as more-or-less given, it sought to sketch out the elements of an entirely new way of thinking about management and organization.

In the book, Ghoshal and Bartlett argued that there had been a sea change in the nature of economic activity over the last generation. Industrial companies were built at the turn of the twentieth century on a logic of efficiency and standardization, in which capital was the scarce resource. But in the post-war years, and particularly the last 20 years of the twentieth century, financial capital had become abundant, and the scarce resource had become knowledge, or human capital. While this structural shift in the make-up of the economy had *de facto* occurred, and while a few leading-edge companies had emerged to take advantage of it, most large firms were stuck with the traditional practices and processes that had been developed for the industrial era, some 80 years earlier.

They put forward a new model – one in which the individual employee was the building block, and the organization was designed around them. In direct contrast to the notion of the "organization man" forced into a corporate way of thinking and acting through constraining policies and systems, they described the "individualized corporation" as one in which the organization was built around the ideas and initiative of its empowered and energized people. While there were many aspects to this shift, Ghoshal and Bartlett crystallized it through a memorably simple argument. Where the industrial age model was about strategy, structure, and systems, the new model was about purpose, process, and people. The role of the top executive, in other words, was about setting a purpose for the firm, defining the core processes by which value would be created, and developing and nurturing its people so that they could fulfil their potential. More than controlling strategic content, the key role became one of framing organizational context.

While the individualized corporation and a set of related articles with Chris Bartlett were the major thrust of Ghoshal's work in this era, he was also working on a number of related strands of thought, some of which fed directly into his more recent work. Foremost among these was his work on the pathologies of traditional management theory. "Bad for practice" with Peter Moran, which is Chapter 8 in this book, was the first formal statement of why transaction cost theory, built as it is on assumptions of opportunistic individual behaviour, could end up creating the very behaviours it was designed to curb. Ghoshal also began to examine the broader implications of this line of argument, by showing how most other strands of organization theory either built on negative assumptions about human nature, or viewed managerial discretion as having very little impact on firm performance (Bartlett and Ghoshal, 1993). In fact, he felt that much of the contemporary literature had lost its way, with its undue emphasis on the short-term appropriation of value, and its implicit belief in the primacy of "markets" as the means by which economic activity is best organized. Ghoshal argued instead for the concept of *Organizational Advantage* – how firms were able to build a context for behaviour and a set of shared values that enabled them to combine resources and structure their use in ways that markets never could.

Ghoshal's paper with Henry Mintzberg entitled "Diversifiction and diversifact" (Chapter 9 in this volume) illustrated the concept of organizational advantage. Focusing on the particular case of the diversified firm, they demonstrated the need for a shared context to enable the firm to continue to add value to its operating businesses. This paper also demonstrated the power of a simple metaphor (the spinning top) to explain a complex argument.

What emerged from this stream of research were the first elements of what Ghoshal and Bartlett called a *Managerial Theory of the Firm*. By this, they meant a body of theory that was built on its own intellectual origins, rather than on the negative and sometimes inappropriate assumptions of economics; and one that was built on the actual behaviours and belief systems of executives. Interestingly, this approach harkened back to a much earlier research tradition in management, as exemplified by Chester Barnard, Elton Mayo, and others, whose ideas were typically developed in close collaboration with companies, not at a distance.

Part III The new management agenda

By the mid-1990s, Ghoshal had moved to London Business School, and while continuing to work with Bartlett, he also developed a much broader set of working relationships with others, often doctoral students at London Business School and Insead.

There were several common themes to Ghoshal's research in the period 1995–2004. First, a continued emphasis on the real management agenda facing executives in large firms. Second, a much deeper investigation of the theoretical foundations of social and intellectual capital. And third, a *modus operandi* built around detailed interactive case studies of a small number of leading-edge firms, such as BP, Lufthansa, and Oracle.

His research during this era took place along a number of parallel tracks. One was a continuation of his work with Peter Moran on the nature of the organizational advantage – the essence of the firm that makes it qualitatively different from a market. In their 1997 paper, "Firms, markets and economic development," they showed that organizations allocate resources in fundamentally different ways than markets, and that for economic progress to occur we need plurality – both have to coexist. This paper continued the theme of "Bad for Practice" (Chapter 8), but with broader concern with the relative merits of organizational and market modes of governance.

In a subsequent paper, Janine Nahapiet and Sumantra Ghoshal drilled down even deeper into the nature of the organizational advantage (Chapter 10). They showed how under certain conditions the "social capital" embedded in individual relationships could lead to significant increases in the knowledge base or "intellectual capital" of the firm, in ways that were unlikely to happen in a market-based system of exchange. As they argued in the paper "organizations build and retain their advantage through the dynamic and complex interrelationships between social and intellectual capital." This paper became highly influential in the management field because it was the first to formally link the concepts of social capital and organizational knowledge. It was also another line of argument to support Ghoshal's long-standing interest in demonstrating that firms were qualitatively superior to markets as engines of value creation.

A second track was his work with Heike Bruch on action-taking, human willpower, and organizational energy, ultimately leading to their co-authored book *A Bias For Action* (2004). In a series of engaging articles they looked first at the need for individuals to engage in "purposeful action taking" rather than unfocused busyness (Chapter 13); they subsequently identified the tactics individuals can use to overcome inertia and non-action, and the approaches firms can use to "unleash organizational energy." Central to all this work was the concept of *volition* or willpower – a commitment that arises from a deep personal attachment to a certain intention. Volition is subtly different from motivation, because it suggests the ability to overcome obstacles and short-term disinterest in pursuit of a higher-order goal. For Sumantra and Heike, the critical task of the leader was to harness willpower and create a bias for action among their employees.

A third track was a series of case studies and articles with Lynda Gratton, an expert on human resource management at the London Business School. Their joint work focused on the development of social capital in large organizations, and in the approaches – formal and informal – that top executives could use to improve the quality of collaboration between individuals. The paper reproduced in this volume, "Integrating the Enterprise" (Chapter 12), puts forward a framework to show how integration can be built at multiple levels – through operational, social, intellectual, and emotional mechanisms.

A fourth track was Ghoshal's long-standing interest in improving the performance of businesses in his mother country, India. While building on his established portfolio of ideas and frameworks, this work provided Ghoshal a new challenge, specifically how could he inspire radical and dramatic change in companies that had grown comfortable with what he called *satisfactory underperformance?* This work resulted in a book *Managing Radical Change* co-authored with Gita Piramal and Chris Bartlett, the first chapter of which is reproduced in this volume (Chapter 11). It also spawned a highly successful TV series called "Lessons in Excellence" produced by CNBC India. The book and the TV series were classic Ghoshal: challenging, visionary, idealistic, but positioned in a way that made the argument just about believable to the ambitious manager.

Ghoshal was in the process of pulling together these strands of work in 2004, but his death in March 2004 meant that the synthesis did not happen. He had explicit plans to write a book with Peter Moran, provisionally entitled *A Good Theory of Management*. The first chapter of the current volume would have been the first chapter in this new monograph. Most of the concepts were in place, and some of the writing had been done, but the complete argument was not ready. And Ghoshal would have been the first to admit that the "alternative" theory to the economic arguments that currently dominate management does not yet exist. Elements of this alternative theory are taking shape – the nature of organizational advantage, the creation of social and intellectual capital, the power of volition – but without Ghoshal's central role in pulling them together, they remain fragmented. It is up to his many co-authors, and to the many others inspired by his ideas, to deliver on his enduring vision of a Managerial Theory of the Firm.

Acknowledgments

We are grateful to the following for permission to reproduce copyright material:

Chapter 1 Susmita Ghoshal and Peter Moran.

Chapter 2 Reprinted from Managing Across Borders; The New Strategic Requirements by C.A. Bartlett and S. Ghoshal, *MIT Sloan Management Review*, Summer 1987, by permission of the publisher. Copyright © 1987 by Massachusetts Institute of Technology. All rights reserved.

Chapter 3 Reprinted from Managing Across Borders; The New Organizational Responses by C.A. Bartlett and S. Ghoshal, *MIT Sloan Management Review*, Fall 1987, by permission of the publisher. Copyright © 1987 by Massachusetts Institute of Technology. All rights reserved.

Chapter 4 from ACADEMY OF MANAGEMENT LEARNING & EDUCATION by S GHOSHAL AND C BARTLETT. Copyright 1990 by ACAD OF MGMT. Reproduced with permission of ACAD OF MGMT in the format Trade Book via Copyright Clearance Center.

Chapter 5 from Strategic Management Journal, S. Ghoshal and N. Nohria, 1989. Reproduced by permission of John Wiley & Sons Limited.

Chapter 6 Reprinted from Rebuilding Behavioral Context: Turn Process Reengineering into People Rejuvenation by C.A. Bartlett and S. Ghoshal, *MIT Sloan Management Review*, Fall 1995, by permission of the publisher. Copyright © 1995 by Massachusetts Institute of Technology. All rights reserved.

Chapter 7 Reprinted from Rebuilding Behavioral Context: A Blueprint for Corporate Renewal by S. Ghoshal and C.A. Bartlett, *MIT Sloan Management Review*, Winter 1996, by permission of the publisher. Copyright © 1996 by Massachusetts Institute of Technology. All rights reserved.

Chapter 8 from ACADEMY OF MANAGEMENT REVIEW by J NAHAPIET AND S GHOSHAL. Copyright 1998 by ACAD OF MGMT. Reproduced with permission of ACAD OF MGMT in the format Trade Book via Copyright Clearance Center.

Chapter 9 Copyright © 1994, by The Regents of the University of California. Reprinted from the California Management Review, Vol. 37, No. 1, By permission of The Regents.

Chapter 10 from ACADEMY OF MANAGEMENT REVIEW by S GHOSHAL AND P MORAN. Copyright 1996 by ACAD OF MGMT. Reproduced with permission of ACAD OF MGMT in the format Trade Book via Copyright Clearance Center.

Chapter 12 Reprinted from Integrating the Enterprise by S. Ghoshal and L. Gratton, *MIT Sloan Management Review*, Fall 2002, by permission of the publisher. Copyright © 2002 by Massachusetts Institute of Technology. All rights reserved.

Chapter 13 Reprinted by permission of *Harvard Business Review*. From Beware the Busy Manager: by H. Bruch and S. Ghoshal, February 2002. Copyright © 2002 by the Harvard Business School Publishing Corporation; all rights reserved.

In some instances we have been unable to trace the owners of copyright material, and we would appreciate any information that would enable us to do so.

CHAPTER 1

Towards a good theory of management

Sumantra Ghoshal and Peter Moran

This is one of Sumantra's final papers, and also one of his most ambitious. It builds on many of his earlier papers, especially in its critique of traditional organizational theory, but it pushes the argument further by spelling out the role played by business schools in disseminating "bad" theory. In this paper, Sumantra and Peter Moran argue that many theories – from transaction cost economics to Michael Porter's "five forces" – have influenced management practice for the worse. Far from being irrelevant or obscure, such theories have profoundly influenced the behavior and beliefs of an entire generation of managers. And while these theories have undoubtedly been valuable in many contexts, their overall impact has been debilitating to the practice of management.

This paper was orginally intended to be the opening chapter of the authors' new book, A Good Theory of Management. *While the book was never completed, this paper makes clear their intentions and aspirations. We need positive theories that address human intentionality, they argue, and we need to start with building blocks that have stronger moral foundations.*

Why do companies elicit such powerful love–hate responses? On the one hand, amid the decay of legitimacy and influence of other institutions such as the State, the Church, political parties, and even the family, companies have emerged as the most powerful economic institutions in modern societies. Versatile and creative, they are a prodigious amplifier of human effort, across national and cultural boundaries. It is companies, not abstract economic forces or governments, which create and distribute most of a society's wealth, innovate, trade and raise living standards. As Jane Jacobs and Francis Fukuyama have shown, historically companies have been a pervasive force for civilisation, promoting honesty, trust and respect for obligations and contracts. With the market sphere growing to annex areas such as health and sport, they loom even larger in the lives of individuals. People look to them for community and identity, as well as economic well-being.

At the same time, companies and their managers suffer from a profound social ambivalence. Hero-worshipped by the few, they are deeply distrusted by the many. Public outrage with the scandals at Enron or Worldcom and widespread criticism of soaring executive pay are only the most obvious and the most salient features of this distrust. The roots of suspicion run much deeper, and have been growing for a much longer period of time.

In popular mythology, the corporate manager is Gordon Gecko, the financier who preaches the gospel of greed in Hollywood's *Wall Street*. Dilbert is the best-selling management book. When asked by pollsters to rank professionals by ethical standing, people consistently rate managers the lowest of the low – below even politicians and journalists.

Does this ambivalence matter? Yes, it does. History teaches a profound lesson. Institutions, no matter what role they actually play in society, lose their influence as well as their effectiveness when they lose their social legitimacy. This is what happened to the institutions of monarchy and aristocracy in nineteenth century Europe. This is what happened to the Church and the State. This is precisely what would happen to companies and management unless the tide of suspicion and distrust is turned.

Indeed this is precisely what we are witnessing post-Enron. Worldwide, the debate is not whether companies and managers need to have their wings clipped, but how. The protesters against globalization in Seattle and the managers of the SEC in New York have entirely different starting premises but ironically converging goals.

Some of the measures being contemplated, such as the requirements for greater disclosure and more transparent processes of corporate governance, are obviously needed, but the underlying forces are dangerous. They are dangerous simply because they are based on the fundamental premise that management, left to itself, is evil and that society's primary task is to prevent the exploitation of people by companies. This premise runs the risk of becoming a self-fulfilling prophecy, thereby further damaging the credibility and legitimacy of companies, as institutions, and of management, as a profession.

People are right in their intuition that something is wrong. But this is not because companies or management are inherently harmful or evil. It is because of the narrow, pessimistic and deeply unrealistic assumptions about human nature, about the role of companies in society and about the causes and processes of business success that underlie current management theory and which in practice cause managers to undermine their own profession.

"The ideas of economists and political philosophers, both when they are right and when they are wrong, are more powerful than is commonly understood", wrote Lord Keynes.[1] "Indeed the world is ruled by little else. Practical men, who believe themselves to be quite exempt from any intellectual influences are usually the slaves of some defunct economist . . . It is ideas, not vested interests, which are dangerous for good or evil."

Obsessed though they are with the "real world" and sceptical as most of them are of all theories, managers are no exception to the intellectual slavery of "practical men" to which Keynes referred. Ironically, in their day-to-day actions and choices, the hardest driving of today's managers conform to theories to which the real real world does not correspond. To the extent that conformity is unconscious and the assumptions behind them unrecognized, the theories are self-fulfilling and doubly debilitating.

This background provides the justification for this paper. Kurt Lewin observed that nothing is as practical as a good theory. He had in mind the usefulness of good theory in shaping effective practice. But the obverse is also true: nothing is as dangerous as a bad theory. We believe that bad management theory is at present destroying good management practice. What makes these theories bad is that they rest on an ideological doctrine that is deeply embedded within them in the form of starting assumptions – which, therefore, are exempt from the needs of either face validity or empirical evidence – and these assumptions are both untrue and grotesque. We also believe that the solutions that are being proposed are based on the same theories that lie at the root of the problems and, as a result, they are doomed not only to fail in solving the problems, but are likely to make them much worse. That is why it is time to expose the old, disabling assumptions of existing theories and to replace them with a different and more realistic set of premises which call on managers to act out a more positive role that can release the vast potential still trapped in the old model. In this paper, we sketch the outlines of such a theory that is based on the following three core arguments that define its points of departure from the current doctrine.

First, contrary to popular wisdom, we believe that modern societies are not market economies; they are what Herbert Simon described as organizational economies. In these economies, most of the wealth is created not by the invisible hand of markets, idealized by Adam Smith as arm's length transactions among small and powerless actors that are mediated through the price mechanism, but by the visible hand of coordination in relatively large formal organizations which act as the marshalling yards for society's resources. In organizational economies, companies are not what currently dominant theories see them to be: pale shadows of markets that come into existence as inferior alternatives when markets fail and that are best managed through the logic of market efficiency. Instead, they are the chief actors for creating wealth and advancing economic progress. They exist and prosper because of their ability to create value from a society's endowment of resources in a way that markets, no matter now efficient, cannot. As institutions they follow a logic very different from that of markets, and they are weakened and ultimately fail when managed as if they were markets.

Second, we believe that the prosperity of companies and, therefore, of economies, depends crucially on the quality of their management. In other words, management matters; it matters not just as the key agent for achieving corporate success but also as the main force for economic and social progress. In organizational economies, the interests of the company and those of society do not collide but coexist in a symbiotic manner. There is no inherent conflict between the economic well-being of companies and their serving as a force for good in societies. In organizational economies, management is, or can be, more than a profession; it can be a calling. But, to take on such a role, managers must escape from the quagmire of evasion that they find themselves trapped in, and develop not only an economic but also a moral foundation for their practice. And, given the alignment between corporate and social interests, the economic and moral dimensions of management are not distinct and separate, but both rest on the same set of principles and processes.

And, third, we believe that theory matters. In a practical discipline like management, its normative influence can make it uniquely beneficial or uniquely dangerous. Bad theory and a philosophical vacuum is currently causing managers to subvert their own profession, trapping them in a vicious circle. But there is a choice. When the solution to a recurring problem is always "Try harder," there is usually something wrong with the terms, not the execution. Managers absolutely need a new theory, and a good theory in the sense that it would not only provide an adequate basis for executing the economic dimension of their role but would also create a moral foundation for the profession which the amoral presumptions of current theory have destroyed.

Companies are the engines of economic progress

At one level, any discussion on the economic importance of companies can be accused of being an elaboration of the obvious – a waste of time and an intellectual affront. Anyone, except perhaps those living in the remotest and least developed parts of the world, knows the truth of the premise simply through the experiences of daily life. To millions of people in the world, companies matter because much of their wealth is invested in them both directly, through personal investments, and indirectly, through pension funds, for example. To hundreds of millions, companies matter because, as employees, they derive their livelihoods from companies. And to billions, companies matter because the quality of their lives – indeed their lives themselves – depend on the products and services provided by companies that they use or consume on a daily basis.

And, while some of the entities that provide us with goods and services to consume, or with employment, or with investment opportunities are indeed akin to Adam Smith's baker, brewer and butcher, most are not. Some – like IBM or Unilever or Sony – are giant institutions employing thousands of people. Others, while much smaller, are still significantly larger than an individual entrepreneur or a small family unit. They are formal organizations.

Indeed, it is organizations of this kind that dominate our socio-economic landscape. Their influence in people's everyday lives has grown steadily for two centuries, particularly among the wealthiest and most developed regions of the world. This "ubiquity of organizations" prompted Herbert Simon to question the use of the term "market economy" to describe the structure of our economic institutions. If, as Simon colourfully put it, patterns of global economic activity were illuminated as solid green areas to depict companies and red lines to indicate market transactions, the resulting image would appear more as "large green areas interconnected by red lines" than "a network of red lines connecting green spots." "Wouldn't organizational economy be the more appropriate term?" asked Simon, rhetorically. He also noted that this apparent ubiquity of organizations did not pervade all societies equally. Rather the number and size of companies coincided sharply with the magnitude of market transactions around them. Hence, "in Central Africa, or the more rural portions of China or India, the green areas would be much smaller, and there would be large spaces inhabited by the little black dots we know as families and villages. But the red lines would be fainter and sparser in this case, too, because the black dots would be close to self-sufficiency, and only partially immersed in markets."[2]

This positive association between the prosperity of an economy and the role of companies operating in that economy, noted by Simon in a metaphorical vein, is also confirmed through more systematic analysis. The relationship is robust to many different ways of operationalizing both the prosperity of nations and the size of firms. At the extreme, Figure 1 represents this positive relationship when prosperity is measured simply

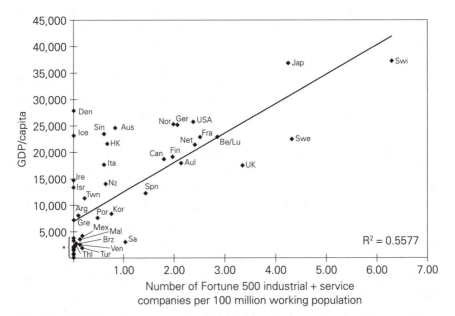

Figure 1 GDP/capita versus number of large companies for 48 countries (1994)

* Hungary
Czech Rep.
Chile
Poland
Peru
Columbia
Russia
Jordan
Philippines
Egypt
Indonesia
China
India

Source: World Economic Forum.

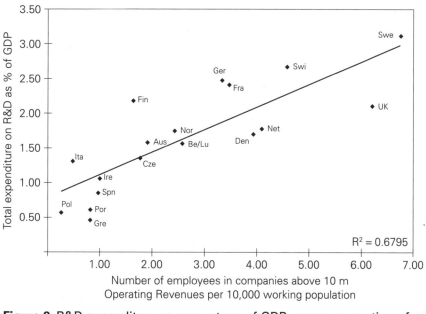

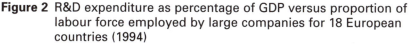

Figure 2 R&D expenditure as percentage of GDP versus proportion of labour force employed by large companies for 18 European countries (1994)

Source: AMADEUS European Companies Database and World Economic Forum.

by the GDP per capita of the country and when we consider only the very largest firms, viz those that find a place in Fortune's list of the 500 largest companies in the world. Figure 2 shows the relationship between R&D expenditure as a percentage of GDP – which is often used as an indicator of economic and technical progress of nations – and the proportion of working population employed by companies earning above US$10 millions in annual revenues. Together, these two aspects of the relationship between the prosperity of nations and the role of relatively large firms operating in those nations rule out the possibility of an entirely accidental association.

While correlation does not imply causation, the observations made by Simon and the associations shown in Figures 1 and 2 reinforce what commonsense already suggests: that the most prosperous and wealthiest regions and nations of the world have the most advanced markets integrally combined with the healthiest and most productive companies. Few would be surprised or take issue with the inference from this strong positive association between the wealth of nations and the relative pro-portion of successful firms operating in those nations, that society and firms coexist and prosper alongside one another.

Although certainly remarkable, there is little that would be controversial in a characterization of our organizational economy as comprising both intensely competitive markets and healthy companies, coexisting in a constant state of vigorous but creative tension with one another. It consists of an evolving state of continuous interaction among companies, on the one hand, creating and realising new value; and markets, on the other hand, relentlessly forcing these same companies to surrender, over time, most of that value to consumers; and, as a result, ensuring that companies never let up their relentless search for new ways to create and realize value, as part of their continuing struggle to remain viable and healthy, and to grow. Indeed, this is the essence of the process of creative destruction that Joseph Schumpeter, the Austrian economist, theorized and wrote about over half a century ago.[3]

If the proposition that companies matter – not just for their investors, employees, and customers but for all members of a society – is so uncontroversial, why do we propose it as a central justification and point of departure for our endeavors? It is because, apparent as the proposition may seem, formal models of economic growth offer little to reflect this process of creative destruction or to suggest any significant role for corporate organizations, much less model the process itself. To be sure, improvements in such models have been significant, as reflected in recent efforts to endogenize some of the proximate sources of growth – like technological advances and human capital – and to incorporate features like proprietary technology, imperfect competition, externalities, and economies of scale. But an explicit acknowledgement of the role of companies, particularly large companies, is still ignored, prompting Richard Nelson to lament: "The new formal models continue in the spirit of the older ones in treating the actions taken by firms as determined by the environment they are in and in ignoring anything like Schumpeter's 'entrepreneurship' or Abramovitz' 'enterprise'."[4]

One of the consequences of this omission of any role of firms in theories of economic progress is that it severely vitiates our understanding of why firms exist. To the extent that an idealized, and oversimplified, model of a market economy largely dominates the macro-framework, the role of firms at the micro-level can only be defined as a departure from the ideal state. Thus, in much of what we now have by way of theories of the firm, the starting points are efficient markets, and companies are only seen as aberrations that come into existence and continue to survive because, under some circumstances, markets fail.

To both practicing managers and management scholars, theory of the firm may appear to be an irrelevance. Why care about why companies exist when we know that they do? Why worry about why New York exists – it just does. What matters to us, they might say, is how to effectively organize and manage companies, not why they exist in the first place.

It is our belief that much of what we call the bad theories of management have come about precisely because we have a bad theory of the firm. Grounded in the market-failure framework, we have built a theoretical infrastructure which views companies as inferior substitutes to the "marvel of the market." This negative framing of the *râison d'être* of the institution, supported neither by any causal argument nor any systematic evidence and justified simply as a matter of analytical convenience, has been the springboard for developing ideas about company strategy, organization, and management that are equally negative. While the logics of these theories may be opaque to most managers, they nevertheless influence and shape management choices – in a manner that is often unconscious. Much of the perversity of corporate management stems directly from this unconscious adherence to theories derived from this negative and erroneous view of the role of companies in society.

When we abandon the oversimplified lens of the market economy and accept instead the reality of the organizational economy, only then can we clearly discern the value-creating role of companies in society and begin our enquiry on why and how they create value.

While beyond the scope of this paper to develop such an enquiry in detail, several strands of the argument can be introduced here. First, the process of value creation can be viewed in terms of the combination and exchange of resources, and it is possible to establish the conditions under which such resource combination and exchange – and, therefore, value creation – becomes viable. As we have demonstrated in our earlier work,[5] while markets create value through their focus on efficiency, they also suffer from significant limitations in making resource combination and exchange viable. In other words, if all we had were markets, no matter how efficient they were, relatively little value would be created from a society's given endowment of resources. Companies, because of the very different institutional context and logic they create within themselves, are able to broaden the conditions of viability and are therefore able to engender resource combination and exchange, i.e., value creation, in a manner that markets cannot.

Second, it is possible to make this theory of value creation more concrete by focusing on one specific resource, viz knowledge. As is now widely acknowledged in both management theory and practice, knowledge is perhaps the most valuable of all resources, both for the overall economy and for individual companies. Again in earlier work, we have used the concept of social capital to show how companies have some distinctive advantages over markets in terms of their capacity for sharing, transferring, synthesizing and creating knowledge.[6]

These ideas suggest that far from being inferior substitutes to markets, companies represent a very different institutional form that creates value through a logic that is very different from the logic of market efficiency. This understanding of the "organizational logic" as different from the "market logic" provides the basis for a new way of thinking about corporate strategy, organization, and leadership.

'Asshole management' is not inevitable

There is a broad consensus that Jack Welch, the recently retired CEO of General Electric, was one of the most effective – if not the most effective – corporate leaders of the twentieth century. In one of the earliest books celebrating Welch's undeniably remarkable achievements, Noel Tichy, a world-renowned management academic, consultant, author, and Welch fan, and Statford Sherman, a business journalist, wrote: "Jack Welch is the best CEO GE has ever had. Jack Welch is an asshole."[7]

Actually, Tichy was recalling a debate among a group of young GE managers around a conference table in Crotonville, the company's management training centre. The statement was meant as a compliment – not that Jack Welch was personally an asshole, but that he knew how to take tough decisions for the good of the company. The debate itself was evidence of the openness and candor that Welch had injected into GE's corporate culture which allowed even junior managers to frankly discuss such an issue.

Yet, Tichy's observation does lead to a broader question. Corporate leadership is increasingly seen as one of initiating and managing change. In an environment of global competition, technological discontinuities, and intense capital market pressures, companies have to continuously renew and transform themselves. Does transformation of ossified organizations and entrenched cultures require a degree of ruthlessness that lies beyond the reach of reasonable people? In that case, is the only role for reasonable men and women in companies to step aside and offer themselves up as self-sacrifice? Must only assholes reach the top of the management ladder?

This is not an idle speculation and it would be a mistake to see only blatant cases of managerial corruption in companies like Enron, Tyco, and Global Crossing as its justification. Worldwide, managers, management academics, consultants, and business journalists are engaged in a debate on how to manage companies better, for the benefit of – what? With the best of intentions, in their search for greater efficiency, speed, and thoroughness, are we all part of an infernal cycle, a profoundly coercive system that is reinforcing the rise of "asshole management?" Are we all collaborating to make both work and leadership, although materially rewarding, a crippling and inhuman experience? Are we all – managers, investors, academics, journalists, consultants – acting as co-conspirators to create a corporate world that can only be led not by Jack Welch, the man, but Jack Welch, the image, personified in men like Scott Paper's "chainsaw" Al Dunlop and Tyco's Dennis Kozlowski?

There is, of course, no novelty in recognizing the dangers of un-principled leadership. We have been amply warned of these dangers through the entire history of humanity and not least in the experiences of the two World Wars in the last hundred years. As a result, we learnt to cherish leadership, with a small "l". In the corporate sector, embarrassed by the scandal of a highly effective leader who also developed the wrong sympathies in the last War, Royal Dutch Shell created a governance system in which no individual could exercise exclusive power. Continental European companies devised complex systems of checks and balances, as did companies in Japan, and even North America. What is new is that we are once again falling in love with Leadership, with a capital "L". In business, we see it rising everywhere, not just in the form of Jack Welch or Andy Grove in the United States, but also in the shape of Bernard Arnault and John Browne in Europe, and Dhirubhai Ambani and Lee Kun Hee in Asia.

And for good reasons. If the fear of the possible negative consequences of forceful leadership were to condemn us forever into foregoing the positive power such leadership can bring to society, we will lose a key engine of both economic and social progress. If, to prevent the rise of another Hitler, we create conditions that would pre-empt the emergence of a Nelson Mandela, it would be no different than eschewing the use of money or credit because they can be used for bad ends.

Nowhere is the need for forceful leadership more salient and more urgent than in companies and, particularly so, in large companies. The weak administrators who inherited the products of Thomas Watson or Anaton Philips' entrepreneurial creations brought both IBM and Philips close to bankruptcy. At the same time, whatever else we may criticize them for, few can deny Michael Eisner's role in revitalizing a tired theme park into a vibrant, global entertainment power house, or that of Jack Welch in enormously enhancing the efficiency with which General Electric uses its very substantial resources. While strong companies can perhaps withstand short periods of weak leadership, in the long term there is no substitute for the invigorating, life-giving force that foresightful, determined, and energetic leaders bring to corporate organizations.

The social concern that follows is how to combine this force with behaviors that most will view as moral or ethical, or, at the very least, as reasonable and, indeed, whether it is at all possible to do so in any systematic way. Howsoever romantic the notion may be, Plato's philosopher kings are not compatible with the capitalist system. Is asshole management, therefore, to be accepted as the lesser evil than weak, bureaucratic, and ineffective leadership, which is its only alternative?

Similarly, the dehumanization of work is not a new complaint. What is new is the enormous pressure that is being created within companies, propelled by a powerful dynamic of competition and reward among investing institutions and corporate managers. The pressure has placed an unprecedented premium on executives who are "unreasonable:" men and women who are ambitious and determined enough to go to extraordinary lengths to fulfil their missions to capital markets. They put it above everything else. That is what boards seek in their CEOs and, in turn what CEOs seek of their subordinates. Such people are celebrated in the business press. Collectively, their traits are bundled into the composite of today's ideal business leader: hard driving, decisive, ruthless, heroic, independent, volitional, male. In other words, an asshole.

Such managers are hugely influential as role models and recruiters in their own image. Yet, they do not exist in isolation. Lower down the organization, ambitious fast trackers remain only too willing to collude in their own dehumanization, in return for the promise that they too will get their turn at the helm. Academics and consultants devise new justifications for unreasonableness and new arguments to keep the treadmill moving faster. The press, too, plays an important part. By identifying companies with their leaders, oversimplifying the determinants of success and hero-worshipping strong, top-down "Leaders", they not only celebrate the asshole model of management, they simultaneously delegitimize those who are unwilling or unable to play by its rules.

Managers themselves justify their actions by pleading powerlessness in the face of external "forces." The capital markets are relentless in their demands, and individual companies and managers have no scope for choice, they claim. Their actions are fully determined because of the constraints of a market system that leaves no space for autonomous behaviors.

Once again, academic theories support this justification of determinism that denies any role of moral or ethical considerations in the practice of management. The theory of principals and agents that now dominates economic analysis of the role of managers sees them as having a single obligation: that of serving as the agents of the shareholders, who are the principals, and therefore having a single goal, viz that of maximizing the returns derived by the principals from their investments in the business. "The only business of business is business," reminds Milton Friedman, and the only social [read moral] responsibility of a business' general manager is to "increase its profit".[8]

It is this theory of determinism that has been the primary cause for the rise of asshole management. It has formally absolved managers of all moral obligations and, to the extent that ultimately all human responsibilities rest on the grounds of motives and morality, it has freed managers from any sense of responsibility for their actions.

If economists have denuded the managerial role of any sense of human responsibilities, theorists of strategy and organization have also done so in their desire to make business studies a branch of the social sciences. Rejecting what they saw as the romanticism of analyzing corporate behaviors in terms of the choices, actions, and achievements of individuals, they have adopted the "scientific" approach of trying to discover patterns and laws, and have replaced all notions of intentionality with a firm belief in causal determinism for explaining all aspects of corporate performance. In effect, they have professed that business is reducible to a kind of physics in which even if individual managers do play a role, it can safely be taken as determined by the economic, social, and psychological laws that inevitably shape their actions.

It is interesting that a confluence of very diverse endeavors – that of economists to make the practice of management amoral, that of strategy and organization theorists to make it scientific, and that of journalists and consultants to make it heroic – have collectively reinforced the rise of asshole management. Both reductionism and exaggeration in theory and explanation have reinforced each other to make practice simultaneously inhumane and irresponsible. Out of this cauldron has emerged the normative order in which all managers today find themselves locked into.

To both the managers and the management academics who profess these beliefs, we refer the words of Sir Isiah Berlin: "One may argue about the degree of difference that the influence of this or that individual made in shaping events. But to try to reduce the behaviors of individuals to that of impersonal 'social forces' not further analyzable into the conduct of the men who . . . make history . . . is a form of 'false consciousness' of bureaucrats and administrators who close their eyes to all that proves incapable of quantification, and thereby perpetrate absurdities in theory and dehumanization in practice."[9]

Asshole management is not inevitable but, to rise above it, management must rise above these absurdities of theory and dehumanization of practice. Both managers and management academics must acknowledge that management matters. It is the managers of a company who influence not only what a company does but also how it does those things, and how well. This premise does not imply a heroic view of management that ascribes to managers all the outcomes of a company's activities. In any company of any size, much that goes on and influences performance depends on the work of non-managers, on circumstances such as the overall economic conditions that lie beyond the control of anyone inside the company including its managers, and on pure luck or chance. Managers are subject to external forces of competition in capital, labor, and product markets and their options are constrained by these forces. Also, in every company of any size, there are internal forces of both evolution and inertia that, at least in the short and even medium term, lie outside of management's control. Yet, despite all these limitations on their influence, managers have great influence. They decide what businesses the company will engage in, the overall business model the company would adopt, the way it will be organized to implement that model, the kind of behaviors that would be encouraged inside the organization, and the efficiency with which particular tasks will be executed.

They have this influence because they have genuine choices. And, if they have choices, they can escape neither the economic nor the social and moral responsibilities of making those choices.

Also, these different dimensions of their responsibilities do not exist in inevitable conflict. If they appear to do so, it is only because of the pernicious effects of the theories of strategy, organization and leadership that have arisen from the fundamentally flawed view about the role of firms in modern economies to which we have referred in the preceding section of this paper.

Consider the example of a theory of strategy that most managers are familiar with – one proposed by Michael Porter of the Harvard Business School.[10] If companies exist only because of market imperfections, then it stands to reason that they would prosper by making markets as imperfect as possible. This is precisely the foundation of Porter's theory of strategy that focuses on how companies can build market power, i.e., imperfections, by developing power over their customers and suppliers, by creating barriers to entry and substitution, and by managing the interactions with their competitors. It is market power that allows a company to appropriate value for itself and prevent others from doing so. The purpose of strategy is to enhance this value-appropriating power of a company, by restricting competition and, thereby, sustaining and enhancing its profits.

The difficulty is that, in this view, the interests of the company are incompatible with those of society. For society, the freer the competition among companies, the better. But for individual firms, the purpose of strategy is to restrict the play of competition to get as much as possible for themselves. To do their jobs, managers must prevent free competition, at the cost of social welfare. The diminishing of social welfare is not just a coincidental by-product of strategy, it is the fundamental objective of profit-seeking firms and therefore, of their managers. Within the intellectual framework of theories that are grounded in a simplistic conceptualisation of the market economy, there is no escape for managers from this conflict between economic goals and their social and moral implications.

As we have argued earlier, there is no such conflict when one adopts the conceptual lens of the organizational economy. Once we acknowledge the coexistence – indeed the symbiotic, mutually reinforcing coexistence – of corporate prosperity and the economic progress of societies, the conflict vanishes. Good economics and moral behavior coexist – the former impossible without the latter, as Adam Smith himself cautioned in his justification for the economic system of capitalism.

Indeed, we would argue that the goal of strategy is value creation, not value appropriation. Acknowledging the constraints of internal and external forces of inertia and evolution does not reduce management to either a mere symbol with no substantive influence on strategy, or a god with unlimited foresight and power over events. Yes, managers face constraints, but they still can guide the evolution of companies towards desired goals. The tired and fruitless debate between strategy as a top-down process of heroic intentionality versus strategy as an ex-post rationalization of chance outcomes and bottom-up explorations dissolves into a new view of strategy as a process of guided evolution, with managers as the guides of the process.

Other implications of this new perspective on management can be pursued. Why, for example, do some companies, including those that are already large, continue to grow while other falter and even disappear? What are the tasks of management in preventing decline and in fostering growth? Viewed through the lens of the theory of the organizational economy, the striving for growth is not a continuous struggle for developing and protecting market power. Instead, it is a process of expanding and accommodating the entrepreneurial judgement of people within a framework of organizational integration that allows individuals to use the accumulated resources of the company in the pursuit of new value creation opportunities.

The organization–employee relationship also needs rethinking. Existing theories of the internal labor market are direct derivatives from the market failure framework and see the employment relationship through that lens. The historical employment relationship, at least in large companies, was based on a contract that we will describe as "employment security for loyalty and obedience" – a master–servant relationship between managers and employees in which employees were told what to do, which they did, in exchange for continuity of employment. This contract, we would argue, protected market imperfections and allowed companies to extract value from their human capital.

At the heart of the new employment relationship lies a view that employees are not "factors of production," as in neo-classical economies, nor "strategic resources," as in much of currently popular management literature, but they are "volunteer investors." Just as shareholders invest financial capital in a company in the expectations of both income and capital growth, similarly employees invest their human capital in a company, with exactly the same expectations. The company's responsibility to employees, therefore, is both to ensure competitive remuneration and to continuously add value to them by enhancing their repertoire of useful knowledge and skills. The employees' obligations, in this new relationship, is to continuously learn, in order to protect and improve their human capital, and to use their expertise and their entrepreneurial capabilities to create new value and thereby improve the company's competitiveness and performance.

As the focus of strategy shifts from value appropriation to value creation, facilitating cooperation among people takes precedence over enforcing compliance, and entrepreneurial initiatives become more valued than obedience. The leader's primary task is redefined from institutionalizing control to embedding trust, from maintaining the status quo to inspiring change. As opposed to being the formulators of strategy, they take on the role of the architects of purpose within the company. Defined in terms of how the company will create value for society, purpose allows strategy, in the form of new and better use of resources, to emerge from within the organization, from the energy and alignment created by the sense of purpose. As opposed to defining the authorities and power of different people over others in the company's hierarchical structure, leaders focus on building the core organizational processes that would enhance the entrepreneurial judgement and volitional action-taking ability of people in the organization, integrate the resources of the organization and make them available for new value creating combinations and exchanges, and create the emotional and moral force that would drive the whole organization into continuously striving for new value creation. From being the builders of systems, leaders transform into the developers of people, adding values to all employees and helping each individual in the organization become the best he or she can be. The leadership doctrine of strategy, structure, systems that is derived from current theories is replaced by a new doctrine focused around purpose, processes and people.

Management theories must be both right and good

Finally, the last of the three premises behind this paper is that theories that relate to the practice of management must be both right and good. This is also undoubtedly the most contentious of our points of departure from current doctrine. Most of our academic colleagues will chafe at the notion that, beyond being right or wrong, theories can also be good or bad. It is a fundamental aspiration of all the sciences to be scrupulously objective and values-free and the social sciences must not be an exception, they will claim. In rejecting our categorization of management theories in normative terms such as good and bad, they are likely to cite David Hume's condemnation of this distinction: "there is no method of reasoning more common, and yet none more blameable than, in philosophical disputes, to endeavor the refutation of any hypothesis, by a pretence of its dangerous consequences to religion and morality."

Our counter to this argument rests on two grounds – one fundamental, rooted in the philosophy of science, and the other pragmatic, based on what existing management theories embody and how they actually influence practice – neither of which disputes the spirit of free inquiry that Hume so ardently believed in. We will present both these arguments in some detail so that even those who disagree with our position will at least be clear about what it is precisely that they disagree with.

The philosophy of science argument draws heavily on Jon Elster's book *Explaining Technical Change*, which provides a very useful way to think about the differences among the different scientific disciplines.[11] First, one must distinguish between the natural sciences and the humanities. Within the natural sciences, there is a need to distinguish the study of inorganic nature, such as physics, and the study of organic nature, such as biology. Within the humanities, similarly, a distinction has clearly emerged between the social sciences, such as economics and psychology, and aesthetic disciplines, such as art. Eschewing for the moment the arguments of those who would classify management as a practicing art, let us accept the more common view and consider management-related theories as part of the social sciences.

His interests limited to the academic concerns of scholarship, Elser has argued that what really differentiates these different fields is neither the methods of inquiry nor the interests they serve but the mode of explanation or theorizing that is appropriate for each. Categorizing such modes as causal, functional, and intentional, Elser demonstrates why for the sciences of organic matter such as physics, the only acceptable mode of explanation is the causal mode. Functional explanations, based on notions such as benefits, evolution, or progress have no role in physics; nor is there any room for intentional explanations, such as those based on some notion of actor imagination or will.

On the other hand, in the sciences of organic matter such as biology, functional theories have the pride of place. All one has to do to explain a particular feature of an organism, or some aspect of its behavior, is to demonstrate that the feature or behavior enhances its reproductive fitness. The reason such functional explanations are adequate, however, lies in the availability of an overarching causal theory – that of natural selection. There can be no role of intentionality within biology – as had been argued by pre-Darwin biologists – as long as the process of evolution is driven by random error or mutation over which the sources of variation or the units of selection have no influence.

The basic building block in the social sciences, the elementary unit of explanation, is individual action guided by some intention. In the presence of such intentionality, functional theories are suspect, except under some special and relatively rare circumstances. Moreover there is no general law in the social sciences comparable to the law of natural selection in biology. But even if there were some overarching selection mechanism as exists in biology, to the extent intentionality is able to influence variation and selection, it would make functional explanations problematic. As Elster explains, intentional adaptation differs from functional adaptation "in that the former can be directed to the distant future, whereas the latter is typically myopic and opportunistic. Intentional beings can employ such strategies as 'one step backward, two steps forward,' which are realized only by accident in biological evolution."

"In the cabinet of horrors of scientific thought," writes Elster, "the biological excesses of many social scientists around the turn of the century have a prominent place." In no area of academic work does this statement apply more forcefully than in the area of management theory. Over the last three decades, functional analysis grounded in an evolutionary perspective has become perhaps the strongest growth area in the explanations for a wide range of business and management related topics: from why firms exist to how their strategy and organization take shape; from processes of technological change to the development of industries and sectors. Most of these theories either ignore or reject the possibility that people, both individually and collectively, are capable of taking action "guided by a goal that is absent, not-yet-realized, merely imagined and represented" in Elster's words – i.e., that people can reject favorable options in the hope of creating even more favorable options later on, and can accept an unfavorable option in order to gain access to a highly favorable option in the future; circumstances under which the iron law of natural selection simply does not hold.

There is, of course, a role for causal and functional theories in the social sciences but it is a role that is necessarily limited by the fact that the behavior they seek to explain is influenced by the imagination and will of actors in addition to all the other forces that drive the behavior of all other matter. Intentions are mental states, and to say that a particular action of an individual was caused by a particular intention is not a causal explanation. Again to quote Elster, "Using causal explanation, we can talk about all there is, including mental phenomena, but we shall not be able to single out mental phenomena from what else there is."

Herein lies the philosophy of science justification for our argument that management theories must be both right and good. Our management theories are overwhelmingly causal. The first requirement of goodness lies in acknowledging the limits of causal analysis of social phenomena and, therefore, in stipulating extreme caution when offering such analysis as aid to practice. Put another way, causal theories of intentional phenomena can be bad for practice even when they are not wrong.

It is this aspect of *badness* that Donald Campbell – the eminent methodologist and champion of scientific methods in social analysis – highlighted when he provided several illustrations of how the application of social theories had led to poor public policy decisions in the United States. Referring to the application of scientific methods for the assessment of public programs he wrote, "If we present our resulting improved truth-claims as though they were definitive achievements comparable to those in the physical sciences, and thus deserving to override ordinary wisdom when they disagree, we can be socially destructive."[12]

Freidrich von Hayek dedicated his entire Nobel Memorial Lecture to this danger posed by scientific pretensions in our social theories. Speaking as an economist and acknowledging that "as a profession we have made a mess of things," he placed the blame on "The pretence of knowledge," which is how he titled his talk.[13] "It seems to me that this failure of economists to guide public policy more successfully is clearly connected with their propensity to imitate as closely as possible the procedures of the brilliantly successful physical sciences." The *badness* in this case, arises from the error of applying causal analysis to social phenomena. Because of the very nature of social phenomena, which Hayek described as "phenomena of organized complexity," the application of scientific methods to such phenomena "are often the most unscientific and, beyond this, in these fields there are definite limits to what we can expect science to achieve."

More recently, Max Bazerman has made a similar argument when he wrote, "behavioral researchers often make unsupportable inferential leaps when we convert descriptive knowledge into advice. Our more analytical colleagues often make the reverse mistake, failing to realize that their false assumptions (typically about rationality) limit the power of their prescriptions."[14]

Management theory at present represents a fairly extreme case of this badness – of the overextension of science and of exaggerated claims based on scientific methods. While management academics are partly to blame for the destructive effects such overextension and exaggeration has had on practice, perhaps a greater share of the guilt must be borne by those including management consultants, journalists, and others who have translated initial ideas and tentative and partial explanations from academic journals to recipes and exhortations to managers, both through the business media and public presentations. Irrespective of how one allocates the guilt among the proponents of such theories, however, what needs to be acknowledged is that often the theories themselves have been bad because of their blindness to the intentional nature of the phenomena and their misapplication of deterministic, causal analysis.

The basic problem remains, however; to apply any form of systematic analysis to social phenomena, the issue of intentionality has to be either included in the analysis or somehow sidestepped. In most causal theories, sidestepping is accomplished by making some assumptions about human nature – assumptions that are often not stated explicitly in the theory but remain implicit, hidden within its causal logic. Our more pragmatic ground for making the distinction between good and bad theories relates to the nature of the assumptions that underlie much of management theory.

Currently influential theories of business and management spread across diverse academic disciplines including psychology, sociology, and economics. Collectively, however, they all share a set of assumptions regarding human nature, the roles of institutions, and the processes of economic, and social progress that are negative, pessimistic, and empirically unsupported, lacking not only in any moral grounding but also in common sense. These negative assumptions are manifest in the strong form of determinism in both ecological and institutional analysis of organizations, in the denial of the possibility of purposeful and goal-directed adaptation in the behavioral theories of the firm, in the focus on value appropriation rather than value creation in most theories of strategy and in the assumptions about shirking, opportunism, and inertia in economic analysis of companies.

In the natural sciences, the assumptions on which a theory is based have only the effect of influencing the theory's conclusions – if the assumptions are wrong, the conclusions are likely to be wrong too. In the social sciences, however, the assumptions of a theory can have some very different effects because of a phenomenon that is technically described as the double-harmeneutic.

Consider any theory in physical science of sub-atomic particles or of the universe. Right or wrong, this theory cannot affect the behavior of those particles or of the universe. For example, a theory that assumes that the sun goes round the earth will not change what the sun actually does. So, if the theory is wrong, the truth is preserved for discovery by someone else.

Social science theories deal with people and their motivations and actions. The difference, with regard to the role of theory, between the sun, or elementary particles, or bees, and people, is that our theories do not (yet at least) affect the behaviors of the sun, or the particle or bees, but they can and often do affect the behavior of people. If a social science theory gains a sufficient level of currency, it becomes self-fulfilling because people start behaving in a manner that is consistent with that theory. A theory that assumes that people can behave opportunistically and draws its conclusions for managing people based on that assumption can enhance opportunistic behavior among people. A theory that assumes that managers cannot be relied upon by shareholders can make managers less reliable.

In other words, negative and pessimistic assumptions of management theory can have and have had an important part to play in how managers think and behave. Much of the pathologies of management practice, as we have asserted earlier in this paper, have arisen precisely from the self-fulfilling nature of these assumptions of management theory.

We must emphasize that this stricture does not in any way relate to what a theory chooses to study or the conclusions it arrives at; we are not suggesting that management theory should not study organizational malpractices or individual pathologies or restrict itself in any way from the spirit of free enquiry. Our accusation of badness relates only to the often unstated assumptions of management theory which, being assumptions, are neither rigorously justified nor empirically validated, and yet influence the social and moral behaviors of people in ways that lie outside of our theorizing. Making these assumptions explicit, subjecting them to the discipline of logical or empirical validation, or simply acknowledging them and their roles in shaping the theory's conclusions would be enough safeguard against these destructive consequences. Our claim for badness rests on the ground that much of the theoretical infrastructure that currently underlies the practice of management does none of these things.

Why are the assumptions about people and organizations systematically pessimistic? Where does the pessimism come from? In his article "The search for paradigms as a hindrance to understanding," Albert Hirschman has traced the source of this pessimism to what he calls a "paradigm-based gloomy vision" that, as the title of his article suggests, he views as a critical barrier to developing an effective understanding of complex social phenomena.[15] Social science paradigms are, and have to be, ideologically motivated. Despite the pretence to be values-free, no social theory can be values-free. As Sir Isiah Berlin argued, anything that needs language for its exposition cannot be values-neutral "because of the particular nexus of descriptive and evaluative concepts which govern the language we use and the thoughts we think."[16] In other words, the ultimate roots of the badness of much of management theory rests essentially on the ideological biases of the academic disciplines that management theorists have increasingly adopted to ply their trade.

Let us illustrate the nature of these ideological biases for one discipline that now occupies perhaps the most prominent role in management theory, viz economics. While no social science discipline makes a stronger claim to objectivity than economics, no domain of the social sciences is more values-laden in both its assumptions and its language than neoclassical economics and all its direct derivatives.

"The closest predecessors for the current members of the economics profession are not scientists such as Albert Einstein or Issac Newton; rather, we economists are more truly the heirs of Thomas Aquinas and Martin Luther," wrote Robert Nelson in *Economics as Religion*. "Economists think that their role in society is to provide technical knowledge to operate the economic system. The members of the economics profession do make important contributions in this regard . . . However, another basic role of economists is to serve as the priesthood of a modern secular religion of economic progress that serves many of the same functions in contemporary society as earlier Christian and other religions did in their time. Economic efficiency has been the greatest source of social legitimacy in the United States for the past century, and economists have been the priesthood defending this core social value in our era."[17]

Robert Nelson is by no means alone in highlighting this ideological – almost religious – nature of economics. Others, such as Donald McCloskey have made the same argument that the values communicated by economic writings are often more important than the research results themselves. "Economics promises objective science but actually delivers a hidden metaphsysics."

Efficiency is perhaps the most central concept in the hidden metaphysics of economics. In Nelson's words: "To fight for efficiency in society would for an economist be to fight for the forces of good and against the forces of evil, much as the Christian priesthood of old had done." It is this focus on efficiency that has allowed economics to neatly sidestep the moral questions on what goals and whose interests any particular efficiency serves. Yet, as Douglass North has so clearly demonstrated, there is in reality no absolute definition of efficiency. What is efficient depends on the initial distribution of rights and obligations; change that distribution and a different efficient solution will emerge. In his words: "As long as transaction costs are positive and large, we have no way by which to define an efficient solution with any real meaning."[18] And as North argues, the transaction costs are not only positive and large; they are growing, particularly in our most economically advanced societies.

Perhaps no derivative of economics is as deeply grounded in ideology as modern finance and the theory of capital markets. "What, then, is truth? A mobile army of metaphors, metonyms, and anthropomorphisms – in short, a sum of human relations which have been enhanced, transposed, and embellished poetically and rhetorically, and which after long use seem firm, canonical, and obligatory to a people: truths are illusions about which one has forgotten." It is with this quotation from Nietzsche that George Frankfurter and Elton McGoun began their much-ignored article "Ideology and the theory of financial economics."[19] In that article they demonstrated with both wit and rigor how "value-impregnated" financial economics is, in general, and the efficient market hypothesis is, in particular, and how this theory has consistently hijacked language in the form of words such as "*fair* competition," "*efficient* markets," and "Shareholder *value*" to yield normative connotations to phenomena of dubious normative merit while all the time protecting an image of being ideology-free in their epistemological rhetoric. For example, as they wrote, "the first use of the word efficient to describe a portfolio selected by an investor is by Markowitz. His definition is purely technical, defined as an optimisation of mean-variance ratio for individuals with quadratic utility of wealth. It is not for us to guess why Markowitz called these collections of assets the 'frontier of efficiency' rather than the quadratic man's choice or any of a score of other names."[20]

Critical analysis has clearly demonstrated how the language of such theories, more than empirical validity, has played a critical part in legitimising their normative role in society. Ideologies take hold by the "efficient drilling of routines into a level of subconsciousness where issues of responsibility will not intrude," to quote Stewart Clegg only slightly out of context.[21] This is precisely the role these theories have played, while all along strenuously adopting the posture of science and denying any role of ideology in their search for truth.

At the same time, our distinction between good and bad theory must not be taken to mean that the normative implications of a theory stands in isolation of its positive merits. A theory must explain and, if it cannot do that, it is not a theory – neither good nor bad. But the trouble with the social sciences typically is that the logic of falsification, which is so very essential for the epistemology of positivism, is very hard to apply with any degree of rigor and ruthlessness in the domain of social theories. Since all theories are, by definition, partial, none can fully explain "a phenomenon of organized complexity" and many different and mutually inconsistent theories explain the same phenomenon, often to very similar extents. As a result, nothing can be weeded out and, ultimately, the choice among the theories falls much more on a scholar's personal preferences than on either the discipline of empirical estimation or on the rigor of formal, deductive logic. It is this ambiguity that, in the social sciences, gives life to the distinction between good and bad theory. A good theory is one that both explains, as well or better than any alternative explanation and, at the same time, induces (as far as we can determine) behaviors and actions of people that lead to better economic, social, and moral outcomes, for them and for society.

Our preferred approach is to build an internally coherent theory, based on a set of assumptions about individual motivations, institutional roles, and economic dynamics of societies that are very different from the existing "paradigm-based gloomy vision." This approach should explain at least as well as the existing model, and yet be as good in terms of its shaping influence on managerial behaviors and, therefore, on the role that companies can play in bringing about economic and social progress – in furthering the "rational reconstruction of society," in James Coleman's terms. Ultimately, we would like to be able to compare and contrast the currently dominant model and the one we argue for, and extrapolate the futures of management as a profession, companies as institutions, and societies as expressions of human aspirations, under each of these two models.

Our goals, in such a comparison, are twofold. There should be enough in this contrast between the two models to serve as food for thought for reflective managers who take the social and moral dimensions of their role seriously, and who would like their companies to serve as a force for good, as well as being economically successful. They really do have a choice and their choice would have a profound influence on the kind of institutions they will leave behind for the generations that follow, and the kind of society that all of us will live in.

Yet, our most important goal is to make an appeal to our academic colleagues who have an interest in the functioning of companies and in the role of management. The ideas we have presented are far from complete, and much more scholarly work is necessary, in terms of both theory development and empirical testing, before it can serve as anything more than food for thought for managers. The nature of the academic process naturally favors building on the existing edifice of theory instead of starting over, on fresh grounds. The currently dominant model has so much commitment vested in it that the temptation of most would be to incrementally adapt this model, if and as necessary, rather than to throw it out and start afresh. Yet we believe that if we have to pursue Coleman's dream, if we are to have an influence in building a better world for the future, adapting the existing model will not get us there. We will feel enormously satisfied if our work can persuade even a few of our colleagues to stop building on management theories that persist with the myth of the market economy and to start afresh by developing alternative theories that acknowledge the reality of the organizational economy.

Note: this piece was written as an early draft intended to serve as the introductory chapter of a book summarizing Sumantra and Peter's work on the theory management, most of which is still in progress.

REFERENCES

1. John Maynard Keynes, 1965. *The General Theory of Employment, Interest and Money*, Harcourt Brace & World.

2. Herbert A. Simon, 1991. "Organizations and Markets," *Journal of Economic Perspectives*, 5 (2): 25–44.

3. Joseph A. Schumpeter, 1934. *The Theory of Economic Development*. Cambridge, MA: Harvard University Press.

4. Richard R. Nelson, 1994. An agenda for Formal Growth Theory. Working Paper no WP-94985. International Institute for Applied Systems Analysis, Luxemburg, Austria: p. 26. See also, R.R. Nelson, 1997. "How new is New Growth Theory?" *Challenge* 40 (5): 29–58.

5. Moran, P. and S. Ghoshal, 1999. "Markets, Firms and the Process of Economic Development," *Academy of Management Review*, Vol 24, no 3.

6. Janine Nahapiet and Sumantra Ghoshal, 1998. "Social capital, intellectual capital and the organizational advantage," *Academy of Management Review*, 23 (2): 242–266.

7. Noel M. Tichy and Stratford Sherman, 1993. *Control Your Destiny or Someone Else Will*. New York: Doubleday, Currency.

8. Milton R. Friedman, 1970. "The Social Responsibility of Business is to Increase Its Profits." *New York Times Magazine*, September 13: 32. *See also* M. Friedman, *Capitalism and Freedom*, Chicago: The University of Chicago Press, 40th Anniversary Edition, 2002.

9. Isaiah Berlin, 2002. *Liberty* (edited by Henry Hardy), Oxford University Press, Oxford, UK: p. 26.

10. Michael E. Porter, 1980. *Competitive Strategy*, New York: Free Press.

11. Jon Elster, 1983, *Explaining Technical Change*, Cambridge University Press: Cambridge, UK.

12. Donald T. Campbell, 1984. "Can we be Scientific in Applied Social Science?" *Evaluation Studies Annual*, 9: 26–48. Reproduced in D.T. Campbell, 1988. *Methodology and Epistemology for Social Science*, The University of Chicago Press, Chicago, IL.

13. Friedrich A. Von Hayek, 1989. "The Pretence of Knowledge," *The American Economic Review*, December: 3–7.

14. Max H. Bazerman, "Fairness, Social Comparison and Irrationality," in J. Keith Murnigham (Ed.) *Social Psychology in Organizations: Advances in Theory and Research*, Prentice Hall, Englewood Cliffs, NJ: pp. 184–203.

15. Albert O. Hirschman, 1970. "The Search for Paradigms as a Hindrance to Understanding," *World Politics*, March.

16. Isaiah Berlin, 2003. *Liberty* (edited by Henry Hardy), Oxford University Press, Oxford, UK: p. 16.

17. Robert H. Nelson, 2001. *Economics as Religion*, The Pennsylvania State University Press, Penn.

18. Douglass North, 1986. "The New Institutional Economics," *Journal of Institutional and Theoretical Economics*, 142: 230–232.

19. George Frankfurter and Elton McGoun, "Ideology and the Theory of Financial Economics," *Journal of Economic Behavior of Organization*, 39 (2): 159–177.

20. Ibid.

21. Stewart R. Clegg, 2002. "Lives in Balance: A Comment on Hinings and Greenwood's 'Disconnects and Consequences in Organization Theory?'" *Administrative Science Quarterly*, 47: 428–441.

PART I

Managing across borders

New concepts and perspectives on the
multinational corporation

CHAPTER 2

Managing across borders:
new strategic requirements

Christopher A. Bartlett and Sumantra Ghoshal

This paper and the next (Chapter 3) present the basic thesis of Chris Bartlett and Sumantra's classic book Managing Across Borders. *It describes the changing business environment facing multinational corporations in the late 1980s. Before then, most multinationals were competing in industries that operated according to a particular set of rules: global economies of scale in consumer electronics, local responsiveness in packaged goods, and worldwide knowledge-sharing in telecommunication equipment. But changing environmental conditions and increasing levels of competition meant that by the late 1980s it was not enough for multinational corporations to deliver on one of these strategic demands (global integration, local responsiveness, worldwide learning). Rather, they had to figure out how to deliver on all three simultaneously: a feat that Chris and Sumantra labelled the* Transnational Solution.

The demands of managing in an international operating environment changed considerably over the past decade. In an increasing number of industries, the benefits of exploiting global economies of scale and scope enhanced the need for integration and coordination of activities. At the same time, volatile exchange rates, industrial policies of host governments, resistance of consumers to standardized global products, and the changing economies of flexible manufacturing technologies increased the value of more nationally responsive differentiated approaches.[1] And with the emergence of competitive battles among a few large firms with comparable resources and skills in global-scale efficiency *and* nationally responsive strategies, the ability to learn – to transfer knowledge and expertise from one part of the organization to others worldwide – became more important in building durable competitive advantage. Managers of multinational companies (MNCs) are now faced with the task of optimizing efficiency, responsiveness, and learning *simultaneously* in their worldwide operations – which suggests new strategic and organizational challenges.

This is the first of two articles that explore this new situation; they are based on a research project that involved extensive discussions with more than 250 managers in nine of the world's largest multinational companies.[2] In this article we will describe the strategic challenges these companies faced because of increasing complexity of environmental demands, and the ways in which they tried to respond to those challenges. Our analysis suggests that, for most MNCs, limited organizational capability (rather than lack of analysis or insight) represents the most critical constraint in responding to new strategic demands. In the follow-up article, we will describe how companies are trying to overcome this constraint by building a very different kind of multinational organization, one that can cope with the increasing complexity of the international environment.

New challenges: mixed responses

The international operations of all the companies we studied were in a state of transition. The 1980s brought new demands and pressures that forced them to question their worldwide strategic approach and to adapt their organizational capabilities. Some seemed to be managing the transitions successfully, others were simply surviving, and a few were encountering major difficulties.

- In the branded packaged goods industry, both Unilever and Procter & Gamble responded to the need for greater scale efficiency and more globally integrated marketing strategies and technology development by providing better coordination and control over their worldwide operations. Kao, the leading Japanese consumer chemicals company, was able to use its formidable technological capabilities, scale-efficient plants, and marketing creativity to score major victories against both these competitors in its home market, yet it was unable to leverage those skills worldwide. Despite significant investments and substantial management effort, the company's internationalization thrust stalled out in the small developing markets of neighboring East Asia.

● Turbulence in the consumer electronics industry led both Philips and Matsushita to make major readjustments over the past decade. Philips made heroic changes to its historically decentralized organization to achieve greater global-scale efficiency. More recently, Matsushita has begun to reconfigure its operations to make them more localized and responsive to host country pressures. But for General Electric, the once-cherished dream of becoming a leading player in the global consumer electronics industry was abandoned in favor of the more modest goal of defending its home-market position in televisions, radios, and other such products, based on an outsourcing strategy.

● Over the past decade, Japan's NEC used the technological changes and political upheaval in the telecommunications switching business to build a strong presence in the global marketplace. In the same period, the Swedish electronics company L.M. Ericsson successfully adapted its strategic approach and realigned its worldwide organization to protect, then build, its global-market position in telecommunications. ITT, meanwhile, floundered in this business. Despite being the second largest supplier of telecommunications equipment in the world in the late 1970s, and the leading company outside the U.S., and despite a staggering investment of over $1 billion in new switching technology, ITT was forced to abandon its attempt to enter the U.S. switching market. And it finally had to sell the crown jewel, its formidable European telecommunications business.

Why was it that some companies fell behind, while others adapted to the changing demands of international industry's competitive environment in the 1980s? The inability of certain businesses within Kao, GE, and ITT to adjust to important new demands is not presented as an example of strategic incompetence or managerial ineptitude. Indeed, all three companies are frequently cited as examples of corporate excellence. To understand the source of their problems, one must first analyze the changes occurring in the international environment, and how they affect each of these companies differently. Then it is important to study how each organization adjusted in order to understand why results have been so different from one company to the next.

Traditional strategic demands

Trying to distill the key strategic tasks in large and complex industries is a hazardous venture but, at the risk of oversimplification, one can make the case that until recently most worldwide industries presented relatively unidimensional strategic requirements. In each industry, a particular set of forces dominated the environment and led to the success of firms that possessed a particular set of corresponding competencies.

Rewarding efficiency in global industries

Bell Laboratories' development of the transistor in 1947 paved the way for global efficiency in the consumer electronics industry. Transistors led to printed circuit boards, and then to integrated circuits, which made mass production feasible by reducing both the amount and skill level of labor required for assembly. The automation of component insertion, in-line testing, materials handling, final assembly, and packaging further reduced manufacturing costs and increased product quality. As a result of all these developments, the efficient scale for production of color televisions went from 50,000 sets per annum in the early 1960s to 500,000 sets by the late 1970s.

Meanwhile, scale economies in R&D and marketing were also increasing. State-of-the-art skills in micromechanics, micro-optics, and electronics could not be supported by revenues from a single market. Funding from global volume was essential to support the breadth and depth of expertise required by the three diverse technologies.

Furthermore, the emergence of giant chain stores caused increasing concentration in distribution channels worldwide and raised the need for marketing economies. The resulting shift in bargaining power from manufacturers to resellers changed the rules of the distribution game. Instead of delivering small lot sizes to single-store operators and recovering fairly large marketing overheads, manufacturers could ship large lot-size deliveries to giant chain outlets, but also had to operate within very low margins. Because these outlets sold on price, manufacturers could no longer rely on knowledgeable store personnel to move their merchandise. To educate the consumer and communicate product benefits, they had to invest heavily in advertising, and this too raised break-even volumes. Finally, local service capability, once an entry barrier to global firms, also became less important as increased product reliability reduced the need for service, and as the development of replaceable service boards practically eliminated the need for skilled service technicians.

According to some industry members, by the late 1970s the new manufacturing, research, and marketing economies meant that a global player in the color TV business needed to produce at least 2.0 or 2.5 million sets annually – forty to fifty times the minimum efficient scale in the early 1960s.

In an environment characterized by incrementally changing technologies, falling transportation and communication costs, relatively low tariffs and other protectionist barriers, and increasing homogenization of national markets, these huge scale economies progressively increased the benefits of global efficiency in the consumer electronics business. The industry gradually assumed the attributes of a classic *global industry* – one in which important characteristics like consumer needs, minimum efficient scale, and context of competitive strategy were defined not by individual national environments, but by the global economy.

Firms like Matsushita were ideally placed to exploit the emerging global-industry demands. Having expanded internationally much later than their American and European counterparts, they were able to capitalize on highly centralized scale-intensive manufacturing and R&D operations, and leverage them through worldwide exports of standardized global products. Such *global strategies* fit the emerging industry characteristics far better than the more tailored country-by-country approach that companies like Philips and GE had been forced to adopt in an earlier era of high trade barriers, differences in consumer preferences, and pretransistor technological and economic characteristics.[3]

Building responsiveness in multinational industries

If global efficiency was the dominant strategic demand in the consumer electronics industry, the consumer packaged goods business represented an interesting contrast. Traditionally, global integration of activities offered this industry few benefits. Instead, national responsiveness appeared to be the key strategic requirement.

In laundry detergents, for example, there was very little scope for standardizing products within Europe, let alone worldwide. As late as 1980, washing machine penetration varied from less than 30 percent of all households in the U.K. to over 85 percent in Germany. Washing practices varied from northern European countries, where "boil washing" had long been standard, to Mediterranean countries, where hand washing in cold water represented an important demand segment. Differences in water hardness, perfume preference, fabric mix, and phosphate legislation made product differentiation from country to country a strategic requirement.

Not only product attributes, but even marketing strategies, had to be responsive to the different conditions in different national markets. Concentration in distribution channels varied greatly – five chains controlled 65 percent of the market in Germany, but no chain controlled even 2 percent of the retail market in neighboring Italy. The possibility of using advertising and promotional tools also varied by market. In Holland, for example, each brand was allowed a maximum number of minutes of commercial television air time per annum, while in Germany the use of coupons, refunds, and similar forms of promotion was virtually blocked by national laws.

Against this strong need for differentiated approaches to each national market, global scale offered few benefits. In R&D, most of the consumer chemicals companies were involved only in formulating the final products; basic research for developing the ingredients was carried out by the chemical manufacturers. Similarly, the relatively simple operations of soap making could be carried out efficiently at a scale that could support a separate plant for all but the smallest markets. In any case, with raw material purchases accounting for 40 to 50 percent of costs, and advertising and marketing accounting for another 20 percent, development and production represented only a modest part of total costs.

This and many other industries with similar characteristics were what we call *multinational industries* – worldwide businesses in which the need for local differentiation made multiple national industry structures flourish. In such an environment, Unilever's *multinational strategy* was a natural fit – the company had a long history of building strong national companies that were sensitive to local needs and opportunities, then allowing them the freedom to manage their local businesses entrepreneurially, with minimal direction from headquarters. It took Procter & Gamble time to learn that transferring the parent company's products and marketing approaches abroad would not guarantee success, but the company was able to adapt. At Kao, subsidiaries were almost totally dependent on efficient, but highly centralized, operations. This proved to be an even less appropriate fit, and prevented the company from responding to the dominant industry requirements.

Exploiting learning in international industries

Unlike the consumer electronics industry, which was dominated by the need for efficiency, or the branded packaged goods industry, where responsiveness was the key strategic task, the telecommunications switching industry traditionally required a more multidimensional strategic capability. Monopoly purchasing in most countries by a government-owned post, telegraph, and telephone authority created a demand for responsiveness – a demand enhanced by the strategic importance almost all governments accord to developing local manufacturers of telecom equipment. Significant scale economies in production, and the need to arrange complex credit facilities for buyers through multinational lending agencies, required global integration and activity coordination. However, the most critical task for the manufacturers of telecom switching equipment was the ability to develop and harness new technologies and to exploit them worldwide. The ability to learn and to appropriate the benefits of learning in multiple national markets differentiated the winners from the losers in this highly complex business.

The historical diffusion of telecommunications switching technologies followed the classic international product cycle described by Vernon.[4] In most cases, new products were developed in one of the advanced Western economies, often because of the powerful research capabilities of AT&T's Bell Labs in North America. Next, they were adopted in other developed countries, typically in European countries first, then in Japan. Once the new technology was understood, and the product design was standardized, companies in the developed nations began to export to countries using earlier-generation products. Exports were usually replaced quickly by local manufacturing in response to host government demands. After the local subsidiary developed adequate understanding of the technology, it was allowed to develop and adapt the product locally, to suit unique attributes of the local markets or to help local vendors. By this time, the next new product – an augmented version based on the same technology, or built on an altogether new technology – would be ready for transfer, and the same cycle would be repeated.

We call industries such as this one, where the key to success lies in one's ability to transfer knowledge (particularly technology) to overseas units and to manage the product life-cycle efficiently and flexibly, *international industries*. This name reflects the importance of the international product cycle that lies at the core of the industry's strategic demands.

Recognizing that its small home market could not support the R&D efforts required to survive, L.M. Ericsson built its strategy around an ability to transfer and adapt its innovative product and process technologies to international markets. Its *international strategy* – sequential diffusion of innovation developed in the home market – fit the industry's requirements much better than ITT's multinational approach or NEC's global posture.

Strategic challenge of the 1980s: transition to transnationality

Our portrayal of these industries' strategic demands in the late 1970s is clearly oversimplified. Different tasks in the value-added chains of the different businesses required different levels of efficiency, responsiveness, and learning capabilities. We have charted what appeared to us to be the "center of gravity" of these activities – the environmental forces that had the most significant impact on the industry's strategic task demands.

In the 1980s, each of these industries underwent some major transitions. In all three, the earlier dominance of a single set of environmental forces was replaced by a much more complex set of environmental forces. Increasingly, firms must respond simultaneously to diverse and often conflicting strategic needs. Today, it is more difficult for a firm to succeed with a relatively unidimensional strategic capability that emphasizes only efficiency, or responsiveness, or learning. To win, it must now achieve all three goals at one time.

Need for multidimensional strategic capabilities

In the consumer electronics industry, the trends of increasing scale economies in manufacturing, R&D, and marketing persisted, and the need for global efficiency, if anything, increased. But the very success of efficient competitors contributed to a counterbalancing set of strategic influences that heightened the need for national differentiation and responsiveness. Most noticeably, host governments reacted strongly when the trickle of imported consumer electronics became a flood that upset their trade balances and threatened local industries. In the United States and Europe, antidumping suits, orderly marketing agreements, and political pressures fragmented the manufacturing operations of global companies by forcing almost all companies to set up local plants.

Consumers also reacted to an overdose of standardized global products by showing a renewed preference for differentiated products; the advent of flexible manufacturing processes fed the trend. Amstrad, the fast-growing British computer and electronics company, got its start by recognizing and responding to this local consumer need. It captured a major share of the high-end audio market in the U.K. by moving away from the standardized, inexpensive "music centers" marketed by the global firms, and offering customers a product more reminiscent of the old "hi-fi" systems. Their product was encased in teak rather than metal cabinets, with a control panel tailor-made to appeal to the British consumers' preferences. Largely because of localized challenges such as Amstrad's, Matsushita has had to reverse its earlier bias toward standardized global designs and place more emphasis on differentiation of products. From fifteen models in its portable audio product range in 1980, the company increased the line to thirty in 1985; it also doubled the number of tape recorder models it produces, while sales per model have declined 60 percent.

The major industry shakeout of the past twenty years has left only a handful of viable competitors, all roughly equivalent in their potential to capture scale economies and develop responsive strategies. In the emerging environment, it is increasingly important for these companies to capture and interpret information, and to use the resulting knowledge and skills on a global basis. The growing sophistication of global competitive strategies means that knowledge gained about a competitor, and skills developed in response to its activities in one market, may be of vital importance for company units elsewhere in the world. Furthermore, with more sophisticated markets worldwide, rapidly changing technology, and shorter product life cycles, rich rewards are accruing to companies that can develop and diffuse successful innovations. In brief, a company's worldwide organizational learning capability is fast becoming an essential strategic asset.

In the branded packaged goods industry, similarly, responsiveness continues to be a critical task, but both efficiency and worldwide learning have become more important. In the detergent business, for example, product standardization has become more and more feasible because of standardization in the washing machine industry. Growing penetration of washing machines has also contributed, as has the increasing share of synthetic textiles, which narrows the differences in washing practices across countries. But the biggest impetus toward globalization has come from the firms themselves. Managers at P&G, Unilever, Henkel, and Colgate faced sharply rising input prices caused by the oil crisis of the mid-1970s, and the simultaneous recession in demand that made passing increased costs on to customers impossible. They found that developing standard brands, formulas, and packages created some economies in the production process. Further savings were made possible by developing common advertising and promotion approaches.

Innovations made jointly by a company's headquarters and a number of national organizations have been the most important instrument for creating standardized products that satisfied the diverse demands of customers at acceptable cost levels. For example, P&G sells a heavy-duty liquid detergent called Tide in the United States, Ariel in Europe, and Cheer in Japan. The product was truly global in its development: It incorporated surfactant technology, developed in the company's international technical coordination group to respond to cold water washing in Japan; water softening technology, developed at the European Technical Center to respond to the hardness of washing water in most European countries; and builder technology, developed in the United States to combat the higher soil content in dirty clothes. At the same time, however, the existence of regional development groups ensured that the detergent satisfied primary requirements of customers in each country. Such successes have stimulated other global competitors, and have broadened the competitive game from one based primarily on national marketing capability to a much more complex one where local responsiveness, global efficiency, and worldwide innovation and learning are all part of the rules.

Similarly, the new digital technology, at one stroke, enhanced the need for efficiency, responsiveness, and learning in the telecommunications switching business. The increasing need for efficiency and integration is driven by soaring R&D costs that can only be supported through global volume and higher scale economies in component production. The magnitude of skills and resources required to create a new digital switch is difficult for most companies to assemble in one organizational unit, and this has made global innovations essential. At the same time, the growing strategic importance of the switch – it is now the core of a country's information infrastructure – has enhanced its importance to national governments, thereby enhancing the need for companies to be responsive to local demands.

These transitions were not unique to the three industries we have described. Many other industries, from heavy earth-moving equipment and automobiles to photocopiers and power tools, have confronted similar environmental changes. In the emerging international environment, there-fore, there are fewer and fewer examples of industries that are pure global, textbook multinational, or classic international. Instead, more and more businesses are being driven by *simultaneous* demands for global efficiency, national responsiveness, and worldwide learning. These are the characteristics of what we call a *transnational industry*.

This is not to suggest that the strategic challenges facing companies in the branded packaged goods business are the same as those confronting global competitors in the consumer electronics industry. The nature, the strength, and the mix of the three broad demands obviously vary widely. But it is true that companies in both these businesses – and many others besides – will find it increasingly difficult to defend a competitive position based on only one dominant capability. They will need to develop their strategy to a point where they can manage efficiency, responsiveness, and learning on a worldwide basis.

Responding to the challenge: toward transnational capabilities

These new demands had a profound impact on all the companies we studied. Firms whose key competencies had previously fit the domin-ant industry requirement found they needed to develop entirely new capabilities. Those whose strategic posture was an industry mismatch in the era of unidimensional strategic demands also faced the challenge of developing multidimensional capabilities. For many, however, there was the incentive of being able to leverage previously inappropriate organizational capabilities.

Companies like Philips, Unilever, and ITT, which had traditionally operated in a multinational strategic mode (with responsiveness as their dominant posture), faced the challenge of developing global efficiency and improving their ability to develop knowledge and skills worldwide and diffuse it throughout the organization. Firms such as Kao, NEC, and Matsushita, on the other hand, had traditionally adopted a global strategic posture with efficiency as their trump card, and confronted the need for more national responsiveness and improved access to worldwide innova-tive resources and stimuli. GE, Procter & Gamble, and L.M. Ericsson had been exponents of the international product cycle model, efficiently transferring domestic innovations and expertise to worldwide operations. They faced the challenge of expanding their capability to create more global innovations while ensuring that their international operations retained the appropriate balance of responsiveness and efficiency.

The organizational constraint

One thing was clear. In all the companies we studied, there was either an explicit or an implicit recognition of the changing strategic task demands we have described. Even in those organizations that were lagging in their adaptation to the new demands, or that had abandoned their attempts to adjust, the issue was not a poor understanding of environmental forces or inappropriate strategic intent. Without exception, they knew *what* they had to do; their difficulties lay in *how* to achieve the necessary changes.

● Kao had been trying unsuccessfully since the late 1960s to establish a foothold in the European and North American markets. Management recognized that a lack of responsiveness to the very different customer preferences and market structures was limiting the company's potential outside Japan. Emulating the practices of Unilever and P&G, the company created regional headquarters in Asia, America, and Europe. It also undertook a personnel development program to upgrade the skills and organizational status of its overseas groups, and to internationalize the perspectives of managers at headquarters.

　　However, functional managers at headquarters – the dominant group in this traditionally centralized company – saw the localization thrust as a signal to become more directly involved in overseas operations. The company failed to develop the national responsiveness it was seeking, since its established processes reinforced the strong direct control of headquarters functional staff and prevented regional and country managers from significantly influencing product development or even local product-market strategies.

● Many GE managers foresaw that superior global efficiency of its Japanese competitors would erode the company's competitive position in the consumer electronics business. It was manifest to them that GE's philosophy of building autonomous mini-GEs in each country had become inappropriate; greater integration and coordination of activities were necessary. Plans were made to develop more globally efficient operations by shifting production to Southeast Asia and developing specialized internal sourcing plants.

　　But, in an organization that had historically considered foreign subsidiaries appendages to a dominant home country operation, the importance and urgency of these plans were lost. It was a case of too little too late, and the company could not reverse the traditional role of international operations as sales outlets dependent on the parent. By this stage, the Japanese competitors had developed insurmountable leads in the battle for low-cost position, and GE had lost the opportunity to develop a global presence.

● Soon after Rand Araskog took over as ITTs chief executive, he committed himself to selling off many of its diverse businesses to provide the resources and management focus that would be necessary to make the company a leader in the emerging battle for domination of global telecommunications. He also recognized that ITT would have to change the way it managed this business. In particular, there was an urgent need to change the company's product development process in response to the emerging digital technology. All but the smallest national subsidiaries of the company had traditionally developed their own products in cooperation with their local post, telegraph, and telephone authorities. While this had generated multiple standards and a plethora of product varieties, the company had reaped considerable political rewards from being able to present a locally designed product to each government.

But the resources and technological capabilities required to develop a digital switch were clearly beyond the ability of any single country unit. At the same time, the trend toward deregulation had reduced the rewards of local differentiation. As a result, integrating the technological capabilities and financial resources of different national entities to design a standard global product had become a strategic imperative.

However, despite its best efforts, ITT management failed to persuade the different national units to cooperate with each other in building a standard switch. Conditioned by a long history of local autonomy, and driven by systems that measured performance on a local basis, national units strongly resisted joint efforts and common standards. Fierce turf protection led to constant duplication of efforts and divergence of specifications; total development costs ballooned to over $1 billion. The biggest problem appeared when the company decided to take the System 12 switch to the U.S. market. In true ITT tradition, the U.S. group asserted its right to develop its own product and launched a major new R&D effort, despite concerns from the company's chief technological officer that they risked developing what he called System 13. After years of effort and hundreds of millions of dollars in additional development costs, the product was still not ready for the market. Ultimately, it was this failure to create an integrated process for global product development that led to ITT's withdrawal from the telecommunications switching business.

The problems these companies faced were not caused by a lack of strategic analysis or insight, but instead by the limitations and biases in their own organizations that prevented the development of required strategic competencies. While the consequences were somewhat extreme in their cases, all the other companies we surveyed faced basically the same kind of organizational constraints in developing the multidimensional strategic capability that the environment of the 1980s required.

The critical role of administrative heritage

Managers of all these companies have since learned that while strategic plans can be scrapped and redrawn overnight, a company's organizational capability is much more durable and difficult to restructure. There is no such thing as a zero-based organization. A company's organizational capability develops over many years and is tied to a number of attributes: a configuration of organizational assets and capabilities that are built up over decades; a distribution of managerial responsibilities and influence that cannot be shifted quickly; and an ongoing set of relationships that endure long after any structural change has been made. Collectively, these factors constitute a company's *administrative heritage*. It can be, at the same time, one of the company's greatest assets – the underlying source of its key competencies – and also one of its most significant liabilities, since it resists change and thereby prevents realignment or broadening of strategic capabilities.

A company's administrative heritage is shaped by many factors. Strong leaders often leave indelible impressions on their organizations, as Kenosuke Matsushita has in the company that bears his name, and as Harold Geneen has in a company that still reflects his philosophies.

● Geneen is best known for strengthening the corporate controller's function in ITT, but he also built up a strong tradition that headquarters managers could not interfere with either the strategic autonomy or the day-to-day operating decisions of national management in subsidiaries. He resisted the development of a central research function in the telecommunications business, and instead ensured that the national units controlled almost all the key resources and technological expertise of the company. He also placed the strongest managers in different national units, and held them fully accountable for their performance. This led to a distribution of resources and power that was strongly biased in favor of the area organization at the cost of central functional and business management. It was this administrative heritage that resisted subsequent efforts to achieve global integration.

Home country culture and social systems also have significant influences on a company's administrative heritage. For example, the more important roles that owners and bankers play in corporate-level decision making in many European companies led to an internal culture quite different from that of their American counterparts. These companies tended to emphasize personal relationships rather than formal structures, and financial controls rather than coordination of technical or operational detail.[5] This management style led companies like Unilever to develop highly autonomous national subsidiaries that were managed like a portfolio of offshore investments, rather than like a single worldwide business. In contrast, Japanese cultural norms that emphasized group decision making and commitment to long-term welfare of employees led to highly centralized management processes that resisted the growth in the resources and influence of foreign units.[6]

● Decision-making processes based on *nemawashi* and *ringi* require close face-to-face contact among participating managers. These processes lay at the core of Kao's management systems and obstructed management's efforts to give foreign subsidiaries greater access, legitimacy, and influence. Further, a commitment to maintain and increase domestic employment impeded the company's ability to expand the activities and resources of the offshore units.

Finally, the internationalization history of a firm also influences its administrative heritage.[7] Expanding in the pre-Second World War period of rising tariffs and discriminatory legislation, many European companies were forced to transfer most value-adding activities to their foreign subsidiaries. High tariff barriers in the 1920s and 1930s forced Philips to decentralize not only assembly but even component production; the dangers of German occupation of Holland led to decentralization of R&D; and, finally, the postwar boom further strengthened the roots of decentralization, since the war-ravished headquarters did not have the capability to coordinate the company's rapidly growing international operations. Japanese companies faced quite the opposite situation. Making their main international thrust in the 1970s – the era of falling tariffs and transport costs, and increasing homogenization of national markets – their centrally controlled, export-based internationalization strategy represented a perfect fit with the external environment, besides being consistent with their own cultural norms and internal management processes. American companies, many of which enjoyed their fastest international expansion in the 1950s and 1960s, grew primarily on the strength of new technologies and management processes that they had developed during the war.[8] The creation of new products and technologies at home, and their exploitation abroad, became the core of internationalization strategies.

● While delegating most application engineering, manufacturing, sourcing, and marketing responsibilities to its foreign subsidiaries, GE kept basic research tightly centralized at home. The assumption was that a domestic operation could create new products that would then be available to foreign units for adoption and adaptation. This parent-company-as-leader mentality proved a major impediment to building a worldwide manufacturing function. It compromised the willingness of the U.S. company to rely on offshore sources, and kept it from recognizing the need to tap into the multiple centers of technological excellence that had emerged in different parts of the world.

In developing the capabilities required to cope with the complex demands of transnational industries, each of the companies we studied was confronted with the limiting constraints of its administrative heritage. Yet such limitations were not always immediately recognized. The more normal approach was to respond to new demands by emulating those competitors that were most successful in dealing with the situation. Philips's initial reaction to the growing competitive challenge from Japan was to pull product decisions and sourcing control to headquarters. This step was intended to replicate (and, therefore, enable Philips to compete with) companies like Matsushita, whose global efficiency was dependent on standardized products and centralized production. Meanwhile, managers at Matsushita were extremely aware of the growing need for responsiveness, and launched a localization program aimed at enhancing the self-sufficiency and entrepreneurship of the worldwide subsidiary companies – attributes of Philips's national organizations that were greatly admired and envied in Osaka.

Initially, both approaches not only failed, but also had unfortunate consequences, primarily because they did not take into account the powerful administrative heritage of the organization that had to implement the changes. At Philips, the national subsidiaries were not only the main sources of international knowledge and skill, but also the entrepreneurial spark plugs that fired many strategic initiatives. Denying their traditional roles and diminishing their influence damaged their motivation and deprived corporate management of the benefits of their considerable resources. Instead of improving global efficiency, the action jeopardized the company's key organizational asset. Philips has since recognized that, while global efficiency has to be achieved, it must be done in a way that is consistent with its administrative heritage and that protects and indeed builds on the formidable strengths of its national organizations. Facing limited success in its localization program, Matsushita has also learned that the way to build national responsiveness is not to weaken central management, but to leverage the strengths of its centralized and culture-bound systems.

Philips and Matsushita (and many of the other companies we studied) eventually recognized the importance of both harnessing and offsetting the powerful influence of their administrative heritage as they adapted to new strategic demands. (In the companion article, we will describe some of the ways in which these companies were able to do so.) In con-strast, as the earlier examples showed, the companies that were slow to adapt to the new environment never seemed to recognize the importance of their administrative heritage, and were therefore unable to leverage its strengths while counterbalancing its limitations.

Organizational capability as key competence

The ability of a company to survive and succeed in today's turbulent international environment depends on two factors: The fit between its strategic posture and the dominant industry characteristics, and its ability to adapt that posture to the multidimensional task demands shaping the current competitive environment. Kao's inability to succeed internationally stemmed from a poor fit between its centralized scale and technology-driven strategy in an industry that demanded a more differentiated and market-responsive approach. ITT's problems, on the other hand, were due more to an inability to adapt strongly focused organizational norms and behaviors, shaped by its unique administrative heritage, to the fast-changing, multidimensional demands of today's telecommunications industry. And GE experienced both fit and adaptation problems.

Despite the very different tasks facing the other companies in our study, in broad terms they are all moving toward a common goal, though from diverse directions. In the terminology we have adopted, they are making the transition from being multinational, international, or global companies to being transnational corporations. Obviously, these companies are not adopting a common strategy – the differences in their industry characteristics and administrative heritages prevent that. Indeed, neither a particular competitive posture nor a specific organizational form characterizes these companies. What *is* emerging as common to all of them is a new set of beliefs about managing across borders.[9] Fundamental to this new mentality is the awareness of the importance of administrative heritage both as an asset to protect and as a constraint to overcome. To respond to the complexity, diversity, and dynamism of the external environment, and to build the multidimensional strategic postures that are required, each of these companies has to overcome the unidimensional bias shaped by its administrative heritage. To become a transnational, each must build a multidimensional organization capable of developing new strategic competences while protecting the existing strengths. What are the key attributes of such an organization? How can managers develop those attributes? How should such an organization be managed once it is built? These are some of the questions that we will address in the following article.

Christopher A. Bartlett is Associate Professor of Business Administration at the Graduate School of Business Administration, Harvard University. Dr. Bartlett holds the B. Econ. degree from the University of Queensland, Australia, and the M.B.A. and D.B.A. degrees from Harvard University. Prior to his academic career, Dr. Bartlett had extensive management experience in Alcoa, McKinsey and Co., and Baxter Travenol, where he was general manager of the French subsidiary. His research has focused on the strategic and organizational problems facing multinationals.

This article appeared in *Sloan Management Review*, Summer 1987.

REFERENCES

1. The tension between the strategic requirement for integration and differentiation has a long intellectual history, but is perhaps best captured in the classic Lawrence and Lorsch study [P. Lawrence and J. Lorsch, *Organization and Environment* (Boston: Harvard Business School Press, 1967)]. Their differentiation-integration framework was first applied to the international organization task by Prahalad [C.K. Prahalad, "The Strategic Process in a Multinational Corporation" (Boston: unpublished doctoral dissertation, Harvard Graduate School of Business Administration, 1976)], and subsequently adapted by others, including Doz and Bartlett [see Y. Doz, *National Policies and Multinational Strategic Management* (New York: Praeger, 1979)]; and [C.A. Bartlett, "Multinational Structural

Evolution: The Changing Decision Environment" (Boston: unpublished doctoral dissertation, Harvard Graduate School of Business Administration, 1979)].

2. This research project consisted of three phases. The first aimed at identifying and describing the key challenges faced by managers of worldwide companies and documenting "leading practice" in coping with these challenges. That was also the hypothesis-generating phase, and the sample was selected to represent the greatest variety of strategic and organizational situations. In the consumer electronics industry, globalization offered the greatest benefits; in the consumer packaged products business, the forces of national responsiveness were especially strong; and in the telecommunications switching industry, both global and local forces were very important. Within each industry, we selected a group of firms that represented the greatest variety of administrative heritages, including differences in nationality, internationalization history, and corporate culture. The research sites we chose were Philips, Matsushita, and GE in consumer electronics, Kao, Procter & Gamble, and Unilever in consumer chemicals, and ITT, NEC, and L.M. Ericsson in telecommunications switching.

In each of these companies, we interviewed a great many managers in the corporate headquarters and also in a number of national organizations in the U.S., Brazil, U.K., Germany, France, Italy, Taiwan, Singapore, Japan, and Australia. In addition, we studied company documents, and also collected information about the industries and the companies from a range of external sources. This two-article series is written primarily on the basis of data collected in this first phase of the project.

In the next stage, we conducted detailed questionnaire surveys in three of these nine companies. The principal objective of the survey was to carry out a preliminary test of some hypotheses generated during the first phase of clinical research, to define the hypotheses more precisely, and to develop suitable instruments for testing them more rigorously. Approximately 100 managers each from NEC, Matsushita, and Philips participated in the survey.

Finally, in the third phase of the study, the hypotheses were tested through a large-sample mailed questionnaire survey that yielded data on 720 cases of headquarters-subsidiary relations in sixty-six of the largest U.S. and European multinational corporations.

The overall findings of the project are being reported in our forthcoming book, tentatively entitled *Managing across Borders: The Transnational Solution*, to be published by the Harvard Business School Press.

3. The term "global," applied to industries, companies, and strategies, has been subject to widely differing definition and usage. For further discussion, see M.E. Porter, "Competition in Global Industries: A Conceptual Framework," in M.E. Porter, ed., *Competition in Global Industries* (Boston: Harvard Business School Press, 1986). We will use the term *global strategy* in its purest sense – one that defines product, manufacturing scale, technology, sourcing patterns, and competitive strategy on the assumption of a unified world market. It is the classic standardized product exported from a centralized global-scale plant and distributed according to a centrally managed global strategy.

4. See R. Vernon, "International Investment and International Trade in the Product Cycle," *Quarterly Journal of Economics*, May 1966, pp. 190–207.

5. The internationalization processes and accompanying organizational attributes of many European multinationals have been described by L.G. Franko, *The European Multinationals* (Stanford, CA: Graylock, 1976).

6. For a detailed discussion of the management process in Japanese firms and their impact on strategy, see M.Y. Yoshino, *Japan's Managerial System: Tradition and Innovation* (Cambridge: MIT Press, 1968).

7.   Readers with a particular interest in the history of international business will find a far richer historical analysis in A.D. Chandler, "The Evolution of Modern Global Enterprise," in *Competition in Global Industries*, ed. M.E. Porter (Boston: Harvard Business School Press, 1986).

8.   Documenting the postwar expansion of U.S.-based companies, Jean Jacques Servan-Schreiber attributed the Americans' success to their technological and managerial abilities. See J.J. Servan-Schreiber, *The American Challenge* (New York: Atheneum, 1968).

9.   The issue of a management mind-set being critical to the task of managing MNCs was highlighted almost two decades ago by Perlmutter. See H.V. Perlmutter, "The Tortuous Evolution of the Multinational Corporation," *Columbia Journal of World Business*, January-February 1969, pp. 9–18.

CHAPTER 3

Managing across borders: new organizational responses

Christopher A. Bartlett and Sumantra Ghoshal

T*he previous chapter identified the key strategic challenge facing multinational corporations in the late 1980s: the need to deliver on the demands for global integration, local responsiveness and world-wide learning simultaneously. Here Chris and Sumantra consider the* Transnational Solution. *Rather than focusing on changes to the organization structure, the Transnational involves simultaneous attention to the firm's structures, systems* and *culture. Ultimately, the authors argue, the solution is about creating "a matrix in the mind of the manager" so he or she can act accordingly to the overall objectives of the firm, rather than according to the narrow interests of a single country, function, or business unit.*

In a companion article (Summer 1987), we described how recent changes in the international operating environment have forced companies to optimize *efficiency, responsiveness*, and *learning* simultaneously in their worldwide operations. To companies that previously concentrated on developing and managing one of these capabilities, this new challenge implied not only a total strategic reorientation but a major change in organizational capability, as well.

Implementing such a complex, three-pronged strategic objective would be difficult under any circumstances, but in a worldwide company the task is complicated even further. The very act of "going international" multiplies a company's organizational complexity. Typically, doing so requires adding a third dimension to the existing business- and function-oriented management structure. It is difficult enough balancing product divisions that bring efficiency and focus to domestic product-market strategies with corporate staffs whose functional expertise allows them to play an important counterbalance and control role. The thought of adding capable, geographically oriented management – and maintaining a three-way balance of organizational perspectives and capabilities among product, function, and area – is intimidating to most managers. The difficulty is increased because the resolution of tensions among product, function, and area managers must be accomplished in an organization whose operating units are often divided by distance and time and whose key members are separated by culture and language.

From unidimensional to multidimensional capabilities

Faced with the task of building multiple strategic capabilities in highly complex organizations, managers in almost every company we studied made the simplifying assumption that they were faced with a series of dichotomous choices.[1] They discussed the relative merits of pursuing a strategy of national responsiveness as opposed to one based on global integration; they considered whether key assets and resources should be centralized or decentralized; and they debated the need for strong central control versus greater subsidiary autonomy. How a company resolved these dilemmas typically reflected influences exerted and choices made during its historical development. In telecommunications, ITT's need to develop an organization responsive to national political demands and local specification differences was as important to its survival in the pre- and post-World War II era as was NEC's need to build its highly centralized technological manufacturing and marketing skills and resources in order to expand abroad in the same industry in the 1960s and 1970s.

When new competitive challenges emerged, however, such unidimensional biases became strategically limiting. As ITT demonstrated by its outstanding historic success and NEC showed by its more delayed international expansion, strong *geographic management* is essential for development of dispersed responsiveness. Geographic management allows worldwide companies to sense, analyze, and respond to the needs of different national markets.

Effective competitors also need to build strong *business management* with global product responsibilities if they are to achieve global efficiency and integration. These managers act as champions of manufacturing rationalization, product standardization, and low-cost global sourcing. (As the telecommunications switching industry globalized, NEC's organizational capability in this area gave it a major competitive advantage.) Unencumbered by either territorial or functional loyalties, central product groups remain sensitive to overall competitive issues and become agents to facilitate changes that, though painful, are necessary for competitive viability.

Finally, a strong, worldwide *functional management* allows an organization to build and transfer its core competencies – a capability vital to worldwide learning. Links between functional managers allow the company to accumulate specialized knowledge and skills and to apply them wherever they are required in the worldwide operations. Functional management acts as the repository of organizational learning and as the prime mover for its consolidation and circulation within the company. It was for want of a strongly linked research and technical function across subsidiaries that ITT failed in its attempt to coordinate the development and diffusion of its System 12 digital switch.

Thus, to respond to the needs for efficiency, responsiveness, and learning *simultaneously*, the company must develop a multidimensional organization in which the effectiveness of each management group is maintained *and* in which each group is prevented from dominating the others. As we saw in company after company, the most difficult challenge for managers trying to respond to broad, emerging strategic demands was to develop the new elements of multidimensional organization without eroding the effectiveness of their current unidimensional capability.

Overcoming simplifying assumptions

For all nine companies at the core of our study, the challenge of breaking down biases and building a truly multidimensional organization proved difficult. Behind the pervasive either/or mentality that led to the development of unidimensional capabilities, we identified three simplifying assumptions that blocked the necessary organizational development. The need to reduce organizational and strategic complexity has made these assumptions almost universal in worldwide companies, regardless of industry, national origin, or management culture.

● There is a widespread, often implicit assumption that roles of different organizational units are uniform and symmetrical; different businesses should be managed in the same way, as should different functions and national operations.

- Most companies, some consciously, most unconsciously, create internal interunit relationships on clear patterns of dependence or independence, on the assumption that such relationships *should* be clear and unambiguous.

- Finally, there is the assumption that one of corporate management's principal tasks is to institutionalize clearly understood mechanisms for decision making and to implement simple means of exercising control.

Those companies most successful in developing truly multidimensional organizations were the ones that challenged these assumptions and replaced them with some very different attitudes and norms. Instead of treating different businesses, functions, and subsidiaries similarly, they systematically *differentiated* tasks and responsibilities. Instead of seeking organizational clarity by basing relationships on dependence or independence, they built and managed *interdependence* among the different units of the companies. And instead of considering control their key task, corporate managers searched for complex mechanisms to *coordinate and coopt* the differentiated and interdependent organizational units into sharing a vision of the company's strategic tasks. These are the central organizational characteristics of what we described in the earlier article as transnational corporations – those most effective in managing across borders in today's environment of intense competition and rapid, often discontinuous change.

From symmetry to differentiation

Like many other companies we studied, Unilever built its international operations under an implicit assumption of organizational symmetry. Managers of diverse local operating companies in products ranging from packaged foods to chemicals and detergents all reported to strongly independent national managers, who in turn reported through regional directors to the board. In the post-World War II era, the company began to recognize a need to supplement this geographically dominated structure with an organizational ability to capture potential economies and to transfer learning across national boundaries. To meet this need, a few product-coordination groups were formed at the corporate center. But the assumption of organizational symmetry ensured that all businesses were similarly managed, and the number of coordination groups grew from three in 1962 to six in 1969 and to ten by 1977.

By the mid-1970s, however, the entrenched organizational symmetry was being threatened. Global economic disruption caused by the oil crisis dramatically highlighted the very substantial differences in the company's businesses and markets and forced management to recognize the need to differentiate its organizational structures and administrative processes. While standardization, coordination, and integration paid high dividends in the chemical and detergent businesses, for example, important differences in local tastes and national cultures impeded the same degree of coordination in foods. As a result, the roles, responsibilities, and powers of the central product-coordination groups eventually began to diverge as the company tried to shake off the constraint of the symmetry assumption.

But as Unilever tackled the challenge of managing some businesses in a more globally coordinated manner, it was confronted with the question of what to coordinate. Historically, the company's philosophy of decentralized capabilities and delegated responsibilities resulted in most national subsidiaries' becoming fully integrated, self-sufficient operations. While they were free to draw on product technology, manufacturing capabilities, and marketing expertise developed at the center, they were not required to do so, and most units chose to develop, manufacture, and market products as they thought appropriate. Thus functions, too, tended to be managed symmetrically.

Over time, decentralization of all functional responsibilities became increasingly difficult to support. In the 1970s, for example, when archcompetitor Procter & Gamble's subsidiaries were launching a new generation of laundry detergents based on the rape seed formula created by the parent company, most of Unilever's national detergent companies responded with their own products. The cost of developing thirteen different formulations was extremely high, and management soon recognized that not one was as good as P&G's centrally developed product. For the sake of cost control and competitive effectiveness, Unilever had to break with tradition and begin centralizing European product development. The company has since created a system in which central coordination is more normal, although very different for different functions such as basic research, product development, manufacturing, marketing, and sales.

Just as they saw the need to change symmetrical structures and homogeneous processes imposed on different businesses and functions, most companies we observed eventually recognized the importance of differentiating the management of diverse geographic operations. Despite the fact that various national subsidiaries operated with very different external environments and internal constraints, they all traditionally reported through the same channels, operated under similar planning and control systems, and worked under a set of common and generalized mandates.

Increasingly, however, managers recognized that such symmetrical treatment can constrain strategic capabilities. At Unilever, for example, it became clear that Europe's highly competitive markets and closely linked economies meant that its operating companies in that region required more coordination and control than those in, say, Latin America. Little by little, management increased the product-coordination groups' role in Europe until they had direct line responsibility for all operating companies in their businesses. Elsewhere, however, national management maintained its historic line management role, and product coordinators acted only as advisers. Unilever has thus moved in sequence from a symmetrical organization to a much more differentiated one: differentiating by product, then by function, and finally by geography.

Recently, within Europe, differentiation by national units has proceeded even further. Operations in "key countries" such as France, Germany, and the United Kingdom are allowed to retain considerably more autonomy than those in "receiver countries" such as Switzerland, Sweden, Holland, and Denmark. While the company's overall commitment to decentralization is maintained, "receiver countries" have gradually become more dependent on the center for direction and support, particularly in the areas of product development and competitive strategy.

Figure 1 is a schematic representation of the different ways in which Unilever manages its diverse businesses, functions, and markets.[2] The vertical axis represents the level of global integration, and hence of central coordination; the horizontal axis represents the extent of national differentiation, and consequently of the desired influence of subsidiaries in strategic and operational decisions.

The detergent business must be managed in a more globally integrated manner than packaged foods, but also needs a more nationally differentiated strategy than the chemicals business. But not all tasks need to be managed in this differentiated yet coordinated manner: there is little need for national differentiation in research or for global coordination of sales management. And even those functions such as marketing that exhibit the more complex simultaneous demands need not be managed in this way in all national markets. Marketing strategy for export sales

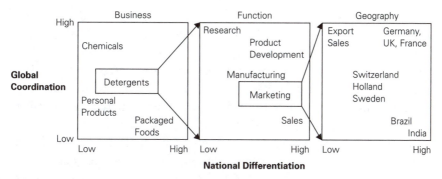

Figure 1 Unilever's differentiated organization

can be highly coordinated, while approaches taken in closed markets like India and Brazil can be managed locally. Only in key strategic markets like Germany, the U.K., and France is there a need for differentiated yet coordinated marketing strategies. This flexible and differentiated management approach stands in marked contrast to the standardized, symmetrical approach implied in Unilever's earlier blanket commitment to decentralized responsibility.

But Unilever is far from unique. In all of the companies we studied, senior management was working to differentiate its organizational structure and processes in increasingly sophisticated ways.[3] For example, Philips's consumer electronics division began experimenting with an organization differentiated by product life-cycle stage – high-tech products like CD players being managed with very different strategies and organization processes from those for stable high-volume products like color TVs, which, in turn, were managed differently from mature and declining products like portable radios. Procter & Gamble is differentiating the roles of its subsidiaries by giving some of them responsibilities as "lead countries" in product strategy development, then rotating that leadership role from product to product.[4] Matsushita differentiates the way it manages its worldwide operations not on the basis of geography, but on the unit's strategic role. (Single-product, wholly owned manufacturing units, the A Group, are managed differently from multiproduct, multifunction companies, the B Group, and from simple sales and marketing subs, the C Group.) L.M. Ericsson, which had centralized most of the basic research on its digital switch, is now decentralizing development and applications responsibilities to a few key country subsidiaries that have the capability to contribute.[5]

Thus, instead of deciding the overall roles of product, functional, and geographic management on the basis of simplistic dichotomies such as global versus domestic businesses or centralized versus decentralized organizations, many companies are creating different levels of influence for different groups as they perform different activities. Doing this allows the relatively underdeveloped management perspectives to be built in a gradual, complementary manner rather than in the sudden, adversarial environment often associated with either/or choices. Internal heterogeneity has made the change from unidimensional to multidimensional organization easier by breaking the problem up into many small, differentiated parts and by allowing for a step-by-step process of organizational change.

From dependence or independence to interdependence

The limitations of the assumption of clarity in organizational relationships eventually confronted top managers in the Japanese soap and detergent company Kao. In the early 1980s they began to recognize that their foreign subsidiaries' strong dependence on the parent company provided significant benefits of global efficiency only at the cost of less sensitivity and responsiveness to local market needs. For example, when investigating the reason for the company's slow penetration of the shampoo market in Thailand despite offering a technologically superior product, headquarters managers found that the subsidiary had adopted the product positioning, packaging, and pricing policies developed for the Japanese domestic market. Since local management had been unable to make the necessary local adaptations, managers were brought in from headquarters to identify the source of the problem and to make necessary changes in the marketing mix.

In other companies we studied – Unilever and ITT, for example – clarity of organizational relationships was achieved by giving foreign subsidiaries substantial independence. But, as our earlier discussion of Unilever illustrated, such organizational clarity was achieved at the cost of substantial inefficiency; individual subsidiaries often reinvented the wheel or operated at suboptimal scale.

New strategic demands make organizational models of simple inter-unit dependence *or* independence inappropriate. The reality of today's worldwide competitive environment demands collaborative information sharing and problem solving, cooperative support and resource sharing, and collective action and implementation. Independent units risk being picked off one-by-one by competitors whose coordinated global approach gives them two important strategic advantages – the ability to integrate research, manufacturing, and other scale-efficient operations, and the opportunity to cross-subsidize the losses from battles in one market with funds generated by profitable operations in home markets or protected environments.[6] The desire to capture such strategic benefits was one of Philips's main motivations as it attempted to coordinate the competitive responses of historically independent national organizations.

On the other hand, foreign operations totally dependent on a central unit must deal with problems reaching beyond the loss of local market responsiveness described in the Kao example. They also risk being unable to respond effectively to strong national competitors or to sense potentially important local market or technical intelligence. This was the problem Procter & Gamble's Japan subsidiary faced in an environment where local competitors began challenging P&G's previously secure position with successive, innovative product changes and novel market strategies, particularly in the disposable diapers business. After suffering major losses in market share, management recognized that a local operation focused primarily on implementing the company's classic marketing strategy was no longer sufficient; the Japanese subsidiary needed the freedom and incentive to be more innovative. Not only to ensure the viability of the Japanese subsidiary, but also to protect its global strategic position, P&G realized it had to expand the role of the local unit and change its relationship with the parent company to enhance two-way learning and mutual support.

But it is not easy to change relationships of dependence or independence that have been built up over a long history. Many companies have tried to address the increasing need for interunit collaboration by adding layer upon layer of administrative mechanisms to foster greater cooperation. Top managers have extolled the virtues of teamwork and have even created special departments to audit management response to this need. In most cases these efforts to obtain cooperation by fiat or by administrative mechanisms have been disappointing. The independent units have feigned compliance while fiercely protecting their independence. The dependent units have found that the new cooperative spirit implies little more than the right to agree with those on whom they depend.

Yet some companies have gradually developed the capability to achieve such cooperation and to build what Rosabeth Kanter calls an "integrative organization."[7] Of the companies we studied, the most successful did so not by creating new units, but by changing the basis of the relationships among product, functional, and geographic management groups. From relations based on dependence or independence, they moved to relations based on formidable levels of explicit, genuine interdependence. In essence, they made integration and collaboration self-enforcing by making it necessary for each group to cooperate in order to achieve its own interests. Companies were able to create such interdependencies in many ways, as two brief examples will illustrate.

● NEC has developed reciprocal relationships among different parts of its organizations by creating a series of internal quasi markets. It builds cooperation between the R&D function and the different product groups by allocating only a part of the R&D budget directly to the company's several central laboratories. This portion is used to support basic and applied research in core technologies of potential value to the corporation as a whole. The remaining funds are allocated to the product groups to support research programs that reflect their priorities. In response to the product divisions' proposed projects, each research group puts forward proposals that it feels will lead to the desired product or process improvements. What follows is a negotiation process that results in the product divisions' "buying" some of the proposals put up by the laboratories, while different R&D groups adopt some of the projects demanded by the product managers. In other words, NEC has created an internal market for ensuring that research is relevant to market needs. (A similar process seems to have had comparable success at Matsushita.)[8]

● Procter & Gamble employs an entirely different approach to creating and managing interdependencies. In Europe, for example, it formed a number of Eurobrand teams for developing product-market strategies for different product lines.[9] Each team is headed by the general manager of a subsidiary that has a particularly well-developed competence in that business. It also includes the appropriate product and advertising managers from the other subsidiaries and relevant functional managers from the company's European headquarters. Each team's effectiveness clearly depends on the involvement and support provided by its members and, more important, by the organizational units they represent. Historically, the company's various subsidiaries had little incentive to cooperate. Now, however, the success of each team – and the reputation of the general manager heading it – depends on the support of other subsidiaries; this has made cooperation self-enforcing. Each general manager is aware that the level of support and commitment he can expect from the other members of the Euro-brand team depends on the support and contribution the product managers from his subsidiaries provide to the other teams. The inter-dependencies of these Eurobrand teams were able to foster teamwork driven by individual interests.

In observing many such examples of companies building and extending interdependence among units, we were able to identify three important flows that seem to be at the center of the emerging organizational rela-tionships. Most fundamental was the product interdependence that most companies were building as they specialized and integrated their worldwide manufacturing operations to achieve greater efficiency, while retaining sourcing flexibility and sensitivity to host country interests.[10] The resulting *flow of parts, components, and finished goods* increased the interdependence of the worldwide operations in an obvious and fundamental manner.

We also observed companies developing a resource interdependence that often contrasted sharply with earlier policies that had either encour-aged local self-sufficiency or required the centralization of all surplus resources. Systems such as NEC's internal quasi markets were designed to develop a greater *flow of funds, skills, and other scarce resources* among organizational units.

Finally, the worldwide diffusion of technology, the development of international markets, and the globalization of competitive strategies have meant that vital strategic information now exists in many differ-ent locations worldwide. Furthermore, the growing dispersion of assets and delegation of responsibilities to foreign operations have resulted in the development of local knowledge and expertise that has implications for the broader organization. With these changes, the need to manage the *flow of intelligence, ideas, and knowledge* has become central to the learning process and has reinforced the growing interdependence of worldwide operations, as P&G's Eurobrand teams illustrate.

It is important to emphasize that the relationships we are highlight-ing are different from the interdependencies commonly observed in multiunit organizations. Traditionally, MNC managers have attempted to highlight what has been called "pooled interdependence" to make sub-unit managers responsive to global rather than local interests. (Before the Euroteam approach, for instance, P&G's European vice president often tried to convince independent-minded subsidiary managers to transfer surplus generated funds to other more needy subsidiaries, in the overall corporate interest, arguing that, "Someday when you're in need they might be able to fund a major product launch for you.")

As the example illustrates, pooled interdependence is often too broad and amorphous to affect day-to-day management behavior. The interdependencies we described earlier are more clearly reciprocal, and each unit's ability to achieve its goals is made conditional upon its willingness to help other units achieve their own goals. Such interdependencies more effectively promote the organization's ability to share the perspectives and link the resources of different components, and thereby to expand its organizational capabilities.[11]

From control to coordination and cooption

The simplifying assumptions of organizational symmetry and dependence (or independence) had allowed the management processes in many companies to be dominated by simple controls – tight operational controls in subsidiaries dependent on the center, and a looser system of administrative or financial controls in decentralized units.[12] When companies began to challenge the assumptions underlying organizational relationships, however, they found they also had to adapt their management processes. The growing interdependence of organizational units strained the simple control-dominated systems and underlined the need to supplement existing processes with more sophisticated ones. Furthermore, the differentiation of organizational tasks and roles amplified the diversity of management perspectives and capabilities and forced management to differentiate management processes.

As organizations became, at the same time, more diverse and more interdependent, there was an explosion in the number of issues that had to be linked, reconciled, or integrated. The rapidly increasing flows of goods, resources, and information among organizational units increased the need for *coordination* as a central management function. But the costs of coordination are high, both in financial and human terms, and coordinating capabilities are always limited. Most companies, though, tended to concentrate on a primary means of coordination and control – "the company's way of doing things." (At ITT it was through "the system," as Harold Geneen used to call his sophisticated set of controls, while at Kao it was primarily through centralization of decisions.) Clearly, there was a need to develop multiple means of coordination, to rank the demands for coordination, and to allocate the scarce coordinating resources. The way in which one of our sample companies developed its portfolio of coordinative processes illustrates the point well.

During the late 1970s and early 1980s, Philips had gradually developed some sophisticated means of coordination. This greatly helped the company shape its historically evolved, nationally centered organization into the kind of multidimensional organization it needed to be in the 1980s. Coordinating the flow of goods in a global sourcing network is a highly complex logistical task, but one that can often be formalized and delegated to middle and lower-level management. By standardizing product specifications and rationalizing sourcing patterns through designating certain plants as international production centers (IPCs), Philips facilitated goods-flow coordination. By making these flows reasonably constant and forecastable, the company could manage them almost entirely through formal systems and processes. These became the main coordination mechanisms in the company's attempt to increase the integration of worldwide sourcing of products and components.

Coordinating the flow of financial, technical, and human resources, however, was not so easily routinized. Philips saw the allocation of these scarce resources as a reflection of key strategic choices and therefore managed the coordination process by centralizing many decisions. The board became heavily involved in major capital budgeting decisions; the product divisions reasserted control over product development, a process once jealously guarded by the national organizations; and the influential corporate staff bureau played a major role in personnel assignments and transfers.

But while goods flows could be coordinated through formalization, and resource flows through centralization, critical information flows were much more difficult to manage. The rapid globalization of the consumer electronics industry in the 1970s forced Philips to recognize the need to move strategic information and proprietary knowledge around the company much more quickly. While some routine data could be transferred through normal information systems, much of the information was so diverse and changeable that establishing formal processes was impossible. While some core knowledge had to be stored and transferred through corporate management, the sheer volume and complexity of information – and the need for its rapid diffusion – limited the ability to coordinate through centralization. Philips found that the most effective way to manage complex flows of information and knowledge was through various socialization processes: the transfer of people, the encouragement of informal communication channels that fostered information exchange, or the creation of forums that facilitated interunit learning.

Perhaps most well known is the company's constant worldwide transfer and rotation of a group of senior managers (once referred to internally as the "Dutch Mafia," but today a more international group) as a means of transferring critical knowledge and experience throughout the organization. Philips also made more extensive use of committees and task forces than any other company we studied. Although the frequent meetings and constant travel were expensive, the company benefited not only from information exchange but also from the development of personal contacts that grew into vital information channels.

In other companies, we saw a similar broadening of administrative processes as managers learned to operate with previously underutilized means of coordination. Unilever's heavy reliance on the socialization of managers to provide the coordination "glue" was supplemented by the growing role of the central product-coordination departments. In contrast, NEC reduced central management's coordination role by developing formal systems and social processes in a way that created a more robust and flexible coordinative capability.

Having developed diverse new means of coordination, management's main task is to carefully ration their usage and application. As the Philips example illustrates, it is important to distinguish where tasks can be formalized and managed through systems, where social linkages can be fostered to encourage informal agreements and cooperation, and where the coordination task is so vital or sensitive that it must use the scarce resource of central management arbitration.[13]

While the growing interdependence of organizational units forces the development of more complex administrative processes, the differentiation of roles and responsibilities forces management to change the way it uses the new coordination and control mechanisms. Even though they recognize the growing diversity of tasks facing them, a surprising number of companies have had great difficulty in differentiating the way they manage products, functions, or geographic units. The simplicity of applying a single planning and control system across businesses and the political acceptability of defining uniform job descriptions for all subsidiary heads were often allowed to outweigh the clear evidence that the relevant business characteristics and subsidiary roles were vastly different.

We have described briefly how companies began to remedy this situation by differentiating roles and responsibilities within the organization.

Depending on their internal capabilities and on the strategic importance of their external environments, organizational units might be asked to take on roles ranging from that of strategic leader with primary corporatewide responsibility for a particular business or function, to simple implementer responsible only for executing strategies and decisions developed elsewhere.

Clearly, these roles must be managed in quite different ways. The unit with strategic leadership responsibility must be given freedom to develop responsibility in an entrepreneurial fashion, yet must also be strongly supported by headquarters. For this unit, operating controls may be light and quite routine, but coordination of information and resource flows to and from the unit will probably require intensive involvement from senior management. In contrast, units with implementation responsibility might be managed through tight operating controls, with standardized systems used to handle much of the coordination – primarily of goods flows. Because the tasks are more routine, the use of scarce coordinating resources could be minimized.

Differentiating organizational roles and management processes can have a fragmenting and sometimes demotivating effect, however. Nowhere was this more clearly illustrated than in the many companies that unquestioningly assigned units the "dog" and "cash cow" roles defined by the Boston Consulting Group's growth-share matrix in the 1970s.[14] Their experience showed that there is another equally important corporate management task that complements and facilitates coordination effectiveness. We call this task *cooption*: the process of uniting the organization with a common understanding of, identification with, and commitment to the corporation's objectives, priorities, and values.

A clear example of the importance of cooption was provided by the contrast between ITT and NEC managers. At ITT, corporate objectives were communicated more in financial than in strategic terms, and the company's national entities identified almost exclusively with their local environment. When corporate management tried to superimpose a more unified and integrated global strategy, its local subsidiaries neither understood nor accepted the need to do so. For years they resisted giving up their autonomy, and management was unable to replace the interunit rivalry with a more cooperative and collaborative process.

In contrast, NEC developed an explicitly defined and clearly communicated global strategy enshrined in the company's "C&C" motto – a corporatewide dedication to building business and basing competitive strategy on the strong link between computers and communications. For over a decade, the C&C philosophy was constantly interpreted, refined, elaborated, and eventually institutionalized in organizational units dedicated to various C&C missions (e.g., the C&C Systems Research Laboratories, the C&C Corporate Planning Committee, and eventually the C&C Systems Division). Top management recognized that one of its major tasks was to inculcate the worldwide organization with an understanding of the C&C strategy and philosophy and to raise managers' consciousness about the global implications of competing in these converging businesses. By the mid-1980s, the company was confident that every NEC employee in every operating unit had a clear understanding of NEC's global strategy as well as of his or her role in it. Indeed, it was this homogeneity that allowed the company to begin the successful decentralization of its strategic tasks and the differentiation of its management processes.

Thus the management process that distinguished transnational organizations from simpler unidimensional forms was one in which control was made less dominant by the increased importance of interunit integration and collaboration. These new processes required corporate management to supplement its control role with the more subtle tasks of coordination and cooption, giving rise to a much more complex and sophisticated management process.

Sustaining a dynamic balance: role of the "mind matrix"

Developing multidimensional perspectives and capabilities does not mean that product, functional, and geographic management must have the same level of influence on all key decisions. Quite the contrary. It means that the organization must possess a differentiated influence structure – one in which different groups have different roles for different activities. These roles cannot be fixed but must change continually to respond to new environmental demands and evolving industry characteristics. Not only is it necessary to prevent any one perspective from dominating the others, it is equally important not to be locked into a mode of operation that prevents reassignment of responsibilities, realignment of relationships, and rebalancing of power distribution. This ability to manage the multidimensional organization capability in a flexible manner is the hallmark of a transnational company.

In the change processes we have described, managers were clearly employing some powerful organizational tools to create and control the desired flexible management process. They used the classic tool of formal structure to strengthen, weaken, or shift roles and responsibilities over time, and they employed management systems effectively to redirect corporate resources and to channel information in a way that shifted the balance of power. By controlling the ebb and flow of responsibilities, and by rebalancing power relationships, they were able to prevent any of the multidimensional perspectives from atrophying. Simultaneously, they prevented the establishment of entrenched power bases.

But the most successful companies had an additional element at the core of their management processes. We were always conscious that a substantial amount of senior management attention focused on the *individual* members of the organization. NEC's continual efforts to inculcate all corporate members with a common vision of goals and priorities; P&G's careful assignment of managers to teams and task forces to broaden their perspectives; Philips's frequent use of conferences and meetings as forums to reconcile differences; and Unilever's extensive use of training as a powerful socialization process and its well-planned career path management that provided diverse experience across businesses, functions, and geographic locations – all are examples of companies trying to develop multidimensional perspectives and flexible approaches at the level of the individual manager.

What is critical, then, is not just the structure, but also the mentality of those who constitute the structure. The common thread that holds together the diverse tasks we have described is a managerial mindset that understands the need for multiple strategic capabilities, that is able to view problems from both local and global perspectives, and that accepts the importance of a flexible approach. This pattern suggests that managers should resist the temptation to view their task in the traditional terms of building a formal global matrix structure – an organizational form that in practice has proven extraordinarily difficult to manage in the international environment. They might be better guided by the perspective of one top manager who described the challenge as "creating a matrix in the minds of managers."

Our study has led us to conclude that a company's ability to develop transnational organizational capability and management mentality will be the key factor that separates the winners from the mere survivors in the emerging international environment.

Christopher A. Bartlett is Associate Professor of Business Administration at the Graduate School of Business Administration, Harvard University. Dr. Bartlett holds the B. Econ. degree from the University of Queensland, Australia, and the M.B.A. and D.B.A. degrees from Harvard University. Prior to his academic career, Dr. Bartlett had extensive management experience in Alcoa, McKinsey and Co., and Baxter Travenol, where he was general manager of the French subsidiary. His research has focused on the strategic and organizational problems facing multinationals.

This paper appeared in *Sloan Management Review*, Fall 1987.

REFERENCES

1. The findings presented in this article are based on a three-year research project on the organization and management of multinational corporations. A description of the three-phase study and of the nine American, European, and Japanese MNCs that made up the core of the clinical research stage is contained in the companion article, "Managing across Borders: New Strategic Requirements" (Summer 1987). Complete findings will be presented in the forthcoming book, *Managing across Borders: The Transnational Solution* (Boston: Harvard Business School Press, forthcoming).

2. This global integration/national responsiveness framework was first applied to the analysis of MNC tasks by Prahalad. See C.K. Prahalad, "The Strategic Process in a Multinational Corporation" (Boston: Harvard Business School, unpublished doctoral dissertation, 1976).

3. Working with a group of Swedish companies, Hedlund has come to similar conclusions. He describes MNCs with dispersed capabilities and differentiated operations as "heterarchies." See G. Hedlund, "The Hypermodern MNC – A Heterarchy?" *Human Resource Management*, Spring 1986, pp. 9–35.

4. Rugman and Poynter have observed a similar phenomenon in the trend toward assigning mature national subsidiaries worldwide responsibility for products with worldwide markets. See A.M. Rugman and T.A. Poynter, "World Product Mandates: How Will Multinationals Respond?" *Business Quarterly*, October 1982, pp. 54–61.

5. This issue of differentiation in the roles and responsibilities of MNC subsidiaries has been discussed and a normative framework for creating such differentiation has been proposed in C.A. Bartlett and S. Ghoshal, "Tap Your Subsidiaries for Global Reach," *Harvard Business Review*, November–December 1986, pp. 87–94.

6. Such global competitive strategies have been described extensively by many authors. See, for example, T. Hour, M.E. Porter, and E. Rudden, "How Global Companies Win Out," *Harvard Business Review*, September–October 1982, pp. 98–108; and G. Hamel and C.K. Prahalad, "Do You Really Have a Global Strategy?" *Harvard Business Review*, July–August 1985, pp. 139–148.

7. See R.M. Kanter, *The Change Masters* (New York: Simon & Schuster, 1983).

8. The use of such internal quasi market mechanisms as a means of managing interdependencies has been richly described by Westney and Sakakibara. See D.E. Westney and K. Sakakibara, "The Role of Japan-Based R&D in Global Technology Strategy," *Technology in Society* 7 (1985): 315–330.

9. For a full description of the development of Eurobrand in P&G, see C.A. Bartlett, "Procter & Gamble Europe: Vizir Launch" (Boston: Harvard Business School, Case Services #9-384-139).

10. Kogut provides an excellent discussion on how multinational corporations can develop operational flexibility using a worldwide configuration of specialized resource capabilities linked through an integrated management system. See B. Kogut, "Designing Global Strategies: Profiting from Operational Flexibility," *Sloan Management Review*, Fall 1985, pp. 27–38.

11. The distinction among sequential, reciprocal, and pooled interdependencies has been made in J.D. Thompson, *Organizations in Action* (New York: McGraw-Hill, 1967).

12. The role of headquarters management in establishing control over worldwide operations and the means by which it is done have been richly described in Y.L. Doz and C.K. Prahalad, "Headquarters Influence and Strategic Control in MNCs," *Sloan Management Review*, Fall 1981, pp. 15–30.

13. The use of centralization, formalization, and socialization as means of coordination has been discussed by many authors, including P.M. Blau and R.A. Schoenherr, *The Structure of Organizations* (New York: Basic Books, 1971); and W.G. Ouchi, "Markets, Bureaucracies, and Clans," *Administrative Science Quarterly* 25 (March 1980): 129–141.

In the specific context of the multinational corporation, the process implications of these mechanisms were described by Bartlett in a model that distinguished "substantive decision management," "temporary coalition management," and "decision context management" as alternative management process modes in MNCs. See C.A. Bartlett, "Multinational Structural Evolution: The Changing Decision Environments" (Boston: Harvard Business School, unpublished doctoral dissertation, 1979).

See also the contributions of G. Hedlund, T. Kogono, and L. Leksell in *The Management of Headquarters–Subsidiary Relationships in MNCs*, ed. L. Otterbeck (London: Gower Publishing, 1981); and Doz and Prahalad (Fall 1981).

14. See P. Haspeslagh, "Portfolio Planning: Uses and Limits," *Harvard Business Review*, January–February 1982, pp. 58–73.

CHAPTER 4

The multinational corporation as an interorganizational network

Sumantra Ghoshal and Christopher A. Bartlett

*S*umantra *and Chris Bartlett bring together in this paper the insights into multinational management that were documented in* Managing Across Borders *with the rich body of academic literature on organizational networks. It presents a simplified model of the multinational corporation in which individual subsidiary companies are the nodes in a network, and the structure of that network is a function of the broader environmental forces surrounding it. When first published, this paper provided an important advance in the way academics thought about the multinational corporation, because it challenged the simplistic assumption that everything flowed from the corporate centre. In reality, multinational corporations operate in a diversified set of markets, where individual subsidiaries have considerable freedom to respond to local demands.*

As pointed out recently by Kogut (1989), the late 1980s have witnessed a significant evolution of academic interest in the multinational corporation (MNC). An important element of this shift has been a change in the focus of research away from the dyadic headquarters-subsidiary relationship in MNCs, or the specific decision of a company to invest in a foreign location, to the coordination tasks of managing a network of established foreign subsidiaries and analysis of the competitive advantages that arise from the potential scope economies of such a network.

This new research focus demands new theoretical, conceptual, and methodological anchors. Analysis of international competition, for example, has already embraced a range of new theories such as those of multiplant production, multipoint competition, and valuation of options to explore the costs and benefits of the MNC's geographic scope of activities (e.g., Kogut, 1983; Ghemawat & Spence, 1986; Teece, 1980). The present authors advocate a similar adoption of interorganizational theory for future MNC-related research, albeit with some modifications to reflect the ownership-based intraorganizational ties that exist between the MNC headquarters and its different foreign subsidiaries. We believe that interorganizational theory, properly adapted, can provide new insights about a complex and geographically dispersed organizational system like the MNC, and our main objective here is to propose an initial formulation regarding how the concepts and tools of interorganizational analysis can be applied to fit this slightly different but analogous case.

To frame the context of our discussions, it may be useful to begin with an illustration. Figure 1 shows the simplest possible representation of N.V. Philips, a multinational company headquartered in the Netherlands. The company has its own operating units in 60 countries as diverse as the United States, France, Japan, South Korea, Nigeria, Uruguay, and Bangladesh. Some of these units are large, fully integrated companies developing, manufacturing, and marketing a diverse range of products from light bulbs to defense systems. Such subsidiaries might have 5,000 or more employees and might be among the largest companies in their host countries. Others are small, single-function operations responsible for only R & D, or manufacturing, or marketing for only one or a few of these different businesses. Some such units might employ 50 or fewer people. In some cases, the units have been in operation for more than 50 years; a few began their organizational lives less than 10 years ago. Some of these units are tightly controlled from the headquarters; others enjoy relationships with the headquarters more akin to those between equal partners than those between parent and subsidiary.

With only minor alterations, Figure 1 could also be a representation of an American multinational such as Procter & Gamble, or another European company such as Unilever, or a Japanese company such as Matsushita Electric (see descriptions of these companies in Bartlett & Ghoshal, 1986 and 1987). In many ways our description of Philips is a generic account that characterizes many large MNCs. As suggested by a number of authors, MNCs are physically dispersed in environmental settings that represent very different economic, social, and cultural milieus (Fayerweather, 1978; Hofstede, 1980; Robock, Simmons & Zwick, 1977); are internally differentiated in complex ways to respond to both environmental and organizational differences in different businesses, functions, and geographic

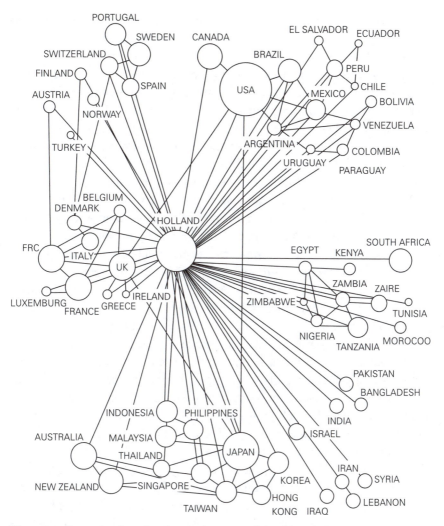

Figure 1 Organizational units and some of the interlinkages within
N.V. Philips

locations (Bartlett & Ghoshal, 1986; Prahalad & Doz, 1987), and, as a
result of such dispersal and differentiation, possess internal linkages and
coordination mechanisms that represent and respond to many different
kinds and extents of dependency and interdependency in interunit exchange
relationships (Ghoshal & Nohria, 1989).

We believe that an entity such as any of these large multinational
corporations can be more appropriately conceptualized as an interorganizational grouping rather than as a unitary *organization*; also, valuable
insights can be gained on the internal structures and operations of such

entities from the concepts of organization sets and networks that are more commonly used for exploring interorganizational phenomena (Aldrich & Whetten, 1981; Evan, 1967). In particular, we believe that the concept of a network, both as a metaphor and in terms of the tools and techniques of analysis it provides, reflects the nature and complexity of the multinational organization and can provide a useful lens through which to examine such an entity. We propose here a framework that conceptualizes the multinational as a network of exchange relationships among different organizational units, including the headquarters and the different national subsidiaries that are collectively embedded in what Homans (1974) described as a structured context. Further, continuing the thinking of Tichy, Tushman, and Fombrun (1979), we visualize this context as an *external network* consisting of all the organizations such as customers, suppliers, regulators, and competitors with which the different units of the MNC must interact. Our main proposal is that different attributes of a multinational such as the configuration of its organizational resources and the nature of *inter*unit exchange relations that lead to such a configuration can be explained by selected attributes of the external network within which it is embedded and on which it depends for its survival.

A note of caution must, however, be sounded at this stage. Because network analysis is a rapidly emerging and highly complex field of study and because of the considerable divergence on definitions and approaches that exists within this field, it is unlikely that this initial attempt to apply network concepts to the study of MNCs will be either complete or above reproach. In the concluding section of our article, we discuss some of the limitations of the present effort and suggest how these might be overcome through future conceptual and empirical research. This article must be viewed, therefore, as an initial attempt to identify the possibility of developing a *network theory of the MNC*, rather than as a rigorous presentation of such a theory.

Although the attempt to formally apply the interorganizational network perspective to the study of MNCs is relatively new, it should also be noted that the conceptual foundation for such an approach already exists in the international management literature. For example, Perlmutter's (1969) scheme for categorizing MNCs as ethnocentric, polycentric, and geocentric organizations is clearly consistent with a network theoretic view. Similarly, the stylized models of MNC organizations developed by Bartlett (1986) and Hedlund (1986), the concept of a *coordinated multinational system* proposed by Kogut (1983), and the application of the resource dependency model by Herbert (1984) for explicating strategy-structure configurations in MNCs have all been implicitly or explicitly grounded in the conceptualization of MNCs as interorganizational systems. Although it builds on this foundation, the article also differs from these earlier pieces in two important ways.

First, in most of these proposals, the structure and attributes of the MNC were explained as arising from the technical and economic rationality and constraints in resource allocation (Kogut, 1983) or from the administrative heritage (Bartlett, 1986) and cognitive orientation (Perlmutter, 1969) of its managers. Our explanation focuses instead on the social and institutional structure of the environments in which the MNC operates. As institutional theorists have argued, the relational networks in the institutional environment play an important role in influencing the structure and behavior of organizations (Meyer & Scott, 1983; Zucker, 1988). The uniqueness of the MNC as an organizational form arises from the fact that its different constituent units are embedded in different national environments in which the structures of these relational networks can be and often are very different (Westney, 1989). Further, in an era of expanding transnational linkages among individuals and organizations, these relational networks in the different countries are also increasingly interconnected among themselves in complex ways. These differences in national industry systems and the interconnections among them are central to our explanation of both economic action and administrative coordination within the dispersed system of the MNC.

Second, the concept of a network has so far been used in this literature mostly as a metaphor to describe and categorize MNC structures and to support normative arguments on the importance of lateral relationships, shared values, and reciprocal task interdependencies for effective management of MNCs. Even though we believe that such a metaphorical use of the term has been useful for descriptive and normative purposes, this paper represents an effort to move to the next step of theory building by using network concepts to explain specific structural attributes of multinational organizations.

Interorganizational theories applied to the multinational corporation

Much of the existing theory and almost all empirical analyses of interorganizational networks have focused on interorganizational groupings that are not connected by ownership ties (e.g., Pfeffer & Salancik, 1974; Bacharach & Aiken, 1976; Van de Ven & Walker, 1984). Before applying any of the concepts or empirical findings from such studies to the analysis of MNCs, it is first necessary to make a prima facie case that the ownership ties that exist within the multinational do not necessarily preclude the entire range of discretionary behaviors that are possible among interacting organizations that are not so connected.

A number of authors have argued that the linkage between ownership and hierarchical power ("fiat") in complex organizations is much weaker than is often assumed (e.g., Granovetter, 1985, p. 499). We believe that this link is particularly weak in the case of MNCs because of the large physical and cultural distances between the owned and the owning units. Case histories of extreme subsidiary autonomy have been well documented in the literature on multinationals: the refusal of North American Philips to sell the V2000 video cassette recorder developed by its Dutch parent, preferring instead to purchase from a Japanese archrival, is a good example. Even more dramatic, however, is the case of the British and German subsidiaries of Ruberoid that unilaterally severed all ties with the parent and, with the support of local financial institutions, ultimately secured complete legal independence. Such situations are relatively more common for MNCs headquartered in small countries, many foreign subsidiaries of which often control more resources and contribute more revenues than the parent company. However, many such cases also have been observed in companies such as ITT and Unilever, even though the parents were headquartered in large countries such as the United States and the United Kingdom (Bartlett & Ghoshal, 1989).

The efficacy of fiat is particularly limited in the case of multinationals not only because some of the subsidiaries happen to be very distant and resource-rich but, more so, because they control critical linkages with key actors in their local environments, particularly the host government. To cite but one illustration, the Australian subsidiary of Ericsson, the Swedish telecommunications company, accumulated a very high level of R & D resources primarily because of a coalition between the local management and the Australian Post and Telegraph authorities that had as its principal goal the creation of a major R & D center in Australia. Subsidiary company links with local customers, suppliers, and investors also contribute to the local management's automony. For example, following deregulation of the U.S. telecommunications industry, the influence of the American subsidiary of NEC expanded significantly within the company, despite its relatively small size and short organizational life. This was so because of its role in building the company's relationships with the Bell operating companies, which came to be viewed by NEC not only as major potential customers but also as its main contacts for joint development of new products.

We do not claim that the relationships among the parent company and the national subsidiaries in an MNC are identical to those among an interacting group of universities, or social service organizations, or regulatory agencies. Some anecdotal evidence of extreme subsidiary autonomy notwithstanding, the parent company of a multinational typically enjoys considerable hierarchical authority. However, we suggest that the existence of such hierarchical authority does not necessarily lead to fiat as the dominant or even the "last resort" mechanism of control. Typically, in such large, dispersed, and interdependent organizations, hierarchical authority coexists with significant local autonomy and such a situation, we believe, is not inappropriate for the application of interorganizational theories.

For example, in one of the seminal articles on the topic, Warren (1967) developed a typology of interorganizational relationships that distinguished four ways in which members of an organizational field could interact: unitary, federative, coalitional, and social choice. Table 1 summarizes the different attributes of each of these different contexts of interorganizational interactions. In our view, the multinational organization lies somewhere between Warren's unitary and federative structures, both of which admit some level of hierarchical decision making at the top of the inclusive structure. Further, even though the formal structure of MNCs may often resemble the unitary form or what has been described in the literature as *mandated networks* (Aldrich, 1976; Hall, Clark, Giordano, Johnson, & Roekel, 1977), the actual relationships between the headquarters and the subsidiaries and among the subsidiaries themselves tend to be more federative because, contrary to the case of both unitary and mandated networks, issues of competency and power tend to be contested within the MNC and interdependencies among the units tend to be reciprocal as well as sequential (Ghoshal & Nohria, 1989). This claim is consistent with Provan's analysis of different kinds of federations and his observation that the network characteristics of divisionalized firms generally are similar to those of independent federations (see Table 1, p. 83 in Provan, 1983). As demonstrated by Provan, Beyer, and Kruytbosch (1980), the interorganizational approach can be particularly useful for analyzing such federated relationships among

Table 1 Different contexts of interorganizational interactions

Dimension	Type of Context			
	Unitary	Federative	Coalitional	Social Choice
Relation of units to an inclusive goal	Units organized for achievement of inclusive goals	Units with disparate goals, but some formal organization for inclusive goals	Units with disparate goals, but informal collaboration for inclusive goals	No inclusive goals
Locus of inclusive decision making	At top of inclusive structure	At top of inclusive structure, subject to unit ratification	In interaction of units without a formal inclusive structure	Within units
Locus of authority	At top of hierarchy of inclusive structure	Primarily at unit level	Exclusively at unit level	Exclusively at unit level
Structural provision for division of labor	Units structured for division of labor within inclusive organization	Units structured autonomously, may agree to a division of labor, which may affect their structure	Units structured autonomously, may agree to ad hoc division of labor, without restructuring	No formally structured division of labor within an inclusive context
Commitment of a leadership subsystem	Norms of high commitment	Norms of moderate commitment	Commitment only to unit leaders	Commitment only to unit leaders
Prescribed collectivity-orientation of units	High	Moderate	Minimal	Little or none

units when the participants have only limited option for discretionary behavior and no opportunity to terminate the relationship.

Despite the broad theoretical scope of the interorganizational perspective as shown in Warren's classification of the field, empirical applications of this perspective have so far been limited to contexts that range from federative to social choice and interaction contexts that range from unitary to federative have been excluded from the domain of inter-organizational inquiry and placed in the domain of intraorganizational analysis (Cook, 1977). As such, the relationships between the diverse units of a multidivisional or a multinational corporation have rarely been examined from an interorganizational perspective.

Meanwhile, the limitations of applying traditional intraorganizational theory to the analysis of such complex and dispersed business organizations have become increasingly clear. As summarized by Nohria and Venkatraman (1987), the most critical of these limitations stem from the need in such analysis to provide a relatively clear separation between the "organization" and its relevant "environment." As a result, "the environment is typically viewed as an exogenous entity and is reified as a source of undefined uncertainties (e.g., volatility, resource scarcity, etc.) as opposed to being seen as a field of specific interacting organizations which locate the source of those contingencies" (Nohria & Venkatraman, 1987, p. 2). The organization is seen as a well-defined collective and is assumed to be internally homogeneous, coherent, and consistent. "Therefore, it is typically described in distributional (e.g., organization chart division of responsibility, authority, etc.) and categorical (e.g., centralized versus decentralized, mechanistic versus organic, differentiated versus integrated, etc.) terms as opposed to relational terms that focus on the actual inter-action patterns based on both internal and external flows of products, information, and authority" (Nohria & Venkatraman, 1987, p. 2).

In contrast to these limitations of traditional intraorganizational analysis, a dominant construct in most interorganizational theories is an exchange relation (e.g., A_x and B_y) that is defined as consisting of "transactions involving the transfer of resources (x, y) between two or more actors (A, B) for mutual benefit" (Cook, 1977, p. 64). The term *resources* as used in this context includes "any *valued* activity, service or commodity" (Cook, 1977, p. 64, emphasis added) and therefore includes not only the flows of finances and products but also the flows of technology, people, and information. Furthermore, as Cook observed, "the term actor in the theory refers not only to individuals but also to collective actors or corporate groups [thus making] it uniquely appropriate when organizations or subunits of organizations are used as the primary unit of analysis" (1977, p. 63). It is this suggestion of Cook that we adopt and develop in this article.

The multinational as a network: constructs and terminology

Let us consider a multinational corporation M with operating units in countries A, B, C, D, E, and F and a focal organization in the corporate headquarters H. For the purpose of analytical simplicity, let us assume that all the units of M are engaged in a single and common business (i.e., M is a single-industry company). Note that H serves as a coordinating agency and plays the role that Provan (1983) described as belonging to the Federation Management Organization (FMO) and, therefore, must be distinguished from the organizational unit, say A, that is responsible for operations in the home country of M, even though the two may be located in the same premises. By the term *multinational network* we shall refer to all the relationships and linkages that exist among the different units of M (i.e., among A, B, C, D, E, F, and H).

Each of the national operating units of M is embedded in a unique context and, for any specific type of exchange relationship, has its unique organization set (Aldrich & Whetten, 1981). For example, the unit A can have existing or potential exchange relationships with a specific set of suppliers $[s_A]$, buyers $[b_A]$, regulatory agencies $[r_A]$, and it competes for resources with an identifiable set of competitors $[c_A]$. Collectively, the group consisting of $[s_A, b_A, r_A, c_A$, etc.] constitutes what we call the organization set of A and denote by the symbol $[OS_A]$.

Different members of the organization set $[OS_A]$ can be internally connected by exchange ties. In keeping with Aldrich and Whetten's thinking (1981) we can define the density of $[OS_A]$ as the extensiveness of exchange ties within the elements of the organization set of A. Density measures the extent to which actors within the set are connected, on average, to one another (i.e., the mean relation from any one actor to any other actor). As suggested by Aldrich and Whetten, such a construct of density can be operationalized in different ways. For present purposes, we can choose the simplest of these ways and define it as the percentage of actual to potential ties among members of $[OS_A]$. The concluding section of this article includes a more detailed discussion on identification of boundaries and measurement of densities for the different local organization sets.

The density of such connections within the different local organization sets of A, B, C, and so on may vary. For example, it has been noted by many authors that the level of connectedness among different members of an industry group is significantly higher in Japan in comparison to some Western countries (e.g., see discussions and the quotation from Lohr cited in Granovetter, 1985, p. 497). Similarly, it has been shown in the management literature that within the same national environment, the level of cohesiveness among customers, suppliers, competitors, and so forth may be higher in certain businesses such as construction (Eccles, 1981), publishing (Powell, 1985), textiles (Sabel, Herrigel, Kazis, & Deeg, 1987), and investment banking (Eccles & Crane, 1987), compared to others.

The different organization sets of the different units of M may themselves be interconnected through exchange ties. For example, one of the supplying organizations in the local environment of A may be an affiliated unit of another multinational company, and it may have exchange linkages with its counterpart in the local environment of B. Similarly, the actions of regulatory agencies in one location (say, r_C) may influence the actions of their counterparts in other locations (say, r_D). Such influence may be manifest in actions such as retaliation by r_C to what is seen as protectionist action of r_D, or deregulation by r_D to reciprocate or just emulate similar action by r_C (Mahini & Wells, 1986). Such linkages also may exist among suppliers and competitors. In fact, much of the current literature on global strategy considers such cross-border linkages among customers, competitors, and other relevant organizations as a key factor that does or should influence the behaviors of MNCs (e.g., this is a focal issue for a number of essays in Porter, 1986).

Because of such linkages among the different local organization sets, all members of all the organization sets of the different units of M collectively constitute what we shall call the *external network* (Tichy, Tushman, & Fombrun, 1979) within which the multinational network is embedded. In the same manner as we defined the construct of density for each of the different organization sets of the different units of M, we can also describe the density of this external network as the ratio of actual to potential ties among all its constituents. To differentiate between these two densities, we shall refer to the density of ties within each of the local organization sets as *within density* and the density of ties within the total external network, that is, across the different organization sets, as *across density*.

The main thesis in this article is that different attributes of the MNC can be explained in terms of selected attributes of the external network within which it is embedded. Following the arguments of Benson (1975), the interactions within the different organizational units of the MNC are best explained at the level of resource exchange. This suggests two attributes of the MNC as particularly relevant to our analysis: (a) the distribution of resources among its different affiliated units and (b) the structural characteristics that mediate internal exchange relationships within the MNC and continually restructure the resource configuration (Zeitz, 1980). These two characteristics of the MNC and how they relate to within and across densities will provide the focus of our attention for the remaining part of this article.

Resource configuration in MNCs

Resources such as production equipments, finance, technology, marketing skills, and management capabilities may be located in any one or more of the different units of M. By the term resource configuration we refer to the way in which the resources of M are distributed among A, B, C, D, E, F, and H. (We use the word resource in the sense of Cook [1977, p. 64] to refer to "any valuable activity, service, or commodry".) In some companies that Bartlett (1986) described as "centralized hubs," most of such resources may be concentrated in any one location, typically the parent company. For example, 90 percent of the manufacturing investments of Matsushita, the Japanese consumer electronics company, and 100 percent of its research facilities are located in Japan. In contrast, in companies such as Philips, Matsushita's European competitor and one that Bartlett categorized as a "decentralized federation," over 77 percent of total assets are located outside the company's home, which is in the Netherlands, and no single national subsidiary has more than 15 percent of the company's worldwide assets. This difference illustrates one aspect of resource configuration in MNCs that is of analytical interest, namely, *dispersal,* by which term we refer to the extent to which the company's resources are concentrated in one unit versus dispersed among the different units.

However, although both Philips and Electrolux (the Swedish home appliances company) have a relatively high level of dispersal in the sense that both companies have significant parts of their total assets distributed in a number of countries, the pattern of distribution of such assets is very different in the two cases. Let us consider their resources within Europe. For Electrolux, even though the resources are dispersed, they also are very specialized, that is, the resources and associated activities located in any one country are of sufficient scale to meet the company's worldwide or, at least, regional requirements for that activity, thereby avoiding the need for carrying out the same activity or task in multiple locations. For example, Electrolux's washing machine factory in France produces top-loading washing machines only and it meets the company's requirements in that product category for all of Europe. Similarly, the washing machine factory in Italy produces only front-loading models to meet Europe-wide demand. Its research centers, product development laboratories, and component-producing units are all similarly differentiated and specialized. By contrast, despite considerable recent efforts to increase such specialization, Philips owns five factories in Europe that produce identical or near-identical models of television sets, each basically for a local market. In other words, the resources of Philips are dispersed on a local-for-local basis (Ghoshal, 1986) – they are dispersed but undifferentiated, with identical resources being used by each unit to carry out essentially similar tasks in and for its own local environment. We refer to this dimension of resource configuration as *specialization*, and it represents the extent to which the resources located in each unit are differentiated from those in others.

Resource configuration in MNCs traditionally has been analyzed from an economic perspective, typically under the assumption that resource location decisions are based on rational, self-interested considerations such as needing increasing profitability, gaining access to new markets or desired factors of production, protecting competitive position, and minimizing costs and risks (for reviews, see Buckley & Casson, 1985; Caves, 1982; Dunning, 1981; Hennart, 1982). Explanations of both dispersal and specialization have therefore focused on factors such as differences in costs of inputs (e.g., Stevens, 1974), potential scale economies in different activities (e.g., Porter, 1986), impacts of transportation and other "friction" costs (e.g., Hirsch, 1976), imperfections in information and other intermediate product markets (e.g., Magee, 1977; Rugman, 1980), defense against opportunism (e.g., Teece, 1986), and potential benefits of risk diversification (e.g., Lessard & Lightstone, 1986).

Following from Granovetter's (1985) ideas, much of this analysis can be criticized as *undersocialized* or *oversocialized* conceptualizations that ignore the important and ongoing effects that surrounding social structures have on economic behaviors of organizations. We present here an alternative framework that relates dispersal and specialization to the densities of interactions both within and across the different local organization sets of the company. As suggested in the introductory section, our conceptualization is strongly influenced by the work of institutional theorists who have argued that the structure and behavior of organizations are influenced by both technical and institutional factors (Meyer & Scott, 1983) and that "organizations compete not just for resources and customers, but for political power and institutional legitimacy, for social as well as economic fitness" (DiMaggio & Powell, 1983, p. 150). Although Meyer and Scott have been cautious in suggesting that business organizations belong to "technical sectors" in which the economic need for efficiency and effectiveness in controlling work processes dominates institutional need for legitimacy, they also have contended that "while the two dimensions (technical and institutional) tend to be negatively correlated, they are apparently not strongly so" (1983, p. 140). As suggested by Westney (1989), we believe that for MNCs, strong needs for legitimacy and local isomorphism in each host country environment coexist with strong demand for efficiency within its worldwide system and, therefore, the institutional structure of the environment (i.e., the attributes of the local organization sets and the external network) plays an important role in moderating the influence of technical and economic considerations. Even though they are different from traditional economic analysis, our arguments are much more consistent with recent work of economists such as Porter (in press) and Kogut (1988), both of whom have shown the importance of interinstitutional structure in determining the competitiveness of different countries and companies in different businesses.

Effects of within density in national organization sets

As Bower (1987) has shown through his in-depth study of American, European, and Japanese companies in the petrochemical industry, the density of linkages among key players in a national industrial context greatly influences industry performance and company strategy. For a variety of economic, legal, sociological, cultural, and historical reasons, some countries such as Japan are characterized by dense linkages among the suppliers, producers, regulators, customers, and others involved in a particular field of industrial activity (Westney & Sakakibara, 1985). Such linkages among the different actors may involve different kinds of exchanges such as those involving funds, people, or information, and they may be established and maintained through many different mechanisms such as integrating governmental agencies, interlocking boards of directors, cross-holding of equity, institutionalizing systems of personnel flows, using long-term contracts and trust-based relationships, and mediating roles of organizations such as trade associations, banks, and consultants (e.g., the collected essays in Evan, 1976). Bower's study shows how Japanese petrochemical companies were able to capitalize on such linkages, not only to build entry barriers in the local market, but also as a means of restructuring and rationalizing the industry.

In locations in which the local organization sets are densely connected, the implications for local units of MNCs are clear. As argued by Granovetter (1973), strong and multiplexed ties among the existing members of the national organization sets will lead to exclusion from the sets of those who cannot establish equally strong and multiplexed ties with each member. Westney and Sakakibara's (1985) study on the R & D activities of Japanese and American computer companies illustrates this effect of within density in the local organization sets. According to these authors, the Japanese R & D centers of some of the American computer companies could not tap into local skills and technologies because the absence of associated manufacturing and marketing activities prevented the isolated research establishments from building linkages with the local "knowledge networks" that were embedded in the dense interactions among different members of the organization set for the computer industry in Japan.

Where the linkages within the local organization sets are sparse, no such barriers are created, as shown in the U.S. Department of Commerce's account of the television industry in the United States in the early 1970s (Paul, 1984). Absence of ties among producers because of rivalry and antitrust laws, and their arm's-length relationships with suppliers, labor, and government, created an environment that made it easy for Japanese producers to enter the U.S. market with local sales offices importing finished products from the parent companies. However, when the American companies responded in a unified manner through the Electronics Industry Association, with the support of labor unions and suppliers, they were able to obtain government support on antidumping suits, and the resulting politically negotiated import quotas forced the Japanese companies to establish local manufacturing facilities.

We can, therefore, make the following propositions about the effects of within density on dispersal and specialization in the configuration of resources in a multinational. When interaction densities within the different national organization sets are low, the social context exerts limited influence and intended economic rationality becomes dominant in resource configuration decisions. In this situation, therefore, the

MNC will concentrate research, production, assembly, and other similar activities based on consideration of potential scale and scope economies and locate them on the basis of *resource niches* (Aldrich, 1979) that may exist in different countries as a result of their comparative advantages (e.g., R & D in the United States or Japan, manufacturing in Singapore or Brazil). As a result, its overall resource configuration will show relatively low dispersal and high specialization. When within densities are high, however, the company will be forced to fragment its activities and locate more of the different kinds of resources in each market so as to provide the variety that is necessary to match the structures of the local organization sets. Consequently, in this case, dispersal will increase while specialization will decrease.

Effects of across density in the external network

When the linkages across the different national organization sets are sparse, the MNC's resource configuration follows the pattern we have described previously based on consideration of the within densities alone. If there are high interactions across members of the different national organization sets, this situation changes significantly.

Consider first the case of low within density and high across density. We have argued that low within density will lead to low dispersal and high specialization, and the company will locate its resources according to the resource niches in different countries. But, with high across densities, many of these national resource niches are eliminated because of freer flows. If technologies developing in one location can be accessed instantaneously from another, or if excess capital available in one environment can be borrowed in markets located elsewhere, there is no longer any need to locate specific activities in specific locations to benefit from access to local resources. Therefore, with high across density, resource-seeking concentration will decline (though not necessarily be eliminated because regulatory and other barriers may selectively prohibit certain flows of people and products).

Consider now the case of high within densities coupled with high across densities. We have suggested that high within density will lead to high dispersal and low specialization because of the need for matching the structures of the local environments. However, when across densities are high, it is no longer necessary to establish a comprehensive range of resources in each market because exchange linkages can now be established across borders, without the need for complementary facilities on a location-by-location basis. In other words, if there is high across density, the logic of resource allocation for both high and low within densities becomes inappropriate. Instead, a completely different set of criteria emerges: In this situation, resource configuration is greatly influenced by the nodal characteristics of the complex external network.

Consider, for example, the situation in which customers in locations A, B, D, and E are strongly influenced by the standards and preferences of customers in location C. Bartlett and Ghoshal (1986) and Prahalad and Doz (1987) have described the existence of such *lead markets* in many businesses, and this existence is predicted by the *normative systems* that Laumann, Glaskiewicz, and Marsden (1978) proposed as one of the modalities that influence the behaviors of members in a network. In such a situation, the MNC will tend to locate a significant amount of resources in C so as to be able to sense the demands of local customers and respond to them in a fashion that attracts their patronage. The level of resources in C will exceed what is required to match the needs for membership of the local organization set (OS_C) and will, instead, be targeted to benefit from the greater role of C as a central node in the larger external network that is created by the linkages among (OS_A), (OS_B), (OS_C), and so on. Given that for different activities of the MNC, different locations might emerge as the nodes in the relevant external networks, and given that even for the same activity there might be multiple nodes instead of a single node, the consequence of increasing across density for the resource configuration of the company will be one of moderate dispersal (i.e., not as high as in the case of local-for-local distribution but higher than concentration only in countries offering specific resource niches) coupled with increasing specialization. Tasks will be divided into finer and finer segments so that each could be located at the appropriate nodal locations which, however, might well be different from those that would be predicted by the traditional considerations of comparative advantages or resource niches as applicable to those tasks.

Chandler (1986), among others, has documented that because of improvements in communication and transportation infrastructures around the world, increasing across densities has been a dominant trend that has affected a wide range of industries in the recent past. The observed consequences of this trend are entirely consistent with our arguments. For example, until the late 1970s, the telecommunications switching industry was characterized by high within and low across densities. Interactions among members of the industry were high within each country because of its status as a *strategic industry* and the resulting coordinating role of the national governments. However, until the advent of digital techno-logy, the industry was highly regulated in most countries, and the need to synchronize the switching equipment with the idiosyncrasies of local terminal equipments constrained opportunities for cross-border linkages. As a result, the resources of most multinational companies were highly dispersed, and they had low levels of specialization. ITT provides a good illustration. Each of its national subsidiaries in Europe had its own local facilities for product development, manufacturing, and marketing, and the corporate staff including the top management of the company con-sisted of fewer than 100 employees.

The context of this industry has changed significantly in the 1980s: Although within densities have remained high, across density has increased substantially due to the emergence of digital technology and the growing trends of standardization and deregulation, all of which have facilitated cross-border integration among suppliers, customers, and other industry participants. As a result, resource configurations of the producers have also changed. Even though the overall level of dispersal has been reduced to a limited extent, the level of specialization has increased drastically. Ericsson, for example, has closed only a few of its factories around the world but it has converted many of them into focused manufacturing centers that produce a narrow range of components. Similarly, each of the laboratories of Alcatel, the company created by merging ITT and CIT-Alcatel, has now been given the mandate and resources to pursue a specific and well-defined technology or development task in contrast to the earlier situation when most of them operated quite independently developing the entire range of products for their local markets.

Centrality and power within the multinational network

Our preceding arguments on resource configuration in MNCs were based on a notion of isomorphic fit with the characteristics of the external network; we did not address the question of how such a fit is achieved. An MNC's configuration of resources at any point in time is the outcome of previous resource flows and, as argued by Benson (1975), the flow of resources within an interorganizational network is influenced by the distribution of power within the network. In this section, we will suggest that within and across densities in the different national organization sets of an MNC predicate the relative power of the headquarters and the national units, and that the nature of resource flows generated by the resulting distribution of power leads to the pattern of isomorphic fit we have described.

Effects of within density in national organization sets

Applying Zald's (1970) political economy approach to the analysis of interorganizational relations, Benson (1975) suggested that an actor in such a network can enhance its power in dyadic relationships with other actors on the strength of its relationships with other organizational or social networks. Subsequently, Provan et al. (1980) provided empirical support to this proposal when they demonstrated that power relations within the network of United Way organizations were significantly modified by the linkages between the individual agencies and other elements in their local communities upon which the United Way depended for its survival. The dependence of the United Way on the local communities of its different organizations is in some ways akin to the dependence of the multinational on the local organization sets of its different national units. Just as dense linkages with the key elements of their communities enhanced the power of the United Way organizations, dense exchange relationships with the members of their local organization sets can be expected to enhance the powers of the national units of the multinational.

It is inappropriate, however, to draw a direct correspondence between the United Way and an MNC because the central management organization of the United Way lacks the hierarchical power of the headquarters of the MNC. To incorporate this difference in our analysis, it is necessary to consider how hierarchical power might modify the interunit exchange patterns proposed by Benson.

We suggest that the efficacy of the hierarchical power of the headquarters to counteract the linkage-based power of the subsidiary is contingent on the density of interactions among members of the subsidiary's organization set. When this within density is low, the potential power of the subsidiary is derived from its individual dyadic relationships. In this situation, the headquarters is more effective in counteracting the power of the subsidiary because it is potentially easier to have "direct control" over such relationships through mechanisms such as periodic visits by the headquarters staff. However, such direct control becomes more difficult in this case, when the subsidiary's power is not derived from an individual dyadic relationship, but from the web of exchange relations in the local organization set of which it is a part. Remote control loses efficacy when "localness," by itself, is the key requirement for maintaining the relationships. For example, in the case of the Australian subsidiary of Ericsson that we referred to earlier, extensive cross-licensing arrangements among all the producers, and the resulting close relationships among equipment suppliers, customers, and regulators, was a main reason (other than distance) that impeded closer control of the local subsidiary from Stockholm and allowed the subsidiary to build up the high level of research and other resources.

Therefore, the positive relationship between environmental linkages and power of the local unit of an interorganizational network proposed by Benson (1975) will remain operational in the context of an MNC under the condition of high within density. Following the arguments of Emerson (1962) and Cook (1977), the local unit will use this power to reduce its dependence on the other units of the network. Therefore, it will bargain for and obtain a full range of resources so that it will be able to autonomously carry out as many of its functions as possible. If all or most of the units of the MNC are located in environments of high within density, the consequence of this process will be a high level of dispersal of its resources on a local-for-local basis.

Effects of across density in the external network

Existing literature on the distribution of power in social networks reveals two main sources of power in such collectivities (Fombrun, 1983). First, power is an antipode of dependency in exchange relations (Emerson, 1962), and it accrues to members of the network who control critical resources required by others but do not depend on others for resources (Aldrich, 1979; Pfeffer & Salancik, 1978). In keeping with Cook (1977), this might be called *exchange power* to distinguish it from the second source of power that arises from structural rather than exchange dependencies. *Structural power* emanates from the position of a member within the network; as shown by Lazarsfeld and Menzel (1961), it is an attribute that is induced by a member's context.

Our preceding discussions on power-dependency relationships within an MNC were based only on consideration of dyadic exchange between the headquarters and the national units. The situation changes when consideration of structural power is brought into the analysis. Structure of the external network now enters the calculation as an important variable because different members of the multinational network can potentially develop different levels of structural power based on their positions within the larger network of interactions among customers, suppliers, and so forth across different countries.

Ignoring for present purposes the exceptions to the rule pointed out by Cook, Emerson, Gilmore, and Yamagishi (1983), the structural power of actors in a network can be assumed to arise from their centrality within the network (Laumann & Pappi, 1976; Lehman, 1975). As pointed out by Freeman (1979), the term centrality has been defined and used in the literature in many different ways. For this article, we can limit our attention to what Freeman describes as point centrality of the different actors within the multinational network, and we can also define the point centrality of each actor as a function of its degree (i.e., the number of other actors within the multinational network with which it has direct exchange relations). Following the arguments of Freeman, the headquarters enjoys the highest levels of point centrality when linkages among the subsidiaries are minimal. In a situation of extensive interactions among the subsidiaries, the centrality of the headquarters declines relative to those of the subsidiaries, and the centrality of the different members of the network becomes dependent on the actual structure of such linkages. This explanation becomes clear from a comparison of the three network structures shown in Figure 2 (each of which is reproduced from Freeman, 1979).

High across density typically implies a high level of interactions among the subsidiaries of a multinational. As an illustration, consider the case of a manufacturer of automotive tires such as Italy's Pirelli and Company. The company produces and markets car and truck tires in a number of countries including the United States, Italy, and Germany. It also supplies tires to the Ford Motor Company in each of these countries.

Until such time that Ford's local units in these countries operated relatively autonomously, with minimal coordination, there was little need for Pirelli's local units to coordinate their own activities with regard to their supply to Ford. But as the interactions and coordination among Ford's operations in these countries increased, leading to internal comparisons of the prices, quality, and support provided by common vendors (thereby enhancing across density, as relevant to Pirelli), Pirelli's subsidiaries also needed to enhance their internal coordination and communication on issues of quality levels, pricing, service, and so on to prevent customer dissatisfaction (see Terpstra, 1982). In other words,

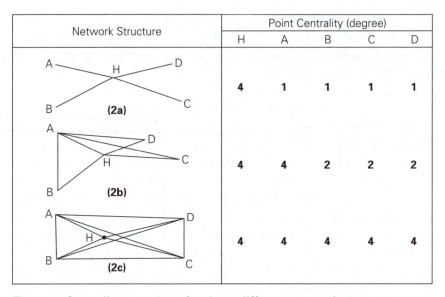

Network Structure	Point Centrality (degree)				
	H	A	B	C	D
(2a)	4	1	1	1	1
(2b)	4	4	2	2	2
(2c)	4	4	4	4	4

Figure 2 Centrality measures for three different network structures

as a general principle, it can be stated that as across density increases, intersubsidiary linkages become more extensive, and the centrality of the headquarters declines, relative to other units.

It is more interesting to note, however, under this condition, multiple points can emerge within the MNC with the same or similar degree of point centrality. Note that for the star-shaped structure (Figure 2c), the headquarters and all the subsidiaries have the same point centrality, whereas in the hub-shaped structure (Figure 2a), the headquarters has a very high level of point centrality compared to the subsidiaries. In Figure 2b, however, whereas one subsidiary has the same point centrality as the headquarters, other subsidiaries have less.

An outcome such as the network structure shown in Figures 2b or 2c will follow from the existence of nodes in the external network. For example, for Pirelli, the United States, Italy, and Germany may emerge as external nodes because the headquarters for its major worldwide customers may be located in these markets. Further, only one of these external nodes (Italy) may coincide with the location of the company's own headquarters. Normative hierarchy in customer tastes and preferences (e.g., adoption by customers in other countries of a perfume or wine that is popular in France) and the advanced states of certain technologies in certain countries (e.g., ceramic technology in Japan, computer software technology in the United States and the United Kingdom) are some other examples of such external nodes that can affect the point centralities of different units within the MNC. For the different activities of the MNC, different locations can emerge as the nodes of the external network; for any particular activity, a number of different locations can possess such nodal characteristics. Consequently, following the arguments of Burt (1978), the multinational network typically will develop multiple centers that have different internal coalitions and nodes corresponding to the different coalitions and nodes that may exist in the external network.

Therefore, in such a situation, the nodal units of the multinational will develop structural power and use this power to attract resources from within the MNC network. As a result, the level of dispersal in the MNC's resources will be moderate – lower than local-for-local dispersal (because not all units will emerge as nodes) but higher than in the case of concentration in locations of specific resource niches (except for businesses where a specific country enjoys a dominant position in all activities). Further, a high level of specialization also will develop in the resource configuration because nodal positions within the MNC network can be expected to vary by activities and tasks as a reflection of similar variance in the external network. Note that both the process and the outcome aspects of this conclusion resonate with some recent empirical findings such as those of subsidiaries being given *world product mandates* (Poynter & Rugman, 1982) and *global leader* or *contributor* roles (Bartlett & Ghoshal, 1986) for specific activities and tasks.

Large MNCs as differentiated networks

Several highly simplifying assumptions were made in the foregoing discussions on resource configuration in MNCs under different conditions of local and global interlinkages. The enormous complexity of several disparate country-level organization sets and the diversity of the heterogeneous international business environment were dichotomized into high-low categories of within and across densities. In reality, the levels of connectedness within and across the national organization sets can be expected to vary across countries and groups of countries. Density of interactions across the national organization sets may be high for the developed countries, or among regional groupings, but low in developing countries, particularly the more regulated and autarchic. Similarly, interactions among members within the national organization sets may be high in homogeneous societies that have a tradition of strong interinstitutional linkages, and it may be low in countries where such linkages are discouraged through legislation, impeded because of societal heterogeneity, or rendered ineffective because of poor communication infrastructures or the absence of linking institutions.

Therefore, the configuration of resources in multinationals engaged in such businesses will be influenced by multiple criteria. In some locations internal interactions within the local organization sets may be high, but external linkages with other organization sets may be low. In such locations, the MNC may provide all the required resources in appropriate measures so that its local unit can build and maintain linkages with key members of its own community. The organization sets in some other countries may be sparsely connected internally, but different elements of the local environment may be strongly connected with their counterparts in other countries. For these locations, the MNC may create a resource structure that is concentrated and specialized, and in some cases the location of the specialized resources may reflect the desire to access special resource niches, whereas in other cases the location choice may be motivated by the modalities in the external network. Finally, the organization sets in a third group of countries may be characterized by high within and across linkages. In these locations, the MNC may establish all the complementary resources for integrated operations, but it may link these locations with others so as to leverage the resources and achieve economies of concentration and specialization.

The overall resource configuration for a company like Philips, then, will reflect a mix of some resources that are dispersed among some units on a purely local-for-local basis (e.g., product development, manufacturing, marketing, and other resources for the lighting business in India), some that are concentrated in different countries to access specialized local resource pools (e.g., the global scale audio factory in Singapore), and others that are concentrated in lead markets (e.g., development and manufacturing facilities for teletext television sets in the United Kingdom). Elsewhere we have described such a structure as the *differentiated network* and have shown that a number of large multinational companies such as Procter & Gamble, Unilever, Ericsson, NEC, and Matsushita are increasingly converging to this structural form despite the differences in their businesses and parent company nationalities (Bartlett & Ghoshal, 1989).

Such a convergence is consistent with the theoretical arguments we have presented here. Following the arguments of Chandler (1986), one effect of worldwide improvements in communication and transportation infrastructures is the increasing interlinkages among actors, both within and across national boundaries. When such linkages are low, the influence of structural embeddedness is low, and MNCs have a greater degree of freedom to locate their activities and resources to benefit from local resource niches and are in line with the economic and technological characteristics of their businesses. Thus, in such situations, the resource configurations of different MNCs can be expected to differ as a reflection of those differences in their businesses and as a result of their freedom to exercise strategic choices. However, in the context of high within and across densities, such freedom is reduced because of the network influences: Both dispersal and specialization now become essential, at least for the very large companies that have been the focus of our attention in this article. If within density is a country trait and across density is a world-system trait, the pattern of linkages in the overall structure of the external network is going to be increasingly similar for large multinational companies, irrespective of their businesses. In other words, mimetic and normative forces of isomorphism (DiMaggio & Powell, 1983) may be getting stronger as the world jolts along to Levitt's (1983) *global village*, and the observed trend of convergence to the differentiated network structure may be an outcome of these broader societal changes.

Implications for research

We have proposed a reconceptualization of the MNC as an interorganizational system rather than as an organization. This reconceptualization creates the possibility of applying exchange theory and network methodologies to the study of MNCs and has some important implications for future research on MNC-related issues.

First, at the aggregate level of macrostructural differences among MNCs, traditional analysis has tended to assume internal homogeneity within such companies. This has resulted in generalized conclusions at the level of the overall company based on empirical studies that have focused on individual actors or specific dyadic links. For example, a sampled group of American MNCs have been inferred to be more centralized than their Japanese and European counterparts based on analysis of the parent companies' relationships with their subsidiaries located in one region (e.g., Hulbert & Brandt, 1980). However, as we have argued, headquarters-subsidiary relations within an MNC can vary widely from subsidiary to subsidiary. The interorganizational network conceptualization can provide new concepts such as graph centrality (Freeman, 1979) or hierarchy (Coleman, 1966), which appear to be theoretically more appropriate for such macrostructural comparisons among internally differentiated and heterogeneous organizational systems like MNCs.

Second, given such heterogeneity, macrostructural analysis alone may not be enough and may need to be complemented with microstructural analyses of these internal differences so as to build a more nearly complete theoretical understanding of the ways in which an MNC functions. For example, in the differentiated network MNC, there is no formal macrostructure that "fits" all parts of the company's heterogeneous environments. Yet, it has to choose a formal departmental structure and might, quite arbitrarily, choose one that appears to be simple and consistent with its own administrative heritage (Bartlett, 1983, 1986). Therefore, not only might macrostructure have become more difficult to predict theoretically – as seems true, given the significant empirically induced modifications to the Stopford and Wells (1972) contingency model proposed by subsequent studies of MNC macrostructures, such as those by Daniels, Pitts, and Tretter (1985) and Egelhoff (1988) – but it might also have become a less interesting attribute to study precisely because of such indeterminateness. For example, contrary to the predictions of structural contingency, NEC, Procter & Gamble, and Unilever have not changed their macrostructures in over two decades despite some very significant changes in their business conditions. What have changed in these companies are the internal management processes; subsidiaries have assumed new and specific roles to respond to changing local conditions, and the headquarters' control mechanisms have evolved from ubiquitous "company ways" to multidimensional gestalts that are applied differently to different parts of the organization so as to respond to shifting global contexts (Bartlett & Ghoshal, 1989). The network perspective is particularly suited for investigation of such differences in internal roles, relations, and tasks of different affiliated units (e.g., through block modeling and analysis of functional equivalence) and of how internal coordination mechanisms might be differentiated to match the variety of subunit contexts (e.g., the papers by Burt on "distinguishing relational contents" (pp. 35–74) and "studying status/role-sets using mass surveys" (pp. 100–118) in Burt, Minor, & Associates, 1983).

The same argument we made for structure can also be made for strategy. Discussions on company- or even business-level generic strategies and how they "fit" generic types of competitive structures are too far removed from the reality of highly differentiated strategic approaches that can be expected in different parts of the differentiated network organization. Instead, it may be more useful to explore the actual content of strategy in such complex organizational systems: Network theoretic analysis of internal flows of resources, products, people, and information might be more relevant for developing middle-range theories on resource commitment, decision making, strategic control, normative integration, and creation and diffusion of innovations in such companies (e.g., the application of network analysis in Carley, 1986; Burt, 1987, and Walker, 1985). In this article we have focused primarily on the hierarchical network relationships between the headquarters and the national subsidiaries of an MNC. Investigation of the lateral network relations among the different subsidiaries can open up avenues for similar fine-grained analysis of both the causes and consequences of horizontal interdependencies and synergy.

Finally, as has been shown in some recent contributions, the interorganizational approach can be particularly useful for the study of another MNC-related phenomenon that is assuming increasing importance (viz., their forming complex webs of alliances and joint ventures with customers, suppliers, and competitors [Ohmae, 1989; Harrigan, 1985]). By focusing on relations among actors, the network analysis approach can provide both appropriate concepts and methodological tools for rigorous and theory-grounded investigation of the strategic and organizational aspects of such alliances (see, for example, the contributions by Walker [pp. 227–240], Westney [pp. 339–346], and Hakausson & Johanson [pp. 369–379] cited in Contractor & Lorange, 1988).

Building a network theory of the MNC

The concepts and arguments presented here suffer from a number of shortcomings that should be overcome before the network conceptualization can yield a useful and testable theory of the MNC. The necessary improvement and extension of these preliminary ideas will require both deductive theory building with more sophisticated use of network theory than has been achieved here; empirical studies are also needed to induce and test more fine-grained propositions and hypotheses.

First, our definitions of constructs such as within and across densities are too coarse because, as we point out in the concluding section, these densities cannot but differ for different parts of the total external network of any company. Such differences can be expected along both geographic and functional dimensions. For example, the external organizations relevant for the R & D department of a company may be far more interconnected across national borders compared to those that are relevant for the service department. Similarly, while within density, on average, may be higher in Japan than in the United States, there may be significant differences between the two contexts for different parts of the local organization sets. One of the main attractions of the network perspective is that the implications of such differences can be explicitly included in both theoretical and empirical analyses, and elaboration of these distinctions must be a priority for future research on this topic.

Second, we have considered exchange very broadly to include many different kinds of transactions involving products, information, affect, and so on, without distinguishing among these different flows. As follows from the general arguments of Mitchell (1973) and Kadushin (1978), each of these different kinds of exchanges can have some very different implications for the strategy, organization, and management of an MNC; further, those effects are also likely to be interactive. Therefore, the next phase of theory development must explicate the separate and joint effects of these different kinds of exchanges.

Third, we have focused on density as the key parameter of the external network because density appeared to relate most closely to the implications of social embeddedness described by Granovetter (1985). Further, it is also a relatively simple construct that is easy to conceptualize and to measure once the relevant organization sets and external network are identified (see below). But density is not a complete description of a network, and it is possible that some other characteristics of the external network can significantly influence specific attributes of the MNC. Therefore, for more nearly complete development of theory, it would be desirable to identify a set of parameters that completely and unambiguously define the external network and then to explore the impact of each of these parameters on selected attributes of the multinational. Krackhardt (1989) has proposed four parameters (connectedness, hierarchy, least-upperboundedness, and graph efficiency) as necessary and sufficient descriptors of a network, and his work provides some interesting opportunities for modifying and extending our theoretical arguments.

Finally, besides (indeed, before) such extension and refinement of the concepts, it might also be necessary to improve the specificity and precision in our definition of some of the constructs so as to facilitate their operationalization in empirical research. One key issue concerns delineation of the boundaries of the different national organization sets, which is a general and widespread problem in network research

(Laumann, Marsden, & Prensky, 1983). As suggested by Aldrich and Whetten (1981), the relevant organization sets may well differ according to different kinds of exchange, and the definition of the boundaries may, therefore, depend on the kind of exchange that is the focus of inquiry. In presenting our ideas here, we have been guided by the belief that these boundaries can be identified either through the naturalistic approach of an a priori commonsense definition, or empirically, through measurement of structural cohesion (DiMaggio, 1986). In the former approach, for example, all relevant suppliers, customers, regulators, and competitors in any country can be prespecified based on expert knowledge of the local structure of the business. In the latter approach, a broader population of potentially relevant members of the local organization set may be identified through a repeated process of snowball sampling until sufficient convergence is achieved, and the organization set can then be identified empirically from this population as the group of organizations that interact maximally with one another and minimally with other members of the population. Once the relevant local organization sets are identified by one or the other method, the external network can be defined as the collectivity of all these local organization sets.

Clearly, the former method for identifying the national organization sets is the more convenient, and it is our belief that experienced researchers should usually be able to prespecify most of the relevant actors with sufficient accuracy. Some researchers, however, may prefer the latter approach for it avoids the arbitrariness of an a priori selection. However, as Laumann *et al.* (1983) have argued, neither approach is fully satisfactory, and some better way for delineation of the boundaries remains as another important topic for further reflection.

Christopher A. Bartlett (DBA, Harvard) is Professor at the Harvard Business School.

Nitin Nohria was an active and equal partner in the idea development phase and would have been a coauthor of the paper but for the temporary distraction of having to write a doctoral dissertation. The paper benefitted from the comments of Martin Kilduff and Eleanor Westney.

This paper appeared in *Academy of Management Review*, October 1990.

REFERENCES

Aldrich, H.E. (1976) Resource dependence and interorganizational relations. Relations between local employment service offices and social service sector organizations, *Administration and Society*, 7, 419–454.

Aldrich, H.E. (1979) *Organizations and environments*. Englewood Cliffs, NJ: Prentice-Hall.

Aldrich, H.E., & Whetten, D.A. (1981) Organization-sets, action-sets, and networks. Making the most of simplicity. In P.C. Nystrom & W.H. Starbuck (Eds.), *Handbook of organizational design* (pp. 385–408). London: Oxford University Press.

Bacharach, S.B., & Aiken, M. (1976) Structural and process constraints on influence in organizations. A level specific analysis, *Administrative Science Quarterly*, 21, 623–642.

Bartlett, C.A. (1983) MNCs: Get off the reorganization merry-go-round, *Harvard Business Review*, 6(2), 138–146.

Bartlett, C.A. (1986) Building and managing the transnational. The new organizational challenge. In M.E. Porter (Ed.), *Competition in global industries*. Boston: Harvard Business School Press.

Bartlett, C.A., & Ghoshal, S. (1986) Tap your subsidiaries for global reach, *Harvard Business Review*, 4(6), 87–94.

Bartlett, C.A., & Ghoshal, S. (1987) Managing across borders: New organizational responses, *Sloan Management Review*, 29(1), 43–53.

Bartlett, C.A., & Ghoshal, S. (1989) *Managing across borders: The transnational solution*. Boston: Harvard Business School Press.

Benson, J.K. (1975) The interorganizational network as a political economy, *Administrative Science Quarterly*, 20, 229–249.

Bower, J.L. (1987) *When markets quake*. Boston: Harvard Business School Press.

Buckley, P.J., & Casson, M.C. (1985) *The economic theory of the multinational enterprise*. London: Macmillan.

Burt, R.S. (1978) Stratification and prestige among elite experts in mathematical sociology circa 1975, *Social Networks*, 1, 105–158.

Burt, R.S. (1987) Social contagion and innovation: Cohesion versus structural equivalence, *American Journal of Sociology*, 92, 1287–1335.

Burt, R.S., Minor, M.J., & Associates (Eds.) (1983) *Applied network analysis: A methodological introduction*. Beverley Hills, CA: Sage.

Carley, K. (1986) An approach for relating social structure to cognitive structure, *Journal of Mathematical Sociology*, 12(2), 137–189.

Caves, R.E. (1982) *Multinational enterprise and economic analysis*. Cambridge: Cambridge University Press.

Chandler, A.D. (1986) The evolution of modern global competition. In M.E. Porter (Ed.), *Competition in global industries* (pp. 405–448). Boston: Harvard Business School Press.

Coleman, J.S. (1966) Foundations for a theory of collective decisions, *American Journal of Sociology*, 71, 615–627.

Contractor, F.J., & Lorange, P. (Eds.) (1988) *Cooperative strategies in international business*. Lexington, MA: Lexington Books.

Cook, K.S. (1977) Exchange and power in networks of interorganizational relations, *Sociological Quarterly*, 18, 62–82.

Cook, K.S., Emerson, R.M., Gilmore, M.R., & Yamagishi, T. (1983) The distribution of power in exchange networks: Theory and experimental results, *American Journal of Sociology*, 89, 275–305.

Daniels, J.D., Pitts, R.A., & Tretter, M.J. (1985) Organizing for dual strategies of product diversity and international expansion, *Strategic Management Journal*, 6, 223–237.

DiMaggio, P. (1986) Structural analysis of organizational fields: A blockmodel approach. In B.M. Staw & L.L. Cummings (Eds.), *Research in organizational behavior* (Vol. 8, pp. 335–370). Greenwich, CT: JAI Press.

DiMaggio, P.J., & Powell, W.W. (1983) The iron cage revisited: Institutional isomorphism and collective rationality in organizational fields, *American Sociological Review*, 48, 147–160.

Dunning, J.H. (1981) *International production and the multinational enterprise*. London: Allen and Unwin.

Eccles, R.G. (1981) The quasi firm in the construction industry, *Journal of Economic Behavior and Organization*, 2, 335–357.

Eccles, R.G., & Crane, D.B. (1987) Managing through networks in investment banking, *California Management Review*, 30(1), 176–195.

Egelhorf, W.G. (1988) Strategy and structure in multinational corporations: A revision of the Stopford and Wells model, *Strategic Management Journal*, 1–14.

Emerson, R.M. (1962) Power-dependence relations, *American Sociological Review*, 27, 31–41.

Evan, W.M. (1967) The organization-set: Toward a theory of interorganizational relations. In J.D. Thompson (Ed.), *Approaches to organizational design* (pp. 173–191). Pittsburgh: University of Pittsburgh Press.

Evan, W.M. (Ed.) (1976) *Interorganizational relations*. Harmondsworth, England: Penguin Books.

Fayerweather, J. (1978) *International business strategy and administration*. Cambridge, MA: Ballinger.

Fombrun, C.J. (1983) Attributions of power across a social network, *Human Relations*, 36, 493–508.

Freeman, L.C. (1979) Centrality in social networks: Conceptual clarification, *Social Networks*, 1(3), 215–239.

Ghemawat, P., & Spence, A.M. (1986) Modeling global competition. In M.E. Porter (Ed.), *Competition in global industries* (pp. 61–79). Boston: Harvard Business School Press.

Ghoshal, S. (1986) *The innovative multinational: A differentiated network of organizational roles and management processes*. Unpublished doctoral dissertation, Harvard University, Graduate School of Business Administration, Boston.

Ghoshal, S., & Nohria, N. (1989) Internal differentiation within the multinational corporation, *Strategic Management Journal*, 10, 323–337.

Granovetter, M. (1973) The strength of weak ties, *American Journal of Sociology*, 81, 1287–1303.

Granovetter, M. (1985) Economic action and social structure: The problem of embeddedness, *American Journal of Sociology*, 91, 481–510.

Hakausson, H., & Johanson, J. (1988) Formal and informal cooperation strategies in international industrial networks. In F.J. Contractor & P. Lorange (Eds.), *Cooperative strategies in international business* (pp. 369–379). Lexington, MA: Lexington Books.

Hall, R.H., Clark, J.P., Giordano, P.C., Jonnson, P.V., & Roekel, M.V. (1977) Patterns of interorganizational relationships, *Administrative Science Quarterly*, 22, 457–471.

Harrigan, K.R. (1985) *Strategies for joint ventures*. Lexington, MA: Lexington Books.

Hedlund, G. (1986) The Hypermodern MNC – a heterarchy? *Human Resource Management*, 25, 9–36.

Hennart, J.F. (1982) *A theory of multinational enterprise*. Ann Arbor: University of Michigan Press.

Herbert, T.T. (1984) Strategy and multinational structure: An interorganizational relations perspective, *Academy of Management Review*, 9, 259–271.

Hirsch, S. (1976) An international trade and investment theory of the firm, *Oxford Economic Papers*, 28 (July), 258–270.

Hofstede, G. (1980) *Culture's consequences: International differences in work-related values*. Beverly Hills, CA: Sage.

Homans, G. (1974) *Social behavior: Its elementary forms* (2nd ed.). New York: Harcourt Brace Jovanovich.

Hulbert, J.M., & Brandt, W.K. (1980) *Managing the multinational subsidiary*. New York: Holt, Rinehart & Winston.

Kadushin, C. (1978) *Introduction to macro-network analysis*. Unpublished manuscript, Columbia University Teachers College.

Kogut, B. (1983) Foreign direct investment as a sequential process. In C.P. Kindleberger & D. Andretsch (Eds.), *The multinational corporation in the 1980s*. Cambridge, MA: MIT Press.

Kogut, B. (1988) Country patterns in international competition: appropriability and oligopolistic agreement. In N. Hood & Vahlne (Eds.), *Strategies in global competition*. London: Croom-Helm.

Kogut, B. (1989) A note on global strategies, *Strategic Management Journal*, 10, 383–389.

Krackhardt, D. (1989) *Graphing theoretical dimensions of the informal organization*. Presentation at the European Institute of Business Administration (INSEAD), Fontainebleau, France.

Laumann, E.O., & Pappi, F. (1976) *Networks of collective action: A perspective on community influence systems*. New York: Academic Press.

Laumann, E.O., Glaskiewicz, J., & Marsden, P.V. (1978) Community structure as interorganizational linkages, *Annual Review of Sociology*, 4, 455–484.

Laumann, E.O., Marsden, P.V., & Prensky, D. (1983) The boundary specification problem in network analysis. In R.S. Burt, M.J. Minor, and Associates (Eds.), *Applied network analysis: A methodological introduction* (pp. 18–34). Beverly Hills, CA: Sage.

Lazarsfeld, P.F., & Menzel, H. (1961) On the relation between individual and collective properties. In A. Etzioni (Ed.), *Complex organizations: A sociological reader* (pp. 422–440). New York: Holt, Rinehart & Winston.

Lehman, E.W. (1975) *Coordinating health care: Explorations in interorganizational relations*. Beverly Hills, CA: Sage.

Lessard, D., & Lightstone, J.B. (1986) Volatile exchange rates can put operations at risk, *Harvard Business Review*, 64(4), 107–114.

Levitt, T. (1983) The globalization of markets, *Harvard Business Review*, 61(3), 92–102.

Magee, S.P. (1977) Information and the multinational corporation: An appropriability theory of direct foreign investment. In J.N. Bhagwati (Ed.), *The new international economic order* (pp. 317–340). Cambridge, MA: MIT Press.

Mahini, A., & Wells, L.T. (1986) Government relations in the global firm. In M.E. Porter (Ed.), *Competition in global industries*. Boston: Harvard Business School Press.

Meyer, J.W., & Scott, W.R. (1983) *Organizational environments*. Beverly Hills, CA: Sage.

Mitchell, J.C. (1973) Networks, norms and institutions. In J. Boissevain & J.C. Mitchell (Eds.), *Network analysis* (pp. 15–35). The Hague: Mouton.

Nohria, N., & Venkatraman, N. (1987) *Interorganizational information systems via information technology: A network analytic perspective*. Working paper No 1909–87, Massachusetts Institute of Technology, Sloan School of Management, Cambridge.

Ohmae, K. (1989) The global logic of strategic alliances, *Harvard Business Review*, 67(2), 143–154.

Paul, J.K. (Ed.) (1984) *High technology international trade and competition*. Park Ridge, NJ: Noyes Publications.

Perlmutter, H.V. (1969) The tortuous evolution of the multinational corporation, *Columbia Journal of World Business*, 4(4), 9–18.

Pfeffer, J., & Salancik, G.R. (1974) The bases and use of power in organizational decision making: The case of a university, *Administrative Science Quarterly*, 19, 453–473.

Pfeffer, J., & Salancik, G.R. (1978) *The external control of organizations: A resource dependency perspective*. New York: Harper and Row.

Porter, M.E. (in press) *The competitive advantage of nations and their firms*. New York: Free Press.

Porter, M.E. (Ed.) (1986) Competition in global industries: A conceptual framework. In M.E. Porter (Ed.), *Competition in global industries* (pp. 15–60). Boston: Harvard Business School Press.

Powell, W.W. (1985) *Getting into print: The decision-making process in scholarly publishing*. Chicago: University of Chicago Press.

Poynter, T.A., & Rugman, A.M. (1982) World product mandates: How will multinationals respond? *Business Quarterly*, 47(3), 54–61.

Prahalad, C.K., & Doz, Y.L. (1987) *The multinational mission: Balancing local demands and global vision*. New York: Free Press.

Provan, K.G. (1983) The federation as an interorganizational linkage network, *Academy of Management Review*, 8, 79–89.

Provan, K.G., Beyer, J.M., & Kruytbosch, C. (1980) Environmental linkages and power in resource dependence relations between organizations, *Administrative Science Quarterly*, 25, 200–225.

Robock, S.H., Simmons, K., & Zwick, J. (1977) *International business and multinational enterprise*. Homewood, IL: Irwin.

Rugman, A.M. (1980) A new theory of the multinational enterprise: Internationalization versus internalization, *Columbia Journal of World Business*, 15(1), 23–29.

Sabel, C., Herrigel, G., Kazis, R., & Deeg, R. (1987) How to keep mature industries innovative, *Technology Review*, 90(3), 26–35.

Stevens, G.V.G. (1974) The determinants of investment. In J.H. Dunning (Ed.), *Economic analysis and the multinational enterprise* (pp. 47–88). London: Allen & Unwin.

Stopford, J.M., & Wells, L.T. (1972) *Managing the multinational enterprise*. New York: Basic Books.

Teece, D.J. (1980) Economies of scale and the scope of the enterprise, *Journal of Economic Behavior and Organization*, 1, 223–247.

Teece, D.J. (1986) Transaction cost economies and the multinational enterprise, *Journal of Economic Behavior and Organization*, 7, 21–45.

Terpstra, V. (1982) *International dimensions of marketing*. Boston: Kent.

Tichy, N.M., Tushman, M.L., & Fombrun, C. (1979) Social network analysis for organizations, *Academy of Management Review*, 4, 507–519.

Van de Ven, A.H., & Walker, G. (1984) The dynamics of interorganizational coordination, *Administrative Science Quarterly*, 29, 598–621.

Walker, G. (1985) Network position and cognition in a computer software firm, *Administrative Science Quarterly*, 30, 103–130.

Walker, G. (1988) Network analysis for cooperative interfirm relationships. In F.J. Contractor & P. Lorange (Eds.), *Cooperative strategies in international business* (pp. 227–240). Lexington, MA: Lexington Books.

Warren, R.L. (1967) The interorganizational field as a focus for investigation, *Administrative Science Quarterly*, 12, 396–419.

Westney, D.E. (1988) Domestic and foreign learning curves in managing international cooperative strategies. In F.J. Contractor & P. Lorange (Eds.), *Cooperative strategies in international business* (pp. 339–346). Lexington, MA: Lexington Books.

Westney, D.E. (1989) *Institutionalization theory: The study of the multinational enterprise*. Paper presented at the conference on organization theory and the multinational enterprise, INSEAD, September 1–2, 1989.

Westney, D.E., & Sakakibara, D. (1985) *Comparative study of the training, careers, and organization of engineers on the computer industry in Japan and the United States*. MIT-Japan Science and Technology Program, MIT (mineo).

Zald, M.N. (1970) Political economy: A framework for comparative analysis. In M.N. Zald (Ed.), *Power in organizations* (pp. 221–261). Nashville, TN: Vanderbilt University Press.

Zeitz, G. (1980) Interorganizational dialectics, *Administrative Science Quarterly*, 25, 72–88.

Zucker, L.G. (1988) *Institutional patterns and organizations*. Cambridge, MA: Bellinger.

CHAPTER 5

Internal differentiation within multinational corporations

Sumantra Ghoshal and Nitin Nohria

This is one of several papers Sumantra wrote with Nitin Nohria examining different facets of the differentiated network *model of the multinational corporation. They argue here that the relationship between the national subsidiary and corporate HQ is systematically differentiated to fit the different environmental and resource contingencies faced by the national subsidiary. Three facets of the HQ–subsidiary relationship are examined – the centralization of decision-making at the centre, the formalization of rules and procedures, and the extent to which there are shared values between the two parties. The analysis supports these arguments, and also offers evidence that a closer fit to one of the "ideal" profiles is associated with higher performance. This paper is important – it provided the first systematic evidence for the different relationships national subsidiaries have with their corporate HQs.*

Over twenty years ago, Thompson proposed that "under norms of rationality, organizations facing heterogeneous task environments seek to identify homogeneous segments and establish structural units to deal with each" (1967: 70). The multinational corporation (MNC) is the quint-essential case of an organization facing heterogeneous task environments: its different national subsidiaries are often embedded in very different environmental conditions (Robock, Simmons and Zwick, 1977), and may have developed under very different historical circumstances (Stopford and Turner, 1985). From the perspective of contingency theory, therefore, one can expect that the internal structure within a multinational corporation will not be homogeneous, but will be differentiated to match the contexts of its different national subsidiaries (Lawrence and Lorsch, 1967).

The objective of this paper is to explore this issue of internal differentiation within MNCs. We propose a contingency framework and develop conditions of "fit" (Drazin and Van de Ven, 1985) between the particular contextual conditions that characterize a subsidiary and the structure of the headquarters–subsidiary relation. We argue that the subsidiary context can be differentiated into four categories based on the joint conditions of its (1) local resource levels and (2) environmental complexity relative to the other subsidiaries in the MNC. The fit structure of the headquarters–subsidiary relation in each contextual category is a correspondingly differentiated combination of the following elements: (1) centralization, the lack of subsidiary autonomy in decision-making; (2) formalization, the use of systematic rules and procedures in decision-making; and (3) normative integration, consensus and shared values as a basis for decision-making.

The framework we present here is based on a research project that consisted of three phases, with a different methodological approach adopted in each phase. The first phase of the project involved case studies of the organizational structures, systems, and management processes in nine large multinational companies and led to a normative scheme proposing four generic organizational roles that could be assumed by MNC subsidiaries (Bartlett and Ghoshal, 1986). In the second phase of the study a similar pattern of internal differentiation among subsidiaries was documented through a detailed questionnaire survey of headquarters–subsidiary relations in three of these nine companies, and it was shown that the governance systems and communication patterns in these three companies tended to be different for subsidiaries belonging to the different categories (Ghoshal, 1986; Ghosal and Bartlett, 1988). In this paper, representing the third stage of this project, the framework is formally grounded in organization theory and is empirically tested using data on 618 cases of headquarters–subsidiary relationships collected by a survey of 66 of the largest European and North American MNCs. While we do not demonstrate methodological triangulation within this paper, it is relevant to note that the framework we present here was not developed purely on prior theoretical principles, but draws heavily from, and builds on, the earlier stages of the overall research project.

The paper is organized in four sections. The first section develops the theoretical motivation for the proposed contingency framework. Central to our argument is the conceptualization of the headquarters–subsidiary relation as a mixed-motive dyad in which members have both inter-dependent and independent interests. It is then shown that each of the four contextual conditions presents a very different situation in terms of the nature of interdependency and independency in the headquarters–subsidiary exchange relation. Centralization, formalization, and normative integration are examined as the primary attributes of headquarters–subsidiary relations. Based on the dual consideration of (i) the relative efficacy of each of these elements in addressing the mixed-motive situation described earlier, and (ii) the administrative costs associated with each element, several hypotheses are proposed that describe a fit between the contingent conditions that characterize a subsidiary and the structure of the headquarters–subsidiary relation. The next section describes the design, the survey, the questionnaire instrument, and the operationaliza-tion and measurement of the constructs employed in the study. The third section presents both the methods used to test the hypotheses developed earlier and the results of these tests. The final section discusses these results and their implications for the literature on headquarters–subsidiary relations in MNCs.

Internal differentiation in MNCs: a contingency framework

It has been well established by authors such as Thompson (1967) and Lawrence and Lorsch (1967) that the structures of organizations, in which term they include formal structural arrangements as well as formal and informal management processes, are and should be differentiated based on the characteristics of the external environment they face. This argument is a direct corollary of the open-systems view of organizations and has demonstrated empirical and theoretical support (see Pfeffer, 1982, for an exhaustive review).

A different motivation for differentiation has been proposed by authors such as Pfeffer and Salancik (1978) and Pfeffer (1981), who have shown that organizational processes are dependent on internal power relationships which, in turn, are critically contingent upon the internal distribution of organizational resources. In this view, then, resource dependency is the key determinant of the structure of internal exchange relationships within complex organizations.

A synthesis of these two views has been proposed by Lawrence and Dyer (1983), but they have treated the entire organization as their unit of analysis and have used different industrial contexts to derive different environmental complexity and resource scarcity situations. It is our view that this synthesis may readily be extended to multi-unit organizations, such as MNCs, in which different components, such as the various national subsidiaries, face vastly different environmental and resource contingencies.

Headquarters–subsidiary relations as a mixed-motive dyad

Adopting an exchange theoretic perspective (Levine and White, 1961; Emerson, 1962, 1975; Aiken and Hage, 1968), the relation between the headquarters and any subsidiary of an MNC may be treated as a dyadic exchange relation involving a series of resource transactions that are embedded in a structured context. Such a relationship may then be conceived as a mixed-motive situation (Schmidt and Kochan, 1977). This view would recognize that headquarters–subsidiary relations involve both (i) interdependent interest situations, e.g., multi-point competition with a global competitor (Knickerbocker, 1973; Graham, 1974; Hamel and Prahalad, 1985), in which each member is internally motivated to transact because each perceives that it will be better able to attain its goals by interacting than by remaining autonomous (Thompson, 1967); and (ii) independent interest situations, e.g., a transfer-pricing decision, in which the motivation to interact may be asymmetrical; including the extreme case when one member is motivated to interact but the other is not. Interaction in this case may, however, be mandated by the headquarters as a result of the authority relationship that exists relative to the subsidiary.

The above conceptualization of the nature of headquarters–subsidiary relations enables us to examine more clearly the contingencies posed by the different conditions of environmental complexity and local resource levels on the nature of interdependency and independency.

Exchange contingencies posed by different contexts

Following Lawrence and Lorsch (1967), Thompson (1967), and Jacobs (1974), increased environmental complexity results in increased interdependency as both the headquarters and the subsidiary are posed with a situation of mutual vulnerability. Imperfect knowledge and fluctuations in the environment induce both the headquarters and the subsidiary to engage in reciprocal exchange relationships to make the realization of even independently disparate goals more predictable over time. The interaction in these circumstances is usually characterized by a high degree of cooperation and problem-solving as opposed to high levels of conflict and bargaining (March and Simon, 1958; Schmidt and Kochan, 1977).

On the other hand, as the resource levels of the subsidiary increase, the independent interests of the subsidiary and the headquarters may diverge. The subsidiary may desire greater autonomy including the right to commit resources to pursue local interests that may not necessarily be in concord with headquarters interests. From the headquarters perspective, however, the subsidiary represents a pool of rich resources in an overall resource distribution that cannot be altered at will, and indeed tends to persist over time; a point that has been theoretically made by Zeitz (1980) and theoretically as well as empirically substantiated for MNCs by Kogut (1983). This creates a situation of headquarters dependency on the subsidiary (Prahalad and Doz, 1981) and a possible power conflict (Blau, 1964). Bargaining and conflict are the potential forms of interaction in this situation, since each party may attempt to attain its own goals at the expense of the other (March and Simon, 1958; Schmidt and Kochan, 1977).

Based on the above arguments, and as summarized in Figure 1, a four-fold classification scheme for the contextual conditions faced by the subsidiary in headquarters–subsidiary relations is proposed; viz. (i) C1: low environmental complexity and low local resource levels, (ii) C2: low environmental complexity and high local resource levels, (iii) C3: high environmental complexity and low local resource levels and

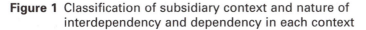

Environmental Complexity (High)	C3	C4
	Interdependency: High and Subsidiary Dependent	Interdependency: High and Headquarters Dependent
	C1	C2
(Low)	Interdependency: Low and Subsidiary Dependent	Interdependency: Low and Headquarters Dependent
	(Low)	(High)

Local Resources

Figure 1 Classification of subsidiary context and nature of interdependency and dependency in each context

(iv) C4: high environmental complexity and high local resource levels. Each of these four contingent conditions presents a very different situation with regard to the nature of dependency and interdependency in the exchange relation between the headquarters and the subsidiary. Since structure both constrains and is constrained by the nature of dependency and interdependency in an exchange relation (Aiken and Hage, 1967; Hall, 1972; Cook, 1977), it follows that each of the above situations will be correlated with different structural features.

The different structural elements of headquarters–subsidiary relations

Since the landmark studies of the Aston Group (Pugh *et al.*, 1968, 1969) centralization and formalization have become central constructs in the analysis of the structure of internal relations in complex organizations. Following Edstrom and Galbraith (1977) and Ouchi (1980), who argued for the importance of normative integration as another primary structural element in multi-unit organizations, we believe that centralization, formalization, and normative integration, analyzed singly and together, constitute a fairly comprehensive characterization of the structure of headquarters–subsidiary relations.

Centralization has been the focus of several studies of headquarters–subsidiary relations (see Gates and Egelhoff, 1986, for a review) and refers to a governance mechanism in which the decision-making process is hierarchically organized with the headquarters often making most of the crucial strategic and policy decisions. Since centralization shifts the locus of power asymmetrically in favor of the headquarters, it can lead to severe dissonance if the subsidiary is a powerful actor in the exchange relation. It is thus positively correlated primarily with situations in which the subsidiary is dependent on the headquarters. This proposition is consistent with the negative association between subsidiary size and centralization observed by Alsegg (1971) and Hedlund (1980), since size can serve as a proxy for the subsidiary's resources and power. Centralization is also inversely related to situations of high interdependency since it causes decisions to reflect the competencies and perspectives of the headquarters only, and constrains reciprocity in exchange relations. It is therefore hypothesized that:

> H1: Centralization is (a) negatively correlated with environmental complexity; and (b) negatively correlated with local resource levels.

Formalization may be interpreted as the routinization of decision-making and resource allocation (Nelson and Winter, 1982) and has been studied in this sense as an element of headquarters–subsidiary relations by Hedlund (1980, 1981). Formalization decreases the power of both the headquarters and the subsidiary as it constrains the exchange relation to an impersonal set of rules that often assume a power independent of the motivations of the actors in the exchange relation (Weber, 1968). Thus formalization is, most importantly, positively correlated with situations of potential conflict between the headquarters and the subsidiary. Formalization also increases with higher interdependence as it provides the structured context (Burgelman, 1984) for reciprocity in exchange. It is therefore hypothesized that across the different subsidiaries in an MNC:

> H2: Formalization is (a) positively correlated with environmental complexity and (b) positively correlated with local resource levels.

Normative integration leads to domain consensus and shared values (Van Maanen and Schein, 1979). By pooling the goals of the subsidiary and the headquarters into an inclusive and shared goal, it facilitates cooperation and participative decision-making (Ouchi, 1980). Thus, normative integration may primarily be expected to be positively correlated with interdependence. It can also mitigate potential conflict by promoting integrative bargaining (Walton and McKersie, 1965). It is therefore hypothesized that across the different subsidiaries in an MNC:

> H3: Normative integration is (a) positively correlated with environmental complexity and (b) positively correlated with local resource levels.

The structure–context "fit" in headquarters–subsidiary relations

The theoretical argument so far for the existence of a context–structure fit in headquarters–subsidiary relations in multinationals has been based on independent and separate consideration of how each element of structure might be linked to each of the different context variables. However, as argued by Drazin and Van de Ven (1985: 519), for a more complete contingency theory it is necessary to consider the context–structure relationships more holistically, and to explore how the different elements of structure, considered jointly and simultaneously, might be linked to the different categories of subsidiary contexts shown in Figure 1.

In developing such a holistic model it is necessary to recognize that while organizational adaptiveness might be enhanced by matching the heterogeneity in the context with appropriate differentiation in structure, for organizational effectiveness such differentiation must also be accompanied by suitable integrative processes (Lawrence and Lorsch, 1967). Further, these processes are expensive, and it is necessary for the MNC to economize on its limited resources for achieving organizational integration. Such an economizing perspective, inherent in Thompson's (1967) norm of "administrative rationality", suggests that the most efficient structure for each context may not simply be the sum of the unidimensional context–structure patterns proposed earlier, and is more likely to be a combination of the structural elements that reflects the optimal trade-offs between the costs of each element and its efficacy under the specified context.

Normative integration of members to share an inclusive goal is the most costly administrative mechanism, involving a significant investment of administrative resources for both initial socialization and continued cultural fidelity (Ouchi, 1980). Its key comparative advantage is its ability to pool the resources and competencies of both actors involved in the exchange relation, thereby allowing the organization to benefit from the complementarities in those competencies. Formalization is a less costly administrative mechanism, an assertion that is at the core of Weber's (1968) claim that the bureaucracy (i.e., the organization that governs primarily through well-developed rules and systems) is the most efficient of all organizational forms. Compared to normative integration, formalization requires less administrative resources to institutionalize, and once established needs little administrative energy to maintain. Though formalization provides a structured context for exchange, a comparative disadvantage is the potential inertia it creates and the constraints it may impose on rapid adaptation to changing environmental conditions (Hannan and Freeman, 1977). Centralization is the least expensive administrative mechanism in that it permits administration by fiat (Williamson, 1975). Requiring almost no resources to institutionalize, it does, however, require administrative resources for continuous monitoring and decision-making. While comparatively advantageous in terms of control over decision-making, decision outcomes under centralization reflect the competencies available at the headquarters and underutilize the supplementary or complementary competencies of the subsidiary.

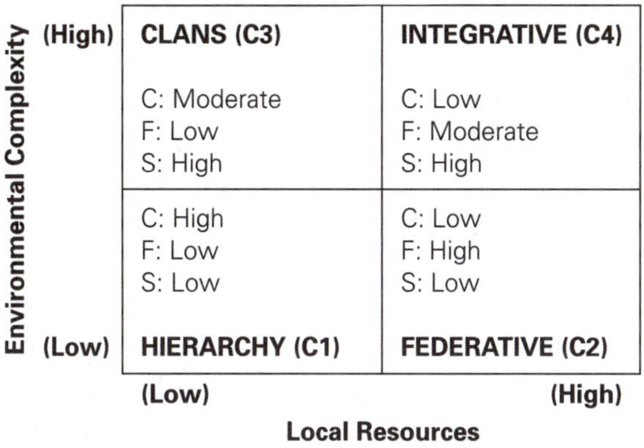
Environmental Complexity
(High)
(Low)
CLANS (C3)
C: Moderate
F: Low
S: High
INTEGRATIVE (C4)
C: Low
F: Moderate
S: High
C: High
F: Low
S: Low
HIERARCHY (C1)
C: Low
F: High
S: Low
FEDERATIVE (C2)
(Low)
(High)
Local Resources

Note: "C" indicates centralization, "F" indicates formalization, and "S" indicates socialization, in each of these contextual categories.

Figure 2 Hypothesized "fit" structure of headquarters–subsidiary relation in each context

Having developed these premises regarding the comparative costs and benefits of the different governance mechanisms, we can now hypothesize the way in which an MNC may deploy its limited administrative resources most efficiently for the management of national subsidiaries facing different contexts (for a summary of the various hypotheses, see Figure 2).

Clearly, the greatest returns to coordinating resources accrue if they are deployed where the MNC has abundant local resources and faces complex external environments (C4). Centralization is most unsuited to this context, as it is likely to invoke considerable dissonance since the subsidiary is resourceful and would be unwilling to accept the dependency that centralization implies. While formalization is desirable to constrain autonomous interests and to provide a framework for coordinated decision-making, it must be limited because it creates an inertia with regard to adapting quickly to the environmental pressures. Normative integration, though most expensive, is clearly the most appropriate administrative element in this context, since its comparative advantage in greatly facilitating interdependence is most beneficial in this situation. This combination of high normative integration, moderate formalization, and low centralization resembles most closely the structure that Kanter (1983) calls *integrative*.

Subsidiaries with low levels of local resources and facing environments of relatively low complexity (C1) represent the situation when administrative resources are expected to yield the lowest benefit. Economizing on administrative costs is most important in this context. Centralization, therefore, is the fit structure in this situation. It is feasible since the local capabilities are often so impoverished that they almost mandate continuous monitoring and headquarters support in decision-making. While centralization does restrict the ability to respond to interdependencies, the use of formalization and normative integration is inappropriate in this context as there are few benefits to be gained by facilitating such interdependencies. The overall structure, then, that fits this situation may be described as resembling a *hierarchy* (Williamson, 1975).

The abundance of local resources in a subsidiary facing low environmental complexity (C2) is often the legacy of history. These are usually the older subsidiaries of a multinational that owe their resource concentration to historical processes of accumulation. They represent a pool of sticky resources on whose performance the MNC is often dependent. This warrants a greater investment of administrative resources than in the previous context. Centralization is inappropriate because of the potential conflict and dissonance it may create between the headquarters and the subsidiary. Normative integration wastes administrative resources since the critical interdependencies in this situation are limited. Formalization is clearly the most suitable administrative mode in this situation since it facilitates exchange in a conflict-prone situation as well as makes it more predictable over time by constraining it to a set of well-developed rules and routines. This structure resembles that of federated interorganizational networks such as the United Way (Provan, 1983) and may therefore be described as being *federative* in nature.

Subsidiaries that have scarce local resources in complex environments (C3) are often either very young and established recently, or represent contexts where local organizational resources have not kept pace with rapidly changing external conditions. These are subsidiaries that face a crisis and require significant administrative resource commitments. The critical dependency of the subsidiary on the headquarters for both resources and decision-making makes centralization both feasible and necessary. The critical interdependencies, however, cannot be addressed by formalization since the situation is still too premature for standardization and routinization. Normative integration as an administrative structure is critical to this situation, as it allows pooling of the competencies of the headquarters and the subsidiary and also facilitates mutuality in decision-making that eases implementation. Similar structural forms have been described by Ouchi (1980) and labeled clans.

Measurement procedure and sample

Empirical investigation of these propositions required, for each of a reasonably large number of MNCs, measures of environmental complexity, local resources, different structural attributes of the headquarters–subsidiary relations, and performance, for its different national subsidiaries. This enormous volume of information required from each MNC posed a key measurement dilemma given our competing interest in sampling a reasonable number of MNCs for the purposes of robust statistical analyses. A review of the options available suggested that the only feasible way to collect data was a mail questionnaire survey that would require a single knowledgeable respondent at the headquarters of each MNC to furnish, for each of a number of national subsidiaries of the MNC, single measures for each of the constructs we wished to measure. Such a procedure, however, involved a number of possible shortcomings, such as (i) dependence on a single respondent, (ii) dependence on single indicators for complex constructs, and (iii) the questionable reliability of subsidiary-level information being provided by a corporate-level respondent. To adopt this procedure it was necessary to assess the implications of each of these shortcomings on the reliability and validity of the data. This was done through the following process.

Two different instruments were developed. One was designed for response by headquarters managers and all constructs were operationalized by single variables measured on centrally anchored five-point scales (the final version of this instrument that was used for this study is described in Part A of the Appendix). The other questionnaire was designed for response by subsidiary managers and sought subsidiary responses for the same constructs used in the instrument described earlier. In this instrument, though, the structural constructs were operationalized through multiple indicators (summarized in Part B of the Appendix).

In the first instance, both questionnaires were implemented in three large MNCs. In each of these MNCs two senior headquarters managers responded to the first questionnaire providing single indicators for the various constructs for at least five different national subsidiaries of the company. At the same time, between six and eight managers from each of those subsidiaries responded to the second questionnaire and provided multiple indicators for each of the constructs as applicable to their own subsidiary. Analysis of the data so obtained revealed the following:

Table 1 Spearman's rank correlation for assessing inter-rater convergence on selected variables

MNC to which raters belong:	HQ–HQ raters			HQ–sub. raters[1]		
	A	B	C	A	B	C
Clustering variables						
1. Environmental complexity[2]						
(a) Technological dynamism	0.63	0.79	0.76			
(b) Competition	0.88	0.63	0.71			
2. Local resources	0.79	0.84	0.76			
Structural variables						
3. Centralization	0.71	0.69	0.86	0.95	0.70	0.75
4. Formalization	0.92	0.88	0.83	0.65	0.50	0.70
5. Socialization	0.62	0.59	0.43	0.60	0.75	0.70
Dependent variable						
6. Performance	0.84	0.76	0.73			

1 Only structural variables were assessed for convergence of headquarters and subsidiary rater assessments.
2 No correlations are available for environmental complexity directly since this is merely an additive scale of technological dynamism and competition.

1. In each MNC, inter-rater convergence was high for the two headquarters-level respondents. For each variable measured, the ranks of the different subsidiaries were assessed similarly by both respondents as is manifest from the rank correlations shown in Table 1.

2. In each MNC, inter-rater convergence was also consistently high among headquarters- and subsidiary-level respondents. The rank correlation between the ranks for the different structural elements for the subsidiaries obtained by aggregating the responses of the subsidiary managers and the corresponding ranks obtained by aggregating the responses of the two headquarters managers are reported in Table 1.

Based on these findings of high inter-rater convergence among headquarters-level respondents as well as the congruence of data obtained through multiple indicators and multiple respondents at the subsidiary level and single indicators and single respondents at the headquarters level, the final survey was carried out using the instrument described in the Appendix.

This instrument was mailed to the Chairman or CEO of all the 438 North American and European MNCs listed in Stopford's (1983) *World Directory of Multinational Enterprises*. We did not receive any response from 281 (64 percent) companies while another 50 wrote to us declining participation on different grounds; 31 questionnaires were returned due to wrong mailing addresses and completed questionnaires were received from the remaining 76 (17 percent) companies. Of these, 66 (15 percent) were complete in all respects and were used for the statistical analysis reported in this paper.

In 50 of these 66 companies the respondent was the corporate vice-president responsible for all international operations or someone with even greater responsibility such as the CEO or the Chairman. Thirty-six of the 66 companies were headquartered in North America and the remaining 30 were headquartered in Europe. Four had annual sales below $1 billion and 11 had annual sales above $10 billion; the remaining were within this range. A wide range of industries were represented by these companies including aerospace (2 companies), building products (3), health care (3), industrial equipments (9), metals (11), motor vehicles (3), office equipment (2), paper and wood products (2), petroleum products (7), rubber (2), textiles (2), and others (3).

The unit of analysis in this study is each headquarters–subsidiary relation. Collectively, these 66 companies reported data on 618 national subsidiaries (only wholly owned operations were considered, so as to maintain uniformity within the sample). Five of the companies had less than 5 subsidiaries, 44 had between 5 and 15 subsidiaries, and 12 had more than 15 subsidiaries in the 19 countries that were specified in the questionnaire (see Part A of the Appendix). Our focus on differences within MNCs was addressed by measuring the properties of each case (i.e., headquarters–subsidiary relation) as standardized deviations (z-scores) from the mean conditions of the company of which it was a part. Table 2 shows the intercorrelations among all the measured variables for the total sample of 618 cases.

While our system for operationalization and measurement of the different variables is fully described in Part A of the Appendix, some potential weaknesses of these measures need to be highlighted. First, all measures represent the perceptions of a senior manager and can, therefore, suffer from all the well-known deficiencies of perceptual measures (see Downey and Ireland, 1979, for a review). Second, our measures for some variable such as subsidiary performance represent our best judgement of how they could be meaningfully operationalized, given the research context, but the reliability and validity of these measures are not beyond question. These issues, along with the low response rate, constrain the strength and generality of our findings. These weaknesses of the study and their implications are discussed more fully in the concluding section of the paper.

Data analysis and results

Univariate context–structure relationships

The correlations shown in Table 2 provide significant support for all the univariate context–structure relationships proposed in hypotheses 1(a) through 3(b). Centralization is negatively associated with both environmental complexity and local resources. Formalization and normative integration, in contrast, are positively associated with both these context variables. Further, all the correlations are significant at the 0.001 level.

Different types of subsidiary contexts

Theoretically, it was argued that subsidiary contexts could be meaningfully differentiated into four categories based on the joint conditions of (1) relatively low or high local resource levels of the subsidiary and (2) the associated low or high environmental complexity. While a median split on these two contextual variables could be used to classify the different subsidiaries into these contexts based purely on these theoretical grounds, a clustering approach was used to determine if there was a natural empirical pattern that coincided with this *a-priori* scheme. McQueen's *k*-means clustering method was employed using resource scarcity and environmental complexity as the clustering variables. The existence of clusters and the number of clusters were determined using Calinski and Harabasz's C-ratio, as recommended by Milligan and Cooper (1985), who found this to be the best stopping rule among 30 examined. As we varied the number of clusters in the solution from 2 to 8, the C-ratio varied as 600, 473, 656, 571, 610, 560 and 544 respectively. The maximum at the four-cluster solution indicated the existence of four different categories of subsidiaries based on these clustering variables (Everitt, 1980). The robustness of the membership in the various clusters was checked by comparing the *K*-means four-cluster soution with the solution from Ward's method. Ninety-one percent of the cases were classified into the same cluster by both methods. A graphical representation of the four clusters and the cluster centroids is presented in Figure 3.

Given two input variables, the emergence of a four-cluster solution is not surprising. However, as evident from Figure 3, the four clusters represent combinations of local resource and environmental conditions

Table 2 Correlation matrix for selected standardized variables ($n = 618$)

	1	1a	1b	2	3	4	5	6	μ^1	(SD)[1]
Clustering variables										
1. Environmental complexity[2]									0.00	0.96
(a) Technological dynamism	0.88*								0.00	0.95
(b) Competition	0.86*	0.55*							0.02	0.95
2. Local resources	0.50*	0.56*	0.33*						0.02	0.95
Structural variables										
3. Centralization	−0.27*	−0.32*	−0.15*	−0.48*					0.00	0.91
4. Formalization	0.31*	0.35*	0.20*	0.50*	−0.18*				0.00	0.88
5. Socialization	0.26*	0.35*	0.08*	0.51*	−0.22*	0.42*			0.00	0.93
Dependent variable										
6. Performance	−0.01	0.10	−0.12	0.12	−0.06	0.06	0.28*		0.00	0.95

* $P < 0.001$.
1 While all variables are normalized, the normalization is within each MNC accounting for the slight departures of the overall means from 0.00 and the standard deviations from 1.00.
2 Environmental complexity is an additive scale (Cronbach's $\alpha = 0.7$) of the two items technological dynamism (1a) and competition (1b).

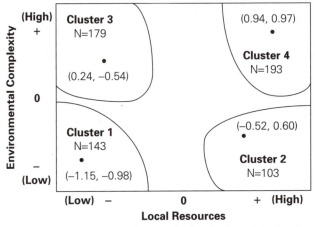

Note: (x, y) represents the standardized value of the local organizational resources "x" and the environmental complexity "y" at each of the cluster centroids shown.

Figure 3 Empirically derived clusters of subsidiaries based on contextual conditions

that are very consistent with the *a-priori* theoretical scheme. For further analysis this natural empirical classification is therefore preferred to a forced theoretical classification based on median-splits.

A multivariate test of "fit"

To test the multivariate hypotheses of fit summarized in Figure 2, the top-performing subsidiaries (z-score > 1.0) were selected to determine the ideal combination of the three structural elements for each contextual situation. The mean scores of each structural variable for these top-performing subsidiaries in the different clusters were considered as empirically derived representations of the ideal structural combination for the four categories of subsidiary context. These ideal types were tested using one-way ANOVA and MANOVA to determine if the patterns actually differed across the clusters. A comparison was also made between these results and the theoretically derived structural forms shown in Figure 2 to determine if the derived values matched the hypothesized relationships. The results are shown in Table 3. The significant F-statistic ($p < 0.01$) for every structural variable shows that these ideal types are very different. An overall MANOVA using all three structural variables was also significant ($F = 32.9$; $p < 0.001$). Furthermore, the empirically

Table 3 Differences in the mean values of top-performing subsidiaries across clusters[1]

	Cluster Membership					
	1 (n = 30)	2 (n = 16)	3 (n = 15)	4 (n = 49)	Scheffe's test	F
Structural variables						
3. Centralization	0.40	−0.46	0.12	−0.56	(3,2) (3,4)	10.8*
4. Formalization	−0.52	0.21	−0.20	0.44	(3,4)	13.2*
5. Socialization	−0.17	0.08	0.32	0.84	(3,4)	12.0*

* F-values in ANOVA ($p < 0.001$).
1 Top-performing subsidiaries are those with z-scores > 1.0.
Note: Scheffe's test is a pairwise comparison of differences in group means (Scheffe, 1953). The pairs listed in the column are those groups for which the means *are* significantly different ($p < 0.01$).

derived profiles are very well matched to the theoretically proposed profiles (Figure 2).

However, there is one discrepancy that is worth noting. The results indicate that, contrary to our hypothesis, in situations of high local resources, subsidiaries that confront more complex environments are governed by greater formalization than those in less complex environments. This finding contradicts the received view that formal systems inhibit adaptation and responsiveness which is so crucial in situations of environmental complexity. While this finding needs to be explored further, a possible explanation may be found in the work of Burgelman (1983) who contends that even autonomous behavior or innovation must take place within a structured context if it is to be effective. Perhaps this is the reason why these subsidiaries are managed with the greatest degree of formalization.

Having found support for the empirically derived structural profiles, deviations from these ideal profiles for the remaining subsidiaries were calculated using an Euclidean weighted distance metric. The resultant distance calculations are between the structure of a focal subsidiary and its respective ideal type, according to the focal unit's contingency category. The distance measure is calculated as follows:

$$\text{Dist.} = \sqrt{\Sigma[B_s(X_{is} - X_{js})]^2}$$

where X_{is} is the score of the ideal unit on the sth structural dimension, X_{js} is the score of the jth focal unit on the sth dimension, and B_s is a weight given by the standardized beta or contribution of the sth dimension in a multiple regression with performance as the dependent variable and all the structural dimensions as the independent variables.

Table 4 Correlations of distance measures with subsidiary performance (excluding high-performing units)

Distance	Performance	n	p-Value
All subsidiaries	−0.14	508	0.001
Cluster 1	−0.08	113	0.201
Cluster 2	−0.11	87	0.160
Cluster 3	−0.18	164	0.012
Cluster 4	−0.17	144	0.022

To test the usefulness of this multivariate approach towards a more complete contingency theory of headquarters–subsidiary relations, the calculated distance measure was correlated with the performance of the subsidiary. A negative correlation would demonstrate "fit" since the greater the distance from the respective ideal type, the lower the hypothesized performance. The results of this analysis are shown in Table 4. As predicted, there is a significant negative correlation between subsidiary performance and the distance measure of the deviation of the structure of the headquarters–subsidiary relation from its ideal type ($r = -0.14$; $p < 0.001$). Table 4 also shows the component correlations between distance and performance within each contextual category. A significant negative correlation was observed for C4 ($r = -0.17$; $p < 0.05$) and C3 ($r = -0.18$; $p < 0.01$) subsidiaries. The correlations were insignificant for C1 and C2 subsidiaries. This suggests that, while overall there is information to be gained by the multivariate approach, it is perhaps more relevant to situations of high environmental complexity.

Conclusions

The empirical analysis provides consistent support for the logic of internal differentiation within MNCs that has been proposed in this paper. It is clear that, within an MNC, the various national subsidiaries are and should be differentiated in terms of both the complexity of their environmental contexts and their local resource levels. Furthermore, depending on the nature of these contingencies, there is a "fit" structure of the headquarters–subsidiary relation that leads to improved subsidiary performance. Thus, as described in the theory section, an *integrative* structure fits subsidiaries that face *complex environments* and have *abundant local resources*; a *hierarchical* structure fits subsidiaries that face relatively *stable environments* and have *limited local resources*; a *federative* structure fits subsidiaries that face *stable environments* and have *abundant local resources*; and a *clan*-like structure fits subsidiaries that face *complex environments* and have *limited local resources*.

These results must, however, be considered in the context of some of the weaknesses of the study. These weaknesses arise from two sources, viz., (1) the theoretical infrastructure in which the study was grounded, and (2) the data from which the conclusions were drawn.

By explicitly grounding the study in contingency theory and a cross-sectional survey, we are unable to observe the interactions between context and structure and are restricted to the narrower and more static concept of a "fit". As has been highlighted in Bartlett and Ghoshal (1986), the different subsidiary contexts are often the products of structure, since structure influences the enactment process that leads organizations to define environmental complexity (Weick, 1980) and also affects internal resource allocation and, therefore, the configuration of resources in different sub-units of the organization (Bower, 1970). At the same time, as argued in this paper, structure is also influenced by the context. Because of the dependence on a cross-sectional survey, our arguments are unable to capture this dynamic and interactive conceptualization of "fit" as an emergent process, and suffer instead from an unintended implication of contextual determinism.

At the level of data there are two potential grounds for concern. The first arises from our operationalization and measurement of the different variables. We believe the use of perceptual responses from key informants to be appropriate for this study for several reasons. First, given the diversity of environments faced by the sampled organizations, reliable and comparable objective measures were particularly difficult to find. This problem was compounded by the consideration that the same national environment could pose very different contingencies for different MNCs, based on factors such as the industry, and even within the same industry, the specific strategic orientation of the firm. Second, subscribing to an important theoretical tradition (Starbuck, 1976; Weick, 1980), we believe that the cognitive orientations of senior managers are key to the processes that yield context–structure congruence in organizations. Finally, our interest was primarily to measure differences among the subsidiaries within the MNC: as such, measures were not sought relative to some absolute/objective anchor that was invariant across all the MNCs, but were obtained relative to an internal anchor that represented the average level of the particular variable for the firm. A key informant, or someone responsible for international operations of the company, was perhaps the only source for such a comparative assessment of subsidiary context, structure, and performance. This argument was perhaps most valid for measurement of performance since many of the subsidiaries did not have to publish independent accounts and therefore there were few ways to assess their performance in an objective manner. Further, given that local maximization of different objectives could often be in conflict with the global objectives of the company, the best measure of performance appeared to be the assessment of a senior manager who was responsible for attainment of those global goals. While these were the reasons for adopting our measurement procedure, and while the fact that 50 of our 66 respondents occupy very senior positions in their companies allows us to claim the potential advantages of such a procedure, these subjective measures, nevertheless, do not provide the same strength to our findings as reliable objective measures could provide. This weakness is exacerbated by the relatively poor response rate, and both these factors collectively suggest that our findings are best considered as suggestive and in need of further verification and testing.

Having said that, we must also highlight the potential relevance of these findings for the substantial literature on headquarters–subsidiary relations in multinationals. It is almost a truism that there are differences both within and among organizations. However, much of the efforts of past research on MNC organizations has been focused on developing contingency models for explaining differences of the first kind. Thus, researchers have tried to explain differences among companies in depart-mentalization (e.g., Stopford and Wells, 1972; Daniels, Pitts and Tretter, 1984), centralization (see review in Gates and Egelhoff, 1986), formal-ization (Hedlund, 1981) and other structural attributes. In contrast, very little effort has been expended on explaining differences of the latter kind. Yet, given that the different national subsidiaries of an MNC face very different organizational and environmental contexts, a contingency model will remain incomplete until such internal differences are also encompassed within a broader theoretical framework. Our arguments and findings presented in this paper, we believe, are at least a small step in the direction of developing this missing half of a more complete contingency model of multinational organizations.

Appendix: Operationalization and measurement of constructs

A: Headquarters-level instrument (instrument finally employed in the study)

Environmental complexity is an additive five-point scale consisting of two equally weighted variables, local competition and technological dynamism (Cronbach's $\alpha = 0.7$). These variables were proposed by Lawrence and Dyer (1983) as important constituents of environmental information complexity. Competition was measured by – "On a scale of 1 [not much competition] to 5 [extremely intense competition], rate the intensity of competition your company faces in each of the following markets." (This was followed by a list of 19 countries, with a centrally anchored five-point scale associated with each and the option of specifying the non-existence of a subsidiary in each case. The same pattern was adopted for all the other questions.) Technological dynamism was measured by – "On a scale of 1 [very slow] to 5 [very rapid], indicate the relative rate of product and process innovations [for the industry as a whole] that characterizes each of the following markets."

Local organizational abilities/resources. This was measured by – "Some national organizations in your company may have relatively advanced physical resources [such as technology, capital] and managerial capabilities. Some others in contrast may not have such resources to the same extent. On a scale of 1 [low] to 5 [high], rate the overall level of resource availability in your national organizations in each of the following countries."

Centralization. This was operationalized as the opposite of autonomy measured by – "Different national organizations in your company may enjoy different levels of autonomy for deciding their own strategies and policies. On a scale of 1 [very low] to 5 [very high], rate the extent of local autonomy enjoyed by each of the following national organizations."

Formalization. This was measured by – "The extent to which policies and systems are formalized may vary within the company, being different for different national organizations. On a scale of 1 [low formalization] to 5 [high formalization], rate the extent of formalization of policies and systems [through instruments such as manuals, standing orders, standard operating procedures, etc.] in each of the following national organizations."

Normative integration. This was measured by – "Some of your national organizations, compared to others, may be relatively more in tune with the overall goals and management values of the parent company. Let us call this the extent of shared values. On a scale of 1 [low shared values] to 5 [high shared values], rate each of the following national subsidiaries."

Performance. This subjective measure was based on the following question – "Please evaluate the average overall performance over the last three years (based on financial, strategic and other considerations, that you feel are relevant) of each of the following national organizations. Rate each organization on a scale of 1 [much lower than expected] to 5 [much better than expected]."

Perceptions of relative strategic importance of the local markets, governmental regulation, impact of budgetary reductions, communications flows, innovativeness, and ease of innovation adoption, were also obtained but were not used in this study.

B: Subsidiary-level instrument (employed for pre-test)

Centralization. Operationalized as the opposite of autonomy and measured by estimates of subsidiary managers on the extent of headquarters and/or subsidiary influence on the following four decision situations: (i) introduction of a new product, (ii) changes in product design, (iii) changes in manufacturing process, and (iv) career development plans for senior managers. For each of these situations, the relative influences could be scored on a five-point scale representing: 1 – headquarters decides alone; 2 – headquarters decides but subsidiary can and does provide suggestions; 3 – both headquarters and subsidiary have roughly equal influence on the decision; 4 – subsidiary decides but headquarters can and does provide suggestions; and 5 – subsidiary decides alone.

Formalization. Measured by the assessment of subsidiary managers of the extent of truth or falsehood of the following three statements: (i) for most tasks, the headquarters have provided a fairly well-defined set of rules and policies; (ii) to the extent possible there are manuals that define the courses of action to be taken under different situations; and (iii) the headquarters continuously monitors to ensure that rules and policies are not violated. Responses could be scored on a four-point scale representing: 1 – definitely true; 2 – more true than false; 3 – more false than true; and 4 – definitely false.

Normative integration. Measured by aggregating the responses of subsidiary managers on the following three indicators: (i) extent of time the respondent actually worked in the headquarters, scored as 1 if the duration was one year or more and 0 otherwise; (ii) perception of having a mentor at the headquarters, positive responses being scored as 1 and negative responses as 0; and (iii) the number of headquarters visits per year, scored as 1 if the count was one or more and 0 otherwise.

Acknowledgements

We are grateful to Christopher A. Bartlett who inspired and initiated the larger research project of which this study was a small part, and for the insightful suggestions of John Chalykoff, Karel Cool, Joel Cutcher-Gershenfeld, Ingemar Dierickx, Bruce Kogut, John Van Maanen, N. Venkatraman, and Gordon Walker, who read and commented on earlier drafts of the paper.

This paper appeared in *Strategic Management Journal*, vol. 10, July–August, 1989.

REFERENCES

Aitken, M. and J. Hage. "Organizational interdependence and intraorganizational structure", *American Sociological Review*, 33, 1968, pp. 912–930.

Alsegg, R.A. "Control relationships between American corporations and their European subsidiaries." AMA Research Study 107, American Management Association, New York, 1971.

Barlett, C.A. and S. Ghosal. "Tap your subsidiaries for global reach", *Harvard Business Review*, November–December 1986, pp. 87–94.

Blau, P.M. *Exchange and Power in Social Life.* Wiley, Chichester, 1964.

Bower, J.L. *Managing the Resource Allocation Process*, Division of Research, Graduate School of Business Administration, Harvard University, Boston, 1970.

Burgelman, R.A. "A model of the interaction of strategic behavior, corporate contest, and the concept of strategy", *Academy of Management Review*, 8, 1983, pp. 61–70.

Burgelman, R.A. "Strategy-making and evolutionary theory: toward a capability based perspective". Research paper, Stanford University, Paper No. 755, 1984.

Cook, K.S. "Exchange and power in networks of interorganizational relations", *Sociological Quarterly*, 18, 1977, pp. 62–82.

Daniels, J.D., R.A. Pitts and M.J. Tretter. "Strategy and structure of U.S. multinationals: an exploratory study", *Academy of Management Journal*, **27**, 1984, pp. 292–307.

Downey, H.K. and R.D. Ireland. "Quantitative versus qualitative: environmental assessment in organizational studies", *Administrative Science Quarterly*, **24**, 1979, pp. 630–637.

Drazin, R. and A.H. Van de Ven. "Alternative forms of fit in contingency theory", *Administrative Science Quarterly*, **30**, 1985, pp. 514–539.

Edstrom, A. and J.R. Galbraith. "Transfer of managers as a coordination and control strategy in multinational organizations", *Administrative Science Quarterly*, **22**, 1977, pp. 248–263.

Emerson, R.M. "Power-dependence relations", *American Sociological Review*, **27**, 1962, pp. 31–41.

Emerson, R.M. "Social exchange theory", *Annual Review of Sociology*, **2**, 1975, pp. 335–362.

Everitt, B. *Cluster Analysis*, 2nd edn. Wiley, New York, 1980.

Gates, S.R. and W. Egelhoff. "Centralization in parent headquarters–subsidiary relationships", *Journal of International Business Studies*, **17**(2), 1986, pp. 71–92.

Ghoshal, S. "The innovative multinational: A differentiated network of organizational roles and management processes". Unpublished D.B.A. dissertation, Harvard Business School, 1986.

Ghoshal, S. and C.A. Bartlett. "Creation, adoption and diffusion of innovations by subsidiaries of multinational corporations", *Journal of International Business Studies*, Fall 1988, pp. 365–388.

Graham, E.M. "Oligopolistic imitation and European direct investment in the United States". Unpublished doctoral dissertation, Harvard Business School, 1974.

Hall, R.H. *Organizations: Structure and Process*. Prentice-Hall, Englewood Cliffs, NJ, 1972.

Hamel, G. and C.K. Prahalad. "Do you really have a global strategy?", *Harvard Business Review*, **63**(4), 1985, pp. 139–148.

Hannan, M.T. and J.H. Freeman. "The population ecology of organizations", *American Journal of Sociology*, **82**, 1977, 929–964.

Hedlund, G. "The role of foreign subsidiaries in strategic decision making in Swedish multinational corporations", *Strategic Management Journal*, **1**, 1980, pp. 23–36.

Hedlund, G. "Autonomy of subsidiaries and formalization of headquarters–subsidiary relations in Swedish MNCs". In Otterbeck, L. (Ed.), *The Management of Headquarters–Subsidiary Relations in Multinational Corporations*. Gower, Hampshire, U.K., 1981.

Jacobs, D. "Dependence and vulnerability: an exchange approach to the control of organizations", *Administrative Science Quarterly*, **19**, 1974, pp. 45–59.

Kanter, R.M. *The Changemasters*. Simon & Schuster, New York, 1983.

Knickerbocker, F. *Oligopolistic Reaction and Multinational Enterprise*. Division of Research, Graduate School of Business Administration, Harvard University, Cambridge, MA, 1973.

Kogut, B. "Foreign direct investment as a sequential process." In Kindelberger, C.P. and Audretsch, D.B. (Eds.), *The Multinational Corporation in the 1980s*. MIT Press, Cambridge, MA, 1983.

Lawrence, P.R. and D. Dyer. *Renewing American Industry*. Free Press, New York, 1983.

Lawrence, P.R. and J.W. Lorsch. *Organization and Environment*. Graduate School of Business Administration, Harvard University, Boston, MA, 1967.

Levine, S. and P.E. White. "Exchange as a conceptual framework for the study of inter-organizational relations", *Administrative Science Quarterly*, 5, 1961, pp. 583–601.

March, J.G. and H.A. Simon. *Organizations*. Wiley, New York, 1958.

Milligan, G.W. and M.C. Cooper. "An examination of procedures for determining the number of clusters in a data set", *Psychometrika*, 50, 1985, pp. 159–179.

Nelson, R.R. and S.G. Winter. *An Economic Theory of Evolutionary Capabilities and Behavior*. Harvard University Press, Cambridge, MA, 1982.

Ouchi, W.G. "Markets, bureaucracies and clans," *Administrative Science Quarterly*, 25, 1980, pp. 129–141.

Pfeffer, J. *Power in Organizations*. Pitman, Boston, MA, 1981.

Pfeffer, J. *Organizations and Organization Theory*. Pitman, Boston, MA, 1982.

Pfeffer, J. and G.R. Salancik. *The External Control of Organizations: A Resource Dependency Perspective*. Harper & Row, New York, 1978.

Prahalad, C.K. and Y.L. Doz. "An approach to strategic control in MNCs", *Sloan Management Review*, Summer 1981, pp. 5–29.

Provan, K.G. "The federation as an interorganizational linkage network", *Academy of Management Review*, 8, 1983, pp. 79–89.

Pugh, D.S., D.J. Hickson, C.R. Hinings and C. Turner. "Dimensions of organization structure", *Administrative Science Quarterly*, 13, 1968, pp. 65–105.

Pugh, D.S., D.J. Hickson and C.R. Hinings. "The context of organizational structure", *Administrative Science Quarterly*, 14, 1969, pp. 91–114.

Robock, S.H., K. Simmons and J. Zwick. *International Business and Multinational Enterprises*. Irwin, Homewood, IL, 1977.

Scheffe, H.A. "A method of finding all contrasts in the analysis of variance", *Biometrika*, 40, 1953, pp. 87–104.

Schmidt, S.M. and T.A. Kochan. "Interorganizational relationships: patterns and motivations", *Administrative Science Quarterly*, 22, 1977, pp. 220–234.

Starbuck, W.H. "Organizations and their environments." In M.D. Dunnett (Ed.), *The Handbook of Industrial and Organizational Psychology*. Rand McNally, Chicago, IL, 1976.

Stopford, J.M. *World Directory of Multinational Enterprises*. Galo Research Company, Detroit, MI, 1983.

Stopford, J.M. and L. Turner. *Britain and the Multinationals*. Wiley, Chichester, 1985.

Stopford, J.M. and L.T. Wells. *Managing the Multinational Enterprise*. Basic Books, New York, 1972.

Thompson, J.D., *Organizations in Action*. McGraw-Hill, New York, 1967.

Van Maanen, J. and E.H. Schein. "Toward a theory of organizational socialization". In Staw, B.M. (Ed.), *Research in Organizational Behavior*, Vol. 1. JAI Press, Greenwich, CT, 1979.

Walton, R.E. and R.B. McKersie. *A Behavioral Theory of Labor Negotiations*. McGraw-Hill, New York, 1965.

Weber, M. *Economy and Society*. Bedminister, New York, 1968.

Weick, K.E. *The Social Psychology of Organizing*, 2nd edn. Addison-Wesley, Reading, MA, 1980.

Williamson, O.E. *Markets and Hierarchies*. Free Press, New York, 1975.

Zeitz, G. "Interorganizational dialectics", *Administrative Science Quarterly*, **25**, 1980, pp. 72–88.

The individualized corporation

Towards a managerial theory of the firm

Rebuilding behavioral context: turn process reengineering into people rejuvenation

Christopher A. Bartlett and Sumantra Ghoshal

This paper presents the core argument of Sumantra and Chris Bartlett's book The Individualized Corporation. *Why, they ask, are some companies able to remain vital, even after extensive reengineering, while others flounder and fail? The answer lies in a firm's ability to rejuvenate its employees by establishing a behavioural context with four characteristics – discipline, support, trust and stretch. By comparing the post-war performances of GE and Westinghouse, Chris and Sumantra show how Westinghouse allowed itself to be sucked into a downward spiral of compliance, control, constraint, and contract-based behaviour, ultimately leading to its break-up. By contrast, other firms including Intel, 3M and Kao have actively built a supportive behavioural context and achieved high levels of individual initiative and cooperation.*

After the slash-and-burn organizational restructuring of the past decade, one thing is becoming increasingly clear to managers: if a company is to proceed beyond the shrinking spiral of downsizing and rationalization to develop the ability of continuous self-renewal, its real battle lies not in reorienting the strategy, restructuring the organization, or revamping the systems, but in changing individual organization members' behaviors and actions. A self-renewing organization can be built only on the bedrock of people who are willing to take personal initiative and to cooperate with one another, who have self-confidence and a commitment to the company, and who are able to execute relatively routine tasks with the same proficiency as they are willing to learn new skills and ways to take the company to the next stages of its ambition. In short, the most vital requirement for revitalizing businesses is to rejuvenate people.

What is not clear to many managers is whether it is possible to stimulate such behaviors in large global firms. Based on our recent research in twenty European, U.S., and Japanese companies, we believe that the answer is an unambiguous "yes."[1] A number of companies we studied demonstrated an ability to shape and protect the required individual attitudes and actions over decades, despite their growing size and diversity. We also found several in which a determined top management was able to recreate such behaviors in stale, tired organizations in a relatively short time.

3M, for example, has overcome the constraints of its humble roots as a sandpaper manufacturer to emerge as one of the world's most consistently innovating companies. With a long-established objective of generating 25 percent of its sales from products introduced in the most recent five-year period, the company has grown from simple industrial abrasives to a portfolio of more than 100 technologies that it has leveraged into some 60,000 products sold through more than forty divisions and national subsidiaries in fifty countries. Rather than slowing the pace of innovation and renewal, CEO Desi DeSimone has recently increased the target for his $15 billion corporation to ensure that 30 percent of future sales comes from products introduced in the previous four years.

Through a very different self-renewing approach, Intel has managed not only to survive in one of the most demanding industries, but also to emerge as its leading competitor. The company has mastered the prerequisite ability to manage extremely compressed product life cycles. At the same time, it has shown remarkable agility in navigating the semiconductor industry's many structural discontinuities brought about by intense competitive pressure, the rapidly changing buyer structure in the computer industry, technological revolutions, and continuously shifting industry alliances and coalitions. In the process, it has evolved from a technology-driven memories developer to a technology- and manufacturing-dominated microprocessor manufacturer and now is becoming a functionally balanced systems company.

What 3M and Intel (and several other self-renewing companies we studied, such as Kao Corporation, Corning, Andersen Consulting, and IKEA) have in common is a carefully nurtured, deeply embedded corporate work ethic that triggers the individual-level behaviors of entrepreneurship, collaboration, and learning that are the foundation of organizational renewal. It is a subtle, complex characteristic that we call the behavioral context.[2] Difficult to define and even more difficult to develop, it is nevertheless something easy to sense and experience: one manager described it as the "smell of the place" manifested in a thousand small details of how a company functions. It is as pervasive and influential as climate – just as one can be energized by the fresh, crisp air at a mountain resort in spring, so too can the behavioral context of a company provide people with a source of stimulation.

Unfortunately, over time, many large companies have created a context more akin to the polluted, oppressive environment of the inner city in mid-summer, sapping personal energy and creating conditions for apathy. The challenge for managers of these companies, to quote one of our interviewees, is "to throw a baseball through the window to let in the life-giving fresh air."

Pathologies of the inherited context

For years, Westinghouse has been a classic example of a company in which employees were trapped in an oppressive behavioral context from which they could not escape. During the past decade or so, Westinghouse top management has declared victory in its battle for strategic and organizational renewal on at least three occasions, each time to stumble and begin the process all over again. After a massive restructuring spanning the entire second half of the 1970s, then-CEO Robert Kirby announced in 1981 an end to the company's history of "unpleasant November and December surprises" and the beginning of an era of uninterrupted growth. By 1983, however, the company's financial results had sharply deteriorated, leading to another round of rationalization together with many "Japanese-style initiatives" for continuous productivity improvement. By 1987, as return on equity topped 20 percent, exceeding that of arch-rival General Electric, then-CEO Douglas Danforth announced Westinghouse's entry into "the winner's circle" – one of the few elite corporations with a reputation for consistently superior financial performance and managerial excellence.

After another setback in 1988, new CEO John Marous announced his vision of elevating Westinghouse "from the good corporation it is today to a great corporation," triggering a fresh round of radical change. By 1989, with double-digit sales growth and a net profit of nearly a billion dollars, Marous's vision appeared close at hand amid external acclaim that the company had achieved "respect, at last." By 1991, however, soon after incoming CEO Paul Lego took over, an embarrassing mess at Westinghouse Credit plunged the company into a 1992 loss position of $1.7 billion and marked its stock down to half the level of two years earlier. Unable to ride out the storm of criticism, in mid-1993, Lego was replaced by Michael Jordan who once again announced "a new beginning."[3]

Westinghouse is not an isolated example. After an orgy of "transformation programs" in the 1980s, many large corporations are waking up in the 1990s with little to show for it except a massive hangover. In the United States, companies like Digital Equipment Corporation, Sears, and Eastman Kodak have struggled for years to reverse their fortunes despite their inspiring visions, dramatic restructuring, and leveraged incentives. In Europe, once revered names like Daimler-Benz, Bull, and Olivetti have made headlines as examples of problems rather than role models. Even much admired Japanese companies like Mazda, Yamaha, and Matsushita have attracted similar unwelcome notoriety in their highly publicized but apparently ineffective efforts to renew themselves.

The roots of such corporate sclerosis lies in the behavioral context these companies have institutionalized in their organizations. Nurtured by the postwar environment of seemingly boundless opportunities, companies pursued aggressive diversification strategies, supporting them with increasingly elaborate divisionalized organization structures. But initially successful strategies became embedded in policies that tended to refine and defend existing positions rather than exploit new ones, and once facilitating organizations became increasingly bureaucratic and compartmentalized, inhibiting both individual initiative and cross-unit learning.

Time and again, once great companies found themselves caught in a spiral in which yesterday's winning formula evolved into today's conventional wisdom and risked being ossified as tomorrow's sacred cow. Like Westinghouse, they found they had gradually developed a context that, while superficially benign, had a corrosive effect on its members' behavior. Only by explicitly recognizing the central characteristics of this inherited context, and understanding how it affects management perceptions and actions, can those who want to revitalize their organization replace its most pernicious qualities with others more conducive to genuine, durable growth and renewal (see Figure 1).

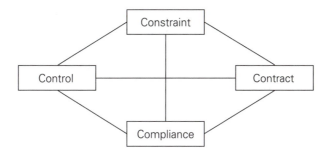

Figure 1 Pathologies of the inherited context

Compliance

The first element of the traditional company's managerial context is what we term *compliance* – an important, even vital, characteristic in the postwar years when many companies diversified their activities into scores of inviting opportunities. As they began their rapid expansion into a diverse range of new businesses and markets, most found an urgent need to have widely dispersed employees complying with common policies and uniform practices in order to prevent powerful centrifugal forces from pulling their organizations apart. The classic military model of line authority that dominated the formal relationships between managers ensured that those deep in the organization would follow the leaders' direction.

But while this widespread contextual norm ensured unity of action at a time when the key management challenge was to choose among competing opportunities, in its pathological form, it developed inflexible procedures and authoritarian intolerance of dissent that inhibited challenge of outmoded policies and shut down meaningful debate on top-down directives.

Ultimately, it was not the policies themselves but the effects they had on people's day-to-day behaviors that made it so difficult for these companies to sense early warning signals and correct problems before they became disasters. One of the most damning public charges leveled against Westinghouse CEO Paul Lego was that "there was no one to challenge him." Although, for years, many in the company apparently could see the impending collapse at Westinghouse Credit ("Even the guys in the mail-room were asking when there would be a write-off," said one former executive), Lego apparently remained unaware of the severity of the mounting problems. In a culture in which authority and order quashed dissent, top management was completely isolated from day-to-day operations. This tradition, built into the behavioral context of the 1970s, continued into the 1990s with massive unexpected losses in financial services followed by major unforecasted problems in environmental services.

Control

The second common characteristic of the managerial context in large modern corporations is *control* – again, an organizational characteristic that allowed companies to expand operations rapidly yet efficiently in an earlier era. This deeply rooted norm that characterizes classic hierarchical relationships was greatly strengthened with the introduction of the divisional organization structure. Corporate executives were willing to delegate substantial responsibility to a new level of general managers only if they had the mechanisms to hold them accountable.[4] Strongly influenced by powerful corporate staffs, most companies developed sophisticated corporate-driven processes based on capital planning and operational budgeting systems to establish top-down control throughout their organizations.

While such systems proved highly effective in allocating funds and driving ongoing performance, they eventually contributed to a deterioration in interpersonal relationships. The objective-setting and forecasting processes often degenerated into a game-playing exercise between adversaries, and the monitoring activity frequently became an excuse for an increasingly powerful corporate financial controller to intervene in the operations of frontline managers.[5]

In a management group dominated by engineers, tight controls had long been a central characteristic of Westinghouse's management style. The principle of tight control was firmly reasserted after a decade-long experiment with freer management created a serious performance decline in the mid-1970s. But the shorter, tighter leash placed on employees led to constant complaints about the haggling in the planning and budgeting processes. The highly sophisticated system was based on company-imposed estimates of capital costs and cash flows that became an unending source of debate, and many felt the system was driving them to achieve short-term results at the expense of long-term business development. About the only topic on which there seemed to be general agreement was that the tightly administered processes were consuming an enormous amount of management time and energy.

Contract

In the traditional large-organization model, another strong influence on attitudes and behavior was the *contractual* nature of the relationship between the corporation and its employees. This characteristic was born of legalistic biases that became greatly strengthened by two more recent organizational trends: the highly incentive-leveraged compensation systems that reinforced the notion of a financial relationship between the company and its employees, and the massive restructuring, rationalization, and redundancy programs that underlined the fact that this relationship could be terminated at any time.

While the implicit or explicit contract between employee and employer initially served to define expectations and give the relationship clarity and stability, it eventually led to a formalization and depersonalization of how individuals felt about their companies. As widening compensation differences fostered resentment and increasing terminations bred fear, people began to distance themselves emotionally from an entity they felt had betrayed them. More and more, they felt like employees of an economic entity, and less and less like members of a social institution.

The familylike relationship that once dominated the Westinghouse culture began eroding in the 1970s when CEO Robert Kirby resolved to revive the company's sagging fortunes with massive layoffs and divestitures that cut the total work force by 30 percent in three years. However, more than the layoffs per se, what destroyed any sense of familylike loyalty at Westinghouse was how the layoffs were implemented. Any notion of an emotional relationship between the company and its people was firmly disabused by Kirby's statement that he would fire his own mother if she weren't producing the expected results. Twenty years later, a never-ending series of layoffs and divestitures reduced the work force from 200,000 in 1974 to 54,000 in 1994, and had long since eroded the once strong sense of company pride and loyalty.

Constraint

The other dominant characteristic common to the behavioral context of many modern corporations is the attribute of *constraint*. As companies expanded and diversified, top management found it increasingly important to develop clear, focused definitions of corporate strategy to provide the boundaries in which those with delegated responsibility could operate. Particularly in an environment in which opportunities for expansion exceeded most companies' ability to finance them, such constraint was helpful in preventing diversification from dissipating resources and becoming unmanageable.[6]

Eventually, however, as companies elaborated broad strategic objectives through detailed strategic plans and translated them into specific portfolio roles for different businesses, the constraints became confinements and the boundaries became barriers. Managers of businesses classified as mature began to think of themselves as mature, averse to risk, and resistant to innovation. The strategic process became a constraint not only for how these managers could act but, ultimately, for how they could think. Constantly bombarded by strategic visions, roles, goals, challenges, and priorities, frontline managers retreated into a much more passive mode than the spirit that had initially powered the organization's growth engine.

The deterioration of this once legitimate element of management context is clearly illustrated at Westinghouse. As a way to control operations that "had gone totally hog wild," Kirby introduced the concept of strategic business units (SBUs) and imposed strict discipline through the company's highly touted planning system, dubbed Vabastram (VAlue BAsed STRategic Management). Initially, Vabastram educated an engineering-oriented management team to a more financially oriented view, improving the discipline of Westinghouse's investment process. For example, because of Vabastram, Westinghouse backed away from several tempting but overpriced acquisitions and avoided a number of risky contracts in the environmental cleanup business that later crippled some of its less disciplined competitors. Ultimately, however, top management's blind faith in Vabastram deprived the business units of all flexibility and creativity. It reshaped behaviors, both within individual businesses and across them, as each of the thirty-seven SBUs focused on its own business, attempting to maximize its own return on allocated equity. Vabastram also reshaped the frontline managers' relationships with top management. It gave top managers the data to decide whether to continue to invest or to sell off the business. As they made seventy divestitures between 1985 and 1987 alone, the message to the organization was clear: deliver current performance or your unit will be sold.

When Michael Jordan replaced Paul Lego as CEO in mid-1993, he identified not only the massive challenges in reviving the company's sagging operating performance and restructuring its damaged strategic portfolio, but also the huge task of transforming an internal management culture that he described as "a throwback to the 1950s." Although a fifties-based culture was ideal in the postwar era when a company's opportunities exceeded its ability to fund them, in an environment in which innovation, responsiveness, flexibility, and learning had become vital sources of competitive advantage, a management context driven by compliance, control, contract, and constraint became more a liability than an asset.

The context for renewal

The portrait we have drawn of the large corporation in the mid-1990s is not a flattering one and, to some extent, is a caricature. While we hope there are only a few companies in which all four elements of the managerial context have deteriorated to the degree we have described, there are equally few that have emerged untarnished by any trace of such pathologies.

This historically evolved behavioral context has proven to be so debilitating because, as all four core characteristics atrophied, they drove management to become passive, compliant, and focused inward – captives of their glorious past, rather than explorers of a brave new future. The only enduring antidote to the pervasive disease of corporate sclerosis is to build a behavioral context that drives a company toward continuous self-renewal rather than a focus on refining existing capabilities and defending current positions.

To develop the kind of management understanding, belief, and commitment that drives the incessant need for renewal, companies have to build a very different behavioral context than the norms of compliance, control, contract, and constraint that hobbled Westinghouse and so many other large organizations. As we examined the management processes at 3M, Intel, Corning, Andersen Consulting, Kao Corporation, and other companies more adept at continually renewing their organizations, we identified four common characteristics of their behavioral context – discipline, support, trust, and stretch (see Figure 2).

Discipline

In traditional organizations, management assumed that desired behavior could be induced largely through the formal reporting relationships of the structural hierarchy and the policies and procedures meant to reinforce

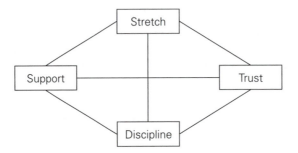

Figure 2 Management context

them. Compliance to authority, or the rules that supported it, was a necessary requirement of overall cohesion in the system. A management context shaped by discipline, on the other hand, does not rely on authority relationships or management policies – either exclusively or even primarily – as the means for influencing individual behavior. Rather, self-discipline becomes integrated into the flow of the company's ongoing activities and is reflected in every aspect of corporate daily life. In disciplined organizations, people do more than follow directives and conform to policies; they also return phone calls promptly, come to meetings on time, refrain from questioning in the corridors decisions made in the conference room, and, above all, deliver on promises and commitments.[7]

Discipline is an organizational characteristic evident to anyone attending a meeting at Intel. Every meeting has an agenda and closes with a decision, action plans, and deadlines. Such a disciplined approach, however, does not imply that debate is limited or dissension discouraged. But once an issue has been fully aired, decisions must be made; the company's clear philosophy is that people are expected to "agree or disagree, but commit."

In a culture based on discipline rather than compliance, individual behavior tends to be embedded – built from the bottom up rather than imposed or driven from the top down. In other words, discipline encourages all employees to strive voluntarily to meet and exceed their own commitments.

The indoctrination process at Andersen Consulting exemplifies the process of embedding discipline in individual behavior. As an organization that grew from a highly respected accounting and auditing partnership, the consulting firm inherited much of its parents' obsession with quality, accuracy, and thoroughness. Its highly disciplined approach was built on careful socialization of all employees, principally through intensive education about the company. The first session in more than 1,000 hours of training during a new recruit's first five years is a six-week program that graduates compare to marine boot camp rather than to an executive education course. Eighty-hour weeks, demanding assignments, and a strict dress code all create a norm of discipline and provide training in new analytic techniques. Although competitors publicly berate the "Andersen Androids," there is a trace of envy in how they talk about the uniformly high standards of these individuals.

Corning is another company whose top management has been successful in shifting from a compliance mode to a self-discipline mode. In 1987, when he became CEO of the hundred-year-old glass company, Jamie Houghton inherited a demoralized company in the midst of a major recession. In an internal environment that the press likened to a country club, managers failed to meet the corporate budget for six consecutive years, despite the multiple demands created by the complex matrix structure and tight formal systems.

Rather than installing more compliance-driven systems and policies, Houghton focused on creating an internal culture that encouraged managers to take more responsibility for their own performance. After shifting attention from the old top-down "do or die" sales and profit budgets to more broadly defined three-year targets in both operating margins and return on assets, he challenged managers to develop and commit to their own budgets. To build self-discipline, Houghton would simply walk out on presentations when managers were unable to define exactly how they would meet their targets, and he refused to consider bonuses or promotions for those who did not deliver on promised performance. In a couple of years, after what one manager described as "an almost Japanese relentlessness in getting people to agree and commit," the organization clearly exhibited a new sense of self-confidence and self-respect. More important, as far as Houghton was concerned, it started routinely delivering on the ambitious targets it had set for itself.

Support

In most traditional organizations, the relationship between boss and subordinate is characterized by top-down control, a linkage almost guaranteeing that communication channels are dominated by formal reporting systems. In companies that have successfully institutionalized a renewal process, however, managers have rejected the assumption that the natural corollary of delegation is control. Instead, they view the appropriate complement as better defined through a relationship characterized by coaching, helping, and guiding.[8]

At Andersen Consulting, for example, the partners see their primary role as strengthening the firm for those who follow them. This well-accepted value, which they call "trusteeship," is evident in the commitment partners make to the development and support of the firm's associates. When recruited into the firm, each new employee is assigned a counseling partner who accepts responsibility for meeting with the new member every six months to discuss performance, career interests, and development needs. In addition, project managers give associates feedback and support, evaluating their specific project performance every three months and coaching them during the project. Through such activities, Andersen guides its operations while simultaneously developing its capabilities.

But the context of support applies to more than just the vertical relationships previously dominated by control. It also frames the horizontal linkages among peers – relationships that become characterized more by cooperation and collaboration than by the competition and contention that often develops across organizational boundaries in companies with strong systems-dominated cultures.

Such horizontal relationships are clearly evident at Corning, where the company's technology-based organization created a long tradition of team-based management, as did its substantial experience with joint ventures and alliance partners. When Houghton became CEO, he further underlined the importance of working in positive and intensive collegial relationships, preferring to manage key issues through teams and groups rather than by reconfiguring formal structure. He created a six-person management committee (immediately dubbed "the six pack") that not only became the key top-level decision-making body but also became the role model for collaboration. Eventually, Houghton decided that such mutually supportive activity needed to be formally recognized in how people thought about the organization. He began to describe Corning as an egalitarian network operating as a mutually dependent family, as opposed to the more traditional paternalistic authority-driven hierarchy. It was an organizational model in which support clearly replaced control as a dominant element of the behavioral context.

A context of support tends to become a pervasive concept in self-renewing companies, mainly because it is built on layers of individual behavior and cultural norms rather than being superimposed through systems and reporting relationships, as control usually is. In the end, support becomes a central part of the ongoing management process; at Intel, the whole system is based on the notion that ideas develop at the front lines and form into championed proposals that bubble up through the organization, gathering both support and opposition. The Intel norm of committing to a course of action only after the proposal has survived the aggressively challenging "constructive confrontation" process means that management can commit the organization's unreserved support, knowing that the decision is safeguarded by support from below rather than control from above. Such commitments may involve massive commitments of human and financial resources: the cost of R&D for a new generation of chips has ballooned to $350 million, for example, and a new fabrication facility adds a further $100 million. But Andrew Grove is confident that Intel's internal process of building support through challenge not only pools the organizational knowledge but also creates the necessary commitment to the project vital to successful implementation.

Trust

The relationship between a company and its employees is defined by a mixture of deterministic contractlike agreements – both explicit and implicit – as well as by a more organic familylike emotional bonding. While the former brings clarity and precision to the execution of objectives, the latter contributes a sense of commitment and dedication to pursuing the company's broad purposes. Historically, companies have drifted toward the contractual end of the spectrum, not only in defining the employer-employee relationship but also in interpreting linkages among organizational units, as departments negotiated with each other on price and delivery times and divisions contracted with their business units on sales objectives and profit targets. In the process, individuals and organizational units were motivated to protect their self-interests and maximize their side of the contract, with the typical net result being an increase in adversarial relationships and an erosion of mutual commitment.

In contrast, most companies that have been able to continually renew themselves have avoided the development of impersonal, distant relationships by building an element best described as trust into their management context. This is the characteristic of an organization that leads people to rely on each other's judgments and depend on each other's commitments.[9]

Trust is most easily recognized in transparent, open management processes that give employees equity and involvement. At Kao, employees' access to information and decision making is particularly striking, reflecting Chairman Yoshio Maruta's belief in equality and commitment to continuous learning. Computer terminals throughout the company allow any employee access to the company's massive information system. "They can even check up on the president's expense account," said a beaming Maruta. He is convinced that the increased creativity and more informed decision making stimulated by such access far outweigh the risk of confidentiality leaks.

Trust is also reflected in and reinforced by a sense of fairness in organizational processes and management practices. Although allocating partners' compensation is often a thorny issue in professional firms, particularly when the contributions to a worldwide profit pool vary widely, the smoothly operating process at Andersen Consulting is built on the strong trust that partners have developed in the overall system. A partner's fraction of the pool is derived from the number of "units" he or she is awarded, based on other partners' evaluation on quantifiable dimensions such as business generated or studies directed and on judgmental criteria such as practice leadership, associate development, and teamwork contributions. All partners receive a list of other unit allocations, and, although there is an official appeal process, nobody in the firm can recall it ever being used.

In the end, trust is perhaps the most vital component of a management context for renewal because it is essential for risk taking. On the organizational trapeze, trust provides the confidence necessary for someone to let go of the security of "business as usual" and take an entrepreneurial leap, knowing that there will be strong, supportive hands at the other end. Such is the environment at Intel, where the company routinely deals with its highly unpredictable technological and competitive environment through a process the company refers to as "buying options." By deliberately backing more than one potential solution to a problem, the company increases the chance it can subsequently back a winner – but it also guarantees that it will have to pull the plug on a loser. To ensure it maintains the confidence and commitment of the unsuccessful team, management is careful to celebrate the discoveries made along "the road not taken" with the same enthusiasm it shows for the contributions of the chosen option. As Intel founder Robert Noyce insisted, "The nature of such high-technology research is that you may not always find what you were looking for, but you find something else equally important." Such a belief buttressed company support for nontraditional approaches and reinforced the frontline experts' high-risk proposals.

Stretch

As many traditional companies found, the more they focused their investment criteria to allocate scarce funds, and the more their corporate leaders refined their strategic visions to clarify the understanding of corporate direction, the more those deep in the organization felt constrained. Tightly defined business boundaries limited the scope of acceptable proposals, and clearly prescribed project boundaries in turn constrained the generation of new ideas. And, on top of this, a budget-driven measurement system further limited managers' focus to a financial target and a twelve-month horizon.

In self-renewing organizations, top management works hard to replace an internal environment that constrains perspectives and restricts activities with one that induces employees to strive for more, rather than less, ambitious objectives. Thus stretch is the liberating, energizing element of managerial context that raises individual aspiration levels and encourages people to lift their expectations of themselves and others.[10]

In a company in which people feel stretched, they are constantly encouraged to see themselves and the organization not in terms of its past or present constraints, but in terms of its future possibilities. Kao's self-image focuses much more on its commitment to being a superior learning organization than on precisely defining the boundaries of the soap and detergent industry segments in which it competes. Its Buddhist-based organizational philosophy also focuses management on how the company can best serve society by applying innovative technology to create true consumer value. Driven by this challenging but unconstrained sense of purpose, the organization seems to have had little difficulty in seeing how its technological capability in fats, fine powders, and liquid crystal emulsification, coupled with its expertise in selling branded package products, could lead them from detergents into cosmetics.

In a stretch environment, corporate leaders are willing to make substantial commitments to amass resources and build capabilities ahead of clear opportunities. By creating a form of "supply-side economics," they build tension that is resolved only by creating new opportunities to meet the developed competencies and committed investments.

Andersen Consulting routinely uses this approach to help it "stay ahead of the commodization envelope," as management puts it. In the 1950s, the young firm invested in building its own computer to develop internal expertise in automated payroll and computerized accounting. Andersen continued to use this approach, and, since the late 1980s, it has been making substantial investments to drive it into the emerging practice of business integration – a field that builds on its leading position in information systems consulting by linking more closely with business strategy and organizational change management. The firm has developed two new Centers of Excellence for Change Management and Strategic Services and hired and trained hundreds of new consultants very different from the traditional operations- and technology-oriented IS specialists. This major commitment has caused some internal stresses and strains, but, according to the firm's partners, it is precisely the kind of change engine Andersen needs to keep growing and evolving.

In the end, stretch is integrated into the fundamental assumptions and beliefs that companies develop about the nature of their industry and their place in it. It fights the development of conventional wisdom and institutionalized verities based on assumptions of a static industry environment or the durability of a strategy, replacing such comforting beliefs with scenarios of discontinuity and norms of dynamic adaptation.

This energizing nervousness has long provided the intellectual and emotional background for decision making at Intel. Since the company's earliest days, it has assumed that it was constantly "on the brink of disaster," as cofounder Gordon Moore put it. He preached that major breakthroughs simply provided breathing space for the next frantic round of development in a business where a new generation chip with four times the capacity of its predecessor would replace it in three years. Because he preached his message so convincingly – and because it turned out to be so accurate – it became known at Intel as Moore's Law and provided for a culture that shunned complacency and rejected incrementalism. Reinforced by the practice of "buying options" and by setting up competing teams for development projects, these values led each new development to start fresh with the explicit objective of making the designers' latest achievements obsolete before anyone else did.

The resulting stretch, along with discipline, support, and trust, provides the framework in which employees can act. Yet these four elements of the renewing companies' management context are far from independent and far from static. Indeed, in their interaction, the whole organizational dynamic of self-renewal is created, an issue on which we now focus.

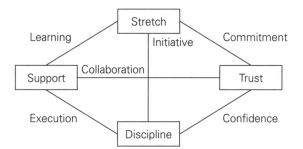

Figure 3 Management context and individual behavior

Framing new individual behaviors

The power of this very different managerial context comes from the internal tensions among the four foundation characteristics. People learn to operate in an environment that is, on one hand, highly disciplined and demanding, yet, on the other, trusting and secure – when expectations are stretching and ambitious, yet within a supportive, nurturing setting. And in the resolution of these complementary yet often contradictory forces, the organization develops the energy and direction to drive its dynamic renewal process.

In the end, therefore, the power of the behavioral context lies in its impact on the behavior of individual organization members (see Figure 3):

- The ability and willingness of people to take *initiative* is rooted in the tension between stretch and discipline: the former is the source of energy and the latter converts that energy into tangible and timebound action. Stretch without discipline leads to daydreaming, while discipline without stretch locks the company into an ever-narrowing spiral of refining existing operations without the courage to make any creative leaps.

- Similarly, the combination of trust and support motivates cooperation and *collaboration*. Trust makes cooperation desirable; support enables individuals to convert that desire into action. Each is a necessary element in the organizational glue, but only in combination do they create a sufficient condition for integrating the disparate actions of dispersed people.

- Beyond initiative and cooperation, renewal also requires some other behaviors – an openness to *learning*, the courage of *confidence*, the willingness to *commit*, and the ability to *execute*. The same four attributes of context, in different combinations, provide the enabling conditions for each behavior.

To illustrate how a broad organizational context can create and sustain the individual behaviors that are the foundation of continuous renewal, we use the example of a small team in 3M's optical systems business. The team's creation of a highly successful computer privacy screen shows the ways the induced organizational values and management processes influenced individual behavior. (For a brief description of how the attributes of discipline, support, trust, and stretch have been embedded at 3M, see the sidebar.)

Deeply embedded management values at 3M

As one of the world's most consistently innovative companies, 3M has been able to escape the confines of its mature industrial base and constantly renew itself by introducing such diverse products as laser imaging equipment, Scotch Brite scouring pads, transdermal drug-delivery systems, and Post-it Notes.

The unique work environment required to create and sustain the energy, creativity, and determination to maintain such an enviable capability has been carefully built and nurtured over many years. Much of it is rooted in values and practices laid down decades ago by William McKnight, the company's spiritual founder and CEO from 1929 to 1966, yet even today provides a classic example of a management context for self-renewal.

● **Stretch.** At 3M's foundation is a deeply embedded belief in and commitment to entrepreneurship that provides the basis of an organizational environment that, according to one senior executive, "stimulates ordinary people to produce extraordinary performance." This strong belief system is reflected in the organizational norms and management practices that energize people to push themselves to achieve. For example, the "15 percent rule" allows employees to devote up to 15 percent of their time pursuing ideas of interest to them that they believe have potential value for the company. The legends about those who have developed creative new products or innovative technologies and the coveted honor of induction into the Carlton Society, 3M's elite club of outstanding scientists and technologists, inspire many. Others are driven by the stretch target that had long demanded every division to ensure that 25 percent of sales came from products introduced in the past five years, a high hurdle recently raised to 30 percent of sales from the past four years' new products.

● **Discipline.** The new-product introduction target is one of several that drive 3M managers. In addition, they must achieve 10 percent growth in sales and earnings, 20 percent return on equity, and 27 percent return on capital employed. Equally important, all parts of 3M's diverse business portfolio are held to this standard. Said one ex-CEO, "We recognize some of our businesses as established, but none of them as mature, and exempt none of them – not even the oldest – from striving to meet our standards for growth and profitability."

But these high standards of performance are not achieved through formal systems and controls; in fact, the company's strategic planning system was not even put in place until the early 1980s. Management expectations rather than controls, and organizational norms of meeting commitments more than formal rewards, give these objectives their power. These attributes of 3M's management process provide an internal discipline that prevents individual entrepreneurship from degenerating into organizational anarchy.

● **Support.** Few divisions can meet 3M's tough objectives without the broad-level support rooted in a corporation explicitly committed to "a respect for the individual and a commitment to creating an entrepreneurial environment where innovation flourishes." This value is reflected in a hierarchical relationship built more on support and coaching than on direction and control. CEO Desi DeSimone commented, "That requires managers to have respect for ideas coming up from below. They have to ask, 'What do you see that I'm missing?'" On the basis of a well-established norm to "make a little, sell a little," management is inclined to fund the bottom-up proposals, even when the end use is not clear, letting the market be the final judge.

Another deeply embedded belief that "products belong to divisions, but technology belongs to the company" encourages a norm of mutual support in product development and ensures the linking and leveraging of the company's numerous pockets of knowledge and expertise. The supportive cultural norms are reinforced by a variety of organizational processes such as cross-unit career path programs, a sophisticated network of electronic directories and e-mail linkages, and the highly effective Technology Forum, a body created to build and strengthen informal contact and mutual support among 3M scientists and technologists.

● **Trust.** 3M's ability to encourage its employees to take the risks required by its ambitious expectations, give the effort demanded by its tough targets, and make commitments to its collaborative activities is based on a trust in the organization and its values. Early in the company's history, McKnight articulated a faith in people's ability and a belief that they sometimes need to fail in order to learn. "Mistakes will be made, but if a person is essentially right, the mistakes he or she makes are not as serious in the long run as the mistakes management will make if it is dictatorial . . . [or] destructively critical."

In this context, management accepts and even celebrates "well-intentioned failure," and stories of how rejected ideas or unsuccessful experiments eventually succeeded are a large part of 3M lore. One recently celebrated "failure" was the development of an extremely weak adhesive by a scientist searching for precisely the opposite. This rejected product subsequently inspired the development of the enormously popular Post-it Notes. The message to the organization is clear: take a chance, reach for a tough objective, and contribute to a worthwhile experiment. Genuine effort and risk taking will be applauded, not punished.

PART II • THE INDIVIDUALIZED CORPORATION

In 1985, Andy Wong became lab manager of 3M's Optical Systems (OS) business unit, and four years later, he was promoted to head of the young operation. During the next few years, he assembled a team, focused on finding the applications and developing the capabilities to turn the struggling unit around, and eventually brought a successful new product to market.

Wong found the initial challenge of building a team difficult because the OS unit had generated losses and was unsuccessful despite its decade-long attempts to find commercial applications for its inherited optical technologies, some of which had been around for more than twenty-five years. He was able to get first-rate scientists, engineers, and marketers to *collaborate* because they could see that, despite its difficulties, the business unit had continued to receive funding from the division and support from several higher level executives who believed in the technologies' potential. Furthermore, they all completely trusted that their personal credibility and future careers with the company would not be compromised if this high-risk venture failed. For example, Rob Noirjean, the marketing manager Wong recruited from another division, acknowledged that while the business looked like a gamble, it also presented an exciting opportunity that would provide good experience for his next assignment. The same sustaining context also facilitated the unit's ability to obtain collaboration from other units. The corporate norm of mutual support and the overarching value of institutional trust made such cooperative activity integral to the ongoing management process.

If collaboration provides one foundation for a self-renewing company, *initiative* provides another. After collecting and supplementing his team, Wong created an environment in which individual enterprise and group energy combined to generate numerous new proposals and alternatives. 3M's stretching corporate goal, which required each division to generate 25 percent of its sales from new products, was further intensified by internal competition among five emerging businesses, including Optical Systems, that made up the Safety and Security Systems Divisions (SSSD). The raw creativity unleashed by such an ambition-driven environment was channeled and focused by the disciplined demands of the company's strict financial objectives implemented by Paul Guehler, the new division general manager. When he took over SSSD in October 1990, Guehler's first objective was to "clean up Optical Systems," a unit he thought needed more structure and definition. By turning up the heat on the unit, Guehler forced a reality check and created a sense of urgency to the process that Wong had unleashed. In this environment of both stretch and discipline, Noirjean generated and then rapidly focused the list of potential applications until the unit finally decided to develop the privacy screen.

The challenge of finding a successful application for an old technology in a unit that had been bleeding red ink for more than a decade was likely to be demotivating. Yet, within the OS unit, there was a widely shared, highly energizing sense of *confidence* that the new project would be successful. This spirit had been fueled by Guehler's insistence that the team commit its ideas to paper, add multiple scenarios, and, most of all, articulate and defend its ideas. The discipline of refining and testing the plans served to reinforce the belief in the project's viability. Furthermore, despite the long, checkered history of both the technology and its sponsoring unit, Wong and his team remained confident that the project would not be killed or the unit disbanded, as long as they could, according to Wong, "Keep our management in the boat by demonstrating steady progress and by painting a picture of the cathedral we were building." Their trust in the system's fairness and in management reinforced their willingness to plan boldly.

Beyond a motivating sense of confidence, Wong and his team developed a deep sense of *commitment* to the privacy-screen project. This became a vital organizational attribute for a unit with limited credibility and developed genuine excitement for the challenge of the stretching objective the new product represented. But the less certain the project's outcome, the more its sponsors had to believe that the organization would not punish them for taking risks. And while 3M's stretching and demanding environment created excitement within OS, its managers were never distracted from their commitment to keep the project alive by worrying about their own jobs.

Despite the unit's commitment to the privacy-screen project, the task of developing and bringing the product to market was complicated by numerous problems, obstacles, and challenges that demanded continual adjustment and refinement. The ongoing *learning* capability was encouraged by the business unit's own self-imposed stretching challenge, framed not only by Wong's expectations of his team, but also by Guehler's more urgent demands. An institutionalized support system gave the team access to technological input from experts in other divisions and to top management backing, particularly from Wong's mentor Ron Mitsch, a group vice president whose faith in the project and the OS team never flagged. Through this push and pull, the unit was able to continually adjust and adapt its product design and marketing strategy after the first two versions met with lukewarm market acceptance. But supported by unflagging confidence and unwavering commitment, the unit developed a third generation of the product, which it proposed for approval in early 1992.

Finally, the example of the OS unit demonstrates how the management context framed a commitment to *execution* – a bias for action and an ability to implement. The complementary tension between discipline and support that encouraged such institutionalized behavior was embodied in what Guehler described as his "give and take" management philosophy; he supported and invested in the privacy-screen project but, at the same time, took resources away and forced the unit to meet its financial objectives. His approach was well understood at 3M and reflected in CEO DeSimone's comment, "[Managers] may have to close their eyes for a while . . . but, in the end, there has to be performance. We can't allow every project to continue indefinitely. So we start to starve it. We force it to show it can survive."

Individualizing the corporation

In the aftermath of the restructuring gains achieved through downsizing, delayering, and reengineering, many companies have suffered a major letdown. Not only have the organizations become too physically strained and emotionally exhausted to maintain the momentum of improvement, but employees' day-to-day behavior has reverted to old, familiar patterns. We suggest that, while corporate renewal may be initiated by a structural revolution, it endures only if it is supported by a cultural transformation. Top management's role, therefore, is not only to reframe the configuration of organizational assets and responsibilities, but also to redefine the context of individual attitudes and behaviors.

Because this implies a fundamental redefinition of the management philosophy at the foundation of a company's ongoing relationship with its employees, the change we describe is profound. In a fast-growth industrial era in which capital was the scarce resource, a company's employees were often managed as if they were just another set of inputs: factors of production to be deployed and controlled to maximize the efficiency of a capital-intensive system. The work environment was deliberately designed to ensure that employees' behavior was as predictable and controllable as machines they supported. By minimizing the idiosyncrasies of human activity, a behavioral context of compliance, control, contract, and constraint fostered the development of what William H. Whyte described as "the organization man" – employees who were shaped and molded to ensure that they operated in clearly defined boundaries and that they did things "the company way."[11]

In redefining the behavioral context around the dimensions of discipline, support, trust, and stretch, however, top management is not only reframing the organization's values and expectations, it is redefining the nature of the relationship between the corporation and its employees. The old notion of "the organization man" that forced the individual to conform to tightly defined corporate norms is being replaced by a concept that we describe as "the individualized corporation." In a radical turnaround, the company must adjust and find ways to take advantage of each employee's unique knowledge and individual capabilities.

This fundamental shift in management philosophy is behind the waves of delayering, reengineering, and empowerment sweeping across today's organization. Rather than managing through the abstractions of plans and controls, top-level managers are recognizing that their key task is to create a work environment that stimulates the company's valuable human resource to be more motivated, creative, and entrepreneurial than its competitors' employees. Only when they liberate and motivate their people to develop and leverage their knowledge and expertise will they have created a dynamic, self-renewing corporation.

Christopher A. Bartlett is a professor at the Harvard Business School.
This paper appeared in *Sloan Management Review*, Fall 1995.

REFERENCES

1. For a brief description of this study and some of its broad conclusions, see:
C.A. Bartlett and S. Ghoshal, "Changing the Role of Top Management: Beyond Strategy to Purpose," *Harvard Business Review*, November–December 1994, pp. 79–88;
C.A. Bartlett and S. Ghoshal, "Changing the Role of Top Management: Beyond Structure to Processes," *Harvard Business Review*, January–February 1995, pp. 86–96; and
C.A. Bartlett and S. Ghoshal, "Changing the Role of Top Management: Beyond Systems to People," *Harvard Business Review*, May–June 1995, pp. 132–142.

2. What we describe as behavioral context is very akin to what has been described in the strategy process literature as organizational context. See:
J.L. Bower, *Managing the Resource Allocation Process* (Boston: Harvard University, Graduate School of Business Administration, Division of Research, 1970); and
R.A. Burgelman, "A Model of the Interaction of Strategic Behavior, Corporate Context, and the Concept of Strategy," *Academy of Management Review* 8 (1983): 61–70.

Organizational theorists have preferred the labels of climate and culture. See:
E.H. Schein, *Organizational Culture and Leadership* (San Francisco: Jossey-Bass, 1985); and R.D. Denison, *Corporate Culture and Organizational Effectiveness* (New York: John Wiley, 1990).

For a recent comparative review of these literatures, see:
D.R. Denison, "What is the Difference between Organizational Culture and Organizational Climate? A Native's Point of View on a Decade of Paradigm Wars" (Ann Arbor, Michigan: University of Michigan, School of Business Administration, mimeo, July 1993).

We choose the term "behavioral context" both to avoid what Denison has described as "paradigm wars" and also to emphasize the notion of a context in which individual behavior – "artifacts" in the terminology of Schein – is embedded. See:
E.H. Schein, "Does Japanese Management Style Have a Message for American Managers?," *Sloan Management Review*, Fall 1981, pp. 55–68.

3. This decade-long history of ups and downs in Westinghouse has been chronicled in detail in the business press. The following insightful articles provide the basis for our analysis:
T.A. Stewart, "Westinghouse Gets Respect at Last," *Fortune*, 3 July 1989, pp. 60–64;
P. Nulty, "Behind the Mess at Westinghouse," *Fortune*, 4 November 1991, pp. 69–71;
M. Schroeder, "Westinghouse Gets a Big Dose of Reality," *Business Week*, 17 February 1992, pp. 110–113;
S. Baker, "Westinghouse: More Pain Ahead," *Business Week*, 7 December 1992, pp. 32–34;
M. Schroeder, "The Decline and Fall of Westinghouse's Paul Lego," *Business Week*, 8 March 1993, pp. 68–70; and
S. Baker, "Go Slow, Now That's Radical," *Business Week*, 24 January 1994, p. 28.

4. Chandler provides perhaps the clearest description of how control was the essential prerequisite for delegating responsibility in the divisionalized corporation. See:
A.D. Chandler, *Strategy and Structure* (Cambridge, Massachusetts, MIT Press, 1962).

5. For a rich analysis of the pathologies of the planning and control systems in large companies, see:
P.C. Haspeslagh, "Portfolio Planning Approaches and the Strategic Management Process in Diversified Industrial Companies" (Boston: Harvard Business School, unpublished dissertation, 1983).

6. Bower's analysis of the resource allocation process provides a detailed description of how the "context" set by top management creates constraints at the level of front-line managers. See:
Bower (1970); and Burgelman (1983).

7. Past research in the organizational behavior field has identified discipline as an important element of organizational climate. See, for example:
P. Amsa, "Organizational Culture and Work Group Behavior: An Empirical Study," *Journal of Management Studies* 23 (1986): 347–362; and G.G. Cordon and N. Di Tomaso, "Predicting Corporate Performance from Organizational Culture," *Journal of Management Studies* 29 (1992): 783–798.

8. For a rich discussion on how a context of support influences the behaviors of organizational members, see:
R. Walton, "From Control to Commitment in the Workplace," *Harvard Business Review*, March–April 1985, pp. 76–84.

9. The literature on organizational culture has consistently highlighted the importance of trust in stimulating both commitment and collaboration among employees. See, for example:

T.E. Deal and A.A. Kennedy, *Corporate Cultures, the Rites and Rituals of Organizational Life* (Reading, Massachusetts: Addison-Wesley, 1982).

10. Hamel and Prahalad have recently emphasized the role of stretch in enhancing corporate performance. See:
G. Hamel and C.K. Prahalad, "Strategy as Stretch and Leverage," *Harvard Business Review*, March–April 1993, pp. 75–87.

11. Whyte's sociological study of life in the classic corporate hierarchy of the postwar decades provides a rich description of the kind of behavioral context such authority-based bureaucracies created. See:
W.H. Whyte, Jr., *The Organization Man* (New York: Simon & Schuster, 1956).

CHAPTER 7

Rebuilding behavioral context: a blueprint for corporate renewal

Sumantra Ghoshal and Christopher A. Bartlett

This is the companion paper to Chapter 6. Where the previous paper focused on the elements *of behavioural context, the focus here is on the* process *of building such a context. The key to making the process of corporate renewal work, Sumantra and Chris argue, is a carefully phased sequence of steps. Step one is simplification – breaking the firm down into small business units in which individual initiative and discipline can be instilled. Step two is integration – realigning cross-business unit relationships, and providing the necessary support, stretch, and trust for them to work effectively together. Step three is regeneration – ensuring continuous learning across the entire organization. This model is illustrated using detailed examples from GE, GM, ABB, and AT&T.*

Few companies around the world have not tried to reinvent themselves – some more than once – during the past decade. Yet, for every successful corporate transformation, there is at least one equally prominent failure. GE's dramatic performance improvement starkly contrasts with the string of disappointments and crises that have plagued Westinghouse. ABB's ascendance to global leadership in power equipment only emphasizes Hitachi's inability to reverse its declining fortunes in that business. And Philips's successful revitalization since 1990 only highlights its own agonizingly slow turnaround in the preceding ten years.

What accounts for the success of some corporations and the failure of so many others? How did some organizations turn around transformation processes that had clearly stalled? In the course of five years of research into the nature and implications of the radically different organization and management models that have begun to emerge during the past decade, we studied more than a dozen companies as they implemented a succession of programs designed to rationalize their inefficient operations, revitalize their ineffective strategies, and renew their tired organizations. In the process, we have gained some insight into the reasons that some made recognizable progress in their transformational change process while others only replaced the dead weight of their bureaucracies with change program overload.

In observing how the successful corporate transformation processes have differed from those that struggled or failed outright, we were struck by two distinctions. First, successful transformation processes almost always followed a carefully phased approach that focused on developing particular organizational capabilities in appropriate sequence. Second, the managers of the successful companies recognized that transformation is as much a function of individuals' behaviors as it is of the strategies, structures, and systems that top management introduces. As a result, rather than becoming preoccupied with downsizing and reengineering programs, they focused much attention on the changes required to fundamentally reshape what we described in our previous article as a company's behavioral context.[1]

A phased sequence of change

The problem with most companies that have failed in their transformation efforts is not that they tried to change too little, but that they tried to change too much. Faced with the extraordinary demands of their highly competitive, rapidly changing operating environments, managers have eagerly embraced the flood of prescriptive advice that consultants and academics have offered as solutions – typically in the random sequence of a supply-driven market for management fads. According to a recent survey, between 1990 and 1994, the average company had committed itself to 11.8 of 25 such currently popular management tools and techniques – from corporate visioning and TQM programs to empowerment and reengineering processes.[2] Despite this widespread frenzy of activity, the study found no correlation between the number of tools a company used and its satisfaction with its financial performance. The authors did conclude, however, that most tools could be helpful "if the right ones were chosen at the right time and implemented in the right way."[3]

While such a generalization borders on the self-evident, we would endorse the importance that the conclusion gives to sequencing and implementing activities in a change process. In many companies, we have seen front-line managers bewildered when faced with multiple, inconsistent priorities. In contrast, we observed that the companies that were most successful in transforming themselves into more flexible, responsive organizations pursued a much simpler, more focused sequence of actions.

One widely recognized phased transformation process has been Jack Welch's revitalization of General Electric. From his emphasis on downsizing, delayering, and portfolio pruning in the early and mid-1980s, Welch shifted his focus to more developmental, integrative activities in the late 1980s. By the early 1990s, he had begun to create what he called a "boundaryless and self-renewing organization." Although he has faulted himself for not moving faster, Welch has remained firmly convinced of the logic in the sequence of his actions and of the need to make substantial progress at each stage before moving to the next.[4]

Our study results suggest that, as a model for corporate transformation, the GE example has broad applicability. It rests on the simple recognition that any company's performance depends on two core capabilities: the strength of each of its component units and the effectiveness of their integration. This is true of the integration of individually strong functional groups along an organization's value chain as well as of the synergistic linking of a company's portfolio of business units or the global networking of its different national subsidiaries. This assumption defines the two axes of the corporate renewal model represented in Figure 1.

As they face the renewal challenge, most companies find themselves with a portfolio of operations (represented by the circles in Figure 1): a few strong but independent units and activities (the tightly defined but separate circles in quadrant 2), another cluster of better integrated operations that, despite their better integration, are not performing well individually (the looser, overlapping circles in quadrant 3), and a group of business units, country subsidiaries, or functional entities that don't perform well individually and are also ineffective in linking and leveraging each others' resources and capabilities (the ill-defined, unconnected circles in quadrant 1).

The overall objective of the transformation process is to move the entire portfolio into quadrant 4 and find ways to prevent the units from

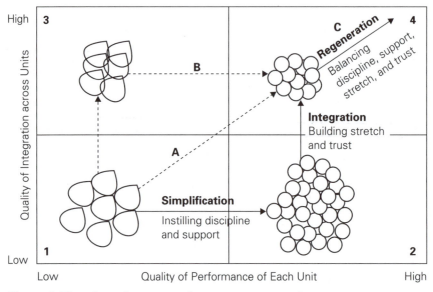

Figure 1 The phased process of corporate renewal

returning to their old modes of operation. But while the goal of develop-ing an organization built on well-integrated, efficient operating entities is clear, the path to this organizational nirvana is not well defined. Yet it matters immensely.

Some companies – General Motors during the 1980s, for instance – tried to take the direct route represented by the diagonal path A in the figure. While intellectually and emotionally appealing, this bold approach of trying to improve performance on both dimensions simultaneously has typically ended in failure due to the complex, often contradictory demands that overload the organization. GM discovered this during the 1980s when it pressured its five auto divisions to boost their individual market share and profitability while simultaneously improving cross-unit synergies. It turned out that the demands of coordinating body styling and chassis design often conflicted with each division's ability to respond to the needs and opportunities of its own particular market segment. Like GM, IBM's attempt in the late 1980s to improve both unit performance and corporate integration also caused that company's transformation program to stumble.

Other companies – Philips in the late 1980s, for example – followed a more focused path, pushing first for integration on the assumption that better synergies among units would help each improve its individual performance. However, this change model, represented by path B, has also proved unsuccessful. In a bold reorganization, company president Cor van der Klugt declared Philips's consumer electronics, professional electronics, components, and lighting businesses the company's "core interdependent" operations and tried to create structures and processes that would help them manage their perceived interdependencies. As the company soon discovered, however, it was extremely difficult to integrate operations that were themselves struggling with enormous internal difficulties. And even where they succeeded, the linkages connecting uncompetitive individual businesses served mostly to emphasize and reinforce the liabilities of each. As corporate performance continued to decline and a new CEO was appointed to try another approach, Philips managers concluded, with classic gallows humor, that "four drunks do not make an effective team." It was a lesson that unfortunately was lost on Daimler Benz, which continued its efforts to integrate its diverse, overstaffed operations until a new top management team signaled a change in direction for the struggling transformation program in 1995.

The third option, path C in our model, defines the most effective sequence of transformational change processes. This is the path Jack Welch followed as he steered GE through an ongoing series of change processes that he initiated in the early 1980s. As we reviewed this much-admired transformation of one of the world's largest corporations, three distinct phases of activity were evident – phases we define as simplification, integration, and regeneration. In the simplification phase, Welch focused on strengthening the performance of each of the company's businesses, attempting to make each "number one or number two in its industry." During the next five years, he sold or closed operations valued at almost $10 billion and acquired new businesses worth $18 billion. He stripped away the heavy superstructure of sectors and groups that had long burdened front-line units and made drastic cuts in the size and responsibilities of corporate staffs. While this streamlining cost the company some ability to integrate and coordinate activities across units, Welch's primary concern was to give the managers of the core businesses the freedom to develop new strategies and to control their operations. By creating a sense of organizational clarity and managerial simplicity, he felt more able to hold them accountable for the results.

By the mid-1980s, with most of the acquisitions and divestitures completed, Welch evolved into a second phase, which we call integration. With thirteen businesses running strongly at the company's core, he began to look for ways he could link them to exploit potential scale economies, leverage their individual resources, and capture opportunities for cross-unit learning. Beginning with his top-level corporate executive committee meetings, he worked to develop an environment for interunit collaboration that would demonstrate the concrete benefits of cooperation. He urged his senior executives to accept some high-visibility, symbolic proposals – putting sixteen pounds of GE plastics into every GE refrigerator, for example, or having the engineers from the locomotive division resolve a serious design problem in the appliance business. During the next several years, he pushed collaboration deeper into the organization through programs designed to open minds, clear communications channels, and eliminate the parochial attitudes that had insulated functions, isolated businesses, and separated operating units from each other.

A decade after he began, Welch had simplified GE's organization and integrated its businesses, but he realized he had not yet created the kind of organization that he hoped to leave to his successor – one that continually replenished and renewed itself. So he initiated actions that moved GE into the third transformation phase, one that would imbue GE with a capability that we call self-regeneration. As he challenges employees with notions of "boundarylessness," Welch is trying to develop an organization with the ability to balance the tensions and management paradoxes implicit in the drive to achieve superior unit performance while simultaneously collaborating with other units to leverage the organization-wide benefits of integration. Like the first two phases, this one is also demanding profound behavioral change among the people who make up General Electric.

A new behavioral context

The major constraint in any corporate transformational process – and the explanation behind the need for the carefully sequenced stages – lies in people's capacity to accommodate change. Indeed, the most successful companies in our study were those that recognized behavioral change as not just an outcome of the transformation but as its driving engine. As a result, they focused their attention beyond the conventional concern about restructuring the hierarchy and reengineering its processes, and devoted most of their attention to the more subtle, demanding task of changing individual attitudes, assumptions, and behaviors.

This realization struck Jack Welch in the mid-1980s, a few years after he had initiated his bold, effective delayering and downsizing program that had eliminated several layers of GE's hierarchy and reduced its payroll by 70,000 employees. Although he had been extraordinarily successful at meeting his initial objectives, Welch understood that he could not achieve his long-term goals unless he won the minds and changed the behaviors of many front-line employees who were suspicious and even cynical about the motivations of a man they had begun to call "Neutron Jack." In 1985, he acknowledged to a group of employees, "A company can boost productivity by restructuring, removing bureaucracy, and downsizing, but it cannot sustain high productivity without cultural change."[5]

Successful corporate transformation, as Welch recognized, could not simply be imposed from the top through macro change programs. It also had to be built from the bottom through activities designed to ensure that everyone understood and supported the change. An effective change process needs to focus simultaneously on the company's "hardware" – its business configuration and organization structure – and on its "software" – the motivations, values, and commitments of the company's employees. In other words, together with the changes in structure and systems, managers also need to change what we described in our previous article as the behavioral context of the company.[6]

As we observed GE and other companies evolve through the long, painful process of transforming bureaucratic hierarchies into self-renewing organizations, we became aware of the importance not only of the sequencing of macro processes – simplification, integration, and regeneration – but also of the changes to individuals' behaviors that supported those broader initiatives. The performance-driven actions implicit in Welch's call for speed, simplicity, and self-confidence, for example, were different from the more collaborative behaviors he was trying to elicit in his subsequent emphasis on "a boundaryless organization." Our observations suggest that discipline, support, stretch, and trust – the four vital elements of the transformational behavioral context – were most effectively developed sequentially in a way that supported the three stages of renewal. Instilling discipline and support, for example, is crucial to managing the company through the simplification phase; instilling stretch and trust is essential to effective cross-unit integration; and balancing all four dimensions is the key to moving to a state of continuous regeneration.

Simplification: building front-line initiative

Of all the companies we studied, the one that faced the most daunting transformation challenge was AT&T. Forced to divest 70 percent of its assets in an antitrust settlement, compelled to confront formidable global competitors in a suddenly deregulated business, and confronted with an industry fundamentally restructured by the converging technologies of computers and telecommunications, AT&T was a dinosaur on the brink of extinction for the first few years after the company's 1984 breakup. Within four years, its near monopoly of long distance service had been reduced to a 68 percent share, its once highly profitable equipment business was staggering under the attack of aggressive competition, and its computer business was floundering in a struggling partnership with Olivetti. At this time, Bob Allen became CEO and initiated a series of initiatives that illustrate the actions most effective in the first stage of transforming a classic bureaucracy into a self-renewing organization.

In a series of early moves, Allen signaled a radical departure from the previous integrative activities that management described as AT&T's "single enterprise" strategy. By deemphasizing cross-unit coordination, he was able to focus attention on simplifying the company's large, unwieldy organization, breaking it into twenty-one business units, each responsible for developing its own business model and for delivering its own results. To reinforce this message, he implemented a rigorous economic value-added (EVA) system that recorded and reported the return on capital employed for the newly created business units, each of which was required to manage not only its profit and loss account but also its own balance sheet. The business unit managers, in turn, created more than 100 focused product groups, each with its own profit and loss account, thereby fragmenting AT&T into more than 100 distinct management units. According to Allen, the dramatic improvement in AT&T's performance during the next five years, reflected in the 200 percent increase in the company's market value, would not have been possible without the restructuring that allowed front-line managers to simplify their tasks and focus their attention.

But simplifying the structure and systems was not enough to change the behavior of individuals who had spent their whole careers in an environment driven by directives, policies, and constraints. In an organization demotivated by several years of competitive defeats, operating losses, and personnel cuts, Allen saw his main objective as "helping our people learn how to win again." This required him to replace the context of imposed compliance and control with a more internalized model of behavior. While stripping out structural overhead, AT&T's top management was also focused on the huge task of establishing strong norms of self-discipline and building a context of support and encouragement.

Building discipline

Over several years, Allen and his top management team designed numerous initiatives to shift the internal cultural norm of compliance to a context that encouraged self-discipline. Among these, the three that seemed the most influential – and common to other successful change processes we observed – were their attention to unambiguous performance standards, their commitment to feedback, and their process of clear, consistently applied rewards and sanctions.[7]

From his first day, one of Allen's strongest and most consistent messages was that financial success could no longer be negotiated in Washington in discussions among lobbyists, lawyers, and regulators, but instead would have to be won in the marketplace through the actions of front-line managers. Central to this communication effort was his introduction of the EVA concept. As a result of management's relentless insistence that each business prove its economic viability and strategic potential, business heads were motivated to translate their broad EVA objectives into a much richer set of internal performance benchmarks that, in turn, were reflected in clearly defined individual targets right down to the front lines of their operations. Supported by intense communication that helped managers understand the performance impact of their business decisions, EVA became more than just a mechanical control system; it became the basis of a behavioral context that resulted in a norm of fulfilling commitments and meeting tough standards – a discipline not widely observed in the predivestiture AT&T.

After focusing the organization on unambiguous performance standards, Allen and his top team worked on developing an effective feedback process so that individuals could see exactly how they were measuring up to the standards. AT&T accomplished this with a new accounting system that provided frequent, detailed, and disaggregated feedback to each unit and was designed to "ruthlessly expose the truth about performance." Again, it was not so much the system as the way senior management used it that was key to shaping the desired behavioral context. Through their practice of conducting open reviews within each unit and between business units and corporate staff, Allen and his top team did more than just define standards and clarify expectations. They used these exchanges to educate management to a new way of thinking and to provide honest, timely performance evaluations against the new expectations. The intensity and quality of this review process greatly contributed to the institutionalization of discipline as an established behavioral norm.

The third common contextual element in organizations that develop a strong sense of individual discipline is a consistently applied set of rewards and sanctions, clearly linked to the performance standards. At AT&T, the EVA system had a strong, direct linkage to the compensation system, a characteristic that gave it credibility and teeth. Equally important, the linkage was reinforced by the way senior managers implemented the system, not only awarding performance-based bonuses of up to 50 percent of base salary but also replacing managers and even selling or merging units unable to meet their EVA targets. The replacement of a number of key nonperforming managers with outsiders from high-discipline organizations strongly reinforced the emerging norm that managers deliver on their commitments – a centerpiece in AT&T's gradual shift in behavioral context from imposed compliance to internalized self-discipline.

Embedding support

Over time, however, such unalloyed emphasis on results can become corrosive. In the course of our study, we found that the radical restructuring called for in the simplification stage was less likely to result in individual burnout or organizationwide rejection if the hard-edged tools of discipline were counterbalanced and complemented by management's nurturing and support of those spurred to action by the rigorous demands of the discipline-based context.[8] As AT&T discovered, a commitment to legitimate empowerment, access to resources, and a management style based on coaching and guidance proved most effective in creating such an environment of support.

One of Allen's first objectives was to break the sense of control and dependence that often characterized the relationships between superiors and subordinates. While he was holding business units accountable for their performance, for example, he was also radically decentralizing responsibility by giving unit leaders the authority to fundamentally change their businesses' strategy and operations. The new accounting system proved to be very important in this effort. Instead of being designed primarily around senior management's control needs, reports were explicitly developed to provide disaggregated information to support the operating level managers' activities and decisions. At the same time, however, the system provided AT&T senior managers an effective early warning tool that gave them confidence to loosen their control, knowing they had timely, reliable information so they could intervene before major problems developed.

Allen's huge commitment to train new managers to use the data and accept the responsibilities they were given reinforced this systems change. Furthermore, Allen took personal responsibility for appointments to all key positions and ensured that his selections were individuals with reputations as delegators and developers. But his own personal management style provided the most powerful empowerment message. He described his philosophy: "I have never thought that I could be so knowledgeable about our businesses and markets that I could make the decisions. I have always been an advocate of shared decision making. In fact, I believe this is one of the reasons I am CEO."

As most companies soon realize, empowerment is legitimized only when those given responsibility are also given access to the resources they need to implement their newly delegated decisions. Again, Allen initiated radical change by decentralizing many assets and resources traditionally controlled at the corporate level. In a major restructuring of Bell Labs, for example, he gave business units the authority to control the budgets of more than 80 percent of the lab's employees, thereby giving them direct access to and influence over AT&T's enormous technological resources. In middle-level managers' view, this increased access to financial and technological resources was key to the company's rapid transition from a highly centralized bureaucracy to a more flexible organization in which those deep in operations could initiate and drive action rather than just write proposals and await approvals.

To give substance to the norms of empowerment and to validate the redeployment of assets and resources, senior managers must be willing to move one stage further. They must retreat from their historic roles as chief planners and controllers and redefine their core responsibilities in more supportive terms. In the new environment of radically decentralized responsibility and authority, they must provide the coaching and guidance that separates legitimate empowerment from the knee-jerk version that often ends up as abdication. This third element of a supportive behavioral context has probably given Allen his most critical challenge. Starting with his own actions and those of his colleagues on the executive committee, he has tried to become a role model for the desired coaching and supporting relationship. When managers try to escalate issues for his decision, he is likely to tell them that his opinion is irrelevant and encourage them to solve the problem themselves.

To spread this management model, he has broadened the evaluation criteria for all senior managers to include a development measure that AT&T calls "people value-added" (PVA), which has the same weight as the well-established EVA measure. PVA is supported by a 360 degree assessment process in which each manager is evaluated not only by his or her boss but also by peers and subordinates. In typical fashion, Allen first applied the new process to himself and his top management team before introducing it to the company.

Through a broad array of such tools, programs, and individual actions, AT&T's management team created a supportive environment that smoothed the hard edges of the highly discipline-oriented demands that they had placed on the organization. Indeed, it was this finely balanced change in the company's behavioral context that management felt was central to AT&T's turnaround from a loss of $1.2 billion in 1988 to a $4.6 billion profit in 1994.

Integration: realigning cross-unit relationships

For most companies, the initial tightening of ongoing operating performance is only the first stage in a long transformation process toward becoming a self-renewing organization. While this simplification phase can improve the productivity of a company's resources, some very different efforts and abilities are required to restart its growth engine. For example, although AT&T's fragmentation into disciplined business units allowed it to reduce waste and cut expense, it also led to the creation of twenty-one highly autonomous units run by what one manager described as "a bunch of independent business-unit cowboys." Yet, to grow – whether by expansion into the dynamic new infocom business at the intersection of the computer, communications, consumer electronics, and entertainment industries or by exploiting the fabulous potential of the emerging Chinese market – the twenty-one entities would have to operate as one AT&T.

Between 1993 and 1995, AT&T struggled to turn around the momentum of its highly successful simplification process by creating the necessary coordinating mechanisms for the integration phase. Management initiated

a number of structural measures, from building a new regional management group to coordinate the disparate international initiatives of
the twenty-one business units, to creating project teams to address the
emerging multimedia, data communication, and other cross-business-unit
opportunities. To support the integrative behaviors required by these
structural changes, the company made a huge effort to embed a shared
vision that focused on how the different parts of AT&T could collectively
allow people to communicate with one another "anytime, anywhere,"
and to articulate shared values as a "common bond" to tie the whole
organization together. Yet, after two years, the company was finally
forced to abandon this effort and break up into three separate entities,
demonstrating the enormous difficulties of managing the transition from
the simplification process to the integration phase.

In contrast to AT&T's difficulties in integrating the company by
leveraging the interdependencies across its different businesses, ABB, Asea
Brown Boveri, the Swedish-Swiss electrotechnical giant is quite far along
this path and illustrates some important requirements for managing
the second phase of renewal. Within three months of his appointment
as CEO of the $17 billion company formed through the merger of Asea
and Brown Boveri, Percy Barnevik expressed his vision for the new
organization as three dualities: "global and local, big and small, radically
decentralized with central reporting and control." For the first few years,
however, Barnevik focused on only one part of each duality: he wanted
to build the new company on a solid foundation of small, local, radically
decentralized units. To break the back of the old bureaucracies and
strip excess resources, Barnevik radically restructured the company into
1,300 legally separate companies, giving them control over most of ABB's
assets and resources. At the same time, he slashed the old hierarchies
from eight or nine levels to a structure that had only three management
levels between him and the front line. Although somewhat more radical,
these early actions were very similar to those Allen took at AT&T.

By the early 1990s, however, Barnevik and his team began to pay more
attention to the challenge of ensuring ABB's long-term growth. This task
needed the revitalization of activities in a mature set of business operations
through the integration of the independent units and numerous acquisitions
into a single company. At this stage, ABB's managers began to focus on
the other half of the dualities as they worked to capture the benefits of the
company's size and reach. By more effectively linking and leveraging the
resources of the 1,300 local companies, ABB used its global scale and scope
to build new capabilities in existing power-related businesses, to develop

new business opportunities in areas like environmental engineering, and to enter new markets such as Eastern Europe, India, and China.

Just as the behavioral change in the simplification phase is facilitated through certain changes in structure and process – fragmenting the organization into smaller units and developing simple, rigorous, and transparent systems, for example – the behavioral context that supports integration also requires some changes in the organizational hardware. At ABB, the organizational structure designed to create the tension that drives cross-unit collaboration is provided by a carefully managed global matrix with a complementary overlay of boards, committees, and task forces at all organizational levels.

Beyond changes in the organizational hardware, just as the simplification phase needs the behavioral software of discipline and support for effective implementation, the integration phase needs a behavioral context of stretch and trust to motivate the vital cross-unit collaboration. ABB's experiences are a good example of how these two attributes of behavioral context can be shaped to drive an organization through this second phase of corporate transformation.

Creating stretch

Stretch is an attribute of an organization's context that enhances people's expectations of themselves and the company. Stretch is the antithesis of timidity and incrementalism and results in the boldness to strive for ambitious goals rather than settle for the safety of achievable targets. In observing the integration efforts at companies like General Electric, Intel, and ABB, we identified three elements at the core of the most successful efforts to create an environment of raised personal aspirations and extraordinary collaborative efforts. First was development of shared ambitions that energized the organization; second was the need to establish unifying values to reinforce an individual's commitment to the organization; and third was an ability to give employees a sense of personal fulfillment by linking their individual contributions directly to the larger corporatewide agenda.[9]

To decouple individuals from the parochial interests that drive performance in the simplification stage, companies need to motivate them to collaborate. In most organizations, this implies creating a shared ambition that exceeds the company's ability to achieve without cooperation: to stretch the organization's collective reach beyond each unit's individual grasp. At the broadest level, Barnevik did this by building a corporatewide commitment to making ABB "a global leader – the most competitive, competent, technologically advanced, and quality-minded electrical engineering company in our fields of activity." But rather than leave this broadly framed vision statement unconnected to the organization's day-to-day operations, he and his top team traveled 200 days a year to communicate and translate it so that each operating unit began to share the ambition and understand its implications for their own particular objectives.

While ambition can be highly energizing, only when the organization's objectives connect with an individual's basic belief system is the required personal commitment likely to endure. It takes a deeply embedded set of unifying values to create such an individual-level commitment to its corporate ambition. For example, ABB has a stated objective "to contribute to environmentally sound sustainable growth and make improved living standards a reality for all nations around the world." Depending on management's actions, such a statement has the potential to become a source either of unifying personal commitment or of organizational cynicism. At ABB, Barnevik ensured that the stated values were not just displayed in the annual report but were part of documented commitments in the company's "Mission, Values, and Policies" book, which insiders referred to as "the policy bible." More important, the values became the basis for face-to-face discussion between top management and employees at every level and, over the years, were confirmed by corporate leaders' actions as they acquired environmental management capability and committed to massive investments in the developing world.

Finally, management must deal with the fact that modern societies in general and large corporations in particular provide individuals with few opportunities to feel they are making a difference. To create a sense of stretch, companies need to counteract the pervasive meaninglessness that people feel about their contributions and replace it with a sense of personal fulfillment in their work. To do this, they must be able to link the macro agenda to each individual's tasks and contributions. At ABB, a whole portfolio of new communication channels and decision-making forums was designed to give front-line managers access to and influence in the company's vital decisions. Through these overlaid devices, ABB's top managers were able to invite the heads of national companies to serve on the internal boards of other local units or even on their worldwide business boards. Similarly, local functional heads can serve on one of the many functional councils that the company uses to identify and transfer best practice worldwide. Through such service, these individuals can see firsthand how they fit into the larger objective and, more important, how their individual efforts contribute to a broader agenda. It has become a highly motivating characteristic of the company's behavioral context.

Developing trust

The ability to link resources and leverage capabilities is central to the integration process, and this intensively collaborative behavior cannot be induced solely by stretching people's goals and expectations. Like discipline, stretch lends a hard edge to the behavioral context that gives rise to individual energy and enterprise but, in its raw form, can also lead to organizational exhaustion. In the second stage of the renewal process, the appropriate offsetting quality to stretch is trust, a contextual characteristic vital to the development and nurturing of the collaborative behavior that drives effective integration.[10]

Unfortunately, the level of trust in a company just emerging from the major restructuring implied by the simplification process is often quite low, with autonomous units intensely competing for scarce resources and once loyal employees feeling that their implicit contracts with the company have been violated by serial layoffs and cutbacks. Most of the companies we studied seemed to accept this erosion in individual and group relationships as an inevitable by-product of a necessary process. While they tried to minimize its impact during that phase, the task of rebuilding individual and intergroup trust was primarily left to the integration stage when frequent and spontaneous cooperation among individuals and across organizational units became vital. Clearly, trust is an organizational characteristic that is built only slowly, carefully, and with a great deal of time and effort. Among the most common behaviors exhibited by managers in organizations that succeeded in developing this vital contextual element were a bias toward inclusion and involvement, a sense of fairness and equity, and a belief in the competence of colleagues.

Involvement is a critical prerequisite of trust, allowing companies to build both organizational legitimacy and individual credibility. ABB's integrative forums provided the infrastructure for routinely bringing managers together to discuss and decide on important issues. As we described earlier, local company managers were appointed to their business area boards where they participated in decisions affecting their business's global strategy and operations, while their functional managers' membership on worldwide functional councils gave them a major role in deciding the policies and developing the practices that governed their area of expertise.

This bias toward inclusion and participation extended beyond the formal boards and committees, however, and ABB's senior managers made employee involvement integral to their daily operating style. For example, in one of ABB's business areas that we studied, the new global strategy was formulated not by the global business manager and his staff or even by the more inclusive business area board. It was developed by a group of managers drawn from deep in the worldwide operations who were asked to define the business's objectives, options, and priorities as perceived by those closest to the customers, the technologies, and competitive markets. The process of developing this strategy and top management's subsequent approval created a strong bond among those on the team and trust in their superiors. The new relationship was reflected in and confirmed by the informal contract that developed around the strategic blueprint they had developed together.

Such widespread involvement in the activities and decisions relating to issues beyond their direct control created a vital openness for creating fairness and equity, the second component in a trust-building context. The formal matrix organization – the core design element that management believed allowed ABB to manage the dilemmas in its objective to be "local and global, big and small, radically decentralized with central control" – required the development of such an organizational norm to resolve the tension implicit in the structural dualities and to manage the conflicting demands in the strategic paradoxes they reflected. The function of the numerous boards, teams, and councils was not only to allow widespread involvement but also to create the channels and forums in which often conflicting views and objectives could surface and be debated and resolved openly and reasonably.

But fairness cannot simply be designed into the structure; it must be reinforced by managers' words and actions, particularly at the most senior level. Backed by the "policy bible's" commitment to build employee relations on the basis of "fairness, openness, and respect," ABB's senior management conducted the constant stream of decisions surrounding ongoing plant closing, employee layoffs, and management reassignments in an environment of transparency and rationality rather than through backroom political maneuvering. The resulting perception of fairness protected and, indeed, enhanced feelings of trust, despite the inherent tensions and painfulness of the decisions.

Finally, trust requires people to believe in the competence of their colleagues and particularly their leaders, because it is in these people that individuals place their confidence as they relinquish the traditional safety of incrementalism to achieve new stretch targets. At ABB, Barnevik set the tone in selecting his senior management team. Recognizing that their drastically delayered, radically decentralized organization placed a huge premium on high-level competence, he personally interviewed more than 400 executives from both Asea and Brown Boveri to ensure that ability assessment rather than horse trading dominated the selection for the top positions in the newly merged companies. His actions not only provided a model that influenced the whole selection and promotion process but also signaled that the identification and development of human resources was a vital management responsibility.

This integration process, supported by greater cross-unit collaboration, has allowed ABB to leverage the one-time productivity gains from the massive simplification program that radically restructured the company between 1988 and 1990. It helped the company develop new products and enter new markets during a recession that caused almost all its competitors to retrench in the first three or four years of the 1990s. It was a critical stage of the renewal process that was made possible by managers' behavioral changes framed by an expectation of stretch and supported by a growing culture of trust.

Regeneration: ensuring continuous learning

The hardest challenge for companies that have reconfigured their structures and realigned behaviors through the simplification and integration processes is to maintain momentum in the ongoing transformation process. This is particularly difficult for companies that have been through two successive processes and are striving to maintain an internal context to support both the individual initiative for driving the ongoing performance of front-line operations and the collaborative team-based behaviors for supporting resource linkages and best-practice transfers across individual entities. The final stage of self-renewal is when organizations are able to free themselves from the embedded practices and conventional wisdom of their past and continually regenerate from within.

As in the earlier transformation stages, the challenge of the regeneration phase is not just in changing the structure or the processes but, rather, in fundamentally altering the way managers think and act. As ABB executive vice president Göran Lindahl saw it, this final stage would be achieved only when he had succeeded in a long, intense development process he described as "human engineering," through which he hoped to change engineers into capable managers, and capable managers into effective leaders. "When we have developed all our managers into leaders," he explained, "we will have a self-driven, self-renewing organization."

Top executives at GE and ABB would readily acknowledge, however, that they have not yet achieved this stage of self-generated continuous renewal. Indeed, of the many companies that have undertaken organizational transformation programs during the past decade, few have moved beyond the rationalization of the simplification stage, and even fewer have successfully revitalized their businesses in the manner we have described in the integration process. Nonetheless, in our study, we observed a handful of companies that had reached the stage of constantly regenerating themselves by developing new capabilities and creating new businesses on an ongoing basis.

In most of these companies, like 3M in the United States or ISS, the Danish cleaning-services company, this elusive self-regenerative capability is based on long-established, deeply embedded corporate values and organizational norms, often linking back to the influence of the founder or other early leaders. But we observed a few companies in which a more recent transformation process led to the creation of this impressive organizational capability. A good example is Kao, the Tokyo-based consumer packaged goods company.

For its first fifty years, Kao had been a family-run soap manufacturer, eventually expanding into detergents in the 1940s as the company modernized by unabashedly copying leading foreign companies (even Kao's corporate logo was amazingly similar to Procter & Gamble's famous moon and stars symbol). Only after Yashio Maruta took over as president in 1971 did the company gradually develop a self-regenerative capability. As Maruta stated, "Distinct creativity became a policy objective, supporting our determination to explore and develop our own fields of activity." By 1990, after it had expanded into personal care products, hygiene products, cosmetics, and even floppy disks, Kao was ranked by *Nikkei Business* as one of Japan's top ten companies along with Honda, Sony, and NEC, and ahead of such icons as Toyota, Fuji-Xerox, Nomura Securities, and Canon.

In our analysis of Kao and other successful self-regenerating companies like 3M, ISS, Intel, and Canon, we developed some notions about two management tasks that inevitably played a central role in the development of such capabilities. The first was an ability to integrate the entrepreneurial performance-driving behavior shaped by the contextual elements of discipline and support with the equally vital cross-unit integrative learning framed by the managerial characteristics of stretch and trust. The second was the somewhat counterintuitive task of ensuring that these basic contextual elements were kept in a state of dynamic disequilibrium to ensure that the system never became locked into a static mode of reinforcing and defending its past.

Integrating the contextual frame

Maruta always introduced himself first as a Buddhist scholar and second as president of Kao; he saw these two roles as inextricably linked. Over the years, he embedded two strong Buddhist values and beliefs into Kao as a basis for its self-regenerating capability. The first core principle is an absolute respect for and belief in the individual, a value supported by an explicit rejection of elitism and authoritarianism and an active encouragement of individual creativity and initiative. The other pervasive value is a commitment that the organization function as an educational institution in which everyone accepted dual roles as teacher and student. At this level of corporate philosophy and organizational values, the vital entrepreneurial and collaborative behaviors are legitimized and integrated.

Reflecting the strong belief that the ideas and initiatives of individual managers drove performance, Maruta created an organization in which all employees were encouraged to pursue their ideas and seek support for their proposals. Central to this environment was one of the most sophisticated corporate information systems in the world. Instead of designing it to support top management's need for control, as most such systems were, Maruta had spent more than twenty years ensuring that its primary purpose was to stimulate operating-level creativity and innovation. For example, one internal network linked the company directly with thousands of retail stores, allowing marketing managers not only to monitor market activity and trends in a direct way, but also to give those retailers analyses of store-level data. Kao also developed an artificial intelligence-based market research system that processed huge volumes of market, product, and segment data to generate clues about customer needs, media effectiveness, and various other marketing questions. A third information gathering process, based on Kao's consumer research laboratory, combined a traditional monitoring of product usage in a panel of households with an ongoing analysis of calls to customer service. Managers used the integrated output to define new product characteristics and fine-tune existing offerings.

In launching the company's new Sofina cosmetics, the new-product team members used these and other data resources and intelligence systems to define a product-market strategy that defied the industry's conventional wisdom. They developed a uniquely formulated product line based on technical data and scientific research rather than on new combinations of traditional ingredients; they positioned it as a skin care product, rather than on the more traditional image platform; they sold it through mass retail channels rather than through specialty outlets; and they priced it as a product for daily use rather than as a luxury item.

Although respect for individual initiative was central to Kao's philosophy, so too was the commitment to organizationwide collaboration, particularly as a way to transfer knowledge and leverage expertise. Collaboration was aimed at achieving what Maruta described as "the power of collective accumulation of individual wisdom" and relied on an organization "designed to run as a flowing system."

Throughout Kao, there was much evidence of this philosophy, but a most visible manifestation of its commitment to the sharing of knowledge and expertise was the open conference areas known as "decision spaces." From the tenth floor corporate executive offices down, important issues were discussed in the decision spaces, and anyone interested, even a passerby, could join the debate. Likewise, R&D priorities were developed in weekly open meetings, and projects were shaped by laboratories hosting monthly conferences to which researchers could invite anyone from any part of the company. In all the forums, information was freely transferred, nobody "owned" an idea, and decision making was transparent.

Through such processes, individual knowledge in particular units was transferred to others, with the process becoming embedded in policies, practices, and routines that institutionalized learning as "the company way." Similarly, isolated pockets of expertise were linked together and leveraged across other units, in the process developing into distinctive competencies and capabilities on which new strategies were developed.

The vital management role at this stage was to create and maintain an internal environment that not only stimulated the development of individual knowledge and expertise to drive the performance of each operating unit, but also supported the interunit interaction and group collaboration to embed knowledge and develop competencies through an organizational learning process. This demanded the creation of a delicately balanced behavioral context in which the hard-edged norms of stretch and discipline were counterbalanced by the softer values of trust and support to create an integrated system that Maruta likened to the functioning of the human body. In what he termed "biological self-control," he expected the organization he had created to react as the body does when one limb experiences pain or infection: attention and support immediately flows there without being requested or directed.

At this stage, the organization becomes highly effective at developing, diffusing, and institutionalizing knowledge and expertise. But, while a context shaped by discipline, support, stretch, and trust is necessary for organizational regeneration, it is not sufficient. It needs a second force to ensure that the contextual frame itself remains dynamic.

Maintaining a dynamic imbalance

Less obvious than the task of creating a behavioral context that supports both individual unit performance and cross-unit collaboration is the complementary management challenge of preventing such a system from developing a comfortable level of "fit" that leads toward gradual deterioration. The great risk in a finely balanced system of biological self-control such as the one Kao developed is that it can become too effective at embedding expertise and institutionalizing knowledge. This capability risks becoming a liability when unquestioned conventional wisdom and tightly focused capabilities constrain organizational flexibility and strategic responsiveness, leading the system to atrophy over time.

Recently, the popular business press has been full of stories about once great companies that fell victim to their own deeply embedded beliefs and finely honed resources – the so-called "failure of success" syndrome. Digital Equipment's early recognition of a market opportunity for mini-computers grew in its strong commitment to VAX computers that blinded managers to the fact that the segment they were serving was disappearing. There are similar stories in hundreds of other companies, from General Motors and Volkswagen to Philips and Matsushita. These stories underscore the role top managers must play to prevent the organizational context they create from settling into a static equilibrium. Despite the widely advocated notion of organizational fit, the top-level managers in the self-regenerating companies we studied were much more concerned about doing what one described as "putting a burr under the saddle of corporate self-satisfaction."

Contrary to their historically assumed role of reinforcing embedded knowledge through policy statements of "the company way" and reaffirming well-established capabilities as core competencies, top managers in dynamic, regenerating companies perceive their task to be almost the opposite. While creating a context in which front-line and middle managers can generate, transfer, and embed knowledge and expertise, they see their role as counterbalancing and constraining that powerful process. By challenging conventional wisdom, questioning the data behind accumulating knowledge, and recombining expertise to create new capabilities, top managers at companies like Kao, Intel, ISS, and 3M created a dynamic imbalance that proved critical in the process of continuous regeneration.

Maruta and his colleagues at Kao maintained this state of slight organizational disequilibrium through two major devices: a micro process aimed at providing continuous challenge to individual thinking, and a macro process based on regular realignment of the organizational focus and priorities. With regard to the former, Maruta was explicit about his willingness to counterbalance the strong unifying force of Kao's highly sophisticated knowledge-building process. He repeatedly told the organization, "Past wisdom must not be a constraint, but something to be challenged." One approach that Maruta adopted to prevent his management team from too readily accepting deeply ingrained knowledge as conventional wisdom was his practice of discouraging managers from referring to historical achievements or established practices in their discussion of future plans. As one senior manager reported, "If we talk about the past, the top management immediately becomes unpleasant." Instead, Maruta constantly challenged his managers to tell him what new learning they had acquired that would be valuable in the future. "Yesterday's success formula is often today's obsolete dogma," he said. "We must continually challenge the past so that we can renew ourselves each day."

At a more macro level, Maruta created a dynamic challenge by continually alternating his emphasis on simplification and integration. Soon after assuming Kao's presidency in 1971, he initiated the so-called CCR movement, a major corporate initiative to reduce work-force size through a widespread computerization of activities. This efficiency-driven initiative was followed in the mid-1970s by a TQM program that focused on organizationwide investments and cross-unit integration to improve long-term performance. By the early 1980s, an office automation thrust returned attention to the simplification agenda, which, by the mid-1980s, was broadened into a total cost reduction (TCR) program. By the late 1980s, however, top management was reemphasizing the integration agenda, and the company's TCR slogan was reinterpreted as "total creative revolution" requiring intensive cross-unit collaboration.

Through this constant shift between simplification and integration, Maruta created an organization that not only supported both capabilities but embedded them dynamically to ensure that no one mode of operation became the dominant model. This organizational context was vital for ongoing business regeneration.

Leading the renewal process

Managers in many large companies recognize the need for the kind of radical change we have described. Yet, most shy away from it. The European head of a large U.S. company gave us perhaps the most plausible explanation for this gap between intellectual understanding and emotional commitment to action: "The tragedy of top management in large corporations is that it is so much more reassuring to stay as you are, even though you know the result will be certain failure, than to try to make a fundamental change when you cannot be certain that the effort will succeed."

Many of the recent books and articles on corporate transformation suggest that the process is inherently complex and messy. While that is true, many also ascribe a mystical characteristic to transformation by claiming that it is impossible to generalize it. That is not true. We have seen several companies that made effective, sustainable change toward the self-regenerative capability we have described. In all such cases – Motorola, GE, AT&T, ABB, Lufthansa, and several others – we observed the same sequential process, with distinct, though overlapping phases of simplification, integration, and regeneration. At the same time, others like IBM, Daimler Benz, DEC, Philips, and Hitachi that have tried alternative routes have made little progress until a change of top management led them to something closer to the model we have described. Similarly, when such a phased approach failed, as it did at Westinghouse, it was because changes in the organizational hardware were not matched with changes in the behavioral software. The model we have presented is general, and while we have inferred it from observations of practice, recent theoretical advances suggest that the particular sequence we have proposed is necessary to break down the forces of organizational inertia.[11]

We do not mean, however, that leading a company through such a renewal process will be easy, quick, or painless. The metaphor of a caterpillar transforming into a butterfly may be romantic, but the experience is an unpleasant one for the caterpillar. In the process of transformation, it goes blind, its legs fall off, and its body is torn apart, as beautiful wings emerge. Similarly, the transformation from a hierarchical bureaucracy to a flexible, self-regenerating company will be painful and requires the enormous courage of its leaders. We hope the road map we have provided will help instill this courage by removing some of the mysticism and uncertainty from the most daunting challenge of corporate leadership today.

Christopher A. Bartlett is a professor at the Harvard Business School. This paper appeared in *Sloan Management Review*, Winter 1996.

REFERENCES

1. See C.A. Bartlett and S. Ghoshal, "Rebuilding Behavioral Context: Turn Process Reengineering into People Revitalization," *Sloan Management Review*, Fall 1995, pp. 11–23.

2. Results are from the Bain & Co./Planning Forum Survey reported in:
D.K. Rigby, "Managing the Management Tools," *Planning Review*, September–October 1994, pp. 20–24.

3. Ibid.

4. Jack Welch described this logic in a presentation at the Harvard Business School in 1992. The logic can also be inferred from the detailed descriptions of the changes at GE. See:
N.M. Tichy and S. Sherman, *Control Your Destiny or Someone Else Will* (New York: Doubleday, 1993).

5. "Competitiveness from Within," speech to GE employees, 1985.

6. Bartlett and Ghoshal (1995).

7. Past research on organizational climate has highlighted the importance of standards, feedback, and sanctions in building organizational discipline. See, for example:
G.H. Litwin and R.A. Stringer, "Motivation and Organizational Climate" (Boston: Harvard Business School, Division of Research, 1968);
R.T. Pascale, "The Paradox of Corporate Culture: Reconciling Ourselves to Socialization," *California Management Review* 13 (1985): 546–558; and
G.G. Gordon and N. DiTomaso, "Predicting Corporate Performance from Organizational Culture," *Journal of Management Studies* 29 (1992): 783–798.

8. For the importance of support in enhancing corporate performance, see:
R. Walton, "From Control to Commitment in the Workplace," *Harvard Business Review*, March–April 1985, pp. 76–84.
For a more academically grounded analysis of the organizational requirements to create this attribute of behavioral context, see:
R. Calori and P. Samnin, "Corporate Culture and Economic Performance. A French Study," *Organizational Studies* 12 (1991): 49–74.

9. Gordon and DiTomaso have shown the positive influence that ambitious goals can have on organizational climate. See Gordon and DiTomaso (1992).

For the importance of values and personal meaning, see:

J.R. Hackman and G.R. Oldham, *Work Redesign* (Reading, Massachusetts: Addison-Wesley, 1980); and

K.W. Thomas and B.A. Velthouse, "Cognitive Elements of Empowerment: An Interpretative Model of Intrinsic Task Motivation," *Academy of Management Review* 15 (1990): 666–681.

10. The importance of trust features prominently in the academic literature on organizational climate. See, for example:

J.P. Campbell, M.D. Dunette, E.E. Lawler, and K.E. Weick, *Managerial Behavior, Performance, and Effectiveness* (New York: McGraw-Hill, 1970).

For a more recent contribution on the effect of trust, see: R.D. Denison, *Corporate Culture and Organizational Effectiveness* (New York: John Wiley, 1990).

11. See, for example:

R.P. Rumelt, "Inertia and Transformation," in C.M. Montgomery, ed., *Resource-Based and Evolutionary Theories of the Firm* (Boston: Kluwer Academic Publishers, 1995).

CHAPTER 8

Bad for practice: a critique of the transaction cost theory

Sumantra Ghoshal and Peter Moran

In this paper, Sumantra and Peter Moran put forward a detailed and thoughtful critique of transaction cost theory, one of the most well-known bodies of theory in organizational economics. Transaction cost theory assumes that individuals are self-interested and opportunistic in nature, and they will cheat the system if they can. It implies managers should put in place control systems and legal mechanisms to guard against such behaviour. Unfortunately, such systems often encourage the very behaviours that they are trying to curb, and as a side-effect drives out such desirable attributes as initiative and cooperation. Organizations, Sumantra and Peter conclude, are not mere substitutes for structuring efficient transactions when markets fail; they possess unique advantages for governing certain kinds of economic activities through a logic that is very different from that of a market. Transaction cost economics is "bad for practice" because it fails to recognize this difference.

In business circles, a story is often told of two hikers who wake up one night to find a tiger lurking near their tent. One of the hikers immediately reaches for his running shoes. On being reminded by his partner that he could not possibly outrun the tiger, he responds that all he has to do is to outrun the partner. At a superficial level, the somewhat macabre humor of the situation also serves as a powerful reminder of the similarities between biological and economic competition. Survival of the fittest, and, hence, the need to be the fittest, is seen as the moral of the tale.

On deeper reflection, however, the story reveals a set of assumptions and their self-fulfilling and ultimately debilitating consequences for the hikers that directly contradict the first-cut analysis. We begin our critique of transaction cost economics (TCE) with this story because much of TCE (Williamson, 1975, 1985, 1991a,b,c,d, 1992, 1993a,b,c) is based on a very similar set of assumptions with similar debilitating consequences for organizations whose managers knowingly or unknowingly adopt its prescriptions.

The first assumption is regarding human nature. In reaching for his shoes instead of considering any collaborative action with his partner, the first hiker represents the "model of humans" that is embedded in Williamson's brand of TCE logic. His behavior is opportunistic (i.e., an expression of "self-interest unconstrained by morality") (Milgrom & Roberts, 1992). In deciding to abandon his partner, he assumes that he has no choice because he cannot be certain, ex-ante, that his partner will not behave opportunistically, and ex-post discovery can be costly (Williamson, 1975).

The second assumption is regarding the requirement for success. What matters is the speed of running, because that is the strength of the tiger. Going up a tree, or lighting a fire, or any other such "strategic" actions are not contemplated: Rather, "efficiency" within predefined rules of the game is the criterion that determines the desirability of the outcome (Williamson, 1991d).

In a world of hikers and tigers, given these two assumptions, tigers will ultimately prevail. Even if one hiker survives the first encounter by outrunning his partner, he would succumb in some subsequent encounter either to a faster partner or simply because he would soon run out of partners and would have to go hiking alone.

In Williamson's world of TCE, the competition between organizations and markets can be predicted to lead to similar unhappy consequences for the former. According to this theory, organizations exist because of their superior abilities to attenuate human opportunism through the exercise of hierarchical controls that are not accessible to markets. As we will show, however, such hierarchical controls need not necessarily curtail opportunistic behavior. Indeed, they are more likely to cause precisely the opposite effect. The assumption of opportunism can become a self-fulfilling prophecy whereby opportunistic behavior will increase with sanctions and incentives imposed to curtail it, thus creating the need for even stronger and more elaborate sanctions and incentives. Caught in such a vicious cycle, "hierarchies," as organizations are described by

Williamson, would, over time, lose their initial raison d'être. Like the hiker, such organizations will ultimately succumb either to other organizations (which may be at an earlier phase of this self-destructive cycle or may be governed by a logic different from that of TCE) or, in the long run, to the very markets from which they sprang. Organizational failure would return to markets what market failure gave to organizations.

TCE has been criticized for many things – for embodying a hidden ideology that distorts more than it illuminates (Perrow, 1986), for ad-hoc theorizing divorced from reality (Simon, 1991), for lacking generality because of ethnocentric bias (Dore, 1983), for ignoring the contextual grounding of human actions and, therefore, presenting an undersocialized view of human motivation and an oversocialized view of institutional control (Granovetter, 1985), and for other such purported acts of omission and commission. Although we sympathize with most of these arguments, our critique of the theory rests on a very different ground. Like Pfeffer (1994), we are concerned with its normative implications.

All positive theories of social science are also normative theories, whether intended or not. The normative implications of TCE, in particular, are inescapable. "[T]hat transaction cost economics can be useful to business decision makers" is the "import" of a recent special issue of "Managerial and Decision Economics" (Rubin, 1993: 95). In that issue, Scott Masten, a key contributor to the TCE literature, wrote, "Were explaining managerial behavior the sole aim of transaction-cost reasoning, this [empirical research to date] . . . would constitute considerable progress. But transaction-cost economics aspires to influence as well as understand behavior" (1993: 120). "In effect, transaction cost economics offers strategy a set of normative rules for choosing among alternative governance arrangements. To the extent that governance choices are an important determinant of firm performance, managers would be well advised to heed those rules and to factor transaction-cost concerns into their decision-making calculus" (1993: 119).

Over the last decade, TCE has become an increasingly important anchor for the analysis of a wide range of strategic and organizational issues of considerable importance to managers – from vertical integration (Masten, Meehan, & Snyder, 1989; Monteverde & Teece, 1982; Walker, 1988) to distribution strategy (Anderson & Schmittlein, 1984; John & Weitz, 1988), from international expansion (Buckely & Casson, 1976; Hennart, 1982; Rugman, 1981; Teece, 1983) to strategic alliances (Balakrishnan & Koza, 1993; Hennart, 1991), from optimum financial structure (Balakrishnan & Fox, 1993; Williamson, 1991d) to the design of internal incentive systems (Harris & Raviv, 1978; Hoskisson & Hitt, 1988). On each of these and many other such applied issues, normative implications can and have been drawn based on the TCE logic. Such implications are no longer buried in the pages of obscure academic journals: They are featured in the popular press and in the rhetoric of chief executives, and specialist consulting organizations have sprung up to disseminate the theory to their corporate clients. As Masten emphasized, "Economists have also begun to bring transaction-cost reasoning to the classroom (e.g., Milgrom & Roberts, 1992) and to general business audiences (Rubin, 1990) not just as positive theory of business practices but also as a normative theory of organizational choice and design" (1993: 120).

Our primary objective in this article is to caution against this growing tendency of applying the TCE logic for such normative purposes. As we will discuss in the concluding section, Williamson's theory is not without its merit as a positive theory though, given its strong assumptions and extreme stylization, its usefulness is far more limited than is sometimes claimed. However, although positive theory (applied at the proper level of aggregation) often can be made parsimonious and powerful by simplifying assumptions that may only approximate reality (Friedman, 1953), normative theory cannot. As Masten observed, "Rules of behavior prescribed by economic models, however logical, cannot be normative if managers are incapable of implementing them or the assumptions upon which the models are built do not apply" (1993: 127). Even though Masten is concerned in this case primarily with the irrelevance of positive theory that is misapplied in normative fields, we are more concerned with its dangers. Williamson's arguments – as we show in this article – are not only inapplicable to most decision-making situations in firms but, if so applied, are also likely to adversely affect their performance. In this regard, the hiker's tale is considerably less dangerous than TCE: At worst, it is only a bad joke.

Our critique of TCE, however, will be limited in one important way. Although many scholars have contributed to the expanding domain of TCE and, as a result, there are now several different strands of the theory, we focus on only the version that has been articulated and developed by Oliver Williamson. This is an important limitation because the arguments of both Douglass North (1990) and Ronald Coase (1988) – two Nobel laureates who have made important contributions to the TCE literature – differ significantly from those of Williamson. We highlight some of these differences in our exposition. However, we choose to focus on Williamson's version of TCE for the following reasons.

Williamson's treatment of TCE is well developed, and it is relatively more accessible to "business decision makers." It is also the version that is most commonly used by scholars who conduct research outside of the mainstream field of economics and, as a result, it is the version that predominates the application of TCE to the more managerially relevant issues. More specifically, TCE, originally developed as a positive theory to explain a firm's boundaries (i.e., why firms exist and persist in markets), is more recently being extended to explain internal organization and management practices within firms. Williamson's argument (as in his M-form hypothesis) is the version that is most often applied for this purpose. Given their focal concerns and their level of analysis, other versions of TCE have had less direct influence on the management literature. Further, of the different versions of TCE, Williamson's rests most critically on its behavioral assumptions. When these assumptions, and the logic they are embedded in, are applied normatively to business decisions, particularly decisions that influence a firm's internal management, they can have an adverse impact on the "base rate" (Kahneman & Tversky, 1973) of the phenomena and, hence, the validity of the assumptions themselves. Therefore, the likelihood of applying the TCE logic for normative purposes is higher, and the practical implications are greater, for Williamson's version of the theory. Even though much of our argument may apply to TCE in general, and other versions of TCE may, indeed, be strengthened by addressing our criticisms where they may apply, and by distinguishing that particular version from Williamson's where they do not, we leave these important associations and distinctions to others.

"Unpacking" opportunism

Opportunism is a central concept in Williamson's TCE logic. According to Williamson, while asset specificity is "the big locomotive" to which TCE owes much of its predictive content (1985: 56), opportunism – the seeking of self-interest with guile – is the ultimate cause for the failure of markets and for the existence of organizations (1993c: 102). "But for opportunism, most forms of complex contracting and hierarchy vanish" (1993c: 97), and markets alone would be sufficient for handling most transactions through autonomous contracting, even in the presence of bounded rationality, asset specificity, and small-numbers bargaining (Williamson & Ouchi, 1981). As described by Williamson, "self-conscious attention" to the ramifications of this key behavioral assumption distinguishes TCE from other theories of firms and markets (1975: 4).

At the same time, however, recognizing the possibility of "instrumentalist excesses" in the explication of behavioral concepts, Williamson acknowledged that the "calculative orientation" of economics may be a disability and suggested that a "non-calculative orientation may help to unpack the[se] issues" (1985: 406). He also argued that "organization theory specialists, being less committed to the rational spirit, have less baggage to contend with" (1985: 405) and, therefore, "would appear to be well-suited to the task" (1985: 406). It is with this task of "unpacking" the concept of opportunism that we begin our arguments.

The concept of opportunism

Opportunism is a stronger form of the self-interest assumption of motivation that is common to economics and other social science disciplines. The two are distinguished primarily by whether or not individuals can reliably be expected to obey rules or keep promises. Self-interested behavior, in the received view, is presumed to be constrained by obedience and faithfulness to promises. Opportunism is not. It allows for "strategic behavior," that is, "the making of false or empty, that is, self-disbelieved, threats and promises in the expectation that individual advantage will thereby be realized" (Williamson, 1975: 26).

As it is used in Williamson's analysis, however, the concept of opportunism is more than a mere acknowledgement of the indisputable presence of opportunism in economic institutions. Without specifying the mechanisms through which opportunism is created or is reduced (Hart, 1990: 9), Williamson assumes human nature to be its sole cause. By attributing opportunism solely to the "human condition" rather than to technology or to the institutions themselves, and the control of opportunism solely to imposed safeguards (1993c: 102), Williamson turns a relatively common yet unexplained phenomenon into a behavioral assumption that has been described as an "extreme caricature," even by those who have made important contributions to advance the cause of TCE (Milgrom & Roberts, 1992: 42).

This extreme behavioral assumption, however, is necessary for TCE to explain the existence of organizations as is manifest in Williamson's distinction of opportunism from both stewardship behavior (which implies trust relations) and the "more neutral" instrumental behavior – where parties are not necessarily self-aware of the benefits from their behaving opportunistically (1975: 26). In either of these cases, market mechanisms can be designed that would allow joint profit optimization for any transaction. It is only in the case of opportunistic behavior (given a set of other conditions) that hierarchical control mechanisms such as fiat, monitoring, and incentives represent the only reliable safeguards for effective exchange. In the presence of such behavior, "sanctions" (as Williamson described these mechanisms of hierarchical control) are "required not as the normal motive for obedience, but as a *guarantee* that those who would voluntarily obey shall not be sacrificed by those who would not [Hart, 1961: 193]" (1990: 191).

Attitude or behavior?

Williamson used the term *opportunism* both in the sense of an attitude and in the sense of a behavior. For example, he refers to the "opportunistic attitudes" (1975: 48), which he understood as one of the "rudimentary attributes of human nature" (1991c: 8). At the same time, he saw it as a type of behavior such as lying, stealing, and cheating (1975, 1985) and "calculated efforts to mislead, distort, disagree, obfuscate, or otherwise confuse" (1985: 47). This implicit yet unacknowledged distinction between opportunism as an attitude (i.e., inclination or proclivity) and opportunism as a type of behavior or action is, nevertheless, important for Williamson's arguments. It's this distinction that allowed him to treat opportunism simultaneously as "[t]he behavioral assumption that human agents are given to" (1985: 64) as well as a behavioral outcome that is determined by the choice of governance modes (1975).

However, although clearly implied in his discourse (e.g., in his discussions of "atmosphere" and his concerns for "attitudinal separability" and "spillovers" (1975: 37–39, 256–257; 1993a: 480–48)), this distinction between opportunism as an attitude and its behavioral manifestation in opportunistic behavior is absent from Williamson's formal theorizing. Further, it is this absence of any distinction between opportunism and its manifestation that permits his logic to hang together and keeps it from being underspecified and indeterminate. For his theory to pass, opportunism has to be both an assumption that is independent of context and an outcome that is not.

Consider the implied role that opportunism plays in Williamson's formal logic. For clarity of our own exposition, we shall hereafter refer to the behavioral manifestation of opportunism as opportunistic behavior and to the attitude (i.e., proclivity, inclination, propensity) of individuals to act

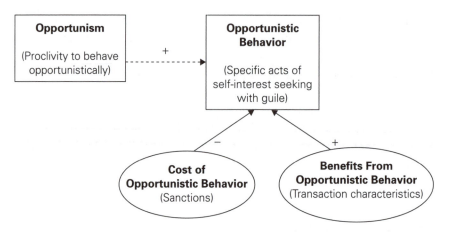

Figure 1 Williamson's model of opportunistic behavior

opportunistically as opportunism. According to Williamson, opportunistic behavior is positively related to the opportunity for (i.e., expected benefits from) such behavior, determined primarily by the characteristics related to a transaction (primarily asset specificity; see Riordan & Williamson, 1985), and is negatively related to (i.e., constrained or moderated by) safeguards such as controls, fiat, monitoring, and so on, which increase the costs (to the individual) associated with such behavior. These relationships (illustrated in Figure 1) are necessary for TCE to predict the most efficient governance form for any specific transaction. They demonstrate both the implied variability of opportunistic behavior, as well as its relationship with context (i.e., the interaction between transaction characteristics and governance).

As for opportunism (i.e., the attitude), TCE does not require that all individuals are so inclined but only that some, sometimes, are (though, according to Williamson, 1979: 234, "even among the less opportunistic, most have their price"), and that it is not practically possible to separate ex-ante those who are from those who are not (Williamson & Ouchi, 1981: 351). However, while accommodating both the existence of individuals of different types (i.e., extent of inclination to be opportunistic) and the individuals' propensity to vary the behavioral manifestation of their individual *attitudes*, the theory does not accommodate their propensity to change their attitudes with changes in time and place. Because Williamson does not theoretically separate opportunism from its behavioral manifestation (i.e., opportunistic behavior), we must infer that either opportunism (i.e., the attitude) is considered to be a fixed trait, unaffected by context, or it is a covariant with opportunistic behavior (i.e., both variables function as a single construct), each affected by context in the same way. That is, even though one contextual variable (i.e., asset specificity) may systematically influence an individual's perceived valence of (or scope for) opportunistic behavior and another variable (i.e., sanctions) may moderate the individual's expectancy from this behavior, context is believed not to have any effect on the individual's attitude toward opportunism that is independent from its effect on opportunistic behavior. Hence, either people are fixed in their attitudes toward opportunism, or their attitudes and behavior must change in concert with one another as if they were hard wired together, so as to act as one and the same concept. Otherwise, that is, if opportunism (the attitude) varied systematically, but independently (from opportunistic behavior) with context, for Williamson's theory to have any explanatory or predictive power with regard to the choice of governance form, a whole range of additional relationships between opportunism and the transaction and governance characteristics would have to be specified together with another set of relationships on how those conditions influenced the interactions between opportunism and opportunistic behavior.

What if opportunism is a variable?

Neither of the two possible interpretations of opportunism that could support Williamson's argument (i.e., either as a single construct, inseparable from opportunistic behavior, or as a fixed attitude) can withstand the scrutiny of received theory in other social science disciplines. A burgeoning literature in the fields of psychology and organization theory (see Kendrick & Funder, 1988, and the 1989 special issue of *AMR*, volume number 14(3), for recent reviews) provides incontrovertible evidence that attitudes and behavior exist as separate and distinct concepts and that both are affected by individual dispositions as well as by the situation that shapes the individual's perceptions and instrumentalities. Hence, both need to be taken into account when predicting the influence of context on behavior.

For example, even though sanctions can undoubtedly promote certain specific types of behavior and deter others, elements of governance mechanisms such as surveillance and fiat have consistently been shown to have negative effects on individual attitudes toward the specific behavior that is targeted (Enzle & Anderson, 1993; Lepper & Greene, 1975; Strickland, 1958) as well as the broader class of behaviors to which the target behavior belongs. An individual's attitude also is influenced by his or her own behaviors (suggesting a feedback loop between opportunistic behavior to opportunism) and also by his or her perceptions of the attitudes and behaviors of others (Aronson, 1980; Bem, 1972; Festinger, 1957; Heider, 1958; Petty & Cacioppo, 1981).

What if we followed Williamson's own advice and used these findings of organization theory scholars to elaborate TCE's behavioral assumptions? What if we considered opportunism as a variable? Next, we examine some of the implications of this more supportable assumption.

The self-fulfilling prophecy

According to the theory of reasoned action, still considered to be "the dominant theoretical framework in the attitude-behavior literature" (Olson & Zana, 1993: 131), volitional behavior is caused by behavioral intentions, which, in turn, are determined by attitudes and subjective norms (Ajzen & Fishbien, 1977). Figure 2 represents the outcome of our efforts to model a moderately dispositionalist view of opportunism on the basis of this theory. We rely on this particular theory only for illustration purposes; alternative theories explaining the attitude-behavior relationship (see Olson & Zana, 1993, for a recent review) are also consistent with our model.

As described by Williamson and shown in Figure 1, opportunistic behavior is influenced positively by the benefits from such behavior determined by transaction characteristics (relationship "h" in the model depicted in Figure 2) and negatively by the cost of opportunistic behavior determined by the sanctions in place (relationship "b"). To these two influencers, we add a third that is also implicit in Williamson's model and is strongly supported by Ajzen and Fishbein's (1977) theory of reasoned action: opportunistic behavior is positively influenced by opportunism (relationship "g").

Opportunism is influenced by three factors. The first is "prior conditioning" (relationship "i") that includes all the attitudes and values formed through exposure to conscious as well as subliminal stimuli (Krosnic, Betz, Jussim, Lynn, & Stephens, 1992), and possibly due to heritability factors (Olson & Zana, 1993; Tesser, 1993). Second, opportunism is influenced by what we describe as the "feeling for the entity," which represents the individuals' favorable or unfavorable assessment of the specific transaction partner, the group or the organization. As shown by Ajzen and

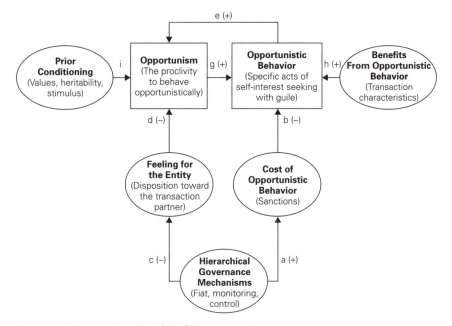

Figure 2 The cycle of self-fulfilling prophecy

Fishbein (1977) and Eagly and Chaiken (1992), a positive feeling for the entity would reduce opportunism whereas a negative feeling would enhance it. Accordingly, we have stipulated a negative influence of this variable on opportunism, identified as relationship "d". The third influencer of opportunism is opportunistic behavior. As described in dissonance theory (Aronson, 1980; Festinger, 1957), any incongruence between attitude and behavior may give rise to dissonance, if the behavior was accompanied by high commitment, freedom of choice and consequence (Petty & Cacioppo, 1981), and, as a result, will lead to modification of attitude as a means of reducing dissonance. This is shown in the model as a positive feedback loop designated as relationship "e".

Finally, the influence of hierarchical governance mechanisms such as fiat, monitoring, and control is specified, following Williamson, as positive on the cost of opportunistic behavior (relationship "a") and, following the literature on motivation we have referred to earlier, as negative on the feeling for the entity (relationship "c").

Before proceeding to draw some implications from this model, it is important to note that there is nothing in the model that is contradictory to Williamson's own views. Relationships "a", "b" and "h" are the explicit basis of TCE. Relationships "i" and "g" are clearly acknowledged by

Williamson (1975: 256) but do not merit any explicit analysis because the linkages among conditioning, attitude, and behavior are seen as direct hard-wired connections or as fixed traits. He does not take into account the dissonance reducing feedback loop "e", but this relationship does not affect the fundamental characteristics of the model since it only reinforces the net influences from the rest of the system. Williamson also clearly acknowledges relationships "c" and "d", for example, in his discussions on the importance of "atmosphere" (1975: 37–39, 40, 256–258) and of the possible negative motivational consequences of monitoring (1979: 245–246), but does not formally introduce these considerations in his theorizing. In other words, our departure from Williamson lies only in making explicit and endogenous to the model considerations that are implicit or exogenous in his theory.

Implications

While a number of implications can be drawn from the model, the one that concerns us here is the effect of hierarchical governance mechanisms on opportunistic behavior in organizations. As we have discussed earlier in the paper, Williamson's logic crucially depends on the claim that hierarchical control reduces opportunistic behavior since, without this claim, organizations would have no rational justification. The model, however, suggests a more complicated and ambiguous relationship between these two variables consisting of two distinct and mutually contradictory effects.

The first is the negative effect stipulated by Williamson: fiat, monitoring, and control increase the costs, to the individual, of certain types of opportunistic behavior (a) which, in turn, reduce these types of opportunistic behavior (b). The total strength of this relationship depends on the strength of "a" and "b" [f (a, b)].

The second is a positive association: hierarchical controls create a negative feeling for the entity (c) which increases the propensity to behave opportunistically (d) which, in turn, increases opportunistic behavior (g). Overall the strength of this relationship depends on the relative strengths of "c", "d," and "g" [f' (c, d, g)].

Consequently, the net effect of hierarchical control on opportunistic behavior will depend in part on the relative strengths of these two opposing influences, i.e., [f (a, b) − f' (c, d, g)]. This net effect, whether positive or negative, will be reinforced by the feedback loop "e".

The directionality of this net effect cannot be theoretically determined. This situation itself should be a matter of concern for TCE scholars, given that any ambiguity in this relationship calls into question the entire edifice of Williamson's theory. Worse still, available empirical evidence from research on the effects of rational control on employees' attitudes and behaviors suggests that the likely net effect may be opposite to what Williamson has asserted. This is because the negative association, on which Williamson's argument depends, between hierarchical controls and opportunistic behavior [f (a, b)] is likely to be weak, whereas the positive association between the same two variables [f (c, d, g)] is likely to be quite strong.

Fiat is a blunt instrument. Although monitoring and incentives may be effective in constraining opportunistic behaviors in specific areas that are considered important, such areas must be few for both cost and practicality considerations. As has been described by Dow (1987), when the balloon of opportunistic behavior is poked in one place by the blunt instrument of rational (i.e., hierarchical) control, it readily yields but reemerges elsewhere in ways that may make it more difficult and costly to detect and curtail. In focusing attention on the relatively few activities or outcomes that lend themselves more easily to observation, measurement, and evaluation, rational controls give rise to opportunism by enhancing any negative feeling (e.g., perceptions of biases, inequities or unfairness) toward the organization [f' (c, d)]. Heightened opportunism, in turn, induces opportunistic individuals to "game the system" [f' (g)] in other important but less accessible areas. Williamson on occasion has acknowledged this risk of "pushing metering at the margin everywhere to the limit," and has described it in terms of "spillover effects from easy-to-meter onto hard-to-meter activities" (1993a: 480). However, he has yet to account for this risk in his core argument.

There is considerable evidence that the use of rational controls adversely affects the feelings of both the controller and the controllee concerning their relationship. For the controller, negative feelings arise from what Strickland (1958) described as "the dilemma of the supervisor" viz., the situation when the use of surveillance, monitoring, and authority led to management's distrust of employees and perception of an increased need for more surveillance and control (Kipnis, 1972; Kruglanski, 1970). Because all behavior (especially that which is consistent with management's objectives) is seen by management as motivated by the controls in place, managers develop a jaundiced view of their subordinates.

For the controllees, the use of rational control signals that they are neither trusted nor trustworthy to behave appropriately without such controls. Enzle and Anderson (1993) have provided strong empirical evidence, for example, that surveillance that is perceived as controlling threatens the controllee's personal autonomy and decreases his or her intrinsic motivation. Similarly, Baker, Jensen, and Murphy (1988) cited several studies that showed that intrinsic motivation and commitment are reduced as extrinsic rewards are increased and that lost motivation and commitment are not restored if the extrinsic rewards are later taken away. In addition to reducing motivation and commitment, rational controls also tend to damage the self-perception of the controllee (Lepper & Greene, 1975). In the face of eroding attitudes, controls may be effective in influencing specific measurable behaviors, but they are likely to be ineffective, or even negatively influence nonmeasurable forms of the same class of behaviors, as evidenced by "work-to-rule" practices (Williamson, 1985: 262–263). An even more damaging and more likely effect of eroding attitudes is a shift from "consummate" cooperation (which is increasingly required of employees and expected by firms) to "perfunctory" compliance (see Blau & Scott, 1962; Kerr & Slocum, 1987; Kim & Mauborgne, 1993; O'Reilly & Chatman, 1986).

The consequence of these negative feelings for both controller and controllee is a "pathological spiraling relationship," which was described by Enzle and Anderson: "Surveillants come to distrust their targets as a result of their own surveillance and targets in fact become unmotivated and untrustworthy. The target is now demonstrably untrustworthy and requires more intensive surveillance, and the increased surveillance further damages the target. Trust and trustworthiness both deteriorate" (1993: 263).

The case of social control

In our discussions so far, we have focused on rational control because Williamson's theory focuses on rational control and because his theory *requires* some form of coercive control to explain an organization's ability to attenuate opportunism. Other authors (most notably Ouchi, 1979), however, have distinguished rational control, based on information and the use of formal administrative mechanisms to limit deceptive or self-interested behavior, from social control, based on people, their preferences, and the use of informal mechanisms to build their motivation and commitment. TCE has been used to account for the efficiency characteristics of some applications of social control, particularly in the context of an organizational form that Ouchi described as *clans* (1980; Wilkins &

Ouchi, 1983; Williamson & Ouchi, 1981). But a careful evaluation will show that (a) TCE can be applied to only a narrow subset of the domain where social controls are used; (b) where it can be applied, TCE can, at best, only explain a very minimal level of cooperation and, consequently, can account for only a small portion of the *potential* efficiency gains; and (c) the ways in which social controls are likely to be most effective are inaccessible to TCE logic and are, therefore, likely to be foreclosed to managers who rely on Williamson's theory.

Social control can influence behavior with or without a change in individual attitudes. In its broader and more far-reaching form, its users seek to create normative integration by inducing individuals to internalize the values and goals of the organization. Because such internalization implies a change in attitudes, users of TCE, in its present form, cannot even *consider* this path without first formalizing the process through which attitudes change and, in turn, affect behavior. It is not surprising then, given the little attention that proponents of TCE have given to social control, that they have emphasized the effects of social control without expecting or allowing for any attitude change. Ironically, however, the value from social control used narrowly in this way is likely to be severely limited by TCE's two behavioral assumptions (i.e., opportunism, which suggests one cannot predict others' behavior, and bounded rationality, which suggests one cannot identify his or her own best behavior), which make the distinction between initiative and opportunism problematic (even ex post).

Although Williamson explicitly differentiates opportunistic behavior from the "less realistic" expectations of instrumental behavior "in which there is no necessary self-awareness that the interests of a party can be furthered by strategems of any sort" (1975: 26), Ouchi assumes that the clan has attained a level of socialization that effectively ensures the instrumental behavior of its members. Indeed, the viability of social control in Ouchi's clan rests not only on the assumption of instrumental behavior, but also on a *necessary* self-awareness among members that the interests of a party *cannot* be furthered by strategems of any sort. As Wilkins and Ouchi argued, "were people in the clan to believe that others would intentionally attempt to misrepresent and seek personal ends, at the expense of the collective good, the cooperation and tolerance of short-run inequities necessary for the clan to function would disappear" (1983: 476).

Essentially then, the clan form of organization is assumed to exhibit an environment where there is *no perceived threat* of opportunism, even from opportunists! Even though Ouchi did not specify how or how often such a clan environment can be expected to come about, he suggested that it is relatively rare and difficult to achieve. At a minimum it requires an organization that values and can credibly support long-term serial equity expectations and has had a long history with stable membership, no institutional alternatives, and a strong social memory (Alvesson & Lindkvist, 1993; Ouchi, 1984; Wilkins & Ouchi, 1983). Williamson has noted that such clan forms of organization can be viable only in specific cultures in which additional "more elaborate informal govern-ance apparatus" is available to offset the greater risk of opportunistic behavior (Williamson & Ouchi, 1981: 361, 363). Not only are such environments likely to be rare, they are likely to induce only a minimal level of cooperation. At best, the kinds of behaviors that can be expected without any change in attitudes are those that will all but ensure indi-vidual net gain and will maintain the likelihood of exploitation from opportunists at very low levels (Axelrod, 1984). In other words, within the logic of Williamson's theory, cooperative behaviors other than what can be expected even among opportunists cannot be reliably ensured through social control, even in the special cultures that are considered as the exceptions to the theory.

In the general case, outside of these special cultures, social control, like rational control, is likely to affect attitudes. Moreover, internaliza-tion (i.e., the effects of controls on attitudes) is not likely to be universal nor uniform. Those members who may internalize their organizations' goals and values less than others (even if the only value requiring inter-nalization is that "opportunism does not pay!") may experience the internalization of others as a coercive form of peer pressure to conform. As such, this form of social control is likely to have similar, if only stronger (because the coercion is so much more fine grained), effects as those shown in Figure 2 for hierarchical governance mechanisms. Hence, in general (if not in all cases), managers who rely on TCE are left to conclude that social control cannot "reliably safeguard" the interests of nonopportunists from the guile of opportunists, and it is, therefore, "nonviable" (Williamson, 1993c: 98). It is important to emphasize that we are not arguing that social controls do not work. Indeed, as we note later in this article, they are at the core of organizations' potential advantages over markets. However, because TCE cannot account for the efficacy of social controls in most realistic settings, managers guided by TCE are likely to avoid their use and, consequently, forego their potential for enhancing efficiency.

To summarize, available theory and evidence suggest the following very plausible scenario. For decision makers shaped by the logic of Williamson's theory, the need for "guarantees" against "the intrusion of unscreened and unpenalized opportunists" (Williamson, 1985: 65) will severely restrict the viability of alternative social controls and will induce them to turn to rational controls. As the increased use of rational controls (a) increases the organization's dependency on those controls, (b) shifts voluntary compliance and extra role behavior to compulsory compliance and work-to-rule, and (c) encourages more difficult to detect opportunistic behavior, the cost of removing these controls will grow until it is no longer an option for the organization. Management's options for responding to opportunistic behavior will narrow to one of more controls that would serve only to increase opportunistic behavior. As this self-fulfilling prophecy plays itself out, management perceptions that employees are opportunistic would become increasingly valid. An equilibrium between dishonesty and control may be reached, temporarily, when the firm exhausts its opportunities to apply rational controls. By then, the most promising individuals within the firm (i.e., those who are most equipped to succeed) will more likely be those who are most skilled at furthering their own interests, with the most guile.

In the end, markets?

One consequence of this self-fulfilling prophecy of opportunism is to increase governance costs, thus making these firms progressively uncompetitive. After all, the task of designing and implementing such controls is among the main causes for the build up of "unneeded bureaucrats and wasteful bureaucratic practices" that Williamson viewed as the source of inefficiency in firms (1991d: 78). It can also enhance risk-averse behavior, adversely affecting long-term performance (Hoskisson & Hitt, 1988), but there is another less obvious outcome. We suggest that firms, caught in this cycle, would gravitate to certain kinds of businesses that are relatively more suitable for governance through rational control. These are also the kind of businesses in which markets will have superior efficiency characteristics and will ultimately prevail over firms. In other words, emphasis on rational control will lead firms to domains in which they would be uncompetitive in comparison with and, therefore, would ultimately succumb to markets.

Control-context fit

In the past, researchers of organizational control have argued for a control-context fit: Certain kinds of control mechanisms are more appropriate than others for certain kinds of businesses and activities (Eisenhardt, 1985; Ouchi, 1979; Thompson, 1967). For example, Ouchi argued that the usefulness of rational and social control would depend on the extent to which performance can be measured and evaluated. When performance can be measured accurately, based on either the behavior of individuals or on the outcomes of those behaviors, rational controls are effective. When, however, neither behavior nor outcomes can be measured precisely, rational controls lose their efficacy, and social controls become preferable (Ouchi, 1979: 845). As described by Eisenhardt, "An organization can tolerate a work force with highly diverse goals if a precise evaluation system exists. In contrast, a lack of precision in performance evaluation can be tolerated when goal incompatibility is minor" (1985: 135). A proper alignment between the context of control and the mechanism of control, therefore, is essential.

As we argued previously, according to Williamson, opportunism can be counteracted only through rational control because only a regime of sanctions can reliably safeguard the interests of the nonopportunists from "the predatory tendencies of a determined minority" (1993c: 98). To use Williamson's own examples of opportunistic behavior (1975: 7), social controls are not likely to be effective protection against embezzlers and bank robbers, who, after all, represent a fairly extreme case of goal incompatibility. In TCE, it is a "rich variety" of precisely these kinds of behaviors that are presumed to cause market failures and to create the need for organizations.

If one reverses the arguments of Ouchi, what kind of activities will such hierarchies engage in? Given that their control tools require high measurability, the need for control-context fit will, over time, lead them toward activities for which either the outcomes, or the behaviors, or, preferably, both are measurable.

Domain bias

As argued by Thompson (1967), uncertainty is the primary enemy of measurability. The presence of uncertainty requires what Williamson called "adaptation (c)" (i.e., coordination, 1991d: 77). However, in the presence of uncertainty, there is an inevitable conflict between measurability and coordination. Consequently, given their need for measurability, organizations that depend upon the use of rational controls will try to adopt structures and strategies that shield them from uncertainty. This argument follows quite directly from the logic of Williamson's argument and is, indeed, both reflected in and consistent with his justifications for efficiency as the first-order objective of strategy (1991d) and for the M-form as the most efficient structure for hierarchies (1975).

There are two sources of uncertainty of organizations. The first lies in the external environment, arising from the complexity and dynamism of technologies and markets (Thompson, 1967: 13). The other lies inside the organization, arising from discretionary behaviors of individuals. In their search to reduce uncertainty, not only will hierarchies create a low-discretion, high-compliance environment inside the organization, they will also choose external environments that will represent relatively low levels of volatility in technologies and market characteristics (Eisenhardt, 1985). Large-volume, mature businesses with relatively standard products and processes involving activities that are programmable will gradually emerge as their domains of choice. However, as argued by Hill (1990), it is precisely for such businesses that markets are likely to possess efficiency characteristics that are superior to those of organizations.

From hierarchies to markets

According to Hill, the threat of opportunism in markets is exaggerated in TCE. Over time, he argued, the invisible hand of a "system of markets" weeds out habitual opportunism. In fact, the very threat of internal organization helps reduce opportunistic behavior in market transactions: "The use of hierarchy, as a response to the threat of opportunism, also dissipates some of the composite quasi-rents that are inherent in the exchange. Using hierarchy involves additional bureaucratic costs that *do not* have to be borne *by* actors who tacitly agree to cooperate and trust each other" (Hill, 1990: 508).

Therefore, as markets mature in size and sophistication and approach a state of competitive equilibrium, they become more and more adept at mediating exchange. According to Hill, there are three conditions under which organizations continue to have a durable advantage over such increasingly sophisticated markets. These are (a) when the outcomes of transactions are highly uncertain, (b) when the reputations of transacting parties are hard to establish, and (c) when the short-term gains from entrepreneurial (i.e., opportunistic) actions are very large.

The first of these conditions may allow opportunism to go undetected, even if both output and behavior are measurable. The second implies low behavior or outcome measurability. The third implies a high-discretion environment within the organization. But as we have established earlier, these are precisely the conditions that an organization locked into Williamson's logic would seek to avoid. The self-fulfilling prophecy of opportunism will guide them, instead, into activities that sophisticated markets can coordinate, without the bureaucratic costs that the firms must incur. Hence, in the end, markets will prevail over these firms. The visible hand of hierarchy will have winnowed the universe of viable business domains down to those that the invisible hand of markets will have made inviable for them.

Beyond the market-failure framework

If opportunism is overstated in markets, as Hill (1990) demonstrated, and if it is so hard to control in organizations, as we have argued, what, then, explains the existence and persistence of so many organizations? On the surface, it may appear that the answer lies in the more sophisticated forms of social and normative control based on identification that Williamson considers nonviable, in general, but that organization theorists have emphasized at least from the time of Fayol (1949) and Barnard (1938) and that economists have begun to explore (Ichniowsky, Shaw, & Prennushi, 1993). But it would be wrong, we believe, to conclude that organizations exist because they are able to attenuate opportunism, if not by rational control, then by other more suitable methods. The real issue is deeper: Although control is, indeed, necessary in all organizations, a preoccupation with control obscures an organization's fundamental source of advantage over markets.

This preoccupation with control arises from the ideological bias of the market-failure framework in which Williamson's arguments have their theoretical roots. This bias has been manifested in both his logic and his terminology. Weighed down by the value-laden label of *hierarchy* that suggests authoritarian subjugation of human volition, organizations in his theory are considered fundamentally inferior vis-à-vis the equity and fairness of markets in which the most efficient is presumed to win. As stated explicitly by Williamson, internal organization is the organizing form "of last resort, to be employed when all else fails" (1991a: 279).

The reality of the modern economy is very different. Efficient, energetic, and well-functioning organizations surround us. Their ability to continuously improve their own productivity underlies the uninterrupted progress of our economies, and their talent for creating new products and services has consistently improved the quality of our lives and surroundings. As argued by Simon, to call ours a market economy is a misnomer: Much of the modern world's business is carried out in an "organizational economy" (1991: 28), in which identifying "markets as beginning where organizations fail" (Rumelt, Schendel, & Teece, 1991: 19) may be the more realistic starting assumption.

The choice of a starting assumption matters a great deal because, as Simon (1991) pointed out, it influences the selection of variables to be included in a first-order theory. Williamson errs not by observing that opportunism exists, for it does, nor by suggesting that organizations need control, for they do. Where he and his followers err is in the assumption that organizations exist because of their ability to attenuate opportunism through control – an assumption that directly follows from their adherence to the market-failure framework.

In their review of strategic management and economics, Rumelt and colleagues suggested that

> Twenty-five years ago economists, asked how a firm should be managed, would have (and did) argue that subunits should be measured on profit, they should transfer products, services and capital to one another at marginal cost, and the more internal competition the better. Today, we know that this advice, to run a firm as if it were a set of markets, is ill-founded. Firms replace markets when *nonmarket* means of coordination and commitment are superior . . . there are limits to building a theory of management and strategy around market failures. (1991: 19)

TCE is bad for practice because it is based on precisely this "ill-founded" advice that remains resistant to change.

However, as Kuhn (1962) pointed out, disconfirmatory analysis does not dislodge a dominant theory unless a more attractive alternative is presented. For our critique of TCE to have any usefulness, we must at least point the way to an alternative formulation that would not deny either the existence of opportunism in society or the need for control in organizations and yet provide the basis for a theory that would not assume organizations to exist only when markets fail. Although we have no claim to such a theory yet, in the next section, we explore some premises that such a theory could be built on.

The organizational advantage

Markets and firms are important in Williamson's analysis because both play important roles in the two key processes that drive the development of capitalist economies: the achievement of efficiency and the adaptation to change. Because transaction circumstances make one more effective than the other, both institutions are necessary to make capitalist societies as efficient as possible in their resource allocation and use. However, according to Williamson, organizations are merely another type of "contractual instrument, a continuation of market relations, *by other means*" (1991b: 162). The fundamental theoretical logics for achieving efficiency and adaptation are assumed by Williamson to be common, and the efficacies of both markets and firms are, therefore, assumed to depend on their ability to apply the same logic, albeit with different means, to transactions with different characteristics.

Lay observation suggests that markets and firms are not as clearly differentiated in terms of transaction characteristics as could be expected from Williamson's arguments. The same kind of transactions often persist for long periods of time in both markets and organizations, for example, the same component continues to be outsourced by some firms and produced in house by others in the same market (Coase, 1988); both individual operators and large organizations remain viable in the same business (de la Torre & Koza, 1990); and both licensing and direct investment are common under essentially similar economic circumstances (Shane, 1992). There is no systematic evidence that for any given kind of transaction the inherent superiority of one governance mode has effectively weeded out the other, even in highly competitive contexts. Instead, what really differentiates markets and firms, we believe, is that they are able to achieve efficiency and facilitate adaptation in different ways, following different institutional logics. One is not a continuation of the relations of the other. The relations themselves and their transacting capabilities undergo a fundamental transformation as they are shifted from one institutional mode to another. The effectiveness of a specific firm or a specific market in accommodating a particular activity depends on how that entity is able to implement its own institutional logic. For any given transaction, a well-managed firm may be able to outperform many autonomous entrepreneurs operating in a poorly structured market, just as those same autonomous entrepreneurs operating in a well-structured market may be able to outperform a poorly managed organization.

To explicate the potential advantages of organizations over markets, therefore, it is necessary to understand the differences in the institutional logics of firms and markets and how those differences influence the ways in which each can pursue the objectives of efficiency and adaptation. Any normative prescriptions to managers of firms can only follow this understanding, just as any advice to the hikers must follow an understanding of a human's advantage over tigers.

The market logic: autonomous adaptation

As described by Hayek (1945), individual firms adapt autonomously in markets in response to market signals. This form of autonomous adaptation occurs automatically as the available supply of goods and services is cleared with current demand. It unfolds, as an emergent process, without any concern for the direction it takes or for its future states. Leaving the direction of adaptation to the judgment of its individual participants, markets are not constrained by the participants' autonomy or their potential conflicts in preferences. In fact, indifference to any specific outcomes enables markets to exploit the independence and "local knowledge" of exchange parties by spontaneously (and, therefore, efficiently) allocating resources among all available options as they emerge.

This process of autonomous adaptation has two distinctive features. First, prices must be known or predictable for the "marvel of the market" to work efficiently (Simon, 1991). Prices must serve as sufficient statistics for transactions to adapt autonomously (Williamson, 1991d: 77). That is, changes in price, which reflect changes in the demand or supply of a commodity, must provide an adequate signal for "individual participants . . . to take the right action" (Hayek, 1945: 527). "Under certain circumstances [such as the absence of externalities and market failures] prices provide people with all the additional information about the economy which they need in order to make efficient use of the available resources" (Milgrom & Roberts, 1992: 58, 75). When these conditions are satisfied, prices enable exchange decisions to be coherent and, hence, permit the process of autonomous adaptation to unfold automatically and efficiently. However, in the absence of meaningful prices (i.e., those that reasonably approximate the value of a good or service), autonomous adaptation may be costly or even impossible.

Second, autonomous adaptation is biased toward static efficiency. Instrumental in making the set of available options as efficient as possible by directing resources away from the less efficient and toward the more efficient uses, autonomous adaptation moves along an evolutionary path that is guided by current relative efficiency and is independent of the efficiencies of future states. In other words, a highly efficient state that must be preceded by the occurrence of relatively inefficient states may not be reached through autonomous adaptation, regardless of how efficient the future state may be (Arthur, 1989).

Organizational logic: purposive adaptation

In contrast to the automatic, autonomous adaptation that emerges within markets, organizations are capable of what Barnard described as "purposive" adaptation. According to Barnard (1938: 137), shared purpose is "the unifying element of formal organization" and "[t]he necessity of having a purpose is axiomatic, implicit in the words 'system,' 'coordination,' [and] 'cooperation'" (1938: 86). Although Williamson recognized the role of coordination in organizational adaptation (1991d), he failed to recognize the role of shared purpose in inducing such coordination. It is purpose that allows what Williamson described as "coordinated adaptation" to move toward some direction (which need not be either explicit or appropriate) and to do so by exercising judgment in deciding *which* market signals to respond to and which to ignore.

The advantage of purposive, coordinated adaptation over the undirected autonomous adaptation that takes place in markets lies in at least three areas. First, purposive adaptation is possible even in the absence of prices or markets. Second, it allows organizations to pursue dynamic efficiency, which creates new options and expands the scope of activities beyond those that markets alone can coordinate efficiently. Finally, shared purpose transforms the institutional context in which relations are embedded and, thereby, influences the behaviors and preferences of actors.

Missing markets. The concept of failed or "missing" markets (Milgrom & Roberts, 1992) as a source of organizational advantage has long been part of most, if not all, versions of TCE, including that of Williamson (1975). However, according to Williamson's argument, the existence of organizations turns on the presence of opportunism (among other conditions). He wrote, "The environmental factors that lead to prospective market failure are uncertainty and small-numbers exchange relations. *Unless joined, however, by a related set of human factors, such environmental conditions need not impede market exchange*" (1975: 9). In his preoccupation with opportunism, Williamson did not consider that coordination can merely be a more efficient means for allocating resources, especially when prices, or even markets, are not available, and autonomous adaptation is difficult. Even though prices are output (i.e., product or service) specific, which is one reason why they may be unavailable if the output is uncommon or ambiguous, coordination is process specific and often depends on specific knowledge or skills. Because organizations' members and routines are repositories of knowledge and skills, they can have an edge over autonomous market participants in coordinated adaptation. Thus, although Williamson views the organizational advantage as lying in the attenuation of opportunism, particularly for transactions with high asset specificity, an alternative view that is consistent with the broader TCE logic suggests that organizations are simply more efficient than markets at coordinated adaptation when market failures are due to missing prices or "missing markets" (Milgrom & Roberts, 1992: 75–76, 601).

Dynamic efficiency. Williamson's claim that "economy is the best strategy" (1991d: 77) did not recognize that efficiency has both static and dynamic properties. What is efficient in the short term may not always coincide with what is efficient in the long term. As Schumpeter argued, "A system – any system, economic or other – that at every given point of time fully utilizes its possibilities to the best advantage may yet in the long run be inferior to a system that does so at no given point of time, because the latter's failure to do so may be a condition for the level or speed of long-run performance" (1942: 83). The efficiency of a transaction is changed by actions that expand the set of available options (Coleman, 1993; Milgrom & Roberts, 1992). Shared purpose permits organizations to relax the binding constraint of current period efficiency and allows the organizations' members and subunits to ignore (i.e., not select) some allocations and select others, in ways they could not outside the organization.

This ability to hold off market forces (at least temporarily) enables organizations to pursue innovative activities. Williamson framed the problem of efficient adaptation as a choice of governance modes for a relatively common class of routine transactions, in which static efficiency is the dominant requirement. The coordination of activities associated with these transactions is largely logistical, and the transaction problems he focused on were mostly concerned with the distribution and appropriability of the transactions' output and not the feasibility or quality of their execution. However, a broader consideration of an economy's complete set of transactions or, more appropriately, all its interdependent activities that require coordination, suggests that different classes of transactions may exist, with different requirements for static and dynamic efficiencies, and that the relative efficacy of markets and organizations in handling these different classes of transactions may have more to do with their influence over the nature and magnitude of transaction outcomes than with the distribution and appropriability of those outcomes.

More specifically, Williamson ignored innovation-related activities that are efficient only in a dynamic sense and that often defy the explicitness necessary for "logistical" coordination. A part of the reason for this exclusion may lie in the fact that many of the activities associated with innovation occur within firms (Dosi, 1988) and are not easily described in transaction-specific terms. Because innovative activities often are characterized by missing prices (or even markets), by "strong" uncertainty (Denzau & North, 1994; Dosi, 1988), and by high ambiguity, markets alone are relatively ill-suited to transmit information and knowledge in sufficient quantity and quality to ensure execution of the most efficient transactions. Organizations enjoy a degree of advantage in executing these activities, at least for certain kinds of innovations, because of the possibility of purposive and more flexibly coordinated action.

It is the same ability to innovate that also may be the key advantage of firms over autonomous contracting in markets, even for those transactions that we have so far referred to as routine. The classification of a transaction as routine or innovation producing is rarely a given and depends instead on a decision maker's (and researcher's) assumptions. One large U.S. automobile company may assume its procurement of components to be a routine task, which is therefore amenable to analysis using transaction-cost logic (Walker & Weber, 1984), whereas its Japanese rival may consider the same activity as vital for producing innovations and choose to manage it in very different ways (Bensaou, 1993). As described by Nelson, "Simply producing a given set of products with a given set of processes well will not enable a firm to survive for long. To be successful for any length of time a firm must innovate" (1991: 68). Therefore, whereas first-order economizing may be relatively more important in some contexts, the ability to innovate – to create discontinuous improvement in processes, for example – may well be the main source of organizational advantage, even for those routine transactions.

The moral factor. Purpose also allows organizations to create an institutional context that influences the values and ambitions of the organization's members. This is what Barnard (1938: 261) described as "the moral factor" – the efficacy of cooperation, coordinated by shared purpose, in changing the preferences and utilities of those whose cooperation is solicited for its achievement. He wrote, "The most important general consequence of cooperation, rarely sought for and only occasionally recognized while in process, is the social conditioning of all who participate and often of those who do not. In this way the motives of men are constantly being modified by cooperation, which is itself thereby altered as are the factors of efficiency" (1938: 45).

Incentives are unavoidably lower powered in organizations than in markets (Williamson, 1992). Williamson saw this, in the perspective of the market logic, as a disadvantage that must be overcome, rather than as an opportunity to exploit. His solution to the "problem" was contained in a combination of minimizing the incentive loss by incorporating as much of marketlike characteristics in the organization as possible and then compensating for at least a part of the rest through fiat and rational control. In stark contrast, Barnard argued that "it appears utterly contrary to the nature of men to be sufficiently induced by material or monetary considerations to contribute enough effort to a cooperative system to enable it to be productively efficient to the degree necessary for persistence over an extended period" (1938: 93). Holmstrom and Milgrom (1991: 38) provided a more direct argument against the use of high-powered incentives in organizations. They showed that "short-term incentives must be muted" to prevent the allocation of individual attention "away from important, but hard to measure, asset values." Similarly, fiat is ineffective in fostering initiative, creativity, or leadership, which are difficult to differentiate ex ante from opportunism. Therefore, as Barnard highlighted, the solution to the incentive loss "problem" is not in organizations emulating markets but by their creating a context of identification, trust, and commitment that clearly differentiates them from markets. As also emphasized by Selznick (1957), the essential role of purpose is to create such a context that guides the evolutionary process, whereby fragile organizations (which he viewed as expendable tools engineered to do a job) are infused with values and transformed into responsive and adaptive institutions. It is ultimately this transformation of institutional context in which social relations are embedded and through which preferences of actors are altered that allows the process of organizational adaptation to unfold via nonmarket incentives in a purposive and quasi-autonomous way, without emphasizing the need for rational controls.

In summary, shared purpose plays the role in organizations that price plays in markets. Each theme is the central focusing device within the institutional logics of the respective institutions. Although autonomous adaptation in markets is driven by changes in price, an organization's adaptation is driven by its members' perceptions of the evolving fit between their view of the organization's purpose and their own. This does not mean that all adaptation in markets is autonomous, based on effective functioning of the price system, nor that all adaptation in organizations is purposive. Also, the two logics are not mutually exclusive. Markets may compete with organizations by developing a level of shared purpose manifest in concepts like relational contracting (Williamson, 1991d) or strategic networks (Jarillo, 1988) and exemplified in extreme examples like the New York diamond market (Coleman, 1993). Organizations, similarly, may adopt certain forms of market mechanisms in directing internal flows of resources and in aligning incentives (Hennart, 1993). However, these mechanisms represent the constraints and overlays on the dominant logic of each. A market that puts purpose above price degenerates rapidly, as the erstwhile Soviet system has shown. Similarly, an organization that puts its faith in prices above purpose fails, too, as is manifest in the experiences of companies that have relied exclusively on market-based transfer pricing systems (Eccles, 1985).

In a market, where a transaction's characteristics are instrumental in determining which among a multitude of autonomous parties are temporarily paired in an exchange, the transaction may be the appropriate unit of analysis. However, in an organization, where relationships are less fluid and the transactions across them more varied, it is the quality of the relationship that determines the characteristics of the transactions that take place across it. By focusing only on transaction characteristics, Williamson took for granted "what a firm does" and focused, instead, on "how well it does it." In that process, the key distinction that only firms, not markets, have the choice is lost in the comparison. Purpose embodies that choice, influencing both the "what" as well as the "how" of the organizational advantage over markets. Purpose provides organizations the ability to adapt, even in the absence of prices or markets – the flexibility to choose a mix of autonomy and coordination in pursuing dynamic efficiency and in concentrating on innovative activities – whether in developing wholly new products or services or in improving existing ones. It is also purpose that allows organizations to create and nurture a social context that shapes the values, goals, and expectations of members and alters their perceptions of the balance between "inducements" and "contributions." It is, therefore, purpose that provides the ultimate source of an organization's advantage over markets and that must, therefore, lie at the core of any theory that, as argued by Rumelt and colleagues (1991), does not assume organizations to emerge when markets fail but identifies markets as beginning where organizations fail.

A theory for the organizational economy

Coase expressed his concern with the direction that TCE has taken since the publication of his original article, which was the basis of this strand of theory. He wrote,

> I consider that one of the main weaknesses of my article ["The Nature of the Firm"] stems from the use of the employer-employee relationship as the archetype of the firm. It gives an incomplete picture of the nature of the firm. But more important, I believe it misdirects our attention . . . the way in which I presented my ideas has, I believe, led to or encouraged an undue emphasis on the role of the firm as a purchaser of the services of factors of production and on the choice of the contractual arrangements which it makes with them. As a consequence of this concentration on the firm as a purchaser of the inputs it uses, economists have tended to neglect the main activity of a firm, running a business. (1988: 37–38)

It is this view of organizations as bundles of employment contracts that led Williamson to focus on opportunistic behavior and on safeguards to minimize one party's exposure to the opportunism of another. Managers preoccupied with controlling opportunism, like the economists Coase referred to, are distracted from the main task of running a business.

The hikers in the story in the beginning of the article will continue to value hiking as long as the pleasure they get from it exceeds whatever "price" they pay for it. As the threat from tigers rises, each hiker can "rationally" justify "paying" more and more to keep track of his access to his running shoes relative to that of his partner. Each partner's expenditure to improve his relative position "ups the ante," and each expenditure is "efficient" as the opportunity cost of not making it rises. Eventually, it is not hiking but having access to one's running shoes that becomes the key objective of the endeavor.

We can now respond to Scott Masten's call for managers to pay heed to the TCE logic in managing their firms. The broad answer would be not to bother. If the assumptions on which the logic is based are accurate, as Masten insisted they must be for productive normative theory, firms are, ultimately, bound to fail anyway, even though they might prolong survival by finding a better fit for an ever-tightening institutional straight-jacket. If, in contrast, the assumptions are overly simplified and incomplete, as we have argued, managers are likely to neglect the main activity of their firms. Like the hikers, managers who pay heed to Williamson's version of TCE will be distracted from the business of generating the collective energy of their organizations and focusing it on the task of running a business. Instead, they would oversee the dissipation of their organizations' energy, or worse, they would witness it being channeled into and consumed by the efforts of each individual to protect himself or herself from colleagues. Because opportunism is difficult to distinguish ex ante from entrepreneurship and leadership, in an effort to control the former, they will destroy the latter.

The double hermeneutic

In arguing that Williamson's particular version of TCE is bad for practice we are not arguing that opportunism does not exist. Also, we are not arguing that Williamson does not account for some behavioral regularities in our societies (e.g., locks on doors, guards in banks). If people were never or even only rarely opportunistic, this particular strand of TCE might not be as bad for practice as we have argued, regardless of its usefulness as a descriptive theory. It is precisely because the threat of opportunistic behavior is *not* uncommon, because its dysfunctional effects *are* substantial, and because, as we have argued, the forces that give rise to the threat and consequences of opportunism are likely to be influenced by management beliefs, policies, and practices, that Williamson's theory is so "bad" for the practice of management. Social sciences carry a special responsibility because of the process of the double hermeneutic: Its theories affect the agents who are its subject matter. By assuming the worst, this theory can bring out the worst in economic behavior. By assuming opportunism and establishing it as his base case, Williamson is blind to forces that work to confirm or discredit the validity of his assumption. In the process, his theory is likely to encourage the very behavior that it takes for granted and seeks so hard to control. Therefore, given its assumptions and logic, Williamson's form of TCE will always be "bad for practice" as far as management of firms is concerned, even if, and especially when, the theory becomes increasingly more predictive of the behavior of the individuals, groups, and organizations that seek guidance from its prescriptions.

At this point we should emphasize that it is not this theory's failure to meet some criteria of social desirability that condemns it. Rather, it is the theory's failure to meet its own criteria of efficiency that causes our criticism. According to the logic of its argument, the threat of opportunism increases transaction costs, and firms exist to attenuate the hazards of opportunism and thereby accrue efficiency gains. Two problems with this approach have been pointed out in the literature. First, as Hart (1990) pointed out, Williamson did not specify the mechanisms through which opportunism is reduced, and, second, he failed to recognize the path-dependent nature of the evolving institutional framework, in which institutions exhibit increasing returns and where history – because it is difficult to change informal constraints – plays an important role in encouraging and locking in the pursuit of persistently inefficient, as well as efficient, activities (North, 1990). In this article we have begun to specify the mechanisms through which governance may influence opportunism and opportunistic behavior. In doing so, we have suggested that, given Williamson's behavioral assumptions (which, according to Williamson himself, is what distinguishes his theory from others with similar objectives), opportunism is likely to increase, not decrease, in firms that adopt his prescription of exclusive or even primary reliance on rational controls, thereby sacrificing long-term economic efficiency in the pursuit of short-term unsustainable gains.

Economic progress requires a combination of both static and dynamic efficiencies. First-order economizing is already a central feature of the process of autonomous adaptation that takes place in markets. Imposing first-order economizing to also be the key objective of organizations and as a principal criterion for the design of their boundaries, structures, and processes, however, is counterproductive. Although the pursuit of static efficiency can provide the resources to fuel investments for achieving dynamic efficiency, it is not likely to guide the direction of those investments. Further, because dynamic efficiency is more difficult to measure than static efficiency, in their effort to lock in the latter, firms that follow Williamson's logic will lose sight of the former. By framing the problem of adaptation in terms of first-order efficiency, Williamson ignored the potential power of organizations to influence both the direction of economic progress and the motivation of individuals to contribute to and benefit from that progress. However, organizations and their members are not the only losers in this normative application of TCE. At a broader and, perhaps, more important level, societies that observe this particular logic of TCE stand to lose the potential vitality of a major source of their economic progress and of their members' satisfaction – the purposive organization.

Building on or starting over?

Although we have criticized Williamson's version of TCE when it is used as normative theory, it is not without merit as a positive theory, but, even for descriptive and analytical purposes, its usefulness is much more limited than we believe is necessary. As Williamson's TCE argument stands today, and as it has stood for nearly 20 years, it is essentially a static theory whose domain of applicability is limited to predicting the existence of a small set of firms in markets in which opportunism is likely to run rampant and unfettered. For markets that are more advanced in their institutional environments and exchange practices, the explanatory power of asset specificity and, therefore, the theory, falls off considerably. Even though an impressive number of empirical studies have found a positive relationship between asset specificity and internalization (Masten, 1994), correlation does not demonstrate causation. Relationship-specific assets (e.g., distance, routines) can reduce the costs of internal coordination, independent of their effects on opportunism or on the hazards of market exchange. Moreover, within an organization, the theory can tell us very little. Our argument, however, suggests some obvious ways in which the theory's domain of applicability can be extended, both across markets and within firms.

By incorporating opportunism as an attitudinal variable, which is conceptually separate and distinct from its behavioral manifestation, the predictive power of the theory can be broadened to cover more firms and different types of markets. Also, such an extension would permit a comparative analysis of different forms of governance within the firm.

Although this modification would go far in extending the usefulness of the framework as descriptive theory, much more is needed before it can be made suitable for normative application. As illustrated in self-fulfilling prophecies, predictive power does not sanction prescriptive license. Williamson himself acknowledged that controls can only lead to perfunctory compliance (1993a), when increasingly what is needed in organizations is consummate cooperation and extra-role behavior (Kim & Mauborgne, 1993; O'Reilly & Chatman, 1986), which are difficult to measure or reward directly. No amount of emphasis on opportunism alone (even ensuring its absence as a threat to the exploitation of an organization's individual members) can unlock the initiative and tap the motivation that large, complex organizations increasingly require from their members. Theorists must adopt long-term efficiency as the criterion, and they must address such variables as innovation, learning, and asset redeployability. They must be able to accommodate multiple levels of analysis and frequent shifts in those levels.

Williamson wrote,

> To argue that the economic approach is flawed because of its preoccupation with intended effects to the neglect of unintended effects . . . assumes that the economic approach is unable or unwilling to take into account all relevant regularities whatsoever. . . . The correct view is that a naive application of calculativeness can be and sometimes is given to excesses but that this is often remediable. On being informed about added consequences, these will be factored into the design exercise from the outset. (1993a: 460)

In this article, we have attempted to inform TCE of such added consequences. We hope that Williamson's confidence that such consequences can be factored into his theory is not misplaced, because until then this version of TCE will remain "bad for practice."

However, we fear that it may not be possible to incrementally adapt Williamson's argument to develop a theory for what Simon (1991) described as the organizational economy. The strength and seductiveness of the markets and hierarchies argument lies in the parsimony of its narrow assumptions of human nature and its equally narrow interpretation of economic objectives: the same features of the theory that also preclude any broadening of its foundations without destroying its core. This is, perhaps, why the theory's mainstream development has remained immune to such important contributions as Ouchi's (1980) insights on social control; Granovetter's (1985) compelling argument for the need to consider the social relations, in which economic behavior is embedded; and even Williamson's own ideas about "atmosphere" (1975) and "dignitary values" (1985).

The context in which social relations and economic exchange are embedded can induce self-aggrandizement or trust, individualism or collectivism, competition or cooperation among participants. Economic progress requires both kinds of behaviors in each set of alternatives, not just one or the other. Because the logic of most markets is based on the first in each set of behavioral alternatives, organizations are necessary to protect some exchange parties from the opportunism of others so as to induce the second set of behaviors. But applying the same logic that gives rise to the need for protection does not provide the needed protection. Theories that ignore this distinction and attempt to create a model of organizations based on the logic of markets are dangerous, because the logic that creates the first set of behaviors destroys the context that is necessary for the second set.

As we have suggested in the preceding section, the advantage of organizations over markets may lie not in overcoming human pathologies through hierarchy, but in leveraging the human ability to take initiative, to cooperate, and to learn; it also may rely on exploiting the organization's internalized purpose and diversity to enhance both learning and its use in creating innovations and purposive adaptation. Similarly, following Barnard (1938), we also argued that organizations fail when they are unable to create the social context necessary to build the trust and commitment that are needed for maintaining cooperation. In a theory of organizations and markets, learning and trust may well take the place that efficiency and opportunism occupy in the theory of markets and hierarchies (see Axelrod, 1984; Coleman, 1990; Krackhardt, 1992), whereas purpose may take the place of price. Such a theory may also yield some very different conclusions on issues of organizational diversification, control, and governance.

It is not our objective to present such a theory here, and we are not yet capable of it. However, such a theory is unlikely to emerge without considerable effort from strategy and organization scholars, who are more exposed to what we have described as the organizational logic. This is why we feel concerned by the trend of those scholars increasingly embracing TCE – by proposing incremental modifications, like the inclusion of variables such as "trust" (e.g., Bromiley & Cummings, 1993), which their research reveals to be important – instead of challenging it on the grounds that such findings falsify its basic tenets. We believe that the time has come for these scholars to stop building on theories of organizations that persist with the myth of the market economy and to start afresh by developing an alternative theory that acknowledges the reality of the organizational economy.

Peter Moran is a doctoral candidate in strategic management at INSEAD. His research focuses on the influence of organizational context and structure on individual and group behavior and on organizational performance.

The authors thankfully acknowledge the suggestions and comments they received from Richard Rumelt, Michael Brimm, Yrjö Koskinen, Charles W.L. Hill, Charlie Galunic, Gerhard Holt, Alice de Koning, and three anonymous reviewers of *AMR*.

This paper appeared in *Academy of Management Review*, January 1996.

REFERENCES

Ajzen, I., & Fishbien, M. 1977. Attitude-behavior relations: A theoretical analysis and review of empirical research. *Psychological Bulletin*, 84: 888–918.

Alvesson, M., & Lindkvist, L. 1993. Transaction costs, clans and corporate culture. *Journal of Management Studies*, 30: 427–452.

Anderson, E., & Schmittlein, D.C. 1984. Integration of the sales force: An empirical examination. *Rand Journal of Economics*, 15(3): 385–395.

Aronson, E. 1980. Persuasion by self-justification. In L. Festinger (Ed.), *Retrospections on social psychology*. New York: Oxford University Press.

Arthur, W.B. 1989. Competing technologies, increasing returns, and lock-in by historical events. *Economic Journal*, 99: 116–131.

Axelrod, R. 1984. *The evolution of cooperation*. Cambridge, MA: Harvard University Press.

Baker, G.P., Jensen, M.C., & Murphy, K.J. 1988. Compensation and incentives: Practice vs. theory. *Journal of Finance*, 43: 593–616.

Balakrishnan, S., & Fox, I. 1993. Asset specificity, firm heterogeneity and capital structure. *Strategic Management Journal*, 14: 3–16.

Balakrishnan, S., & Koza, M.P. 1993. Information asymmetry, adverse selection and joint-ventures: Theory and evidence. *Journal of Economic Behavior and Organization*, 20(1): 99–117.

Barnard, C. 1938. *The functions of the executive*. Cambridge, MA: Harvard University Press.

Bem, D.J. 1972. *Self-perception theory*. New York: Academic Press.

Bensaou, M. 1993. *Interorganizational cooperation: The role of information technology. An empirical comparison of US and Japanese supplier relations*. Working paper (No. 93/62/TM/SM). INSEAD, Fountainebleau, France.

Blau, P.M., & Scott, W.R. 1962. *Formal organizations*. San Francisco: Chandler.

Bower, J.L., & Doz, Y. 1979. Strategy formulation: A social and political process. In D.E. Schendel & C.W. Hofer (Eds.), *Strategic management: A new view of business policy & planning*: 152–168, 180–188. Boston: Little, Brown.

Bromiley, P., & Cummings, L.L. 1993. *Organizations with trust: Theory and measurement*. Working paper, University of Minnesota, Minneapolis/St. Paul.

Buckely, P.J., & Casson, M. 1976. *The future of the multi-national enterprise*. New York: Holmes & Meier.

Burgelman, R.A. 1983. A process model of internal corporate venturing in the diversified major firm. *Administrative Science Quarterly*, 28: 223–244.

Coase, R.H. 1988. The nature of the firm: Influence. *Journal of Law, Economics, and Organization*, 4: 33–47.

Coleman, J.S. 1990. *Foundations of social theory*. Cambridge, MA: Harvard University Press.

Coleman, J.S. 1993. Properties of rational organizations. In S. Lindenberg & H. Schreuder (Eds.), *Interdisciplinary perspectives on organization studies*: 79–90. Oxford, England: Pergamon Press.

de la Torre, J., & Koza, M.P. 1990. *Intercorporate collaboration: Intimacy boundary permeability, and the quality of execution.* Conference on corporate governance and corporate strategy, Minneapolis, MN.

Denzau, A.T., & North, D.C. 1994. Shared mental models: Ideologies and institutions. *KYKLOS,* 47: 3–31.

Dore, R. 1983. Goodwill and the spirit of market capitalism. *British Journal of Sociology,* 34: 459–482.

Dosi, G. 1988. Sources, procedures and microeconomic effects of innovation. *Journal of Economic Literature,* 26: 1120–1171.

Dow, G.K. 1987. The function of authority in transaction cost economics. *Journal of Economic Behavior and Organization,* 8: 13–38.

Eagly, A.H., & Chaiken, S. 1992. *The Psychology of attitudes.* San Diego, CA: Harcourt Brace Jovanovich.

Eccles, R.G. 1985. *The transfer pricing problem: A theory for practice.* Lexington, MA: Lexington Books.

Eisenhardt, K. 1985. Control: Organizational and economic approaches. *Management Science,* 31: 134–149.

Enzle, M.E., & Anderson, S.C. 1993. Surveillant intentions and intrinsic motivation. *Journal of Personality and Social Psychology,* 64: 257–266.

Fayol, H. 1949. *General industrial management.* Boston: Pitman.

Festinger, L. 1957. *A theory of cognitive dissonance.* Stanford, CA: Stanford University Press.

Friedman, M. 1953. *Essays in positive economics.* Chicago: University of Chicago Press.

Granovetter, M. 1985. Economic action and social structure: The problem of embeddedness. *American Journal of Sociology,* 91: 481–510.

Harris, M., & Raviv, A. 1978. Some results on incentive contracts with applications to education and employment, health insurance and law enforcement. *American Economic Review,* 68: 20–30.

Hart, O. 1990. An economist's perspective on the theory of the firm. In O.E. Williamson (Ed.), *Organization theory: From Chester Barnard to the present and beyond:* 154–171. New York: Oxford University Press.

Hayek, F. 1945. The use of knowledge in society. *American Economic Review,* 35(4): 519–530.

Heider, F. 1958. *The psychology of interpersonal relations.* New York: Wiley.

Hennart, J.-F. 1982. *A theory of the multinational enterprise.* Ann Arbor: University of Michigan Press.

Hennart, J.-F. 1991. The transaction cost theory of joint ventures: An empirical study of Japanese subsidiaries in the USA. *Management Science,* 37: 483–497.

Hennart, J.-F. 1993. Control in multinational firms: The role of price and hierarchy. In S. Ghoshal & D.E. Westney (Eds.), *Organization theory and the multinational corporation:* 157–181. New York: St. Martin's Press.

Hill, C.W.L. 1990. Cooperation, opportunism, and the invisible hand: Implications for transaction cost theory. *Academy of Management Review,* 15: 500–513.

Holmstrom, B., & Milgrom, P. 1991. Multitask principal-agent analysis: Incentives, contracts, asset ownership, and job design. *Journal of Law, Economics, and Organization,* 7 (Spring): 24–52.

Hoskisson, R.E., & Hitt, M.A. 1988. Strategic control systems and relative R&D investment in large multiproduct firms. *Strategic Management Journal*, 9: 605–621.

Ichniowsky, C., Shaw, K., & Prennushi, G. 1993. *The effects of human resource management practices on productivity.* Unpublished paper manuscript, Columbia University, New York.

Jarillo, J.C. 1988. On strategic networks. *Strategic Management Journal*, 9: 31–41.

John, G., & Weitz, B.A. 1988. Forward integration into distribution: An empirical test of transaction cost analysis. *Journal of Law, Economics, and Organization*, 4(2): 337–355.

Kahneman, D., & Tversky, A. 1973. On the psychology of prediction. *Psychological Review*, 80: 251–273.

Kendrick, D.T., & Funder, D.C. 1988. Profiting from controversy: Lessons from the person-situation debate. *American Psychologist*, 43(1): 23–34.

Kerr, J., & Slocum, J.W. 1987. Managing corporate culture through reward systems. *Academy of Management Executive*, 1: 99–108.

Kim, W.C., & Mauborgne, R.A. 1993. Making global strategies work. *Sloan Management Review*, 34(3): 11–27.

Kipnis, D. 1972. Does power corrupt? *Journal of Personality and Social Psychology*, 24(1): 33–41.

Krackhardt, D. 1992. The strength of strong ties: The importance of *philos* in organizations. In N. Nohria & R.G. Eccles (Eds.), *Networks and organizations*: 216–239. Boston: Harvard Business School Press.

Krosnic, J.A., Betz, A.L., Jussim, L.J., Lynn, A.R., & Stephens, L. 1992. Subliminal conditions of attitudes. *Personal Social Psychology Bulletin*, 18: 152–162.

Kruglanski, A.W. 1970. Attributing trustworthiness in supervisor-worker relations. *Journal of Experimental Social Psychology*, 6: 214–232.

Kuhn, T.S. 1962. *The structure of scientific revolution.* Chicago: University of Chicago Press.

Lepper, M.R., & Greene, D. 1975. Turning play into work: Effects of adult surveillance and extrinsic rewards on children's intrinsic motivation. *Journal of Personality and Social Psychology*, 31: 479–486.

Masten, S.E. 1993. Transaction costs, mistakes, and performance: Assessing the importance of governance. *Managerial and Decision Economics*, 14: 119–129.

Masten, S.E. 1994. *Empirical research in transaction-cost economics: Challenges, progress, directions.* Working paper, The University of Michigan, School of Business Administration.

Masten, S.E., Meehan, J.W., & Snyder, E.A. 1989. Vertical integration in the U.S. auto industry: A note on the influence of transaction specific assets. *Journal of Economic Behavior and Organization*, 12: 265–273.

Milgrom, P.R., & Roberts, J. 1992. *Economics, organization and management.* Englewood Cliffs, NJ: Prentice Hall.

Mintzberg, H., & Waters, J.A. 1985. Of strategies, deliberate and emergent. *Strategic Management Journal*, 6: 257–272.

Monteverde, K.M., & Teece, D.J. 1982. Appropriable rents and quasi-vertical integration. *Journal of Law and Economics*, 25: 321–328.

Nelson, R.R. 1991. Why do firms differ, and how does it matter? *Strategic Management Journal*, 12: 61–74.

North, D.C. 1990. *Institutions, institutional change and economic performance.* Cambridge, England: Cambridge University Press.

Olson, J.M., & Zana, M.P. 1993. Attitudes and attitude change. *Annual Review of Psychology,* 44: 117–154.

O'Reilly, C., & Chatman, J. 1986. Organizational commitment and psychological attachment: The effects of compliance, identification and internalization on prosocial behavior. *Journal of Applied Psychology,* 71: 492–499.

Ouchi, W.G. 1979. A conceptual framework for the design of organizational control mechanisms. *Management Science,* 25: 833–848.

Ouchi, W.G. 1980. Markets, bureaucracies and clans. *Administrative Science Quarterly,* 23: 293–317.

Ouchi, W.G. 1984. *The M-form society.* Reading, MA: Addison-Wesley.

Perrow, C. 1986. *Complex organizations.* New York: Random House.

Petty, R.E., & Cacioppo, J.T. 1981. *Attitudes and persuasion: Classic and contemporary approaches.* Dubuque, IA: Brown.

Pfeffer, J. 1994. *Competitive advantage through people: Unleashing the power of the workforce.* Boston: Harvard Business School Press.

Riordan, M., & Williamson, O.E. 1985. Asset specificity and economic organization. *International Journal of Industrial Organization,* 3: 365–378.

Rubin, P.H. 1990. *Managing business transactions.* New York: Free Press.

Rubin, P.H. 1993. Introduction. *Managerial and Decision Economics,* 14: 95.

Rugman, A.M. 1981. *Inside the multinationals: The economics of internal markets.* New York: Columbia University Press.

Rumelt, R.P., Schendel, D., & Teece, D.J. 1991. Strategic management and economics. *Strategic Management Journal,* 12: 5–29.

Schumpeter, J.A. 1942. *Capitalism, socialism and democracy.* London: Unwin University Books.

Selznick, P. 1957. *Leadership in administration.* Evanston, IL: Row Peterson.

Shane, S.A. 1992. The effect of cultural differences in perceptions of transaction costs on national differences in the preference for licensing. *Management International Review,* 32: 295–311.

Simon, H.A. 1991. Organizations and markets. *Journal of Economic Perspectives,* 5(2): 25–44.

Strickland, L.H. 1958. Surveillance and trust. *Journal of Personality,* 26: 200–215.

Teece, D.J. 1983. Technological and organizational factors in the theory of the multinational enterprise. In M. Casson (Ed.), *The growth of international business:* 51–62. London: Allen & Unwin.

Tesser, A. 1993. The importance of heritability in psychological research: The case of attitudes. *Psychological Review,* 100: 129–142.

Thompson, J.A. 1967. *Organizations in action.* New York: McGraw-Hill.

Walker, G. 1988. Strategic sourcing, vertical integration and transaction costs. *Interlaces,* 18: 62–73.

Walker, G., & Weber, D. 1984. A transaction cost approach to make-buy decisions. *Administrative Science Quarterly,* 29: 373–391.

Wilkins, A., & Ouchi, W.G. 1983. Efficient cultures: Exploring the relationship between culture and organizational performance. *Administrative Science Quarterly*, 28: 468–481.

Williamson, O.E. 1975. *Markets and hierarchies: Analysis and antitrust implications.* New York: Free Press.

Williamson, O.E. 1979. Transaction-cost economics: The governance of contractual relations. *Journal of Law and Economics*, 22: 233–261.

Williamson, O.E. 1985. *Economic institutions of capitalism.* New York: Free Press.

Williamson, O.E. 1990. Chester Barnard and the incipient science of organization. In O.E. Williamson (Ed.), *Organization theory: From Chester Barnard to the present and beyond*: 172–206. New York: Oxford University Press.

Williamson, O.E. 1991a. Comparative economic organization: The analysis of discrete structural alternatives. *Administrative Science Quarterly*, 36: 269–296.

Williamson, O.E. 1991b. Economic institutions: Spontaneous and intentional governance. *Journal of Law, Economics, and Organization*, 7: 159–187.

Williamson, O.E. 1991c. Introduction. In O.E. Williamson & S.G. Winter (Eds.), *The nature of the firm: Origins, evolution, and development*: 3–17. New York: Oxford University Press.

Williamson, O.E. 1991d. Strategizing, economizing, and economic organization. *Strategic Management Journal*, 12: 75–94.

Williamson, O.E. 1992. Markets, hierarchies, and the modern corporation: An unfolding perspective. *Journal of Economic Behavior and Organization*, 17: 335–352.

Williamson, O.E. 1993a. Calculativeness, trust, and economic organization. *Journal of Law and Economics*, 36: 453–486.

Williamson, O.E. 1993b. The evolving science of organization. *Journal of Institutional and Theoretical Economics*, 149(1): 36–63.

Williamson, O.E. 1993c. Opportunism and its critics. *Managerial and Decision Economics*, 14: 97–107.

Williamson, O.E., & Ouchi, W.G. 1981. The markets and hierarchies perspective: Origins, implications, prospects. In A.H. Van de Ven & W.F. Joyce (Eds.), *Perspectives on organization design and behavior*: 347–370. New York: Wiley.

CHAPTER 9

Diversification and diversifact

Sumantra Ghoshal and Henry Mintzberg

This paper provides an unusual metaphor – the spinning top – to examine the key elements that make up a successful diversified firm. Sumantra and renowned management theorist Henry Mintzberg argue that there are four components to a diversified firm – a set of well-performing businesses (the base of the spinning top), the energy and the vision of top management (the knob at the top), a set of planning systems (the middle part, which adds bulk), and a strong culture (a skin, to stop the parts spinning off in all directions). Of course every diversified firm is different in the way it manages each part, so a careful discussion of the key trade-offs executives have to manage is presented. While the subject matter of diversified firms is not typical of Sumantra's writing, the core themes – the need for a strong culture, an encouragement of individual initiative – are entirely consistent with his other papers.

What a difference an "a" makes! Drop the letter from the word diversification, as a secretary of ours once did, and it comes out as diversifiction. There is much fiction about the management of multi-business enterprises, and there are some facts. Sorting out the facts from the fiction is a major challenge for many large corporations, as they try to find the elusive balance among a diverse set of conflicting needs.

Consider two examples of recent changes in diversified firms. The chief of Matsushita decided that the system of divisional autonomy that had catapulted the company to global leadership in consumer electronics had become the principal barrier to change, and so he began tearing down the walls within the company to consolidate more than a hundred autonomous product divisions into seven large business groups. In contrast, the head of Siemens, frustrated by the sprawling bureaucracy at headquarters, initiated a major restructuring to split up its seven sectors into a large number of focused business units with great autonomy for their managers. These divergent responses indicate different beliefs about the effective management of diversity. But they also reflect the swings that are so common in structural design, from centralization to decentralization, and then back; and from the integration of activity to the autonomy of action, and back again. Companies swing like a pendulum and never seem to get it right.

We propose a new metaphor – the spinning top. It suggests that the energy of diversified corporations should be invested into sustaining a dynamic balance. Our metaphor allows us to address the following questions:

- What are the key organizational dimensions that influence overall performance of diversified companies? In other words, what are the forces that need to be managed?

- What are the major trade-offs that must be considered in managing these forces to develop effective organizational structures and decision-making processes? How can managers balance the conflicting demands without succumbing to these all-too-common swings?

- How can multi-business enterprises develop the organizational capabilities they need for sustained superior performance?

The spinning top of the multi-business enterprise

Organizing an enterprise that consists of a multiplicity of businesses requires a model that encompasses more than the traditionally considered dimensions of bases of grouping (e.g., products, regions) and types of control (e.g., financial, strategic).[1] We begin with four basic elements:

- An enterprise is considered diversified when it has moved beyond different products to identifiably *different businesses*.

- The businesses are overseen by a *central management* (a "headquarters").

- Management generally institutionalizes some kind of formal systems of control, at a minimum typically through *performance planning*.

● In addition to planning for purposes of formal control, there also has to be some means of adaptation, at the very least some mechanism for *autonomous venturing* to develop or acquire new businesses.

Figure 1 shows these four elements placed one atop the other. The individual businesses are at the base to represent the fundamental operations, the delivery of products and services to the marketplace. Above are the other three elements by level of aggregation: autonomous venturing closest to the business operations, which represents adaptation; performance planning at a somewhat greater level of aggregation (and abstraction) which represents control; and central management as the highest level of aggregation, the focal point of a single individual or small executive team. This represents the classic conglomerate, the enterprise as a portfolio of unrelated businesses. Autonomous venturing adds new businesses, while performance planning controls their behavior.

As shown in Figure 1, this can be shaped as a spinning top, sitting on a base of the businesses (taken collectively), with the middle comprising autonomous venturing and performance planning, while the central

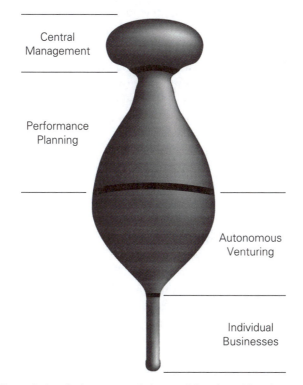

Figure 1 The minimal elements of the multinational business

management acts as the knob by which the whole system receives its spinning energy. But in this form, it may not be very stable. It could well topple over from lack of bulk in the middle. In other words, are autonomous venturing (as the favored form of adaptation) and performance planning (as the primary form of control) sufficient to sustain any corporation? Is this "thin" type of conglomerate really viable?

The few conglomerates that have sustained themselves for a time in this way have done so through the sheer will of their central management – in other words, the constant renewal of spinning energy from a particularly vigorous leadership. While it may be true that their success has often been attributed to their formal systems (none perhaps better known than the tightly managed performance controls at ITT in the 1970s), it was the leadership itself that sustained them (for example, the energy and "chutzpah" of ITT's Harold Geneen). Put another way, there is no formal way to manage an organization that does not know what business it is in. That is diversi*fiction*. We recall the executive of one visible conglomerate who told us that "since Mr. [founder] died, no-one has a clue how to run this place." It was soon restructured.

At the limit of our metaphor, trying to spin a nail is a tricky business (as Rand Araskog, Geneen's successor at ITT, soon discovered). Pretending to manage the balance sheet in such conglomerates, even to calculate "shareholder value" as a direct consequence of proposed strategic moves, has never amounted to much more than a game to impress the stock market analysts. Of course, leaders who buy good businesses in the first place and then appoint good managers to run them can succeed, as did ITT in the early years and Hanson Trust in the 1980s. But for that, there are no good formal systems, only good personal decisions. We do not believe the success of any conglomerate has ever amounted to anything more than this.

Adding bulk for stability

For our spinning top to become more stable, it must add bulk in the middle. That means diversified corporations have to elaborate their systems of formal planning and their mechanisms of informal adapting. Planning can be elaborated beyond the simple control of performance in two stages.

- First is the introduction of *resource planning* to create an initial loose coupling of the businesses. Here efforts are made to rationalize the allocation of resources among different businesses, and thereby impose a certain degree of central coordination. Capital budgeting is one obvious form of this, as were the various "portfolio" techniques introduced in the 1970s to shift resources from low potential to high potential businesses. Similar rationalization is also possible for a variety of other resources, such as the management of technologies or the use of manufacturing facilities.

- Second is *logistics planning*, which introduces tighter coupling of the businesses. Here the flow of information and products between the different businesses is carefully managed, for example through scheduling procedures and the specification of material flows. Of course, extending this kind of planning to its natural limit does away with the distinctiveness of the businesses altogether, as in the evolution of General Motors after the 1920s, whose classic "divisions" – e.g., Chevrolet, Buick – eventually came to be more like marketing functions than real businesses. But at some intermediate level – for example, an aluminium company with its mines, smelters, and fabricating operations – the enterprise maintains some degree of diversification.

As shown in Figure 2, each of these forms of planning, in turn, adds bulk in the middle of the spinning top, resource planning beyond the thin form of performance planning, and logistics planning beyond that.

On the level of adapting, bulk can likewise be added in two stages.

- Beyond simple autonomous venturing is what we call *competency leveraging*. Here initiatives within the businesses are pursued by drawing on the core competences of the enterprise at large, for example, a basic technological capability or a critical function such as merchandising or product design. The venturing, in effect, is now no longer autonomous, but loosely coupled to the existing businesses.

- And, beyond that is the tighter coupling of *cooperative teamworking*, where people from different businesses work collectively, in teams and on task forces, perhaps linked formally by some kind of matrix structure. This can be particularly evident, for example, in new product development efforts that cut across businesses.

Thus, we add bulk to our spinning top by extending it in the middle to encompass three kinds of increasingly integrated planning systems (from performance planning to resource planning to logistics planning) and three kinds of increasingly integrated adapting mechanisms (from autonomous venturing to competency leveraging to cooperative teamworking). In effect, this bulk can be added on two levels. The upper one

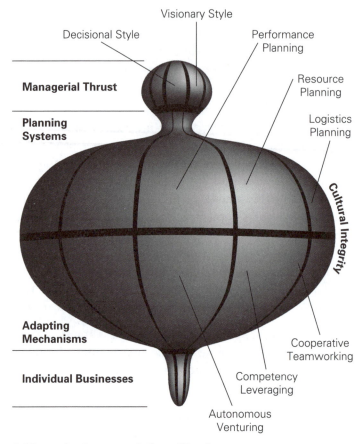

Figure 2 The spinning top of diversification

(called planning) is designed for rationalization, to provide control, and tends to be more formalized and more centralized, and is, therefore, shown closer to the central management at headquarters. The lower level (called adapting), in contrast, is designed more for revitalization, to provide initiative and encourage learning, and tends to be more organic and decentralized, rooted in the businesses themselves. Thus we end up in Figure 2 with something that looks more like a conventional spinning top, and so would seem to be more stable. But two other elements remain to be elaborated.

In our figure, the knob itself, which provides the spinning energy from the central management, can also be extended to reflect greater integration. In its basic form, indicated in Figure 1 and described earlier, the headquarters management exhibits a *decisional style*, focusing on individual, opportunistic decisions, for example, in its acquisition (or divestment) of businesses and the people to run them.

In its more elaborated form, expressing tighter coupling and shown in Figure 2, the central leadership can also exhibit a *visionary style*. Here some "concept of the enterprise" helps to conceive the organization not just as a portfolio of viable businesses, but as an integrated entity. (Perhaps we should label this "diversi*vision*"!) Indeed, such a vision – by which we mean a real sense of the cohesive uniqueness of the company, not just some innocuous "mission statement" – is a necessary prerequisite for developing the more integrated forms of planning and of adapting. For otherwise, there can be no basis for consolidating resources and logistics, nor for defining competences and sustaining teamwork.

Our last element is a sort of metaphorical glue that holds this whole thing together – all the other elements we have introduced, including the managerial thrust, the systems of planning, the mechanisms of adapting, and the businesses themselves. This might alternatively be conceived as the "skin" that keeps the parts from separating and flying off in different directions as the top spins. This is the role of corporate norms and values, which we label cultural integrity (in both senses of the latter word). The stronger the culture, the more solid will be the figure, ensuring that the entire system spins as a cohesive entity.

We can now use the metaphor to describe what we believe to be the organizational requirements of a viable diversified enterprise. First, it must sit on a solid base. In other words, the basic businesses must be strong or nothing else will work. Second, the spin must come from the knob. Management has to provide the initial energy for start-up, and must thereafter add energy to sustain viability and avoid collapse. This it does by the taking of individual decisions integrated by an inspiring vision. Third, the center necessarily comprises two levels of coordination, one of planning systems to ensure rationalized control of the businesses, the other of adapting mechanisms to stimulate revitalizing initiatives by the businesses. For the enterprise to maintain its stability, each must add bulk in the form of more or less integrated systems of planning and mechanisms of adapting, to ensure viable synergies among the different businesses. And finally, a strong culture, or skin, must hold all of these parts together, to ensure that they do not separate and fly off in all directions.

All of this is not, of course, to argue that the design of every multi-business enterprise must be identical, or even similarly balanced. Important trade-offs have to be made, and these can lead to a host of particular forms.

Trade-offs in designing the multi-business enterprise

We have identified various dimensions pertaining to the design of the multi-business enterprise – systems of planning, mechanisms of adapting, styles of managing, as well as the strength of the corporate culture holding all this together. To some extent, these can substitute for each other (as when more teamwork replaces some logistics planning). But perhaps more important are their complementarities (as in enhancing teamwork with logistics planning).

The horizontal trade-off: autonomy vs. synergy

How tightly coupled should the different businesses be to each other? Should they be thought of as merely a "portfolio" of independent activities, or do they together form an integrated enterprise? Loose or no coupling allows for the freedom of movement of each business but renders the enterprise merely a collection of parts. With no synergy, there is really no reason to keep together. Even with a minimum of coordination, the system would not seem to be very stable. As bulk is added, however, the top spins more smoothly, and can remain stable for longer periods of time.

But the greater the bulk, the more difficult to get the top spinning in the first place and to renew its spin when it slows down – that is, the greater the managerial thrust required at those critical moments of change. Moreover, great bulk in the form of tight integration reduces a multi-business enterprise to a single entity, perhaps destroying some of the potential benefits of diversity. Thus, a major issue in organization design is to nuance the trade-off between autonomy and synergy.[2]

On Figure 2, this trade-off flows out horizontally, along three levels. First, at the level of managerial thrust, there is a choice between the loose coupling of opportunistic decisions and the tight coupling of a widening vision. At the level below, of planning systems, there is the choice between the weak coupling of performance planning in the core, or else the adding of bulk in the form of the loose coupling of resource planning or the tighter coupling of logistics planning. Finally at the level of adapting mechanisms, the trade-off appears between the weak coupling of autonomous venturing in the core, or the addition of bulk in the form of the loose coupling of competence leveraging and the tighter coupling of cooperative teamworking.

While our discussion has so far been concerned with substitutability, in fact there is good reason to include the perspective of complementarity here as well (as in Peters and Waterman's discussion of the "simultaneous loose-tight properties" of their "excellent" companies).[3] Indeed, a key challenge for managers in mature multi-business enterprises is to layer the increasingly integrative capabilities along all three levels. Matsushita Electric Industries (MEI) provides a good example of a company engaged in this process.

For much of its seventy-five year history, MEI looked very much like the conglomerate we described in Figure 1. Matsushita Konosuke, the company's legendary founder, provided the managerial thrust through his personal charisma and the breathtaking ambition he instilled in his people. There was no integrated business vision but only a driving desire for growth, mandated in the 250-year plan that the then 37-year-old founder expressed in 1932 when the company was only 14 years old and 160 employees strong.

Until the early 1980s, the company managed each product line as a separate division which was expected to operate as if it were an independent corporation. A new division received start-up capital from the corporate headquarters and loans, when justified under normal commercial conditions. It paid the corporate "bank" interest on those loans at regular market rates, together with sixty percent of pre-tax profits as dividend. All interdivisional transactions were priced at market rates and had to be settled within 30 days. Performance expectations were uniform and high across all divisions, regardless of the maturity of the market or the company's competitive position, and divisions in which operating profits fell below 4 percent of sales for two successive years had the division manager replaced. The system generated a high level of internal competition among divisions and helped drive the development of new products and markets which managers saw as necessary to maintain long-term growth and profitability.

By the mid-1980s, however, the company was facing a very different set of strategic challenges to which its traditional conglomerate organization could not respond. In a period of low growth, the profitability-oriented planning and control system was causing division managers to emphasize short-term results and avoid risky development investments. Furthermore, as the company sought to refocus on new and growing sectors such as semi-conductors, robotics, and computers, interdivisional competition was making it difficult to move information, resources and people from existing to new businesses. And, with the integration of technologies, new products were increasingly taking the form of multi-functional "systems" rather than stand-alone equipment, and the once invigorating force of divisional autonomy was preventing the cooperative teamwork necessary to capture these emerging business opportunities.

The company responded to these new requirements by consolidating its more than a hundred product divisions into seven large sectors. Beyond this structural change, the company has also initiated actions to build tighter coupling at all the three levels. At the level of managerial thrust, the company has adopted the vision of "human electronics" as the multi-trillion dollar business it hopes to create and dominate. At the planning level, the new top management has instituted a process of restructuring the product portfolio to match the evolving strategic direction, developed a five-year planning process that focuses on company-wide new technologies and new environmental expectations, and integrated month-by-month forecasts of production, inventory, and distribution. Finally, at the level of adapting mechanisms, the company has created three customer-oriented sales groups charged with the task of consolidating its marketing competencies, infrastructures, and customer relationships to ensure that these are shared and exploited across the seven sectors. Corporate level coordination over "core technologies" – crucial ones that cut across sectors – has also been strengthened, and the company has established a number of cross-functional and cross-sector groups to promote cooperative teamworking in areas such as development of new multimedia products and reduction of time-to-market.

The vertical trade-off: control vs. initiative

Whatever the balance between synergy and autonomy, both can be managed by central formal controls or they can be left to decentralized informal initiatives. The trade-off then becomes the extent to which there are efforts to rationalize from the center as opposed to allowing for revitalization within the businesses.[4]

We refer to this as the "vertical trade-off" both because it pertains to the degree of decentralization favored in the enterprise (to the individual businesses and especially within them) and because, in our spinning top, it involves choosing either the upper level of planning (imposed on the businesses from above) or the lower level of adapting (achieved within them). In one case, formal programming is the key to coordination, in the other, it is the mutual adjustment among cooperating partners.

Should the enterprise, for example, favor performance controls to drive behavior or should it encourage autonomous venturing? Likewise, if in need of tight coupling, should it use logistics planning to ensure a smoother workplan or should it stimulate cooperative teamworking to ensure the flow of synergistic ideas?

Some key differences between these two levels should be born in mind. Planning is essentially an exercise in disaggregation: it decomposes the organization into component parts (for example, units for purposes of budgeting, activities for purposes of logistics). It is essentially deductive, treating strategy making as a deliberate process and concentrating attention on tangible contents, such as identifiable resources (jobs, cash, machines). Adapting, on the other hand, is less amenable to such disaggregation: it deals in ideas and perspectives. Because these can be known only after the fact, the attention is not on content so much as on process, which tends to be inductive in nature, therefore rendering the strategy-making process more emergent than deliberate. Thus planning and adapting relate to each other much as the yang and ying of Chinese philosophy, one hard, the other soft, one rooted in categories, the other in images.

And much like the ying and yang, while the substitutability is evident, the complementarity is no less important. No organization can do without the revitalizing efforts of adapting, which brings in new ideas, nor the rationalizing efforts of planning, which helps to order these. Our preceding example of MEI illustrates not just the horizontal layering of capabilities for achieving autonomy and synergy simultaneously, but also this vertical balance between planning and adapting. 3M is another company that has developed a reputation for having successfully managed this duality of business unit level initiative and corporate level planning to achieve both local entrepreneurship within its many business units and technological and market synergies across them.

Since its turn of the century origin as a producer of coated abrasives, 3M has pursued innovation as its basic corporate strategy – a company described as being "in the business of creating businesses." Decentralized initiative has been at the heart of the institutionalized corporate entrepreneurship at 3M, with employees allowed to spend up to fifteen percent of their time working on new ideas, those with good ideas eligible for grants. "We consider a coherent sentence to be an acceptable first draft for a new product plan," the company has boasted. But cooperative teamworking has been no less evident. As the company traditionally functioned, the creator of a new idea becomes the product champion and leader of a small team of experts recruited from different parts of the company. To enhance commitment, members of the team are volunteers, assigned indefinitely and full-time to the project, to remain together until the end of the project, operating as a semi-autonomous unit. The champion remains in charge, free to make decisions within broad guidelines, until either the project is abandoned or it becomes a full-fledged business, at which time it is integrated into the larger organization.

As in Matsushita, the high individual and unit autonomy is balanced with a rigorous and disciplined performance planning system applied uniformly to all operating units (which are forbidden by a central directive from creating their own systems). A total of nearly 4000 monthly P&L statements at the level of product families are generated centrally in the United States and are made available on-line to all subsidiaries within ten days of every financial closing. Significant variances from forecast immediately trigger high level corporate reviews.

Moreover, fifteen-year vision statements about future states of technologies, markets and societies provide the basis for resource planning at 3M, particularly with regard to the more than 85 technologies, ranging from abrasive minerals to fluoro-chemistry. Responsibility for developing and protecting these technologies, and leveraging them across units, rests with the company's powerful Technical Council. Like technology, manufacturing capacity is also viewed as a corporate resource, the development and allocation of which is centrally planned and controlled.

The centrifugal trade-off: spin vs. skin

We have suggested that the initial thrust that sets the top spinning, as well as subsequent bursts of it, comes from the central management. Without that vital energy in the form of key decisions and a stimulating vision, the whole enterprise risks toppling over.

But these thrusts set up centrifugal forces that can be damaging. Unless held together, the parts can fly apart. For example, as a new leadership comes in and begins to change all sorts of things, established procedures break down, and even despite a new integrated vision, the net result can be less coordination and a loss of synergy. In other words, organizations can have too much spin – at least at certain times. A necessary complement to the thrust of management must, therefore, be the glue of culture. Spin must, if you like, be supported by skin. And the greater the thrust, the more effective must be the bonding.

Again, the substitutability must be recognized alongside the complementarity. Enterprises can, for example, integrate through the conceptual vision of the current management or the norms of an established culture – i.e., an image of the future or a sense of the past. A strong management can, therefore, partially make up for a weak culture, holding the enterprise together by sheer force of ideas. Likewise, a strong culture – established beliefs, deeply-rooted traditions – can sometimes sustain an enterprise through weak management.

But these forces act on each other too. The stronger the bonds of culture, the heavier becomes the whole edifice, and so the more difficult it becomes to give it added thrust. Turnaround is most difficult in those enterprises that stagnate with strong cultures. They might be described as "thick skinned" – so obsessed with their own traditions as to be impenetrable to proposed changes. These organizations must, therefore, lighten their loads by shedding some of their outdated traditions if they are to regain balance.

Alternatively, however, while it is certainly easy to give spin to an almost weightless top – an organization with barely any cultural integrity – the risk is that it can slip off in almost any direction. Put differently, without culture to hold an enterprise in one place, management can all too easily become opportunist. Thus enterprises can be too "thin skinned" and therefore permeable by almost any change that comes along. Spin and skin must complement each other, a point that was once made to us vividly by a senior manager at an oil company. "It is a bit like flying model airplanes," he said, "I see my son assembling those planes, and they never fly. Sometimes he puts too little glue, and the plane disintegrates when he hurls it, and sometimes he puts too much glue, and the soggy mass drops like a stone."

This task of balancing managerial thrust with cultural integrity is a key responsibility of top management. In normal times, it requires a subtle and patient process of continuous and incremental adjustments. But under turnaround situations, the challenge becomes both more dramatic and more demanding, as was the case for the Scandinavian Airlines System (SAS).

When Jan Carlzon assumed the presidency of SAS in August of 1981, he inherited an airline that was on the brink of bankruptcy. The company had posted hefty operating losses in the preceding years and had been losing market share rapidly, even in its home market. Its fleet mix and route network did not match market needs and its reputation for service and punctuality was one of the worst in Europe. In the first five years of his tenure, Carlzon presided over a remarkable transformation of the company, leading to significant improvements not only in financial performance and market reputation but also in internal morale and employee commitment. While opinions vary about the prudence of his subsequent actions in diversifying the company into several associated service businesses, his initial turnaround of SAS remains as one of the more interesting examples of rebalancing corporate spin and skin.

In managing this transformation, Carlzon relied heavily on his personal effort and leadership. Firing 13 out of the 14 executives in the company's management team, he assumed a highly visible and substantive role in the company's management processes almost immediately after his arrival. He built a new vision around the theme of "the businessman's airline," and restructured the company's assets and resources to match the new focus, for example, by changing the fleet mix to create a low fixed cost, high frequency schedule. He personally set and monitored highly stretched targets for improvement in service quality, and travelled continuously to keep in contact with all levels of the organization, using these contacts to create and maintain bottom-up enthusiasm in support of the new vision.

At the same time, Carlzon recognized that his initiatives had to be supported by a new set of cultural and behavioral norms. The new service focus of SAS required that any employee in the "front-line" (i.e., at the SAS/customer interface) have the decision-making power necessary to do, within reasonable limits, whatever the person felt appropriate to please the customer. This was extremely difficult in an organization that had become accustomed to centralized control, in which a large corporate staff and layers of middle management implemented directives issued by top management.

Carlzon established new cultural norms by emphasizing what he described as the "moment of truth," when a customer encountered a service staff. Each moment of truth had to be used to its full potential so as to encourage repeat business. "Throw out the manual and use your head instead" was the message communicated to employees of SAS. It was believed that an individual with information could not avoid assuming responsibility, and hidden resources could be released when an individual was free to assume responsibility instead of being restricted by instructions. Supervisors were encouraged to coach rather than control the staff. In Carlzon's view everyone worked for those in the frontline. The message was driven home through an intensive training program that was attended, over time, by each employee of the company.

The balance trade-off: base vs. bulk

The diversified enterprise sits on a base of its businesses. Very solid businesses are critical: they create a stable base. But alone, they can go nowhere. If you cannot spin a nail, try spinning a cylinder! Alternatively, all the bulk imaginable, in the form of wonderful systems of planning and adapting, will do no good on a weak base. No enterprise can stay upright with businesses that are not well positioned to compete in their marketplaces. The effective organization must, therefore, have sufficient bulk over a good base – strong businesses and sufficient synergy among them. After that, it can begin to attend to substitutions between stronger businesses, on the one hand, and stronger mechanisms to connect and manage them, on the other.

In terms of our metaphor, there is an interesting issue here. Perhaps Figure 1 should have shown the base as multiple points, to emphasize that the businesses of a conglomerate corporation are independent. That, of course, could not spin at all! We show it as one point, however, partly because, in our metaphor, the businesses are treated as a collective entity, but also because, in our argument, there is the need for some kind of synergy to mold them into a cohesive entity. The base may be made up of strands from different businesses, but ultimately they have to converge on a single point that symbolizes the market position of the corporation. Indeed, there is an interesting irony here, because as the middle widens – as coordinating bulk is added – the base narrows, that is, the different market activities come increasingly to resemble a single business. But that, of course, fits our argument quite well: a top of this shape spins rather well!

Faced with intense competitive pressures, many companies have spiralled out of control because of their inability to manage this balance between bulk and base. Some have focussed exclusively on the base, periodically restructuring their business portfolios and reducing their people and investments. Each round of such restructuring may have improved financial results temporarily, but, in the absence of the bulk needed to protect, enhance, and exploit internal capabilities, this has only led to the next round of performance decline and restructuring. For a considerable period of time, Westinghouse was caught in such a restructuring spiral in which strategy-making was ultimately reduced to one simple question: which business should we sell or restructure next?

Some other companies have focussed on the bulk, ignoring the base, with revitalizing rather than restructuring as their battle cry. Unable or unwilling to make the hard decisions that are often necessary to strengthen a business base, managers have spent endless hours creating integrating mechanisms across businesses in the hope that synergies would lead to improved performance of each business. This, for example, was the approach of Philips in the second half of the 1980s, when effective integration across the "core interdependent businesses" (such as components and consumer electronics) was seen as the key to improving corporate performance. However, as the company eventually learned, integrating a number of weak businesses creates an even weaker company, just as creating a team of a number of incompetent individuals wastes everyone's time.

Building and balancing capabilities

Our discussion of the various trade-offs suggests that the most comfortable posture is to create a balance among the different elements – to achieve, in other words, a dynamic equilibrium. With a strong base of good businesses, dynamism provided by an energetic and ambitious management, and appropriate systems of planning and mechanisms for adapting, held together by a strong corporate culture, such companies find a relatively stable position and keep spinning for long periods of time. In no need of sudden or dramatic changes, they are rarely written up in the popular press, except in brief reports about their steady growth in sales and profits. Over the last three decades, Royal Dutch/Shell, for example, has been able to build and maintain such a balanced position.

Most companies, of course, favor some particular place on our diagram. There are the *acquirers*, such as Electrolux, who have achieved spectacular but often undigested growth through acquisitions determined by strategic decisions at the headquarters. Contrast this with the *venturers*, such as Matsushita, who have proliferated products in a variety of unrelated fields through internal autonomous venturing. Then there are the *visionaries*, such as NEC, who have managed to build strong sets of businesses around integrated visions. In contrast there are the *crystallizers*, such as Hewlett-Packard, who have traditionally focussed on competency leveraging, spinning off a variety of new products and businesses grounded in specific core competencies.

The *controllers*, such as Hanson Trust, have focussed on performance planning, with some venturing to acquire, but almost no resource or logistics planning, competency leveraging, or cooperative teamworking across divisions. Their management style has been more decisional than visionary, aimed at continually stimulating performance of the independent businesses. The *heavies* focus instead on logistics planning, as in many upstream resource-based companies (such as aluminium) and the huge mass producers (such as General Motors) concerned with rationalizing work or product flows. There are *ideologues* among multi-business companies, who emphasize the integrating effects of culture (for example, Bodyshop, the European retailer, holds itself together by strong norms and esprit de corps). Contrast these with the *holders* (such as some of the traditional business groups of Korea and India) who are mostly concerned with the businesses of the base, with barely any discernible headquarters or even performance controls, let alone unique visions.

The problem with favoring any one of these postures is that it risks throwing the organization out of balance. In the long run, it may become vulnerable. Thus, ways have been found to cope with this. Some companies build off-line mechanisms to counteract their dominant on-line approaches. Those with heavy centralized planning, such as Kodak, have tried to sponsor "skunkworks" and "new venture groups" to promote autonomous venturing, while those which have relied on adapting mechanisms, such as Apple and Arthur D. Little, have experimented with ad-hoc processes for resource and capacity planning.

Other companies, while accepting a suboptimal position at any point of time, have sought to shift from time to time, compensating for imbalance by periodic corrections. Like those people who used to sit on high poles years ago, swaying in the wind, it is certainly a more dramatic form of behavior, even if hardly the most comfortable!

In its thirty-year history, Digital Equipment Corporation has gone through at least five such swings: from the freewheeling university-like environment in the 1960s, relying primarily on autonomous venturing; to stronger performance and resource planning in the late 1970s, driven by central product line managers; to a focus on horizontal competency sharing and cooperative teamworking in the early 1980s, as the company re-oriented itself and its offerings in a "network" era; to a renewed emphasis on distributed initiative and middle-up-down venturing in the late 1980s, away from what was seen as excessive central direction and control; and finally back again to centralized resource and logistics planning in the early 1990s as a new top management struggled to stem a rising tide of losses.

In the last two decades, such periodic oscillating has often been adequate for maintaining satisfactory, if somewhat jerky, corporate performance. But not any more, not for large corporations at least. With ever increasing costs of technology and infrastructure, and ever enhanced skills in the marketplace, no company can afford to pursue opportunities randomly. A coherent definition of the boundaries of the company's opportunity horizon (unique vision) together with central coordination of its strategic architecture (formal planning) seem to have become a precondition for effective decentralized initiative. The reverse also seems to be true: in an environment of converging markets and technologies, in which new opportunities arise quickly and increasingly between rather than within well-defined businesses, no amount of planning, however brilliant, can compensate for a lack of autonomous venturing and cooperative teamworking inside the company.

Most managers, we believe, are increasingly aware of this need to build and balance the diverse organizational capabilities. The specific tasks in the process, however, differ depending on a company's starting point. For some, the key challenge is to rebuild the base of excellence; for others to develop the bulk of synergy; while for still others, the need is to provide the spin and skin of energy. Developments at General Electric over the last ten years provide a good illustration of how each of these tasks can be managed.[5] The illustration is particularly useful, to our mind, because the starting point was not a situation of crisis but one of stellar performance. In reviewing Jack Welch's dramatic transformation of GE, what is often overlooked is that he became chief executive in 1981, the same year that a poll of *Fortune 500* chief executives ranked the company as the best managed industrial enterprise in the United States and Reginald Jones, his predecessor, was declared "CEO of the year"!

Strengthening the base

The first step in building balance requires an unrelenting drive to improve the performance of each business – to strengthen the base. This is exemplified in Jack Welch's first volley at GE in the early 1980s: each business had to be number one or two in its industry or had to have a viable strategy to achieve such a leadership position; businesses that failed this requirement would have no place in the GE portfolio. This led to $10 billion worth of divestitures (and $17 billion worth of acquisitions), as well as reduction of over 120,000 people in the remaining businesses, and it created the sound business base that has been the anchor of GE's remarkable performance improvement over the last ten years. While all companies need not aspire to global leadership in each of their businesses, a first step of defining stretched performance standards and restructuring the portfolio by weeding out fundamentally weak businesses and strengthening others is, we believe, essential for effective revitalization of multi-business companies.

Reinforcing the core

To rebuild the base, it is also usually necessary to strengthen each of the elements in the core of the spinning top. Rigorous performance planning, mechanisms for autonomous venturing, and strong top management decision making are prerequisites for effective restructuring. Thus, during the first half of the 1980s, when Welch focused on what he called the "business engine", he also dismantled the sector management structure that Reginald Jones had built and which had since become a major obstacle to decentralized initiative. He cut out management layers, drastically reduced corporate staff, delegated responsibilities, and established a system of individual-level incentives and rewards to drive entrepreneurial behavior at all levels of the company. Note the managerial thrust here: Welch personally energized people through his extensive travel and his interventions in the company's management development programs as well as through his substantive involvement in the strategic decisions on acquisitions, divestments, and resource allocation priorities.

This need to reinforce the core of the spinning top before adding the bulk to its sides appears to be equally applicable to another task frequently confronted by diversified companies: the integration of new acquisitions. Here, too, a process of cleaning up the problems in the acquired unit is a pre-condition for effective integration of that unit into the rest of the company. As described by Leif Johansson, President of Electrolux – an experienced acquirer, having absorbed over 350 companies in the last ten years – "in any company, some money lies on the floor. Your have to pick those up immediately after you get your foot in the door. It will be much more difficult later . . . and the flabby slack comes in the way of effective integration. Electrolux will not begin to make major investments in an acquired company nor build interdependencies with our existing operations until the unit first achieves the efficiencies it can with its existing infrastructure."

Adding bulk

For companies with a sound core – with strong businesses, distributed entrepreneurship, disciplined performance control, and effective managerial decision making – the challenge is to build the bulk of systems of planning and mechanisms of adapting. The key task here is to restore balance, since most companies suffer from a kaleidoscope of imbalances, such as lopsidedness (uneven or incoherent systems), top heaviness (too much planning), or squatness (excessive adaptation).

Given the heritage of heavyhanded corporate planning – GE had invented portfolio planning and developed ever more sophisticated and complex strategic planning processes – Jack Welch's challenge was to build the adapting mechanisms the company lacked. During the first phase, that of restructuring, he focused on autonomous venturing and simplifying the planning processes. In the next phase, that of revitalization, he began to create mechanisms for competency leveraging and cooperative teamworking. From 1988, he instituted a search for best practices, both inside the company and outside, to create mechanisms for the transfer of learning within and across the businesses. At Crotonville, GE's in-house management development center, courses have been developed to benefit from the results. These are offered each month to groups representing all of GE's key businesses. Process mapping is another such adapting mechanism practiced at GE, to identify commonalties in such diverse businesses as domestic appliances and medical equipment, and to create mechanisms for joint exploitation of company capabilities.

Providing spin and skin

Many companies have assumed the creation of a unique vision and shared culture to be the first step in a process of corporate transformation. Senior managers of these companies have gone on long retreats, to debate the wording of vision and mission statements, then have returned with a feeling of great energy and excitement, only to become frustrated when those statements, after ceremonial distribution throughout the organization, have proved to be empty.

Vision and shared culture have meaning when they coexist with a solid base, strong core, and substantial bulk. Strong performance orientation gives teeth to vision, just as a unique vision provides energy and commitment for the demanding performance objectives. Similarly, there can be no shared norms without shared tasks, just as there can be no informal trust without some level of formal order.

At GE, Welch articulated the vision of a "boundaryless organization" late in the 1980s, after the initial steps of rebuilding the core and rebalancing the bulk were well underway. This vision focused not on a specific business or growth objective, but on the philosophy of the company and its internal norms of behavior. "Integrated diversity" would distinguish GE from both single product companies and conglomerates. The norms of behavior were to eliminate the boundaries, not only within the company but also between it and its customers and suppliers, to ensure the free flow of ideas, and of learning. However, as Welch described it, each element in the diversity had to be strong and viable. Hence, the work of the 1980s – creating strong businesses – "was the indispensable forerunner of integrating them in the 1990s."

Putting the "a" back in diversi*fiction*

Over the past two decades, managers have been inundated with ever-new formulas for managing diversification, each positioned as a denial and refutation of some earlier "false promise."

In the 1970s, diversification was strategy. Driven by the seductive portfolio models, companies were urged to exchange dogs for stars in order to maintain perpetual corporate youth on the strength of their internal capital markets. Problems in the many companies that succumbed to this formula then led, in the early 1980s, to the dogma of "stick to your knitting." Once again, companies that adhered to this dogma missed the enormous opportunities that were opening up as markets and technologies converged to create huge new businesses.

Meanwhile, the fascination with strategic planning led companies to develop ever more sophisticated techniques. Yet, as powerful staff groups increasingly bureaucratized planning systems, autonomous venturing emerged as the new fashion under the garb of "intrapreneurship." In the slash and burn that followed, many companies lost their basic control systems, and were no longer able to either predict or monitor performance except ex-post.

In the 1980s, strategic business units became the darling of academics and consultants who, like Johnny Appleseeds, spread the message of the multi-divisional enterprise from company to company and from continent to continent. Creating independent SBUs, with full functional control and complete profit responsibility, may have improved short-term performance for some companies, but, in the long term, internal fragmentation sapped their abilities to create new products and new capabilities. In the 1990s, then, SBUs became the villains amid the new "mantra" of core competence which, in effect, called for corporate level integration of key functions and core processes.

The image all this suggests is not a fully endowed spinning top, but rather one that is hollow, except for a loose ball inside that bounces around between resource planning, autonomous venturing, competency leveraging, and so on. Hardly a way to promote balanced harmony, let alone remain upright!

To challenge this erratic behavior, we have proposed a more nuanced model with several key elements and a set of critical trade-offs. This nuancing is diversi*fact*. There is often the need to diversify to some degree, but also the need to create and manage synergy. There is a need to provide decentralized autonomy, but also to ensure central coordination and control. There is a need to rationalize, but also to revitalize. A good base, balanced bulk, and energized spin and skin enjoy a symbiotic relationship: each is most effective only in the presence of the others. There is no one best way to build and balance these diverse capabilities, probably not even any permanently good way for any one enterprise. Managers need to face the complexity – not deny the difficult balancing tasks. Any simplification of this complexity, however seductive, is diversi*fiction*.

Organizations are inherently unstable, especially diversified ones. Left to themselves, they eventually topple, or go over some edge. At best, like our spinning top, they have to achieve a dynamic equilibrium, maintaining their performance by periodic adjustments to their delicate balances. That is how they stay up and keep on spinning. That is the difference the "a" makes.

This paper appeared in *California Management Review*, Vol. 37, No. 1, Fall 1994.

REFERENCES

1. Diversification and the management of diversity has been one of the most popular and durable research topics in the field of strategic management. Readers interested in a broad review of this literature can find one in C.W.L. Hill and R.E. Hoskisson, "Strategy and Structure in the Multiproduct Firm", *Academy of Management Review*, 2 (1987): 331–341. While much of the empirical work has used products or businesses as the key dimension of diversity, R.P. Rumelt's *Strategy, Structure and Economic Performance*

(Boston, MA: Harvard Business School Press, 1974) remains as the seminal work in that line of inquiry. Geographic diversity has been a relatively recent interest in the field and readers interested in this aspect of management of diversity are recommended to read C.K. Prahalad and Y.L. Doz, *The Multinational Mission* (New York, NY: Free Press, 1987). For analyses of the types of controls appropriate for managing diversity, please refer to V. Govindarajan, "A Contingency Approach to Strategy Implementation at the Business-Unit Level: Integrating Administrative Mechanisms with Strategy," *Academy of Management Journal*, 31 (1988): 828–853, for a rigorous academic treatment and to M. Goold and A. Campbell, *Strategies and Styles* (London: Basil Blackwell, 1987) for a more managerial exposition.

2. The tradeoffs between autonomy and synergy are richly described in J. Lorsch and S. Allen, *Managing Diversity and Interdependence*, Division of Research, Harvard Business School, Boston, MA, 1973. For a nuanced analysis of this tradeoff in the context of multinational companies, see Prahalad and Doz, op. cit.

3. T. Peters and R. Waterman, *In Search of Excellence* (New York, NY: Harper and Row, 1982).

4. For a comprehensive review of this tension between planning and adaptation and on its implications for organizational structure, see H. Mintzberg, *Mintzberg on Management* (New York, NY: Free Press, 1989).

5. The model of GE's transformation is drawn from Jack Welch's presentation at the Harvard Business School in 1987. Readers can find greater details of the four-step process in N.M. Tichy and S. Sherman, *Control Your Destiny or Someone Else Will* (New York, NY: Doubleday, 1993).

PART III

The new management agenda

Building social capital and unleashing organizational energy

CHAPTER 10

Social capital, intellectual capital, and the organizational advantage

Janine Nahapiet and Sumantra Ghoshal

In this paper, Sumantra and Janine Nahapiet tackle the thorny question: What is it that really makes the economic institution of the firm different from the market? *Building on Sumantra's earlier work with Peter Moran on the nature of the organizational advantage, Sumantra and Janine show how under certain conditions the "social capital" embedded in individual relationships can lead to significant increases in the knowledge base or "intellectual capital" of the firm, in ways that are unlikely to happen in a market-based system of exchange. Or as they say, "organizations build and retain their advantage through the dynamic and complex interrelationships between social and intellectual capital." This paper became highly influential in the management field because it was the first to formally link the concepts of social capital and organizational knowledge.*

Kogut and Zander recently have proposed "that a firm be understood as a social community specializing in the speed and efficiency in the creation and transfer of knowledge" (1996: 503). This is an important and relatively new perspective on the theory of the firm currently being formalized through the ongoing work of these (Kogut & Zander, 1992, 1993, 1995, 1996; Zander & Kogut, 1995) and several other authors (Boisot, 1995; Conner & Prahalad, 1996; Loasby, 1991; Nonaka & Takeuchi, 1995; Spender, 1996). Standing in stark contrast to the more established transaction cost theory that is grounded in the assumption of human opportunism and the resulting conditions of market failure (e.g., Williamson, 1975), those with this perspective essentially argue that organizations have some particular capabilities for creating and sharing knowledge that give them their distinctive advantage over other institutional arrangements, such as markets. For strategy theory, the implications of this emerging perspective lie in a shift of focus from the historically dominant theme of value appropriation to one of value creation (Moran & Ghoshal, 1996).

The particular capabilities of organizations for creating and sharing knowledge derive from a range of factors, including the special facility organizations have for the creation and transfer of tacit knowledge (Kogut & Zander, 1993, 1996; Nonaka & Takeuchi, 1995; Spender, 1996); the organizing principles by which individual and functional expertise are structured, coordinated, and communicated, and through which individuals cooperate (Conner & Prahalad, 1996; Kogut & Zander, 1992; Zander and Kogut, 1995); and the nature of organizations as social communities (Kogut & Zander, 1992, 1996). However, notwithstanding the substantial insights we now have into the attributes of organizations as knowledge systems, we still lack a coherent theory for explaining them. In this article we seek to address this gap and to present a theory of how firms can enjoy what Ghoshal and Moran (1996) have called "the organizational advantage."

Our theory is rooted in the concept of social capital. Analysts of social capital are centrally concerned with the significance of relationships as a resource for social action (Baker, 1990; Bourdieu, 1986; Burt, 1992; Coleman, 1988, 1990; Jacobs, 1965; Loury, 1987). However, as Putnam (1995) recently has observed, social capital is not a unidimensional concept, and, while sharing a common interest in how relational resources aid the conduct of social affairs, the different authors on this topic have tended to focus on different facets of social capital. In this article we (1) integrate these different facets to define social capital in terms of three distinct dimensions; (2) describe how each of these dimensions facilitates the creation and exchange of knowledge; and (3) argue that organizations, as institutional settings, are able to develop high levels of social capital in terms of all three dimensions. Our primary focus, however, is on the interrelationships between social and intellectual capital since, as we have already noted, there is already a clear stream of work that identifies and elaborates the significance of knowledge processes as the foundation of such organizational advantage. Our aim here is to provide a theoretical explanation of why this is the case.

Social capital

The term "social capital" initially appeared in community studies, highlighting the central importance – for the survival and functioning of city neighborhoods – of the networks of strong, crosscutting personal relationships developed over time that provide the basis for trust, cooperation, and collective action in such communities (Jacobs, 1965). Early usage also indicated the significance of social capital for the individual: the set of resources inherent in family relations and in community social organizations useful for the development of the young child (Loury, 1977). The concept has been applied since its early use to elucidate a wide range of social phenomena, although researchers increasingly have focused attention on the role of social capital as an influence not only on the development of human capital (Coleman, 1988; Loury, 1977, 1987) but on the economic performance of firms (Baker, 1990), geographic regions (Putnam, 1993, 1995), and nations (Fukuyama, 1995).

The central proposition of social capital theory is that networks of relationships constitute a valuable resource for the conduct of social affairs, providing their members with "the collectivity-owned capital, a 'credential' which entitles them to credit, in the various senses of the word" (Bourdieu, 1986: 249). Much of this capital is embedded within networks of mutual acquaintance and recognition. Bourdieu (1986), for example, identifies the durable obligations arising from feelings of gratitude, respect, and friendship or from the institutionally guaranteed rights derived from membership in a family, a class, or a school. Other resources are available through the contacts or connections networks bring. For example, through "weak ties" (Granovetter, 1973) and "friends of friends" (Boissevain, 1974), network members can gain privileged access to information and to opportunities. Finally, significant social capital in the form of social status or reputation can be derived from membership in specific networks, particularly those in which such membership is relatively restricted (Bourdieu, 1986; Burt, 1992; D'Aveni & Kesner, 1993).

Although these authors agree on the significance of relationships as a resource for social action, they lack consensus on a precise definition of social capital. Some, like Baker (1990), limit the scope of the term to only the structure of the relationship networks, whereas others, like Bourdieu (1986, 1993) and Putnam (1995), also include in their conceptualization of social capital the actual or potential resources that can be accessed through such networks. For our purposes here, we adopt the latter view and define social capital as the sum of the actual and potential resources embedded within, available through, and derived from the network of relationships possessed by an individual or social unit. Social capital thus comprises both the network and the assets that may be mobilized through that network (Bourdieu, 1986; Burt, 1992).

As a set of resources rooted in relationships, social capital has many different attributes, and Putnam (1995) has argued that a high research priority is to clarify the dimensions of social capital. In the context of our exploration of the role of social capital in the creation of intellectual capital, we suggest that it is useful to consider these facets in terms of three clusters: the structural, the relational, and the cognitive dimensions of social capital. Although we separate these three dimensions analytically, we recognize that many of the features we describe are, in fact, highly interrelated. Moreover, in our analysis we set out to indicate important facets of social capital rather than review such facets exhaustively.

In making the distinction between the structural and the relational dimensions of social capital, we draw on Granovetter's (1992) discussion of structural and relational embeddedness. Structural embeddedness concerns the properties of the social system and of the network of relations as a whole.[1] The term describes the impersonal configuration of linkages between people or units. In this article we use the concept of the structural dimension of social capital to refer to the overall pattern of connections between actors – that is, who you reach and how you reach them (Burt, 1992). Among the most important facets of this dimension are the presence or absence of network ties between actors (Scott, 1991; Wasserman & Faust, 1994); network configuration (Krackhardt, 1989) or morphology (Tichy, Tushman, & Fombrun, 1979) describing the pattern of linkages in terms of such measures as density, connectivity, and hierarchy; and appropriable organization – that is, the existence of networks created for one purpose that may be used for another (Coleman, 1988).

In contrast, the term "relational embeddedness" describes the kind of personal relationships people have developed with each other through a history of interactions (Granovetter, 1992). This concept focuses on the particular relations people have, such as respect and friendship, that influence their behavior. It is through these ongoing personal relationships that people fulfill such social motives as sociability, approval, and prestige. For example, two actors may occupy equivalent positions in similar network configurations, but if their personal and emotional attachments to other network members differ, their actions also are likely to differ in important respects. For instance, although one actor may choose to stay in a firm because of an attachment to fellow workers, despite economic advantages available elsewhere, another without such personal bonds may discount working relationships in making career moves. In this article we use the concept of the relational dimension of social capital to refer to those assets created and leveraged through relationships, and parallel to what Lindenberg (1996) describes as behavioral, as opposed to structural, embeddedness and what Hakansson and Snehota (1995) refer to as "actor bonds." Among the key facets in this cluster are trust and trustworthiness (Fukuyama, 1995; Putnam, 1993), norms and sanctions (Coleman, 1990; Putnam, 1995), obligations and expectations (Burt, 1992; Coleman, 1990; Granovetter, 1985; Mauss, 1954), and identity and identification (Hakansson & Snehota, 1995; Merton, 1968).

The third dimension of social capital, which we label the "cognitive dimension," refers to those resources providing shared representations, interpretations, and systems of meaning among parties (Cicourel, 1973). We have identified this cluster separately because we believe it represents an important set of assets not yet discussed in the mainstream literature on social capital but the significance of which is receiving substantial attention in the strategy domain (Conner & Prahalad, 1996; Grant, 1996; Kogut & Zander, 1992, 1996). These resources also represent facets of particular importance in the context of our consideration of intellectual capital, including shared language and codes (Arrow, 1974; Cicourel, 1973; Monteverde, 1995) and shared narratives (Orr, 1990).

Although social capital takes many forms, each of these forms has two characteristics in common: (1) they constitute some aspect of the social structure, and (2) they facilitate the actions of individuals within the structure (Coleman, 1990). First, as a social-structural resource, social capital inheres in the relations between persons and among persons. Unlike other forms of capital, social capital is owned jointly by the parties in a relationship, and no one player has, or is capable of having, exclusive ownership rights (Burt, 1992). Moreover, although it has value in use, social capital cannot be traded easily. Friendships and obligations do not readily pass from one person to another. Second, social capital makes possible the achievement of ends that would be impossible without it or that could be achieved only at extra cost.

In examining the consequences of social capital for action, we can identify two distinct themes. First, social capital increases the efficiency of action. For example, networks of social relations, particularly those charac-terized by weak ties or structural holes (i.e., disconnections or nonequival-encies among players in an arena), increase the efficiency of information diffusion through minimizing redundancy (Burt, 1992). Some have also suggested that social capital in the form of high levels of trust diminishes the probability of opportunism and reduces the need for costly monitoring processes. It thus reduces the costs of transactions (Putnam, 1993).

Whereas the first theme could be regarded as illustrative of what North (1990) calls "allocative efficiency," the second theme centers on the role of social capital as an aid to adaptive efficiency and to the creativity and learning it implies. In particular, researchers have found social capital to encourage cooperative behavior, thereby facilitating the development of new forms of association and innovative organization (Fukuyama, 1995; Jacobs, 1965; Putnam, 1993). The concept, therefore, is central to the understanding of institutional dynamics, innovation, and value creation.

We should note, however, that social capital is not a universally beneficial resource. As Coleman observes, "[A] given form of social capital that is useful for facilitating certain actions may be useless or harmful for others" (1990: 302). For example, the strong norms and mutual identification that may exert a powerful positive influence on group performance can, at the same time, limit its openness to information and to alternative ways of doing things, producing forms of collective blindness that sometimes have disastrous consequences (Janis, 1982; Perrow, 1984; Turner, 1976).

The main thesis of the work we have reviewed thus far is that social capital inheres in the relations between and among persons and is a productive asset facilitating some forms of social action while inhibiting others. Social relationships within the family and wider community have been shown to be an important factor in the development of human capital (Coleman, 1988). In a parallel argument we suggest that social relationships – and the social capital therein – are an important influence on the development of intellectual capital. In elaborating this argument, we focus on the firm as the primary context in which to explore the interrelationships between social and intellectual capital. Later in the article we consider how our analysis may be extended to a wider range of institutional settings.

Intellectual capital

Traditionally, economists have examined physical and human capital as key resources for the firm that facilitate productive and economic activity. However, knowledge, too, has been recognized as a valuable resource by economists. Marshall, for example, suggests that "capital consists in a great part of knowledge and organization. . . . [K]nowledge is our most powerful engine of production" (1965: 115). He goes on to note that "organization aids knowledge," a perspective also central to the work of Arrow (1974). More recently, Quinn has expressed a similar view, suggesting that "with rare exceptions, the economic and producing power of the firm lies more in its intellectual and service capabilities than its hard assets – land, plant and equipment. . . . [V]irtually all public and private enterprises – including most successful corporations – are becoming dominantly repositories and coordinators of intellect" (1992: 241).

In this article we use the term "intellectual capital" to refer to the knowledge and knowing capability of a social collectivity, such as an organization, intellectual community, or professional practice. We have elected to adopt this terminology because of its clear parallel with the concept of human capital, which embraces the acquired knowledge, skills, and capabilities that enable persons to act in new ways (Coleman, 1988). Intellectual capital thus represents a valuable resource and a capability for action based in knowledge and knowing.

This orientation to intellectual capital builds on some central themes and distinctions found in the substantial and expanding literature on knowledge and knowledge processes. Many of these themes have a long history in philosophy and Western thought, dating back to Plato, Aristotle, and Descartes. Two issues are of particular relevance to our consideration of the special advantage of organizations as an institutional context for the development of intellectual capital. These are, first, debates about the different types of knowledge that may exist and, second, the issue of the level of analysis in knowledge processes, particularly the question of whether social or collective knowledge exists and in what form.

Dimensions of intellectual capital

Types of knowledge. Arguably, the most persistent theme in writing about the nature of knowledge centers on the proposition that there are different types of knowledge. For example, a key distinction scholars frequently make is between practical, experience-based knowledge and the theoretical knowledge derived from reflection and abstraction from that experience – a distinction reminiscent of the debate of early philosophers between rationalism and empiricism (Giddens & Turner, 1987; James, 1950). Variously labeled "know-how" or "procedural knowledge," the former frequently is distinguished from know-that, know-what, or declarative knowledge

(Anderson, 1981; Ryle, 1949). It concerns well-practiced skills and routines, whereas the latter concerns the development of facts and propositions.[2]

Perhaps the most-cited and influential distinction of this sort is Polanyi's identification of two aspects of knowledge: tacit and explicit. This is a distinction he aligns with the "knowing how" and "knowing what" of Gilbert Ryle (Polanyi, 1967). Polanyi distinguishes tacit knowledge in terms of its incommunicability, and Winter (1987) has suggested that it may be useful to consider tacitness as a variable, with the degree of tacitness a function of the extent to which the knowledge is or can be codified and abstracted (see also Boisot, 1995). However, close reading of Polanyi indicates that he holds the view that some knowledge will always remain tacit. In so doing, he stresses the importance of *knowing*, as well as knowledge, and, in particular, the active shaping of experience performed in the pursuit of knowledge.[3] Discussing the practice of science, he observes that "science is operated by the skill of the scientist and it is through the exercise of this skill that he shapes his scientific knowledge" (Polanyi, 1962: 49). This suggests both a view of knowledge as object and of knowing as action or enactment in which progress is made through active engagement with the world on the basis of a systematic approach to knowing.

Levels of analysis in knowledge and knowing. Another equally fundamental cause for debate within philosophical and sociological circles centers on the existence, or otherwise, of particular phenomena at the collective level. That is, what is the nature of social phenomena that is different from the aggregation of individual phenomena (Durkheim, 1951; Gowler & Legge, 1982)? In the context of this article, the question concerns the degree to which it is possible to consider a concept of organizational, collective, or social knowledge that is different from that of individual organizational members.

Simon represents one extreme of the argument, stating that "all organizational learning takes place inside human heads; an organization learns in only two ways: (a) by the learning of its members, or (b) by ingesting new members who have knowledge the organization didn't previously have" (1991a: 176). In contrast, Nelson and Winter take a very different position, asserting that

> the possession of technical "knowledge" is an attribute of the firm as a whole, as an organized entity, and is not reducible to what any single individual knows, or even to any simple aggregation of the various competencies and capabilities of all the various individuals, equipments and installations of the firm (1982: 63).

A similar view is reflected in Brown and Duguid's (1991) analysis of communities of practice, in which shared learning is inextricably located in complex, collaborative social practices. Weick and Roberts (1993) also report research demonstrating collective knowing at the organizational level.[4] Our definition of intellectual capital reflects the second of these perspectives and acknowledges the significance of socially and contextually embedded forms of knowledge and knowing as a source of value differing from the simple aggregation of the knowledge of a set of individuals.

These two dimensions of explicit/tacit and individual/social knowledge have been combined by Spender (1996), who created a matrix of four different elements of an organization's intellectual capital. Individual explicit knowledge – what Spender labels "conscious knowledge" – is typically available to the individual in the form of facts, concepts, and frameworks that can be stored and retrieved from memory or personal records. The second element, individual tacit knowledge – what Spender labels "automatic knowledge" – may take many different forms of tacit knowing, including theoretical and practical knowledge of people and the performance of different kinds of artistic, athletic, or technical skills. Availability of people with such explicit knowledge and tacit skills clearly is an important part of an organization's intellectual capital and can be a key factor in the organization's performance, particularly in contexts where the performance of individual employees is crucial, as in specialist craft work (Cooke & Yanow, 1993).

The other two elements of an organization's intellectual capital are social explicit knowledge (what Spender calls "objectified knowledge") and social tacit knowledge ("collective knowledge," in Spender's terms). The former represents the shared corpus of knowledge – epitomized, for example, by scientific communities, and often regarded as the most advanced form of knowledge (Boisot, 1995). Across a wide range of organizations, we are currently witnessing major investments in the development of such objectified knowledge as firms attempt to pool, share, and leverage their distributed knowledge and intellect (Quinn, Anderson, & Finkelstein, 1996).

The latter represents the knowledge that is fundamentally embedded in the forms of social and institutional practice and that resides in the tacit experiences and enactment of the collective (Brown & Duguid, 1991). Such knowledge and knowing capacity may remain relatively hidden from individual actors but be accessible and sustained through their interaction (Spender, 1994). It is the type of knowledge frequently distinguishing the performance of highly experienced teams. This shared knowledge has been defined as "routines" by Nelson and Winter (1982), and it appears that much important organizational knowledge may exist in this form. For example, Weick and Roberts (1993) describe the complex, tacit, but heedful interrelating they observed between members of the flight operations team on aircraft carriers, which they suggest may characterize all high-reliability organizations.

For a given firm, these four elements collectively constitute its intellectual capital. Further, the elements are not independent, as Spender (1996) notes. However, in a stylized comparison of individuals working within an organization versus the same individuals working at arm's length across a hypothetical market (in the spirit of Conner and Prahalad's [1996] analysis), we use the two categories of social knowledge to provide the crux of our distinction: as Spender argues, "[C]ollective knowledge is the most secure and strategically significant kind of organizational knowledge" (1996: 52). Therefore, it is on the social explicit knowledge and the social tacit knowledge that we focus our analysis of organizational advantage. This is an important limitation of our theory because, by restricting the scope of our analysis only to social knowledge, we will be unable to capture the influences that explicit and tacit individual knowledge may have on the intellectual capital of the firm.

There is another important way in which we limit our analysis. The potential advantages of internal organization over market organization may arise from its superior abilities in both creating and exploiting intellectual capital (Kogut & Zander, 1993). We focus here only on the creation of intellectual capital and ignore the exploitation aspects. We have two reasons for imposing this constraint. First, comprehensive consideration of both processes would exceed the space available. Second, and more important, the benefits of intraorganizational exploitation of knowledge stem largely from missing, incomplete, or imperfect markets for such knowledge (Arrow, 1974; Teece, 1988; Williamson, 1975). Therefore, such advantages historically have been a part of the more traditional market-failure-based theories of the firm. Where we go beyond such theories is in our argument that internal organization may, within limits, be superior to market transactions for the creation of new knowledge.

The creation of intellectual capital

How is new knowledge created? Following Schumpeter (1934), Moran and Ghoshal (1996) have argued that all new resources, including knowledge, are created through two generic processes: namely, combination and exchange. While this argument is yet to be widely scrutinized, and although it is possible there may be still other processes for the creation of new knowledge (particularly at the individual level), we believe that these two, indeed, are among the key mechanisms for creating social knowledge; therefore, we adopt this framework for our purposes.

Combination and the creation of intellectual capital. Combination is the process viewed by Schumpeter as the foundation for economic development – "to produce means to combine materials and forces within our reach" (1934: 65) – and this perspective has become the starting point for much current work on organizations as knowledge systems (Boisot, 1995; Cohen & Levinthal, 1990; Kogut & Zander, 1992). In this literature scholars frequently identify two types of knowledge creation. First, new knowledge can be created through incremental change and development from existing knowledge. Schumpeter (1934), for example, talks of continuous adjustment in small steps, and March and Simon (1958) identify "localized search" and "stable heuristics" as the basis for knowledge growth. Within the philosophy of science, Kuhn (1970) sees development within the paradigm as the dominant mode of progression. Second, many authors also discuss more radical change: innovation, in Schumpeter's terms; double-loop learning, according to Argyris and Schon (1978); and paradigmatic change and revolution, according to Kuhn (1970). There appears to be a consensus that both types of knowledge creation involve making new combinations – incrementally or radically – either by combining elements previously unconnected or by developing novel ways of combining elements previously associated. "Development in our sense is then defined by the carrying out of new combinations" (Schumpeter, 1934: 66),[5] a view endorsed by the recent research of Leonard-Barton (1995).

Exchange and the creation of intellectual capital. Where resources are held by different parties, exchange is a prerequisite for resource combination. Since intellectual capital generally is created through a process of combining the knowledge and experience of different parties, it, too, is dependent upon exchange between these parties. Sometimes, this exchange involves the transfer of explicit knowledge, either individually or collectively held, as in the exchange of information within the scientific community or via the Internet. Often, new knowledge creation occurs through social interaction and coactivity. Zucker, Darby, Brewer, and Peng (1996) recently have shown the importance of collaboration for the development and acquisition of fine-grained collective knowledge in biotechnology. Their research endorses the significance of teamwork in the creation of knowledge, as identified much earlier by Penrose (1959). In developing her theory of the growth of the firm, Penrose proposed that a firm be viewed as "a collection of individuals who have had experience in working together, for only in this way can 'teamwork' be developed" (1959: 46).

There are many aspects to the learning embedded in such shared experience. They include the specific meanings and understandings subtly and extensively negotiated in the course of social interaction. Importantly, they also include an appreciation of the ways in which action may be coordinated. For, as Penrose observes, such experience

> develops an increasing knowledge of the possibilities for action and the ways in which action can be taken by . . . the firm. This increase in knowledge not only causes the productive opportunity of a firm to change . . . but also contributes to the "uniqueness" of the opportunity of each individual firm (1959: 53).

An interest in the ways in which such collective learning, especially concerning how to coordinate diverse production skills and to integrate several technology streams, has been at the heart of much recent discussion of core competence as the source of competitive advantage (Prahalad & Hamel, 1990) and is suggestive of the complex ways in which exchange contributes to the creation of intellectual capital.

The conditions for exchange and combination

In their analysis of value creation, Moran and Ghoshal (1996) identify three conditions that must be satisfied for exchange and combination of resources actually to take place. We believe that these conditions apply to the creation of new intellectual capital. In addition, however, we identify a fourth factor, which we regard as a prerequisite for the creation of intellectual capital.

The first condition is that the opportunity exists to make the combination or exchange. In our context we see this condition being determined by accessibility to the objectified and collective forms of social knowledge. A fundamental requirement for the development of new intellectual capital is that it is possible to draw upon and engage in the existing and differing knowledge and knowing activities of various parties or knowing communities (Boland & Tenkasi, 1995; Zucker et al., 1996). In the academic world the "invisible college" long has been recognized as an important social network giving valuable early access to distributed knowledge, facilitating its exchange and development, and thereby accelerating the advancement of science (Crane, 1972). Clearly, recent developments in technology, such as Lotus Notes and the Internet, have considerably increased the opportunities for knowledge combination and exchange. In addition, however, as the history of science demonstrates, the creation of new intellectual capital also may occur through accidental rather than planned combinations and exchanges, reflecting emergent patterns of accessibility to knowledge and knowledge processes.

Second, in order for the parties involved to avail themselves of the opportunities that may exist to combine or exchange resources, value expectancy theorists suggest that those parties must expect such deployment to create value. In other words, they must anticipate that interaction, exchange, and combination will prove worthwhile, even if they remain uncertain of what will be produced or how. Writing about the anticipated outcome of a conference of business practitioners and researchers, Slocum comments, "[E]ach of us expects to learn something of value as a result of our being here. None of us knows exactly what we are going to learn or what path we will take in the pursuit of this knowledge. We are confident, however, that the process works" (1994: ix). This anticipation of or receptivity to learning and new knowledge creation has been shown to be an important factor affecting the success or otherwise of strategic alliances (Hamel, 1991). It exemplifies Giddens' (1984) concept of intentionality as an influence on social action and, in so doing, also acknowledges the possibility that outcomes may turn out to be different from those anticipated.

The third condition for the creation of new resources highlights the importance of motivation. Even where opportunities for exchange exist and people anticipate that value may be created through exchange or interaction, those involved must feel that their engagement in the knowledge exchange and combination will be worth their while. Moran and Ghoshal (1996) see this as the expectation that the parties engaged in exchange and combination will be able to appropriate or realize some of the new value created by their engagement, even though, as noted previously, they may be uncertain about precisely what that value may be. For example, while having considerable potential, the availability of electronic knowledge exchange does not automatically induce a willingness to share information and build new intellectual capital. Quinn et al. (1996) found, in a study of Arthur Andersen Worldwide, that major changes in incentives and culture were required to stimulate use of its new electronic network, and they suggest that motivated creativity, which they describe as "care-why," is a fundamental influence in the creation of value through leveraging intellect. In his research on internal stickiness, Szulanski (1996) also found that lack of motivation may inhibit the transfer of best practice within the firm. However, Szulanski discovered that far more important as a barrier was the lack of capacity to assimilate and apply new knowledge.

Accordingly, we propose that there is a fourth precondition for the creation of new intellectual capital: combination capability. Even where the opportunities for knowledge exchange and combination exist, these opportunities are perceived as valuable, and parties are motivated to make such resource deployments or to engage in knowing activity, the capability to combine information or experience must exist. In their research on innovation, Cohen and Levinthal (1990) argue that the ability to recognize the value of new knowledge and information, but also to assimilate and use it, are all vital factors in organizational learning and innovation. Their work demonstrates that all of these abilities, which they label "absorptive capacity," depend upon the existence of related prior knowledge. Moreover, they suggest that an organization's absorptive capacity does not reside in any single individual but depends, crucially, on the links across a mosaic of individual capabilities – an observation that parallels Spender's (1996) discussion of collective knowledge.

Toward a theory of the creation of intellectual capital

By way of summary, we have argued the following. First, new intellectual capital is created through combination and exchange of existing intellectual resources, which may exist in the form of explicit and tacit knowledge and knowing capability. Second, there are four conditions that affect the deployment of intellectual resources and engagement in knowing activity involving combination and exchange. Third, in reviewing the burgeoning literature on knowledge and knowing, we have encountered much evidence in support of the view that the combination and exchange of knowledge are complex social processes and that much valuable knowledge is fundamentally socially embedded – in particular situations, in coactivity, and in relationships. As yet, we have uncovered no single theoretical framework that pulls together the various strands we can identify in this literature. For example, although a growing body of work exists in which scholars adopt an evolutionary perspective and identify the special capabilities of firms in the creation and transfer of tacit knowledge, this work has not yet produced a coherent theory explaining these special capabilities. Given the social embeddedness of intellectual capital, we suggest that such a theory is likely to be one that is primarily concerned with social relationships. Accordingly, we believe that social capital theory offers a potentially valuable perspective for understanding and explaining the creation of intellectual capital. It is to this theory we now return.

Social capital, exchange, and combination

Social capital resides in relationships, and relationships are created through exchange (Bourdieu, 1986). The pattern of linkages and the relationships built through them are the foundation for social capital. What we observe is a complex and dialectical process in which social capital is created and sustained through exchange and in which, in turn, social capital facilitates exchange. For example, there is mounting evidence demonstrating that where parties trust each other, they are more willing to engage in cooperative activity through which further trust may be generated (Fukuyama, 1995; Putnam, 1993; Tyler & Kramer, 1996). In social systems, exchange is the precursor to resource combination. Thus, social capital influences combination indirectly through exchange. However, we argue below that several facets of social capital, particularly those pertaining to the cognitive dimension, also have a direct influence on the ability of individuals to combine knowledge in the creation of intellectual capital. Although our primary objective is to explore the ways in which social capital influences the development of intellectual capital, we recognize that intellectual capital may, itself, facilitate the development of social capital. Thus, later in the article we consider how the coevolution of these two forms of capital may underpin organizational advantage.

The main thesis we develop here is that social capital facilitates the development of intellectual capital by affecting the conditions necessary for exchange and combination to occur. To explore this proposition, we now examine some of the ways in which each of the three dimensions of social capital influences the four conditions for resource exchange and combination we presented earlier. The specific relationships we identify are summarized in Figure 1.

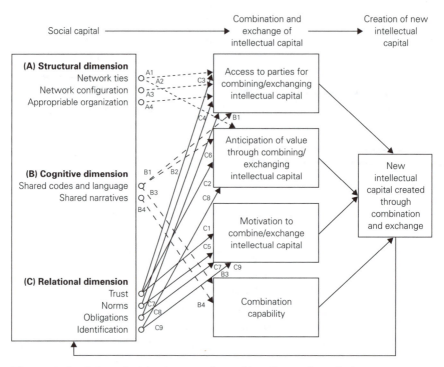

Figure 1 Social capital in the creation of intellectual capital

For the sake of clarity of exposition, we consider, in the following analysis, the impact of each dimension of social capital independently of the other dimensions. We recognize, however, that both the dimensions and the several facets of social capital are likely to be interrelated in important and complex ways. For example, particular structural configurations, such as those displaying strong symmetrical ties, have consistently been shown to be associated with such relational facets as interpersonal affect and trust (Granovetter, 1985; Krackhardt, 1992). Similarly, researchers have highlighted the often-complex interdependencies between social identification and shared vocabulary and language (Ashforth & Mael, 1995).

Moreover, not all dimensions of social capital are mutually reinforcing. For instance, an efficient network in structural terms may not be the best way to develop the strong relational or cognitive social capital that may be necessary to ensure the effective operation of such networks. Nohria and Eccles (1992), for example, highlight important differences between face-to-face and electronic exchange and propose that using electronically mediated exchange to help create a network organization requires more, not less, face-to-face communication. Our primary focus on the independent effects of these dimensions therefore limits the richness of the present exploration and identifies an important area for future work.

Exchange, combination, and the structural dimension of social capital

Our main argument in this section is that, within the context of the framework of combination and exchange adopted by us in this article, the structural dimension of social capital influences the development of intellectual capital primarily (though not exclusively) through the ways in which its various facets affect access to parties for exchanging knowledge and participating in knowing activities. While recognizing that the structural facets also may be systematically associated with other conditions for the exchange and combination of knowledge, we believe that these associations are primarily derived indirectly, through the ways in which structure influences the development of the relational and cognitive dimensions of social capital. For example, the strong, symmetrical ties frequently associated with the development of affective relationships (both positive and negative) may, in turn, influence individuals' motivation to engage in social interaction and, thereby, exchange knowledge (Krackhardt, 1992; Lawler & Yoon, 1996). Similarly, stable networks characterized by dense relations and high levels of interaction are conducive to the development of the different facets of the cognitive social capital we discuss in this article (Boisot, 1995; Orr, 1990).

Network ties. The fundamental proposition of social capital theory is that network ties provide access to resources. One of the central themes in the literature is that social capital constitutes a valuable source of information benefits (i.e., "who you know" affects "what you know"). Coleman (1988) notes that information is important in providing a basis for action but is costly to gather. However, social relations, often established for other purposes, constitute information channels that reduce the amount of time and investment required to gather information.

Burt (1992) suggests that these information benefits occur in three forms: access, timing, and referrals. The term "access" refers to receiving a valuable piece of information and knowing who can use it, and it identifies the role of networks in providing an efficient information-screening and -distribution process for members of those networks. Thus, network ties influence both access to parties for combining and exchanging knowledge (A1 in Figure 1) and anticipation of value through such exchange

(A2 in Figure 1). The operations of the invisible college provide an example of such networks.

"Timing" of information flows refers to the ability of personal contacts to provide information sooner than it becomes available to people without such contacts. This may well increase the anticipated value of such information (A2 in Figure 1), as demonstrated in research on job-seeking behavior (Granovetter, 1973). Such early access to information may be especially important in commercially oriented research and development, where speed to market may be a crucial factor in determining success.

"Referrals" are those processes providing information on available opportunities to people or actors in the network, hence influencing the opportunity to combine and exchange knowledge (A1 in Figure 1). They constitute a flow of information not only about possibilities but frequently include reputational endorsement for the actors involved – thereby influencing both the anticipated value of combination and exchange and the motivation for such exchange (see Granovetter, 1973, and Putnam, 1993). However, we believe that such reputational endorsement derives more from relational than structural factors, which we explore below.

Network configuration. Ties provide the channels for information transmission, but the overall configuration of these ties constitutes an important facet of social capital that may impact the development of intellectual capital. For example, three properties of network structure – density, connectivity, and hierarchy – are all features associated with flexibility and ease of information exchange through their impact on the level of contact or the accessibility they provide to network members (A3 in Figure 1; Ibarra, 1992; Krackhardt, 1989).

Burt (1992) notes that a player with a network rich in information benefits has contacts established in the places where useful bits of information are likely to air and who will provide a reliable flow of information to and from those places. While acknowledging the importance of trust and trustworthiness as a factor in the choice of contacts, Burt (1992) devotes much more attention to the efficiency of different relationship structures, arguing, in particular, that the sparse network, with few redundant contacts, provides more information benefits. The dense network is inefficient in the sense that it returns less diverse information for the same cost as that of the sparse network. The benefits of the latter, thus, derive from both the diversity of information and the lower costs of accessing it.

Jacobs (1965) and Granovetter (1973) have made similar arguments, identifying the role of "hop-and-skip" links and "loose ties" in information diffusion through communities. This aspect of diversity is very important, because it is well established that significant progress in the creation of intellectual capital often occurs by bringing together knowledge from disparate sources and disciplines. Networks and network structures, thus, represent facets of social capital that influence the range of information that may be accessed (A3 in Figure 1) and that becomes available for combination. As such, these structures constitute a valuable resource as channels or conduits for knowledge diffusion and transfer.

However, there are important limitations to the conduit model, in which meaning is viewed as unproblematic and in which the primary concern is with issues of information transfer. For example, Hansen (1996) has found that weak ties facilitate search but impede transfer, especially when knowledge is not codified. Thus, whereas networks having little redundancy may be both effective and efficient for the transfer of information whose meaning is relatively unproblematic, much richer patterns of relationship and interaction are important where the meaning of information is uncertain and ambiguous or where parties to an exchange differ in their prior knowledge. For example, Cohen and Levinthal (1990) have shown that some redundancy is necessary for the development of cross-functional absorptive capacity. Nonetheless, the general point remains that the configuration of the network is an important influence on the accessibility of information resources (A3 in Figure 1), although the appropriate level of redundancy is contingent on the degree to which the parties to knowledge exchange share a common knowledge base.

Appropriable organization. Social capital developed in one context, such as ties, norms, and trust, can often (but not always) be transferred from one social setting to another, thus influencing patterns of social exchange. Examples include the transfer of trust from family and religious affiliations into work situations (Fukuyama, 1995), the development of personal relationships into business exchanges (Coleman, 1990), and the aggregation of the social capital of individuals into that of organizations (Burt, 1992). This suggests that organizations created for one purpose may provide a source of valuable resources for other, different purposes (Nohria, 1992; Putnam, 1993, 1995). Such appropriable social organization can provide a potential network of access to people and their resources, including information and knowledge (A4 in Figure 1), and, through its relational and cognitive dimensions, may ensure motivation and capability for exchange and combination (see below). However, such organization also may inhibit such processes; indeed, research demonstrates how organizational routines may separate rather than coordinate groups within organizations, constraining rather than enabling learning and the creation of intellectual capital (Dougherty, 1996; Hedberg, 1981).

Exchange, combination, and the cognitive dimension of social capital

Earlier in this article, we defined intellectual capital as the knowledge and knowing capability of a social collectivity. This reflects our belief that, fundamentally, intellectual capital is a social artifact and that knowledge and meaning are always embedded in a social context – both created and sustained through ongoing relationships in such collectivities. Although scholars widely recognize that innovation generally occurs through combining different knowledge and experience and that diversity of opinion is a way of expanding knowledge, meaningful communication – an essential part of social exchange and combination processes – requires at least some sharing of context between the parties to such exchange (Boisot, 1995; Boland & Tenkasi, 1995; Campbell, 1969). We suggest that this sharing may come about in two main ways: (1) through the existence of shared language and vocabulary and (2) through the sharing of collective narratives. Further, we suggest that these two elements constitute facets of shared cognition that facilitate the creation of intellectual capital especially through their impact on combination capability. In each case they do so by acting as both a medium and a product of social interaction.

Shared language and codes. There are several ways in which a shared language influences the conditions for combination and exchange. First, language has a direct and important function in social relations, for it is the means by which people discuss and exchange information, ask questions, and conduct business in society. To the extent that people share a common language, this facilitates their ability to gain access to people and their information. To the extent that their language and codes are different, this keeps people apart and restricts their access (B1 in Figure 1).

Second, language influences our perception (Berger & Luckman, 1966; Pondy & Mitroff, 1979). Codes organize sensory data into perceptual categories and provide a frame of reference for observing and interpreting our environment. Thus, language filters out of awareness those events for which terms do not exist in the language and filters in those activities for which terms do exist. Shared language, therefore, may provide a common conceptual apparatus for evaluating the likely benefits of exchange and combination (B2 in Figure 1).

Third, a shared language enhances combination capability (B3 in Figure 1). Knowledge advances through developing new concepts and narrative forms (Nonaka & Takeuchi, 1995). However, as we noted previously, in order to develop such concepts and to combine the information gained through social exchange, the different parties must have some overlap in knowledge. Boland and Tenkasi (1995) identify the importance of both perspective taking and perspective making in knowledge creation, and they demonstrate how the existence of a shared vocabulary enables the combining of information. We suggest it is for all these reasons that researchers increasingly recognize group-specific communication codes as a valuable asset within firms (Arrow, 1974; Kogut & Zander, 1992; Monteverde, 1995; Prescott & Visscher, 1980).

Shared narratives. Beyond the existence of shared language and codes, researchers have suggested that myths, stories, and metaphors also provide powerful means in communities for creating, exchanging, and preserving rich sets of meanings – a view long held by some social anthropologists (Clark, 1972; Nisbet, 1969). Recently, Bruner (1990) proposed that there are two different modes of cognition: (1) the information or paradigmatic mode and (2) the narrative mode. The former suggests a process of knowledge creation rooted in rational analysis and good arguments; the latter is represented in synthetic narratives, such as fairy tales, myths and legends, good stories, and metaphors. According to Bateson (1972), metaphors cut across different contexts, thus enabling the combining of both imaginative and literal observations and cognitions. Orr (1990) demonstrates how narrative in the form of stories, full of seemingly insignificant details, facilitates the exchanging of practice and tacit experience between technicians, thereby enabling the discovery and development of improved practice. The emergence of shared narratives within a community thus enables the creation and transfer of new interpretations of events, doing so in a way that facilitates the combination of different forms of knowledge, including those largely tacit (B4 in Figure 1).

Exchange, combination, and the relational dimension of social capital

Much of the evidence for the relationship between social capital and intellectual capital highlights the significance of the relational dimension of social capital. Szulanski (1996) has found that one of the important barriers to the transfer of best practice within organizations is the existence of arduous relations between the source and the recipient. Whereas we have argued that the structural dimension has its primary direct impact on the condition of accessibility, and the cognitive dimension through its influence on accessibility and combination capability, research suggests that the relational dimension of social capital influences three of the conditions for exchange and combination in many ways. These are access to parties for exchange, anticipation of value through exchange and combination, and the motivation of parties to engage in knowledge creation through exchange and combination.

Trust. Misztal defines trust as the belief that the "results of somebody's intended action will be appropriate from our point of view" (1996: 9–10). A substantial body of research now exists (Fukuyama, 1995; Gambetta, 1988; Putnam, 1993, 1995; Ring & Van de Ven, 1992, 1994; Tyler & Kramer, 1996) that demonstrates where relationships are high in trust, people are more willing to engage in social exchange in general, and cooperative interaction in particular (Cl in Figure 1). Mishira (1996) argues that trust is multidimensional and indicates a willingness to be vulnerable to another party – a willingness arising from confidence in four aspects: (1) belief in the good intent and concern of exchange partners (Ouchi, 1981; Pascale, 1990; Ring & Van de Ven, 1994), (2) belief in their competence and capability (Sako, 1992; Szulanski, 1996), (3) belief in their reliability (Giddens, 1990; Ouchi, 1981), and (4) belief in their perceived openness (Ouchi, 1981).

Misztal observes that "trust, by keeping our mind open to all evidence, secures communication and dialogue" (1996: 10), suggesting thereby that trust may both open up access to people for the exchange of intellectual capital (C3 in Figure 1) and increase anticipation of value through such exchanges (C2 in Figure 1). One can find support for this view in research demonstrating that where there are high levels of trust, people are more willing to take risks in such exchange (Nahapiet, 1996; Ring & Van de Ven, 1992). This may represent an increased willingness to experiment with combining different sorts of information. For example, Luhmann (1979) has shown trust to increase the potential of a system for coping with complexity and, thus, diversity – factors known to be important in the development of new intellectual capital. Trust may also indicate greater openness to the potential for value creation through exchange and combination (C2 in Figure 1). Boisot highlights the importance of interpersonal trust for knowledge creation in contexts of high ambiguity and uncertainty: "[W]hen the message is uncodified, trust has to reside in the quality of the personal relationships that bind the parties through shared values and expectations rather than the intrinsic plausibility of the message" (1995: 153).

As we noted earlier, there is a two-way interaction between trust and cooperation: trust lubricates cooperation, and cooperation itself breeds trust. This may lead to the development, over time, of generalized norms of cooperation, which increase yet further the willingness to engage in social exchange (Putnam, 1993). In this respect, collective trust may become a potent form of "expectational asset" (Knez & Camerer, 1994) that group members can rely on more generally to help solve problems of cooperation and coordination (Kramer, Brewer, & Hanna, 1996).

Norms. According to Coleman (1990), a norm exists when the socially defined right to control an action is held not by the actor but by others. Thus, it represents a degree of consensus in the social system. Coleman suggests that "where a norm exists and is effective, it constitutes a powerful though sometimes fragile form of social capital" (1988: S104). Norms of cooperation can establish a strong foundation for the creation of intellectual capital. Becoming, in effect, "expectations that bind" (Kramer & Goldman, 1995), such norms may be a significant influence on exchange processes, opening up access to parties for the exchange of knowledge (C4 in Figure 1) and ensuring the motivation to engage in such exchange (C5 in Figure 1; Putnam, 1993).

For example, Starbuck (1992) notes the importance of social norms of openness and teamwork as key features of knowledge-intensive firms; he highlights the significance of the emphasis on cooperation rather than competition, on open disclosure of information, and on building loyalty to the firm as significant underpinnings of the success of the American law firm Wachtell, Lipton, Rosen and Katz, which specializes in advice on nonroutine, challenging cases. Other norms of interaction that have been shown to be important in the creation of intellectual capital include a willingness to value and respond to diversity, an openness to criticism, and a tolerance of failure (Leonard-Barton, 1995). Such norms may offset the tendency to "groupthink" that may emerge in strong, convergent groups and that represents the way in which high levels of social capital may be a real inhibitor for the development of intellectual capital (Janis, 1982). At the same time, as Leonard-Barton (1995) has shown, norms also may have a dark side; those capabilities and values initially seen as a benefit may become, in time, a pathological rigidity.

Obligations and expectations. Obligations represent a commitment or duty to undertake some activity in the future. Coleman (1990) distinguishes obligations from generalized norms, viewing the former as expectations developed within particular personal relationships. He suggests that obligations operate as a "credit slip" held by A to be redeemed by some performance by B – a view reminiscent of Bourdieu's (1986) concept of credential we referred to earlier in this article. In the context of the creation of intellectual capital, we suggest that such obligations and expectations are likely to influence both access to parties for exchanging and combining knowledge (C6 in Figure 1) and the motivation to combine and exchange such knowledge (C7 in Figure 1). The notion that "there is no such thing as a free lunch" represents a commonly held view that exchange brings with it expectations about future obligations – a view explicated in detail by Mauss (1954), Bourdieu (1977), and Cheal (1988). Fairtlough (1994) ascribes considerable importance to the formal, professional, and personal obligations that develop between those involved in cooperative research and development projects between different organizations:

> People in the two companies could rely on each other. . . . This was cooperation which certainly went beyond contractual obligations. It might also have gone beyond enlightened self interest, and beyond good professional behaviour, because the scientists liked working together, felt committed to the overall project and felt a personal obligation to help the others involved (1994: 119).

Identification. Identification is the process whereby individuals see themselves as one with another person or group of people. This may result from their membership in that group or through the group's operation as a reference group, "in which the individual takes the values or standards of other individuals or groups as a comparative frame of reference" (Merton, 1968: 288; see also Tajfel, 1982). Kramer et al. (1996) have found that identification with a group or collective enhances concern for collective processes and outcomes, thus increasing the chances that the opportunity for exchange will be recognized. Identification, therefore, acts as a resource influencing both the anticipation of value to be achieved through combination and exchange (C8 in Figure 1) and the motivation to combine and exchange knowledge (C9 in Figure 1). We find support for this in the research of Lewicki and Bunker (1996), whose evidence suggests that salient group identification may not only increase the perceived opportunities for exchange but also may enhance the actual frequency of cooperation. In contrast, where groups have distinct and contradictory identities, these may constitute significant barriers to information sharing, learning, and knowledge creation (Child & Rodrigues, 1996; Pettigrew, 1973; Simon & Davies, 1996).

Thus far, we have argued that social capital theory provides a powerful basis for understanding the creation of intellectual capital in general. The various specific links we have proposed are summarized in Figure 1. In the next section we suggest that the theory also provides a basis for understanding the nature of organizational advantage since firms, as institutions, are likely to be relatively well endowed with social capital.

Social capital, intellectual capital, and the organizational advantage

The last 20 years have witnessed a substantial resurgence of interest in the theory of the firm. During this period, those espousing transaction cost approaches became increasingly influential, positing, at their simplest, that the existence of firms can be explained in terms of market failure and the greater ability of firms, through hierarchy, to reduce the costs of transactions in particular (and relatively restricted) circumstances (Williamson, 1975, 1981, 1985). The transaction cost theory of the firm has proved robust and has been applied across a wide range of issues, but it has also become subject to growing criticism for a range of definitional, methodological, and substantive reasons (see, for example, Conner & Prahalad, 1996, and Pitelis, 1993). More fundamentally, as we noted at the outset of this article, researchers now are seeking to develop a theory of the firm that is expressed in positive terms (Kogut & Zander, 1996; Masten, Meehan, & Snyder, 1991; Simon, 1991b) – away from a market-failure framework to one grounded in the concept of organizational advantage (Moran & Ghoshal, 1996).

Increasingly, the special capabilities of organizations for creating and transferring knowledge are being identified as a central element of organizational advantage. We suggest that social capital theory provides a sound basis for explaining why this should be the case. First, organizations as institutional settings are characterized by many of the factors known to be conducive to the development of high levels of social capital. Second, it is the coevolution of social and intellectual capital that underpins organizational advantage.

Organizations as institutional settings are conducive to the development of social capital

Social capital is owned jointly by the parties to a relationship, with no exclusive ownership rights for individuals. Thus, it is fundamentally concerned with resources located within structures and processes of social exchange; as such, the development of social capital is significantly affected by those factors shaping the evolution of social relationships. We discuss four such conditions here: time, interaction, interdependence, and closure. We argue that all four are more characteristic of internal organization than of market organization as represented in neoclassical theory and that, as a result, organizations as institutional settings are conducive to the development of high levels of social capital relative to markets. However, as we subsequently note, in practice these conditions may also occur in some forms of interorganizational networks, thereby enabling such networks to become relatively well endowed with social capital.

Time and the development of social capital. Like other forms of capital, social capital constitutes a form of accumulated history – here reflecting investments in social relations and social organization through time (Bourdieu, 1986; Granovetter, 1992). Time is important for the development of social capital, since all forms of social capital depend on stability and continuity of the social structure. The concept of embedding fundamentally means the binding of social relations in contexts of time and space (Giddens, 1990). Coleman highlights the importance of continuity in social relationships:

> One way in which the transactions that make up social action differ from those of the classical model of a perfect market lie in the role of time. In a model of a perfect market, transactions are both costless and instantaneous. But in the real world, transactions are consummated over a period of time (1990: 91).

For example, since it takes time to build trust, relationship stability and durability are key network features associated with high levels of trust and norms of cooperation (Axelrod, 1984; Granovetter, 1985; Putnam, 1993; Ring & Van de Ven, 1992). The duration and stability of social relations also influence the clarity and visibility of mutual obligations (Misztal, 1996).

Although, in the main, social capital is created as a by-product of activities engaged in for other purposes, intentional or constructed organization represents a direct, purposeful investment in social capital

(Coleman, 1990, 1993). "These organizations ordinarily take the form of authority structures composed of positions connected by obligations and expectations and occupied by persons" (Coleman 1990: 313). In contrast to the short-term transactions characterizing the markets of neoclassical theory, intentional or constructed organization represents the creation and maintenance of an explicit and enduring structure of ties constituting, through organizational design, a configuration of relationships and resources usable for a variety of purposes – both formal and informal. Moreover, this commitment to continuity facilitates the other processes known to be influential in the development of social capital: interdependence, interaction, and closure.

Interdependence and the development of social capital. Coleman (1990) states that social capital is eroded by factors that make people less dependent upon each other. This appears especially so for the relational dimension of social capital. For example, expectations and obligations are less significant where people have alternative sources of support. Indeed, Misztal (1996) has suggested that the recent resurgence of interest in trust can be explained by the increasingly transitional character of our present condition and the erosion of social interdependence and solidarity. Yet, most authors agree that high levels of social capital usually are developed in contexts characterized by high levels of mutual interdependence.

Whereas markets as institutional arrangements are rooted in the concept of autonomy (and institutional economists largely neglect interdependence between exchange parties; Zajac & Olsen, 1993), firms fundamentally are institutions designed around the concepts and practices of specialization and interdependence and differentiation and integration (Lawrence & Lorsch, 1967; Smith, 1986; Thompson, 1967). Interdependence – and the coordination it implies – long has been recognized as perhaps the key attribute of business organization (Barnard, 1938). Follet goes so far as to suggest that

> the fair test of business administration, of industrial organization, is whether you have a business with all its parts so co-ordinated, so moving together in their closely knit and adjusting activities, so linking, interlocking and inter-relating, that they make a working unit, not a congerie of separate pieces (1949: 61).

Such interdependence provides the stimulus for developing many organizationally embedded forms of social capital. For example, through providing the opportunity to create contexts characterized by the condition of interdependent viability – that is, the requirement that exchanges are positive in outcome for the system overall rather than for each individual member of the system – organizations considerably extend the circle of exchange that takes place among their members (Coleman, 1993; Moran & Ghoshal, 1996), thereby increasing social identification and encouraging norms of cooperation and risk taking.

Interaction and the development of social capital. Social relationships generally, though not always, are strengthened through interaction but die out if not maintained. Unlike many other forms of capital, social capital increases rather than decreases with use. Interaction, thus, is a precondition for the development and maintenance of dense social capital (Bourdieu, 1986). In particular, as we noted already, scholars have shown that the cognitive and relational dimensions of social capital accumulate in network structures where linkages are strong, multidimensional, and reciprocal – features that characterize many firms but that rarely surface in pure market forms of organization. Discussing the development of language, Boland and Tenkasi note that it is "through action within communities of knowing that we make and remake both our language and our knowledge" (1995: 353). According to these authors, such communities must have space for conversation, action, and interaction in order for the codes and language to develop that facilitate the creation of new intellectual capital.

In a different context Boissevain (1974) shows how multiplex relations are more intimate than single-stranded relationships, therefore providing more accessibility and more response to pressure than single-stranded relations. Such relations typically are imbued with higher levels of obligation between network members, as well as trust-based norms (Coleman, 1990). Further, Powell (1996) argues that norm-based conceptions of trust miss the extent to which cooperation is buttressed by sustained contact, regular dialogue, and constant monitoring. He adds that, without mechanisms and institutions to sustain such conversations, trust does not ensue (see also Coleman, 1990). This echoes Bourdieu's earlier emphasis on the fundamental need for "an unceasing effort of sociability" (1986: 250) for the reproduction of social capital in its many forms.

In neoclassical theory, markets as institutional settings are epitomized by impersonal, arm's length, spot transactions. Firms, in contrast, provide many opportunities for sustained interaction, conversations, and sociability – both by design and by accident. Formal organizations explicitly are designed to bring members together in order to undertake their primary task, to supervise activities, and to coordinate their activities, particularly in contexts requiring mutual adjustment (Mintzberg, 1979; Thompson, 1967), change, and innovation (Burns & Stalker, 1961; Galbraith, 1973). Through copresence (Giddens, 1984), colocation (Fairtlough, 1994), and the creation of such processes as routine choice opportunities (March & Olsen, 1976), organizations also create a myriad of contexts and occasions for the more-or-less planned coming together of people and their ideas. Finally, the literature is replete with evidence that organizational life is characterized by a substantial amount of conversation: in meetings, conferences, and social events that fill the everyday life of workers and managers (Mintzberg, 1973; Prescott & Visscher, 1980; Roy, 1960). Together, these can be viewed as collective investment strategies for the institutional creation and maintenance of dense networks of social relationships and for the resources embedded within, available through, and derived from such networks of relationships. Alternatively, these meetings and social events provide the unplanned and unstructured opportunities for the accidental coming together of ideas that may lead to the serendipitous development of new intellectual capital.

Closure and the development of social capital. Finally, there is much evidence that closure is a feature of social relationships that is conducive to the development of high levels of relational and cognitive social capital. Strong communities – the epitome of systems of dense social capital – have "identities that separate and a sense of sociological boundary that distinguishes members from nonmembers" (Etzioni, 1996: 9; see also Bourdieu, 1986). The development of norms, identity, and trust has been shown to be facilitated by network closure (Coleman, 1990; Ibarra, 1992), and the development of unique codes and language is assisted by the existence of community separation (Boland & Tenkasi, 1995). Formal organizations, by definition, imply a measure of closure through the creation of explicit legal, financial, and social boundaries (Kogut & Zander, 1996). Markets, in contrast, represent open networks that benefit from the freedom offered to individual agents but that have less access to the relational and cognitive facets of social capital.

The coevolution of social and intellectual capital underpins organizational advantage

Our main argument thus far has been that social capital is influential in the development of new intellectual capital and that organizations are institutional settings conducive to the development of social capital. We have noted the significant and growing body of work that indicates organizations have some particular capabilities for creating and sharing knowledge, giving them their distinctive advantage over other institutional arrangements, such as markets. We now pull the strands of our analysis together by proposing that it is the interaction between social and intellectual capital that underpins organizational advantage.

Although our primary aim has been to suggest that social capital influences the development of intellectual capital, we recognize that the pattern of influence may be in the other direction. The view that shared knowledge forms the basis from which social order and interaction flow is a central theme in sociology, exemplified in the work of Berger and Luckman (1966) and Schutz (1970). Within organizational analysis, authors long have suggested that the firm's particular knowledge about how activities are to be coordinated underpins its capability to develop and operate as a social system (Kogut & Zander, 1992, 1996; March & Simon, 1958; Penrose, 1959; Thompson, 1967). We represent the influence of intellectual capital on social capital as a feedback relationship in Figure 1. More important, however, we believe that it is the coevolution of social and intellectual capital that is of particular significance in explaining the source of organizational advantage.

Earlier in the article we noted the dialectical process by which social capital is both created and sustained through exchange and, in turn, enables such exchange to take place. As Berger and Luckman observe,

> The relationship between man, the producer, and the social world, his product, is and remains a dialectical one. That is, man (not, of course, in isolation but in his collectivities) and his social world interact with each other. The product acts back upon the producer (1966: 78; see also Bourdieu, 1977).

Giddens, too, examines the self-reproducing quality of social practices, noting that social activities are recursive – that is, "continually recreated by actors via the very means by which they express themselves *as* actors" (1984: 2). For Giddens this implies a concept of human knowledgeability that underpins all social practice.

The discussion of knowledgeability that ensues suggests the reciprocal quality of the relationship between social and intellectual capital and is consistent with our emphasis on the social embeddedness of both forms of capital. Since both social and intellectual capital develop within and derive their significance from the social activities and social relationships within which they are located, their evolutionary paths are likely to be highly interrelated.

Consideration of the reciprocal relationship between knowledge and its social context permeates the sociology of science (Zuckerman, 1988). Mullins (1973), for example, describes the joint evolution of social interaction, communication networks, and the elaboration of scientific ideas and notes that cognitive development is facilitated by the thickening of communication networks, which then leads to their further elaboration. Research within organizations offers many parallel examples (Burns & Stalker, 1961; Leonard-Barton, 1995; Weick, 1995; Zucker et al., 1996). For instance, in a study of change in health administration, Nahapiet (1988) describes, in detail, how a new accounting calculus both shaped and was, in turn, shaped by the social context in which it was embedded.

Discussing Orr's (1990) influential ethnography of service technicians, Brown and Duguid (1991) provide further insight into this coevolution of knowledge and relationships. Specifically, they describe how technicians achieve two distinct forms of social construction. First, through their work, and "through cultivating connections throughout the corporation" (Brown & Duguid, 1991: 67), technicians engage in the ongoing creation and negotiation of shared understanding – an understanding that represents their view of the world, that is their collective knowledge. The second form of social construction, which, according to Brown and Duguid, is also important but less evident, is the creation of a shared identity. "In telling these stories an individual rep contributes to the construction and development of his or her own identity as a rep and reciprocally to the construction and development of the community of reps in which he or she works" (Brown & Duguid, 1991: 68). In an analysis reminiscent of Weick and Roberts' (1993) discussion of collective mind – itself located in processes of interrelating – these authors highlight the mutually dependent and interactive ways in which social and intellectual capital coevolve.

We suggest that this emphasis on the coevolution of the two forms of capital provides a dynamic perspective on the development of organizational advantage. Spender (1996) argues that it is the collective forms of knowledge that are strategically important, and many authors claim that it is these forms of shared tacit knowledge that underpin what we have termed the "organizational advantage." It is these collective forms of knowledge, we believe, that are particularly tightly interconnected with the relational and cognitive forms of social capital with which, we have argued, organizations are relatively well endowed. Organizations, thus, build and retain their advantage through the dynamic and complex interrelationships between social and intellectual capital.

Discussion and implications

The view of organizational advantage we present here is fundamentally a social one. We see the roots of intellectual capital deeply embedded in social relations and in the structure of these relations. Such a view contrasts strongly with the relatively individualistic and acontextual perspectives that characterize more transactional approaches for explaining the existence and contribution of firms. Although we have identified several ways in which facets of social capital may, indeed, reduce transaction costs by economizing on information and coordination costs, we believe that our theoretical propositions go much farther in identifying those factors underpinning dynamic efficiency and growth.

In so doing, we note that our arguments are consistent with resource-based theory in so far as that theory highlights the competitive advantage of firms as based in their unique constellation of resources: physical, human, and organizational (Barney, 1991). Those resources found to be especially valuable are those that are rare, durable, imperfectly imitable, and nontradable (Barney, 1991; Dierickx & Cool, 1989). Among the factors making a resource nonimitable are tacitness (Reed & DeFillippi, 1990), causal ambiguity (Lippman & Rumelt, 1992), time compression diseconomies, and interconnectedness (Dierickx & Cool, 1989), as well as path dependence and social complexity (Barney, 1991; Reed & DeFillippi, 1990). All of these are features integral to the facets of social capital and to its interrelationships with intellectual capital. Thus, we suggest that differences between firms, including differences in performance, may represent differences in their ability to create and exploit social capital. Moreover, at least regarding the development of intellectual capital, those firms developing particular configurations of social capital are likely to be more successful. Evidence for this suggestion is found in studies of knowledge-intensive firms that have been shown to invest heavily in resources, including physical facilities, to encourage the development of strong personal and team relationships, high levels of personal trust, norm-based control, and strong connections across porous boundaries (Alvesson, 1991, 1992; Starbuck, 1992, 1994; Van Maanen & Kunda, 1989). The framework developed here will provide a useful basis for further testing these propositions about firm differences.

In developing our thesis, we have noted several limitations in our approach. First, regarding social capital, our analysis has concentrated primarily, although not exclusively, on how social capital assists the creation of new intellectual capital. However, we recognize that social capital also may have significant negative consequences. For example, certain norms may be antagonistic rather than supportive of cooperation, exchange, and change. Moreover, organizations high in social capital may become ossified through their relatively restricted access to diverse sources of ideas and information. But the general point underpinning our analysis is that institutions facilitate some forms of exchange and combination but limit their scope (Ghoshal & Moran, 1996); thus, effective organization requires a constant balancing of potentially opposing forces (Boland & Tenkasi, 1995; Etzioni, 1996; Leonard-Barton, 1995).

Furthermore, the creation and maintenance of some forms of social capital, particularly the relational and cognitive dimensions, are costly. The development of social capital thus represents a significant investment – conscious or unconscious – and, like all such investments, requires an understanding of the relative costs and benefits likely to be derived from such investment. These are likely to be influenced by the size and complexity of the social structure in which social capital is embedded, since the costs of maintaining linkages usually increase exponentially as a social network increases in size. Although technology may make it possible to stretch the conventional limits of networks of social capital, our arguments about the significance of interdependence, interaction, and closure suggest that there still remain important upper limits. Indeed, adding people to the network may serve to reduce certain forms of social capital, such as personal obligations or high status.

Finally, although we have responded to Putnam's challenge to progress our understanding of the various dimensions and facets of social capital, in our analysis we largely have considered these dimensions separately. Of great interest is the interrelationships among the three dimensions and, indeed, among the various facets within each dimension. We regard this as an important focus for future research.

Second, regarding intellectual capital, we have concentrated on just one aspect: its creation, rather than its diffusion and exploitation. A fuller understanding of knowledge as the source of organizational advantage will require an examination of the ways in which social capital may influence these important and complementary processes. We believe that the framework we develop here provides a sound basis for such examination. Also, we have focused very much on the types and processes of intellectual capital rather than its content – that is, the know-how rather than the know-what. Clearly, the specific knowledge content, including its quality, are important factors to be considered when attempting to gain an understanding of the effective creation of intellectual capital.

Third, our exploration of organizational advantage began with the proposition that knowledge and knowledge processes are major foundations of such advantage. However, our discussion of the coevolution of social and intellectual capital potentially enriches this understanding of organizational advantage in important ways. For instance, our analysis elucidates resource creation within networks, concentrating particularly on the interrelated development of social and intellectual capital as key resources. As such, it is suggestive of the processes whereby organizational networks create value and that, perhaps, underpin their advantage. More generally, we believe that a detailed understanding of social capital itself may be an important element in extending our understanding of the significant, but as yet inadequately understood, concept of organizational advantage. However, we could not explore such issues in this article, and we recognize that much work still needs to be done to elaborate both the concept of organizational advantage and the significance of social capital therein.

Fourth and finally, we have developed our thesis about the relationships between social and intellectual capital in the context of exploring and explaining the source of organizational advantage – that is, we have made the argument regarding these interrelationships within one type of boundary: the firm. It is our view that structures of social capital fundamentally are relatively bounded, and these boundaries typically come from some external physical or social basis for grouping, such as a geographic community (Jacobs, 1965; Putnam, 1993), the family (Coleman, 1988; Loury, 1977), religion (Coleman, 1990), or class (Bourdieu, 1977). As we noted earlier, social capital is typically a by-product of other activities; thus, its development requires a "focus": an entity around which joint activities are organized (Nohria, 1992) and which forms the basis for a level of network closure.

However, our analysis of the conditions conducive to the development of social capital suggests that wherever institutions operate in contexts characterized by enduring relationships – with relatively high levels of interdependence, interaction, and closure – we would expect to see these institutions emerge with relatively dense configurations of social capital. We have argued that these conditions typically occur more within organizations than in neoclassical markets, but they may also be found in particular forms of interorganizational relationship (Baker, 1990; Hakansson & Snehota, 1995; Larson, 1992; Powell, 1996;

Ring & Van de Ven, 1992, 1994). Therefore, we see the potential to extend our fundamental analysis to other institutional settings, including those existing between organizations.

Bourdieu (1993) argues that, by making the concept of social capital explicit, it is possible to focus rigorously on the intuitively important concept of "connections" and to establish the basis for research designed to identify the processes for social capital's creation, accumulation, dissipation, and consequence. The concept also provides a theoretical justification for the study of many social practices, such as the "social round," popularly recognized as important but frequently ignored in formal research. In particular, for Bourdieu, systematic analysis of the volume and structure of social capital enables examination of the relationships between social and other forms of capital.

In identifying the interrelationship between social and intellectual capital, we have made a similar argument. That is, by defining the concepts and developing clear propositions about their interrelationships, we have established an agenda for future research that both complements and extends existing knowledge-based theories of the firm. Moreover, we suggest that the model outlined here also provides the foundation of a viable framework to guide the investments – individual or collective – of practitioners seeking to build or extend their network of connections and, therefore, their stocks of social capital. As Bourdieu observes, "[T]he existence of connections is not a natural given, or even a social given . . . it is the product of an endless effort at institution" (1986: 249).

Janine Nahapiet is a fellow of strategic management at Templeton College, Oxford University, and Director of the Oxford Institute of Strategic and International Management. Her current research focuses on the links between strategy and organization in global firms and on value creation through networks. She has a postgraduate diploma in management from the London School of Economics and a first degree in psychology and sociology from the University of Sheffield, England.

This research was supported in part by a grant from the Sundridge Park Research Fund. We are grateful to John Stopford, Peter Moran, Morten Hansen, Richard Pascale, Max Boisot, Wen-Pin Tsai, Nitin Nohria, Paul Willman, Anthony Hopwood, Tim Ambler, Martin Waldenstrom, and three anonymous referees for their helpful comments on earlier drafts of this article and in discussions of its subject matter.

This paper appeared in *Academy of Management Review*, April 1998.

NOTES

1. We recognize that this terminology deviates from much that is customary in the field of network analysis. In particular, the focus of network analysis is relational data, but included under its heading are attributes that we label structural here. Scott, for example, describes network analysis as being concerned with "the contacts, ties and connections, the group attachments and meetings which relate one agent to another. . . . These relations connect pairs of agents to larger relational systems" (1991: 3). However, we justify our usage both through reference to Granovetter and because we believe this terminology captures well the personal aspect of this dimension.

2. To this recent authors have added the concept of know-why (Hamel, 1991; Kogut & Zander, 1992).

3. Indeed, his much-referenced chapter, in which he introduces the tacit dimension, is entitled "Tacit Knowing," not "tacit knowledge."

4. See also Walsh's (1995) comprehensive discussion of organizational cognition.

5. In their theory of the knowledge-creating company, Nonaka and Takeuchi define combination as "a process of systematizing concepts into a knowledge system. This mode of knowledge conversion involves combining different bodies of explicit knowledge" (1995: 67). They prefer to use different terms for those forms of conversion involving tacit knowledge. However, following Polanyi (1967), we believe that all knowledge processes have a tacit dimension and that, fundamentally, the same generic processes underlie all forms of knowledge conversion. Therefore, our usage of the term "combination" in this context is more general and is rooted in our view of intellectual capital as embracing both the explicit knowledge and the tacit knowing of a collective and its members. Our view, thus, resembles more closely the concept of combinative capabilities discussed by Kogut and Zander (1992).

REFERENCES

Alvesson, M. 1991. Corporate culture and corporatism at the company level: A case study. *Economic and Industrial Democracy*, 12: 347–367.

Alvesson, M. 1992. Leadership as a social integrative action. A study of a computer consultancy company. *Organization Studies*, 13: 185–209.

Anderson, J.R. 1981. *Cognitive skills and their acquisition*. Hillsdale, NJ: Lawrence Erlbaum Associates.

Argyris, C., & Schon, D. 1978. *Organizational learning: A theory of action perspective*. Reading, MA: Addison-Wesley.

Arrow, K. 1974. *The limits of organization*. New York: Norton.

Ashforth, B.E., & Mael, F.A. 1995. *Organizational identity and strategy as a context for the individual*. Paper presented at the Conference on the Embeddedness of Strategy, University of Michigan, Ann Arbor.

Axelrod, R. 1984. *The evolution of co-operation*. New York: Basic Books.

Baker, W. 1990. Market networks and corporate behavior. *American Journal of Sociology*, 96: 589–625.

Barnard, C.I. 1938. *The functions of the executive*. Cambridge, MA: Harvard University Press.

Barney, J. 1991. Firm resources and sustained competitive advantage. *Journal of Management*, 17: 99–120.

Bateson, G. 1972. *Steps to an ecology of mind*. New York: Ballantine Books.

Berger, P.L., & Luckman, T. 1966, *The social construction of reality*. London: Penguin Press.

Boisot, M. 1995. *Information space: A framework for learning in organizations, institutions and culture*. London: Routledge.

Boissevain, J. 1974. *Friends of friends*. Oxford: Basil Blackwell.

Boland, R.J., & Tenkasi, R.V. 1995. Perspective making and perspective taking in communities of knowing. *Organization Science*, 6: 350–372.

Bourdieu, P. 1977. *Outline of a theory of practice*. Cambridge, England: Cambridge University Press.

Bourdieu, P. 1986. The forms of capital. In J.G. Richardson (Ed.), *Handbook of theory and research for the sociology of education*: 241–258. New York: Greenwood.

Bourdieu, P. 1993. *Sociology in question*. London: Sage.

Brown, J.S., & Duguid, P. 1991. Organizational learning and communities-of-practice: Toward a unified view of working, learning and innovation. *Organization Science*, 2: 40–57.

Bruner, J.S. 1990. *Acts of meaning*. Cambridge, MA: Harvard University Press.

Burns, T., & Stalker, G. 1961. *The management of innovation*. London: Tavistock.

Burt, R.S. 1992. *Structural holes: The social structure of competition*. Cambridge, MA: Harvard University Press.

Campbell, D.T. 1969. Ethnocentricism of disciplines and the fish-scale model of omniscience. In M. Sherif & C. Sherif (Eds.), *Interdisciplinary relationships in the social sciences*: 328–348. Chicago: Aldine.

Cheal, D. 1988. *The gift economy*. London: Routledge.

Child, J., & Rodrigues, S. 1996. The role of social identity in the international transfer of knowledge through joint ventures. In S.R. Clegg & G. Palmer (Eds.), *The politics of management knowledge*: 46–68. London: Sage.

Cicourel, A.V. 1973. *Cognitive sociology*. Harmondsworth, England: Penguin Books.

Clark, B.R. 1972. The occupational saga in higher education. *Administrative Science Quarterly*, 17: 178–184.

Cohen, W.M., & Levinthal, D.A. 1990. Absorptive capacity: A new perspective on learning and innovation. *Administrative Science Quarterly*, 35: 128–152.

Coleman, J.S. 1988. Social capital in the creation of human capital. *American Journal of Sociology*, 94: S95–S120.

Coleman, J.S. 1990. *Foundations of social theory*. Cambridge, MA: Belknap Press of Harvard University Press.

Coleman, J.S. 1993. Properties of rational organizations. In S.M. Lindenberg & H. Schreuder (Eds.), *Interdisciplinary perspectives on organization studies*: 79–90. Oxford, England: Pergamon Press.

Conner, K.R., & Prahalad, C.K. 1996. A resource-based theory of the firm: Knowledge versus opportunism. *Organization Science*, 7: 477–501.

Cooke, S.D.N., & Yanow, D. 1993. Culture and organizational learning. *Journal of Management Inquiry*, 2: 373–390.

Crane, D. 1972. *Invisible colleges: Diffusion of knowledge in scientific communities.* Chicago: University of Chicago Press.

D'Aveni, R.A., & Kesner, I. 1993. Top managerial prestige, power and tender offer response: A study of elite social networks and target firm cooperation during takeovers. *Organization Science*, 4: 123–151.

Dierickx, I., & Cool, K. 1989. Asset stock accumulation and sustainability of competitive advantage. *Management Science*, 35: 1504–1511.

Dougherty, D. 1996. Interpretive barriers to successful product innovation in large firms. In J.R. Meindl, C. Stubbart, & J.F. Porac (Eds.), *Cognition within and between organizations*: 307–340. Thousand Oaks, CA: Sage.

Durkheim, E. 1951. (First published in 1897.) *Suicide: A study in sociology.* New York: Free Press.

Etzioni, A. 1996. The responsive community: A communitarian perspective. *American Sociological Review*, 61: 1–11.

Fairtlough, G. 1994. *Creative compartments: A design for future organization.* London: Adamantine Press.

Follet, M.P. 1949. Coordination. In L. Urwick (Ed.), *Freedom and co-ordination: Lectures in business organization*: 61–76. London: Management Publications Trust.

Fukuyama, F. 1995. *Trust: Social virtues and the creation of prosperity.* London: Hamish Hamilton.

Galbraith, J. 1973. *Designing complex organizations.* Reading, MA: Addison-Wesley.

Gambetta, D. (Ed.). 1988. *Trust: Making and breaking cooperative relations.* Oxford, England: Basil Blackwell.

Ghoshal, S., & Moran, P. 1996. Bad for practice: A critique of the transaction cost theory. *Academy of Management Review*, 21: 13–47.

Giddens, A. 1984. *The constitution of society: Outline of a theory of structuration.* Cambridge, England: Polity Press.

Giddens, A. 1990. *The consequences of modernity.* Cambridge, England: Polity Press.

Giddens, A., & Turner, J. (Eds.). 1987. *Social theory today.* Cambridge, England: Polity Press.

Gowler, D., & Legge, K. 1982. The integration of disciplinary perspectives and levels of analysis in problem-oriented research. In N. Nicholson & T. Wall (Eds.), *The theory and practice of organizational psychology*: 69–101. London: Academic Press.

Granovetter, M.S. 1973. The strength of weak ties. *American Journal of Sociology*, 78: 1360–1380.

Granovetter, M.S. 1985. Economic action and social structure: The problem of embeddedness. *American Journal of Sociology*, 91: 481–510.

Granovetter, M.S. 1992. Problems of explanation in economic sociology. In N. Nohria & R. Eccles (Eds.), *Networks and organizations: Structure, form and action*: 25–56. Boston: Harvard Business School Press.

Grant, R.M. 1996. Knowledge, strategy and the theory of the firm. *Strategic Management Journal*, 17(S2): 109–122.

Hakansson, H., & Snehota, I. 1995. *Developing relationships in business networks.* London: Routledge.

Hamel, G. 1991. Competition for competence in inter-partner learning within international strategic alliances. *Strategic Management Journal*, 12: 83–103.

Hansen, M. 1996. *Using the wisdom of others: Searching for and transferring knowledge*. Presentation at the London Business School.

Hedberg, B. 1981. How organizations learn and unlearn. In P.C. Nystrom & W.H. Starbuck (Eds.), *Handbook of organizational design*, vol. 1: 3–27. Oxford, England: Oxford University Press.

Ibarra, H. 1992. Structural alignments, individual strategies, and managerial action: Elements toward a network theory of getting things done. In N. Nohria & R.G. Eccles (Eds.), *Networks and organizations: Structure, form and action*: 165–188. Boston: Harvard Business School Press.

Jacobs, J. 1965. *The death and life of great American cities*. London: Penguin Books.

James, W. 1950. *The principles of psychology*, vols. I and II. New York: Dover Publications.

Janis, I.L. 1982. *Groupthink: Psychological studies of policy decisions and fiascos*. Boston: Houghton Mifflin.

Knez, M., & Camerer, C. 1994. Creating expectational assets in the laboratory: Coordination in "weakest link" games. *Strategic Management Journal*, 15: 101–119.

Kogut, B., & Zander, U. 1992. Knowledge of the firm, combinative capabilities and the replication of technology. *Organization Science*, 3: 383–397.

Kogut, B., & Zander, U. 1993. Knowledge of the firm and the evolutionary theory of the multinational corporation. *Journal of International Business Studies*, 24: 625–645.

Kogut, B., & Zander, U. 1995. Knowledge, market failure and the multinational enterprise: A reply. *Journal of International Business Studies*, 26: 417–426.

Kogut, B., & Zander, U. 1996. What do firms do? Coordination, identity and learning. *Organization Science*, 7: 502–518.

Krackhardt, D. 1989. *Graph theoretical dimensions of informal organization*. Paper presented at the annual meeting of the Academy of Management, Washington, DC.

Krackhardt, D. 1992. The strength of strong ties. In N. Nohria & R.G. Eccles (Eds.), *Networks and organizations: Structure, form and action*: 216–239. Boston: Harvard Business School Press.

Kramer, R.M., Brewer, M.B., & Hanna, B.A. 1996. Collective trust and collective action: The decision to trust as a social decision. In R.M. Kramer & T.R. Tyler (Eds.), *Trust in organizations. Frontiers of theory and research*: 357–389. Thousand Oaks, CA: Sage.

Kramer, R.M., & Goldman, L. 1995. Helping the group or helping yourself? Social motives and group identity in resource dilemmas. In D.A. Schroeder (Ed.), *Social dilemmas*: 49–68. New York: Praeger.

Kuhn, T.S. 1970. *The structure of scientific revolutions* (2nd ed.). Chicago: University of Chicago Press.

Larson, A. 1992. Network dyads in entrepreneurial settings: A study of the governance of exchange relations. *Administrative Science Quarterly*, 37: 76–104.

Lawler, E.J., & Yoon, J. 1996. Commitment in exchange relations: Test of a theory of relational cohesion. *American Sociological Review*, 61: 89–108.

Lawrence, P.R., & Lorsch, J.W. 1967. *Organization and environment: Managing differentiation and integration*. Boston: Division of Research, Graduate School of Business Administration, Harvard University.

Leonard-Barton, D. 1995. *Wellsprings of knowledge: Building and sustaining the sources of innovation.* Boston: Harvard Business School Press.

Lewicki, R.J., & Bunker, B.B. 1996. Developing and maintaining trust in work relationships. In R.M. Kramer & T.M. Tyler (Eds.), *Trust in organizations: Frontiers of theory and research:* 114–139. Thousand Oaks, CA: Sage.

Lindenberg, S. 1996. Constitutionalism versus relationalism: Two views of rational choice sociology. In J. Clark (Ed.), *James S. Coleman:* 229–311. London: Falmer Press.

Lippman, S.A., & Rumelt, R.P. 1982. Uncertain imitability: An analysis of interfirm differences in efficiency under competition. *Bell Journal of Economics,* 13: 418–438.

Loasby, B. 1991. *Equilibrium and evolution: An exploration of connecting principles in economics.* Manchester, England: Manchester University Press.

Loury, G.C. 1977. A dynamic theory of racial income differences. In P.A. Wallace & A.M. LaMonde (Eds.), *Women, minorities and employment discrimination:* 153–186. Lexington, MA: Lexington Books.

Loury, G. 1987. Why should we care about group inequality? *Social Philosophy & Policy,* 5: 249–271.

Luhmann, N. 1979. *Trust and power.* Chichester, England: Wiley.

March, J.G., & Olsen, J.P. 1976. *Ambiguity and choice in organizations.* Bergen: Universitetsforlaget.

March, J.G., & Simon, H.A. 1958. *Organizations.* New York: Wiley.

Marshall, A. 1965. *Principles of economics.* London: Macmillan.

Masten, S.E., Meehan, J.W., & Snyder, E.A. 1991. The costs of organization. *Journal of Law, Economics, and Organization,* 7: 1–25.

Mauss, M. 1954. *The gift.* New York: Free Press.

Merton, R.K. 1968. (First published in 1948.) *Social theory and social structure.* New York: Free Press.

Mintzberg, H. 1973. *The nature of managerial work.* New York: Harper & Row.

Mintzberg, H. 1979. *The structuring of organizations.* Englewood Cliffs, NJ: Prentice-Hall.

Mishira, A.K. 1996. Organizational responses to crisis. The centrality of trust. In R.M. Kramer & T.M. Tyler (Eds.), *Trust in organizations:* 261–287. Thousand Oaks, CA: Sage.

Misztal, B. 1996. *Trust in modern societies.* Cambridge, England: Polity Press.

Monteverde, K. 1995. *Applying resource-based strategic analysis: Making the model more accessible to practitioners.* Working Paper No. 95-1, Department of Management and Information Systems, St. Joseph's University, Philadelphia.

Moran, P., & Ghoshal, S. 1996. Value creation by firms. In J.B. Keys & L.N. Dosier (Eds.), *Academy of Management Best Paper Proceedings:* 41–45.

Mullins, N. 1973. *Theories and theory groups in contemporary American sociology.* New York: Harper & Row.

Nahapiet, J.E. 1988. The rhetoric and reality of an accounting change: A study of resource allocation in the NHS. *Accounting, Organizations and Society,* 13: 333–358.

Nahapiet, J.E. 1996. *Managing relationships with global clients: Value creation through cross-border networks.* Paper presented at the 16th Annual Conference of the Strategic Management Society, Phoenix, AZ.

Nelson, R.R., & Winter, S.G. 1982. *An evolutionary theory of economic change.* Boston: Belknap Press of Harvard University Press.

Nisbet, R.A. 1969. *Social change and history: Aspects of the western theory of development*. London: Oxford University Press.

Nohria, N. 1992. Information and search in the creation of new business ventures. In N. Nohria & R.G. Eccles (Eds.), *Networks and organizations: Structure, form and action*: 240–261. Boston: Harvard Business School Press.

Nohria, N., & Eccles, R.G. 1992. Face-to-face: Making network organizations work. In N. Nohria & R.G. Eccles (Eds.), *Networks and organizations: Structure, form and action*: 288–308. Boston: Harvard Business School Press.

Nonaka, I., & Takeuchi, H. 1995. *The knowledge creating company*. New York: Oxford University Press.

North, D.C. 1990. *Institutions, institutional change and economic performance*. Cambridge, England: Cambridge University Press.

Orr, J. 1990. Sharing knowledge, celebrating identity: Community memory in a service culture. In D. Middleton & D. Edwards (Eds.), *Collective remembering*: 169–189. London: Sage.

Ouchi, W.G. 1981. *Theory Z: How American business can meet the Japanese challenge*. Reading, MA: Addison-Wesley.

Pascale, R. 1990. *Managing on the edge: How the smartest companies use conflict to stay ahead*. New York: Simon and Schuster.

Penrose, E. 1959. *The theory of the growth of the firm*. Oxford, England: Basil Blackwell.

Perrow, C. 1984. *Normal accidents*. New York: Basic Books.

Pettigrew, A.M. 1973. *The politics of organizational decision making*. London: Tavistock.

Pitelis, C. 1993. Transaction costs, markets and hierarchies: The issues. In C. Pitelis (Ed.), *Transaction costs, markets and hierarchies*: 7–19. Oxford, England: Basil Blackwell.

Polanyi, M. 1962. (First published in 1958.) *Personal knowledge: Towards a post-critical philosophy*. London: Routledge and Kegan Paul.

Polanyi, M. 1967. (First published in 1966.) *The tacit dimension*. London: Routledge and Kegan Paul.

Pondy, L.R., & Mitroff, I.I. 1979. Beyond open systems models of organizations. In B.M. Staw (Ed.), *Research in Organization Behavior*, vol. 1: 3–39. Greenwich, CT: JAI Press.

Powell, W.W. 1996. Trust based form of governance. In R.M. Kramer & T.R. Tyler (Eds.), *Trust in organizations: Frontiers of theory and research*: 51–67. Thousand Oaks, CA: Sage.

Prahalad, C.K., & Hamel, G. 1990. The core competence of the organization. *Harvard Business Review*, 68: 79–91.

Prescott, E.C., & Visscher, M. 1980. Organization capital. *Journal of Political Economy*, 88: 446–461.

Putnam, R.D. 1993. The prosperous community: Social capital and public life. *American Prospect*, 13: 35–42.

Putnam, R.D. 1995. Bowling alone: America's declining social capital. *Journal of Democracy*, 6: 65–78.

Quinn, J.B. 1992. *Intelligent enterprise*. New York: Free Press.

Quinn, J.B., Anderson, P., & Finkelstein, S. 1996. Leveraging intellect. *Academy of Management Executive*, 10: 7–27.

Reed, R., & DeFillippi, R.J. 1990. Causal ambiguity, barriers to imitation and sustainable competitive advantage. *Academy of Management Review*, 15: 88–102.

Ring, P.S., & Van de Ven, A.H. 1992. Structuring cooperative relationships between organizations. *Strategic Management Journal*, 13: 483–498.

Ring, P.S., & Van de Ven, A.H. 1994. Developmental processes of cooperative inter-organizational relationships. *Academy of Management Review*, 19: 90–118.

Roy, D.F. 1960. Banana time: Job satisfaction and informal interaction. *Human Organization*, 18: 156–168.

Ryle, G. 1949. *The concept of mind*. London: Hutchinson.

Sako, M. 1992. *Prices, quality and trust: Inter-firm relations in Britain and Japan*. New York: Cambridge University Press.

Schumpeter, J.A. 1934. (Reprinted in 1962.) *The theory of economic development: An inquiry into profits, capital, credit, interest and the business cycle*. Cambridge, MA: Harvard University Press.

Schutz, A. 1970. *On phenomenology and social relations*. Chicago: University of Chicago Press.

Scott, J. 1991. *Social network analysis: A handbook*. London: Sage.

Simon, H.A. 1991a. Bounded rationality and organizational learning. *Organization Science*, 2: 125–134.

Simon, H.A. 1991b. Organizations and markets. *Journal of Economic Perspectives*, 5(2): 25–44.

Simon, L., & Davies, G. 1996. A contextual approach to management learning. *Organization Studies*, 17: 269–289.

Slocum, K.R. 1994. Foreword. In G. von Krogh & J. Roos (Eds.), *Organizational epistemology*: ix. Basingstoke, England: Macmillan.

Smith, A. 1986. (First published in 1776.) *The wealth of nations*, books I–III. London: Penguin Books.

Spender, J.-C. 1994. Knowing, managing and learning: A dynamic managerial epistemology. *Management Learning*, 25: 387–412.

Spender, J.-C. 1996. Making knowledge the basis of a dynamic theory of the firm. *Strategic Management Journal*, 17(S2): 45–62.

Starbuck, W.H. 1992. Learning by knowledge intensive firms. *Journal of Management Studies*, 29: 713–740.

Starbuck, W.H. 1994. Keeping a butterfly and elephant in a house of cards: The elements of exceptional success. *Journal of Management Studies*, 30: 885–922.

Szulanski, G. 1996. Exploring internal stickiness: Impediments to the transfer of best practice within the firm. *Strategic Management Journal*, 17(S2): 27–44.

Tajfel, H. (Ed.). 1982. *Social relations and intergroup relations*. Cambridge, MA: Cambridge University Press.

Teece, D.J. 1988. Technological change and the nature of the firm. In G. Dosi, C. Freeman, R. Nelson, G. Silverberg, & L. Soete (Eds.), *Technical change and economic theory*: 256–281. New York: Pinter.

Thompson, J.D. 1967. *Organizations in action*. New York: McGraw-Hill.

Tichy, N.M., Tushman, M.L., & Fombrun, C. 1979. Social network analysis for organizations. *Academy of Management Review*, 4: 507–519.

Turner, B.A. 1976. The organizational and interorganizational development of disasters. *Administrative Science Quarterly*, 21: 378–397.

Tyler, T.R., & Kramer, R.M. 1996. Whither trust? In R.M. Kramer & T.R. Tyler (Eds.), *Trust in organizations: Frontiers of theory and research*: 1–15. Thousand Oaks, CA: Sage.

Van Maanen, J., & Kunda, G. 1989. Real feelings: Emotional expression and organizational culture. *Research in organizational behavior*, vol. 11: 43–103. Greenwich, CT: JAI Press.

Walsh, J.P. 1995. Managerial and organizational cognition: Notes from a trip down memory lane. *Organization Science*, 6: 280–321.

Wasserman, S., & Faust, K. 1994. *Social network analysis: Methods and applications.* Cambridge, England: Cambridge University Press.

Weick, K.E. 1995. *Sensemaking in organizations.* London: Sage.

Weick, K.E., & Roberts, K.H. 1993. Collective mind in organizations: Heedful interrelating on flight decks. *Administrative Science Quarterly*, 38: 357–381.

Williamson, O.E. 1975. *Markets and hierarchies: Analysis and antitrust implications.* New York: Free Press.

Williamson, O.E. 1981. The economics of organization: The transaction cost approach. *American Journal of Sociology*, 87: 548–577.

Williamson, O.E. 1985. *The economic institutions of capitalism.* New York: Free Press.

Winter, S.G. 1987. Knowledge and competence as strategic assets. In D.J. Teece (Ed.), *The competitive challenge: Strategy for industrial innovation and renewal*: 159–184. New York: Harper & Row.

Zajac, E.J., & Olsen, C.P. 1993. From transaction cost to transactional value analysis: Implications for the study of interorganizational strategies. *Journal of Management Studies*, 30: 131–146.

Zander, U., & Kogut, B. 1995. Knowledge and the speed of transfer and imitation of organizational capabilities: An empirical test. *Organization Science*, 6: 76–92.

Zucker, L.G., Darby, M.R., Brewer, M.B., & Peng, Y. 1996. Collaboration structures and information dilemmas in biotechnology: Organization boundaries as trust production. In R.M. Kramer & T.R. Tyler (Eds.), *Trust in organizations: Frontiers of theory and research*: 90–113. Thousand Oaks, CA: Sage.

Zuckerman, H. 1988. The sociology of science. In N.J. Smelser (Ed.), *Handbook of sociology*: 511–574. Beverly Hills, CA: Sage.

CHAPTER 11

Radical performance improvement is possible

Sumantra Ghoshal, Gita Piramal, and Christopher Bartlett

This is adapted from the opening chapter from Sumantra's book Managing Radical Change, *coauthored with Gita Piramal and Chris Bartlett. The book was written for Indian managers, and it blends many of Sumantra's existing ideas and frameworks with new case studies of Indian companies that have achieved dramatic improvements in their performance. The authors begin by showing how many firms get stuck in a rut called* satisfactory underperformance. *They then argue that dramatic improvement in performance is possible, regardless of a firm's existing position. It does not matter if your industry is unattractive, shrinking, or dominated by larger competitors – and it does not matter if your leaders lack charisma – there is always a way you can generate a radical change in your firm's performance.*

We learnt more about corporate leadership and change management in a single morning in February 1989 than it is possible to learn from reading any number of books and articles.

The top management group of a multi-billion dollar European giant – let us call it Semco – had gathered for their annual two-day retreat. Held every year in the same location, the retreat was an opportunity for the senior most 50 people, including the CEO and all board members, to catch up with one another, and to take stock of the overall situation of the company. One of the two mornings had been scheduled for a review of the company's strategy, and one of us had been asked to facilitate

Table 1 Semco's relative performance

	Semco	General Electric	Matsushita
1. Sales per Employee	$88,471	$184,534	$215,223
2. Inventory to Sales	27.4%	12.4%	14.5%
3. Sales to net fixed assets	3.0%	3.4%	6.7%
4. Operating margin	2.9%	9.5%	7.6%
5. Return on equity	3.9%	18.9%	7.4%

discussions in that session. Indeed, the HR Director of Semco had been very specific in his brief: "No lectures, please – just help us think about our overall corporate strategy."

How can you review the "overall corporate strategy" of a company that operates in over ten distinctly different businesses, with over 3000 products produced and sold in 100 countries around the world – all in one brief morning session?

After considerable thought, we settled on a very simple – to our mind, almost simplistic – way to begin the discussions. We compared Semco's performance in the preceding year with that of two roughly comparable companies, General Electric and Matsushita – with whom it competed in several different businesses. Lacking the resources and information for any elaborate or sophisticated benchmarking, we picked the easiest numbers from all three companies' annual reports. The comparisons looked as shown in Table 1.

In that memorable morning, we put up this comparison right at the beginning, and asked "gentlemen" – all men in the group, no women – "These numbers appear to us to be a good starting point for a review of your corporate strategy. What are you going to do about this situation?"

For us, what followed was education for a lifetime. What followed was a long and vigorous argument as to why "our" numbers were either wrong or irrelevant.

The people in the room were seasoned experts – in their own areas of specialization, they had forgotten more than we could ever hope to learn. So, their arguments were intellectually unassailable. How could we compare their performance with that of Matsushita for a year when, as everyone knew, the yen was severely undervalued and most of the key European currencies including their own were equally severely overvalued? How could their returns be compared with those of an American and a Japanese company when both America and Japan had well developed and competitive component suppliers while Europe did not, forcing

Semco to continue with the capital intensive and low return component businesses to ensure the reliability and quality of its final products? How could we be so simple-minded as to overlook the dramatic differences in wage rates and labor productivity across the U.S., Japan and Europe – and could they, as managers of a European company, do anything about the leisure-loving decadence of European labor? Were the European governments not to blame, rather than corporate managers?

The Finance Director of a large division of the company made a long speech about accounting norms and standards: "If you took into account the differences between the Japanese and our methods of accounting, you would see that our ROE, if we accounted like the Japanese, would be closer to 4.3%!"

There were other kinds of arguments, too. Was business all about making money? Did a company not have other responsibilities? Why were we looking at only the simplest financial figures, ignoring all the other priorities? Also, the Japanese were obsessive people. In Europe people were not like that at all. Everything in Europe was at 5%: inflation was 5%, unemployment was 5%, growth was 5%. The implications were that if only we understood Europe better, we would not be wasting their time with such silly numbers.

Some readers may find this story amusing, given the abysmal performance of Semco the numbers reveal, but ask, were those people in the room stupid? Prestigious and established global corporations do not hire stupid people; in fact, they hire the best and the brightest around the world. And then, only the very best of these hires ascend to the top ranks of the hierarchy. There are too many checks and balances in these companies for stupid people to reach the top. There were no stupid people in the room.

Then, why did they react as they did? Why could they not see how poor their performance was, compared to that of their key competitors? Why did they find it so hard to confront that simple reality, without which they could not even begin a discussion on how they could improve that performance?

The pathology of satisfactory underperformance

The answer to these questions, we have since learnt, is very simple. It lies in a corporate disease called satisfactory underperformance. It is a pervasive disease – we have confronted it in companies all over the

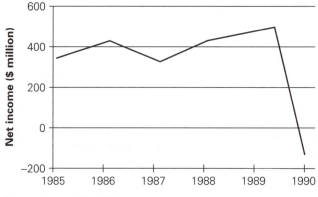

Figure 1 Semco's profitability

world. It is a disease that is very easy to catch – indeed, finding a way to avoid it is the unnatural act.

Consider the case of Semco. The graph in Figure 1 shows its performance in the second half of the 1980s. Our encounter with its senior managers took place in early 1989. At that point, what were these managers seeing?

First, they were seeing an annual profit of about $400 million. 400 million dollars is a lot of money; for anyone. So, they were seeing that the company was making a lot of money. They were not seeing that the profits were a pathetic 4% of equity, nor were they seeing that given their cost of capital of over 11%, at that rate of profit, they were destroying value every year. They were not seeing that their profit margins were worse than practically risk-free bank returns. One does not naturally "see" these things – they are too intellectual, too abstract, too remote. Besides they were also seeing that their profits that year were higher than the profits of the preceding year; indeed, higher than their profits for the three preceding years. They were not seeing that in each of those years, and in the three earlier ones, they had been systematically destroying value, which is why their stock prices were doing so badly.

What was even more remarkable for us was the fact that, deep in their hearts, all the 50 managers in the room knew that they were performing very poorly. You could take any one of them aside, on a one-to-one basis, and they would honestly admit that given their strengths in technology, people, brands, distribution and so on, the results were poor. Yet, they would never acknowledge that reality in any collective forum. Individually, they knew the truth; collectively, they would conspire together to deny the truth.

For established companies, the truth is relatively easy to deny. Often their competitive strengths erode rapidly, as it had done for Semco. But the company continues to make money – because of all the resources it has, in terms of an established customer base, a historically developed distribution channel, strong brands, and so on. All these resources would have been built by earlier generations of managers, yet the incumbent management takes credit for all the returns these resources generate, never asking the question: "What are we doing to add value?" The crisis ultimately comes, as it did for Semco when it fell off the precipice towards the end of 1989. But, before the crisis hits, there is often a long period when the company can coast along in a state of satisfactory under-performance, assigning all uncomfortable signs to factors in the external environment, beyond management control; and finding rationalizations on the one hand, and reducing ambition on the other hand, so as to maintain satisfaction in the face of declining fortunes.

The dynamics of satisfactory underperformance

There is a highly predictable process through which the pathology of satisfactory underperformance takes hold of a company (see Figure 2).

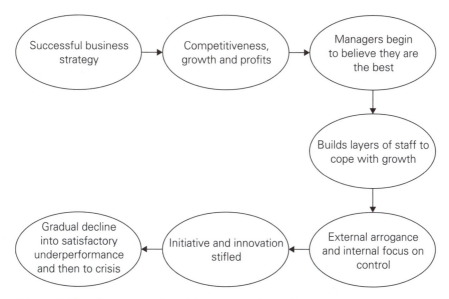

Figure 2 The dynamics of satisfactory underperformance

By luck, chance or foresight and courage, a company develops an effective and successful business strategy. The strategy fits the market demands, and matches the company's strengths. As a result, the company becomes highly competitive with growth and profits as the ensuing rewards.

With growth and profits come recognition and celebration. Top managers of the company start seeing their faces on the covers of business journals. The Harvard Business School writes a case on their success. Soon they start believing all that is being said of them – they are the best. It is their brilliance that caused it all. They go on the lecture circuit to tell others how they did it – despite all the adversity.

With growth comes the perceived need for better control. After all, if they did it all, then they must continue to do it all, to protect the success and build on it. As the company becomes bigger, to do it all they need support to collect all the information, to bring all the important choices and decisions to them. So, they hire layers of staff, as instruments to leverage their own brilliance in the expanded organization. The staff joins the business press in telling them how good they are, and it all becomes a positive reinforcement cycle.

Being the best gives these managers the right to be arrogant, not only internally with their subordinates, but also externally with customers and suppliers: "Why make a fuss if some little thing goes wrong? Don't you understand what a privilege you have, dealing with the best?"

External arrogance and a focus on internal control soon stifles all initiative and enthusiasm at the operating levels of the company. Those who can manage the politics progress, those who side with customers or employees or raise uncomfortable questions are seen as obstacles and are soon sidelined or, better still, pushed overboard. Arrogance leads to hierarchy, to bureaucracy and, ultimately, to staleness and passivity. No one rocks the boat; compliance and fear take over from enthusiasm and passion. Gradually the company slips first into satisfactory underperformance and, finally, into acute crisis.

Satisfactory underperformance is pervasive in India

While there are some exceptions, satisfactory underperformance is pervasive in corporate India. We confronted its full force in a senior management program a few years ago.

In the room were about 35 managers from different Indian companies, belonging to both the private and the public sectors. Some were from multinational subsidiaries. All of them occupied very senior positions, including three who were CEOs. A number of them represented organizations that are household names in the country.

"How satisfied do you feel with your company's performance over the last three years?" we asked them. We focused on the word "satisfied" to tap into their honest feelings. We put up a simple 5-point scale, in which 1 represented "complete dissatisfaction" and 5 indicated "total satisfaction." "Total satisfaction does not mean that everything is perfect and all that needed to be done has been done," we explained. "All it means is that the company is dealing with the right issues and making progress in the right direction at the right speed." Complete dissatisfaction stood for the opposite. We asked all the managers to pick their satisfaction scores – not for the part of the company they worked for, but for the overall company.

The responses followed a predictable near-normal distribution with a skew to the right. 21 managers gave their companies a 3: there were nine 4's, and five 2's. No one rated his or her company either 1 or 5.

"Now," we asked them, "What does a 3 mean for you? After all, if 5 is excellent and 1 is abysmal, 3 lies somewhere in the middle – sort of 'O.K.' performance. What is O.K.?" We put up a blank chart, with Return on Capital Employed (ROCE) on the horizontal axis, and annual revenue growth on the other. What was "O.K." for each of these two key performance parameters?

The first remarkable discovery was that most of the managers had no clue about their companies' ROCE. They knew about their annual profits, but not about either the asset base or the capital employed. These were senior-level managers – typically among the top ten people in their companies – and they had no knowledge about their companies' ROCE! In fact many had not confronted the term earlier.

Once we got past explaining what ROCE meant, we could get back on track: what was "O.K." ROCE in their minds? With weighted average cost of capital (WACC) varying from 15% to 21%, the different participants suggested numbers between 18% and 30%. 18% was the minimum. Anything below that would not be "O.K." they felt.

Then we turned to growth. What average rate of annual growth was O.K.? We emphasized that what we were seeking was their emotional response, not just the intellectual one. "What growth rate makes you personally feel O.K. – not great, not lousy, but acceptable?" Influenced

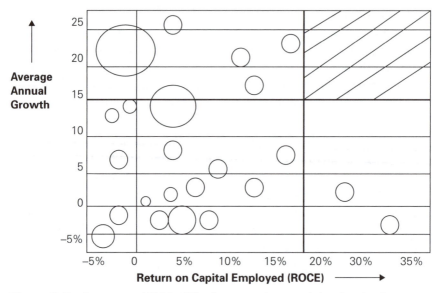

Figure 3 Performance (1994–97) of companies participating in the senior management program in India

by the specifics of their own industries, the different managers came up with different numbers. For some in IT-based industries, for example, 40% growth was O.K. For others, it was 15% to 20%. Once again, 15% was the lowest number. Anything below that would not be O.K.

We then put up a chart showing the performance of the companies represented in the room that we had worked out ahead of time (see Figure 3). We drew thick black lines at 18% for ROCE, and at 15% for growth. Then we shaded the top right hand box – where performance exceeded the minimum acceptable level for both of these parameters. Anything outside of this box was not O.K., according to the participants' own definition of acceptable performance.

THERE WAS NOT A SINGLE COMPANY IN THE ROOM WHOSE PERFORMANCE COULD FIND A PLACE IN THAT TOP RIGHT HAND BOX. NOT ONE! There were a few who had grown rapidly, but their returns were relatively poor. There were others whose returns were acceptable, but not growth. And, for a vast majority of companies represented in the room, both growth and returns were below the acceptable minimums.

"How come 30 of you – out of 35 – marked your company's performance a 3 or more, i.e., O.K. or better, when not one of you meet your own criteria for O.K. performance?" we asked.

The point is simple. While all the 35 managers loudly claimed that their companies needed to change, and change quite radically, to respond to the changing economic and competitive situations in India, deep in their hearts none of them felt the urgency they were professing. Without that urgency in their hearts and without their own belief about the possibility of radical change – of radical performance improvement – no one in their organizations was likely to develop that sense of urgency or that belief. People do not listen to what their senior managers say, they look into the eyes of those managers to see the convictions and passions that lie behind the words. Without the energy of their own convictions, what chances did those managers have of leading change in their own organizations?

There is something very interesting about the topic of managing change. On the one hand, almost every company in India is struggling with this issue: what to change to, and how to change? Consulting organizations are enjoying a boom period, helping companies find answers to these questions. Academic seminars on this topic are proliferating, with eager participants filling auditoriums to listen to the latest guru-speak on managing change. Everyone is looking for answers, for solutions on how to respond to the radically changing business situation in India.

On the other hand, in every airport bookshop, the largest number of books are on this topic. And, while the language and the examples vary, the basic message in most of those books is similar. They advocate similar actions, often in roughly similar sequence: take the lead, build a case for action, shape a shared vision, mobilize commitment, create actions plans, track progress . . . and so on. And these are good books by competent experts, written on the basis of the experiences of companies around the world. We know a lot about managing change; we know what to do and how.

Why then is something that we know so much about – something that, in this sense, is so easy – so hard to do? Where are the bottlenecks? Where are the barriers?

Bottlenecks tend to be at the top of the bottle. Here too the most critical barrier to change lies at the level of top managers: in their lack of belief in and passion for change. They all say the right words, publish them in the annual reports and in the in-house journals, but deep in their hearts they do not believe what they say. This is why companies find it so hard to manage change. Surely there are many other barriers and obstacles but none of them are as debilitating as the mindset of senior managers.

Radical performance improvement is possible

This is the first and essential prerequisite for creating and managing change: senior managers have to develop the belief that radical change is possible. It is certainly possible for small and medium-sized firms, but it is also possible for large, established companies. And, it is possible to achieve such non-incremental improvements within a reasonably short period of time – not a quarter, or even a year, but not ten years either.

There is a religion in the field of management: it is called incrementalism. It is based on the belief that everything in companies happens slowly and incrementally. It comes with its own rituals and metaphors: like the analogy of supertankers. Supertankers turn slowly, in long turning circles. You cannot jerk them around. Ditto for companies, particularly large companies with thousands of employees – you can't push them for too much too fast. You have to have patience, you have to be pragmatic. In big companies, things simply do not happen that quickly.

There are those – Dhirubhai Ambani at Reliance, for example – who have never believed in this religion, but most Indian managers practice it, knowingly or unknowingly. They have been brought up in an era of crippling regulations, bureaucratic dominance and poor systems and infrastructures when the tenants of this religion tended to be valid most of the time. That is how they got converted to this faith. They continue to maintain that faith. They do not like words like "radical change." They find it too childish, too unsophisticated, too un-Indian. For them, it is difficult to convert once again to the faith of radical performance improvement.

Yet, this is the most important implication of deregulation. In a deregulated, competitive economy driven by the cruel logic of markets, a company that fails to change fast enough can and will die – as is manifest in the slow march to extinction that has already become inevitable for some of India's great old companies. At the same time, in this deregulated market economy, a determined management can transform a company much more quickly and much more effectively than was possible in the past.

International experience clearly shows that radical performance improvement is possible. Motorola fell off the precipice in 1985: its profitability had collapsed from 6.3% to 1.3%, a drop of 80%. Competition from Japanese companies had forced Motorola out of the DRAM business. It had slipped from the second to the fifth position as a supplier of semiconductors and was considering a merger – a polite term for divestment – of its semiconductor operations with that of Toshiba. Even in the pagers and cell phone businesses, the Japanese competitors were surging ahead in the battle for miniaturization and featurization, appearing well set to soon capture market leadership.

By 1988, in a mere three years, the position had totally changed. Profitability was back at 5.3% and Motorola had established clear leadership in pagers and cell phones with a slew of innovative and price competitive products. It was back in the DRAM business, and had emerged as a major supplier of semiconductor products to the most demanding customers around the world.

Within these three years, Motorola achieved dramatic improvements in its operations. Development time for new products was shortened from an average of 3 years to 1.8 years. Design improvements led to a fall in the average number of parts per product from 3400 to 630. The order to shipment period was cut from 30 to 3 days. Defects per million fell from 3000 to 200, thanks to the celebrated six sigma total quality program.

Motorola is by no means an isolated case. Over the last two decades, many companies around the world have achieved similarly radical performance improvement, shattering the myth of incrementalism. Collectively, their experiences demonstrate some simple truths that most managers, steeped in the tradition of "business-as-usual" incrementalism, may find hard to believe.

1. High performance companies exist in "unattractive" industries

Industry determinism is perhaps the most debilitating of all management beliefs. "How can I do much better, my industry is in a lousy shape?" We hear it all the time, over and over again from executives in consumer durables, electrical machinery, paper, heavy engineering, bulk chemicals and a variety of other businesses. "Didn't Michael Porter talk about industry attractiveness? Well, mine is a most unattractive industry."

Here is a quiz. Draw a horizontal line on a piece of paper. On that line, at equal spaces, list some of the major industries: semiconductors, banking, automobiles, petroleum, telecommunication, and so on. Find out the average profitability of each of those industries – the average of all the companies in that business – for a five-year period, and plot these numbers on the vertical axis.

What you will get is a zig-zag curve – some industries, like tobacco, will have a high average industry profitability; others, like semiconductors or airlines, will have low profitability for that particular five-year period. Instead of profitability, you can look at some other performance measure, like shareholder value creation. The same highs and lows will emerge.

Now, check the figures for the best performing company in each industry – not the average, but the best. What do you think the plot of these numbers will look like?

Zero marks for those who think that this plot will parallel average industry profitability. The ups and downs will be much smaller. The performance of the best performers in different businesses is a lot more similar than the average performance of those businesses. Put differently, even in industries that have poor average results, there are individual companies that do very well – almost as well as the best performing companies in any business.

There are those managers who live their lives by the law of industry averages. And then there are those who are inspired by the outliers and have the courage to ask: if one company can do it, why can't we? This is the mindset that is necessary for achieving radical performance improvement – the willingness to benchmark, not against the average or the comparable, but against the best, and drawing both inspiration and learning from those benchmarks to drive oneself forward.

An Indian example? Ispat International N.V. While registered in Holland and headquartered in London, Ispat is a very Indian company in its spirit and in its management. Amid the ruins of the steel industry, Lakshmi Niwas Mittal has built one of the most successful of Indian-led enterprises by ignoring the law of industry determinism.

2. A company can achieve outstanding performance even when its industry is shrinking

Historically, Sheffield in England was the source of the world's best cutlery. It was one of the early "industrial clusters" – like Silicon Valley is today for IT – with a large number of cutlery makers dominating the upper end of the market through their superb workmanship and quality. Then, in two decades, the industry collapsed. Competition from Hong Kong and other low cost Asian producers led to absolute catastrophe for the entire industry in Sheffield. Volumes shrunk by over 90%. On an indexed basis, production fell from 160 in 1976 to 20 in 1992 (see Figure 4). A vast majority of the local companies simply went out of business, victims of the industry collapse.

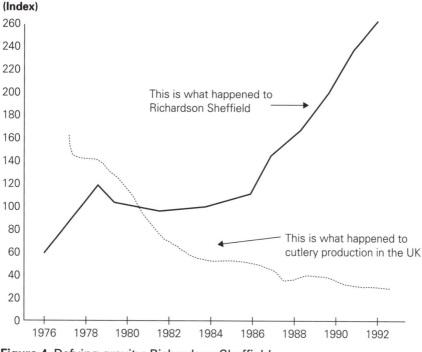

(Index)

This is what happened to Richardson Sheffield

This is what happened to cutlery production in the UK

Figure 4 Defying gravity: Richardson Sheffield

But one company – Richardson Sheffield – went from strength to strength over the same period, defying gravity by growing over 500%.

In India, which industry has shrunk more in size than jute? Drive on the Grand Trunk Road from Calcutta and you will see the corpses of once thriving jute mills lining up the road. Yet, in that industry, Hastings Jute Mills is surging forward, growing profitably and investing in new capacity. Just as Richardson Sheffield defied the rules of the business through innovation and entrepreneurship, by creating the hugely successful "Laser Knife," the Kajaria brothers, owners of Hastings Jute Mills since 1994, made the jute business attractive by transforming employee-management relationship to radically improved productivity, and by creating innovative new products that find new uses in international markets.

3. Outstanding performance can be achieved even when competitors are much bigger and stronger

In 1975, Xerox enjoyed a staggering 93% share of the worldwide photocopier market. Its technology was guarded by over 500 patents. It had a worldwide marketing and support organization of 12,000 sales representatives and 15,000 service people working directly for the Xerox organization in the United States and for the company's joint ventures abroad – Rank Xerox in Europe and Fuji Xerox in Japan. It had a worldwide manufacturing infrastructure, invested more in R&D than the total revenues of most of its competitors, and was one of the few companies whose brand names were indistinguishable from their businesses. Photocopying meant Xeroxing.

When Canon, the little camera company from Japan, jumped into this business in the late 1960s, most observers were skeptical. Less than a tenth the size of Xerox, Canon had no sales and service organization to reach the corporate market for copiers, nor did it have a process technology to bypass Xerox's patents. Reviewing Canon's entry vis-à-vis those of other corporate giants like IBM, Kodak, 3M, Nashua and Smith Corona who also chose to challenge Xerox around the same time, one investment analyst commented that "a photocopier is not a large camera."

Yet, over the next three decades, Canon rewrote the rule book on how copiers were supposed to be produced, emerging as the second largest global player in terms of sales and surpassing Xerox in numbers of units sold. Evidence of this success is visible in the ubiquitous "Xeroxing by Canon" signs over photocopying shops all over India.

Yes, size matters, but no, size does not determine. While David and Goliath stories may be relatively rare in other aspects of life, they are all too common in the world of business. To those Indian managers who shy away from the aspirations of radical performance improvement on the ground that their ambitions must match the reality of their comparative resources and scale, consider Zee TV. Against the Goliaths of Rupert Murdoch and his Star TV, on the one side, and Doorodarshan on the other, if Zee could do what it has done, why not you?

4. Radical performance improvement is possible even when you are already very successful

Perhaps the most pervasive myth of all is the belief that truly radical change is possible only when a company is in actual crisis. With crisis comes defreezing, a delegitimization of the existing order including the existing power structures, beliefs and processes, and this delegitimization of the old clears the path for the new. "Fix it while it ain't broken yet" is a fashionable statement but not very practical, the belief goes, because people cannot see the need for change when everything is going so well.

Perhaps the strongest evidence against this myth lies in the experiences of General Electric over the last twenty years. All over the world, including in India, Jack Welch, GE's formidable CEO, represents the epitomy of determined leadership. For good reasons. He took over the helms of GE in 1981 when the company's market capitalization was $11 billion. Now, it hovers in the range of $450 billion! You could buy almost all of India's established corporate sector with about a fifth of GE's current value!

This jump in market value was achieved through change that is spectacular by any measure. Over his tenure, Welch has transformed GE's business portfolio, organization, culture and behaviors. Indeed there is at least some element of truth in the claim made by a Harvard Business School professor that Welch's transformation of GE, with its employee base of over 200,000 people, represents "one of the biggest planned efforts to alter people's behavior since the cultural revolution in China."

All of this, of course, is old hat now. Everyone knows the GE story. What people tend to forget, however, are the circumstances under which the story began.

When Jack Welch succeeded Reginald Jones in April 1981 as the chairman and CEO of GE, the *Wall Street Journal* claimed that the company was "replacing a legend with a live wire." Indeed, in the decade of the seventies, Jones had doubled GE's sales and tripled its profits. In 1981, GE was the tenth largest industrial corporation in the U.S. and was often referred to as the role model for American management. In a poll of Fortune 500 chief executives in 1981 – the year that Welch assumed the leadership role in the company – GE was ranked as the best managed industrial company in the U.S. and Reginald Jones received Fortune's "CEO of the decade" award.

In other words, Welch did not inherit a company in crisis, not even a company struggling with satisfactory underperformance. He inherited the best managed and one of the highest performing industrial companies in the world. And then, again as described by *Fortune*, He seized the company's "vast bureaucracy by the scruff of the neck and shook it till it saw stars."

In India, this is precisely what successive generations of top management have done in the perennially successful Hindustan Lever. Sushim Dutta inherited a very successful company from the legendary Ashok Ganguly. And then, he changed the company fundamentally by merging tea gardens, the food and beverages businesses of Brooke Bond and

Lipton, and other units into the big detergents operation to create an integrated Unilever group of companies in India, through a spate of acquisitions including Tomco in the detergents business and Kissan in the foods business, and by decentralizing authority down from the chairman's level to the level of the divisional managements. By the time he handed over charge to Keki Dadiseth, he was no less a management legend in India than Reginald Jones was in the United States.

But, instead of maintaining the status quo, Keki Dadiseth once again led a revolution in Hindustan Lever, radically decentralizing the company to create small, highly entrepreneurial businesses. At $4 billion in revenues, Hindustan Lever represents about 5% of Unilever's global turnover; Dadiseth was determined to double it to 10%. "When we imagined it," said Dadiseth, "it was difficult to conceptualize. The key concept here is when there is a huge challenge and people sit down as a team to address it, they may not reach a solution, but the solution comes within sight." And the solution that came within his sight was to ignite the entrepreneurial spark plugs in the middle ranks of the company, by creating small profit centers that would help the company retain the aggressiveness and agility of small companies and simultaneously offer personal growth opportunities to a much broader array of young managers.

5. Charismatic leadership is not a prerequisite for radical performance improvement

Last but not least is the myth of charismatic leadership: the belief that only personal charisma at the top can galvanize a company to achieve radical change. Yes, charisma helps. But no, it is not a prerequisite.

Desi DeSimone, the CEO of 3M, is not charismatic by any standards. There is an obvious wholesomeness in him, an authenticity that creates trust and confidence, and a genuine love for people that creates the same love in return. But, he is not 7 feet tall, nor a great public speaker. He is not the fire that burns with spectacular brightness but only leaves burnt out ash at the end; he is like a gentle stream that cools and comforts people, in a soothing and durable way.

Today, with all the public acclaim creating a halo around him, Infosys' N.R. Narayana Murthy may appear as charismatic but he too is not 7 feet tall. A soft spoken, conservative and traditional middle-class Indian, he is more courteous than aggressive, more empathetic than evangelical. Yet, he is the soul that has nurtured the body of Infosys, a key attraction why people join and stay in the company, and the primary architect of Infosys' spectacular performance improvement since 1991.

We could list many more such myths, but that is not the point. What is not necessary may be interesting, but a far more interesting question is "what does it take?" If radical performance improvement is possible, what are its "how to's"?

What does it take?

What does it take to achieve radical performance improvement? There is no one answer to that question. It requires the courage to roll the dice for a big roll, but also to take care of managing a lot of small details. History and context matter, so there is no one universal formula applicable to all companies.

Over the last twenty years, we have seen – sometimes from the inside and sometimes from the outside – some amazing changes in the fortunes of companies in the United States, Europe, Japan and India. We have seen a few soar, many more stumble, and some – like Digital Equipment Corporation and Westinghouse – die. In India, we have witnessed some, like Reliance, Hindustan Lever and Infosys, go from success to success and seen others, like Indian Oxygen (renamed as BOC India), stumble and struggle. We do not know if there are any absolute laws or truths in the field of management. But, if there are, we have no access to them. Our research methods are not amenable to ferreting out truths; all they can lead to are speculations and interpretations, and raise issues for thought, discussion and reflection.

One of the criticisms about these examples may be that they represent a search for excellence. They are all exceptional cases and, therefore, cannot provide the basis for any generalization. We disagree. In "An Observation on Method", Edgar Wind[1] writes: "It seems to be a lesson of history that the commonplace may be understood as a reduction of the exceptional, but the exceptional cannot be understood by amplifying the commonplace. Both logically and causally the exceptional is crucial because it introduces (however strange it may sound) the more comprehensive category."

Reliance, Bajaj Auto, Infosys, Ranbaxy, Hero Honda, Zee TV, Hindustan Lever, Wipro, HDFC, Sundaram Fasteners – these are all Indian companies and are, therefore, part of the comprehensive category of corporate India. What they can do, others can do too. The Indian situation, with all its pathologies and opportunities, is not what is special about them. What is special is their management approach. At least from a normative perspective, they are a perfectly valid – in fact, indispensable – basis for generalization.

To achieve radical performance improvement, the management of a company will require a sense – a vision, if you will – of the company's destiny. How does one arrive at this sense?

Begin by trying to tell the story of your company's future. Try out all the different stories that you can generate. With each story, you will describe a different future, a different destiny. Mull over these stories told in different ways. Gradually, a special story will emerge – perhaps from just one of the many different stories, or perhaps from a synthesis of some of them. It will be special because it will resonate with you; it will fit something that is inside you, whether you are an individual or a management team. You will feel that resonance because of the flush of energy and excitement it will generate.

Refine that story. Picture – that is what a vision is, a picture – the future state of the company, as it emerges from your special story. Then, have the courage to stand in that future and look at the present from that vantagepoint. How can you pull the present into that future? Have the courage to take those actions to drag your company, "by the scruff of its neck" if necessary, as Jack Welch did, into that future. You cannot manage from the present to the future – that will inevitably land you into the trap of incrementalism. You will have to manage the present from the future – that is the path and the process for radical improvement.

REFERENCE

1. Edgar Wind, *Pagan Mysteries in the Renaissance*. Harmondsworth, England: Penguin Books, 1967.

CHAPTER 12

Integrating the enterprise

Sumantra Ghoshal and Lynda Gratton

In this paper Sumantra and Lynda Gratton revisit one of the oldest but most important management challenges – how to create an integrated enterprise in which the whole is greater than the sum of the parts. While the challenge is old, it has taken on new relevance today as many firms struggle with pulling together their fragmented and diversified operations around the world. Building on their detailed case studies of Goldman Sachs, BP, OgilvyOne and other companies, they show how integration can be built at multiple levels in the firm – through operational, social, intellectual and emotional mechanisms. This paper won the Richard Beckhart Prize for the best paper published in Sloan Management Review *in 2002.*

One of the most fundamental and enduring tensions in all but very small companies is between subunit autonomy and empowerment on the one hand and overall organizational integration and cohesion on the other.[1] The tensions grow with increasing organizational complexity and assume the most intensity in large, diversified global companies.[2] In our research with such organizations, we have seen that it is possible to balance those tensions successfully by implementing four kinds of horizontal integration for achieving cohesion without hierarchy.

Over the last decade, many large companies around the world focused on creating relatively autonomous subunits and empowered managers by breaking up their organizational behemoths into small, entrepreneurial units. Some, though not all, achieved significant benefits from such restructuring.[3] Freed from bureaucratic central controls, the empowered units improved both the speed and the quality of responsiveness to market demands – and fostered increased innovation. Companies were able to reduce their corporate-level overhead and make internal-governance processes more disciplined and transparent.

However, the empowerment of subunits also led to fragmentation and to deficiencies in internal integration. The autonomous managers of subunits saw few incentives to share knowledge or other resources, particularly when evaluation of their performance focused primarily on how their own unit was doing, rather than on how the unit contributed to the company's overall performance.

But today, in company after company, we are finding that management attention has moved to the integration and cohesion side of the tension. (See "About the Research.") Having captured benefits from strengthening the competitiveness of each unit, companies are now improving integration in order to achieve the benefits of better sharing and coordination across those units.[4]

Although many companies are moving toward integration, our research shows that the drivers forcing that change often differ. For some enterprises, the main impetus comes from the demands of customers whose needs cut across the company's internal boundaries. At global engineering company ABB, the 1,300 small companies that Percy Barnevik created in the late 1980s have been consolidated by current CEO Jörgen Centerman into 400, primarily for serving global customers more effectively. Customer needs created similar pressures at OgilvyOne, the world's largest direct-marketing agency. That company had to roll out the American Express Blue credit card worldwide across multiple media in six months – a task that would have been impossible in the formerly fragmented and internally competitive OgilvyOne.

For other companies, the effects of technological change on management of innovation are the primary integration drivers. For example, with home entertainment shifting from stand-alone, analog-technology-based consumer electronics to Web-based, digitized content delivery, Sony saw the need to integrate its historically autonomous product divisions. Sony had to make all its audio and video products (plus its music and movie software) compatible and accessible directly through a personal computer, video-game machine, PDA or mobile phone. Driven by that fundamental technological change, Sony entered the personal-computer business, the established gateway to the Internet, and launched VAIO computers. The company proceeded to develop an integrated innovation process so that its VAIOs could work seamlessly with all other Sony offerings.

About the Research

This article is based on our case research over the last five years in 15 large, global companies in North America (Oracle, Goldman Sachs, Sun Microsystems), Western Europe (ABB, BT, Lufthansa, SKF, BP, LVMH), Asia (Sony, the LG Group, Standard Chartered Bank) and emerging markets such as Brazil (Natura) and India (Indian Infosys, Nicholas Piramal). We interviewed numerous managers in each company, and we made use of documents from public sources and the companies themselves. For each company, we wrote up a separate case study. In some of the companies (Lufthansa, BT, the LG Group, Indian Infosys), we repeated the full process twice over the last five years, so as to document change over time. Our research focus was not on integration, per se, but on management of change and performance-improvement processes. The issue of horizontal integration emerged from our research as one of the important means many of these companies were adopting in order to improve their business performance.

At Oracle, Goldman Sachs and luxury-goods business LVMH, rapid growth and globalization are what's driving consolidation and integration. Oracle grew at a phenomenal pace internationally, with little time to develop its organizational systems and processes. Each of its overseas units developed its own system to meet the needs of local customers. Over the last two years, the company has worked hard to standardize and integrate those systems and to achieve efficiency and better global coordination.

At BP, the integration driver is different still. BP's mergers with Amoco, Arco and Castrol created a fragmented organization with many different management styles and philosophies. So integration has been vital for turning the focus of the 100,000 employees away from their differences and toward their shared future. Confronting the same needs are Indian pharmaceuticals company Nicholas Piramal, which grew rapidly through acquisitions, and OgilvyOne, which keeps acquiring Internet marketing companies that differ from its traditional direct-marketing businesses.

A need for horizontal integration

At one level, nothing is new here. The need for integration to counterbalance internal differentiation is an old chestnut.[5] But today's circumstances create some new possibilities and eliminate some historical ones.

The most important change is the Web and the associated information-technology capabilities. Information sharing has always been at the heart of integration, but now technology allows organizations to respond to integration needs in ways that were unavailable even five years ago.[6]

Meanwhile, some previous integration tools have become less significant: staff relocation and structured career paths, for example. Formerly, in companies as diverse as Unilever, Matsushita and Hewlett-Packard, managers who had worked in different functions, businesses and geographic locations turned their collective personal networks into the glue that held the company together.[7] Although such networks are still a powerful tool for socializing people and building organizational cohesion, they are less common – in part because lifetime careers and on-demand mobility of employees can no longer be assumed.

Then, the drastic pruning of middle management that many companies undertook in the 1990s deprived them of an important but often unrecognized source of organizational integration.[8] The midlevel managers who once played boundary-spanning and coordinating roles are gone.

But perhaps the most important change is in management philosophy. In the past, integration was managed primarily through vertical processes. The way to encourage different businesses, functions or geographical units to share resources and coordinate their activities was to bring them under a common boss and a common planning and control system.[9] Although there has always been a recognition of the relevance of horizontal-integration mechanisms, in practice they have been seen as secondary, as reinforcement to the primary vertical processes.[10]

The most fundamental change we have observed in the ways companies are responding to integration is a move away from the traditional vertical mechanisms of hierarchy and formal systems to a primary reliance on horizontal processes that build integration on top of subunit autonomy and empowerment. The secondary has now become primary.

Four critical components of horizontal integration

How are companies putting it all together again without destroying the vitality of the parts? We have found four areas of action: operational integration through standardization of the technological infrastructure, intellectual integration through the development of a shared knowledge base, social integration through collective bonds for performance and emotional integration through the creation of a common identity and purpose. (See "A Framework for Organizational Integration.") The four areas are simultaneously distinct and interrelated. The challenge is to manage the interrelationships synergistically.[11]

Operational integration through standardized technological infrastructure

Influenced in part by reengineering, many companies in the 1990s made progress rationalizing their production and distribution infrastructures. Now the focus of operational integration has shifted to support functions such as finance, human resources, planning and service. The bottleneck in rationalizing and integrating those activities lies in IT systems.

Although many companies have recognized that constraint and are making progress in updating their fragmented IT infrastructure, standardization of support functions is still a distant ideal.

Oracle – whose rapid international expansion resulted in autonomous national subsidiaries using different systems to manage operations – is illustrative. Even as late as 1997, Oracle had 97 e-mail servers running seven incompatible programs. Each country had its own enterprise-resource-planning (ERP) system and its own Web site in the local language. Some even changed the color of the Oracle logo because of the local manager's taste.

Despite having the same products worldwide, the Oracle organization packaged, bundled and priced them differently in each market. And to find out how many people Oracle employed worldwide on any given day, someone had to scout through 60 differently formatted databases and consolidate the number. By then, the answer would have changed.

Then, in 1999, CEO Larry Ellison articulated Oracle's direction for the next phase of information technology. He envisioned the computer industry becoming a utility like electricity or water. The hardware, data and applications would reside in a central location and would be accessible over the Internet to any customer with a PC and a Web browser. Oracle would provide integrated services, including ERP, customer-relationship management, supply-chain management and human-resource management. As Ellison explained, "If you want to buy a car, would you get an engine from BMW, a chassis from Jaguar, windshield wipers from Ford? No, of course not. Right now with the software out there, you need a glue gun – or hire all these consultants to put it together. They call it best-of-breed. I call it a mess."

To convince customers of the value of building an operating infrastructure through standardized and integrated applications over the Internet, Ellison made Oracle its own beta-test site. His metaphor was, "Eat your own dog food," and he publicly announced a target of $1 billion in cost savings – 10% of revenues.

By 2001 Oracle had met that goal. All e-mail is now consolidated into one standardized, global system using two servers at Oracle's California headquarters. Prices and discounts, once a local preserve, have been standardized globally and made accessible over the Internet. ERP customizations that differed in every country in Europe are standardized and are operated from a single central source. The different local Web sites have been replaced by a single global site, Oracle.com, which is run out of the United States in multiple languages.

Observers may quibble over how much money Oracle has saved, but most estimates are close to that $1 billion target. Over the two years it took

For effective horizontal integration, managers have to connect the company's knowledge bases, build social relationships among people and shape a shared sense of identity, all supported by a standardized technological infrastructure.

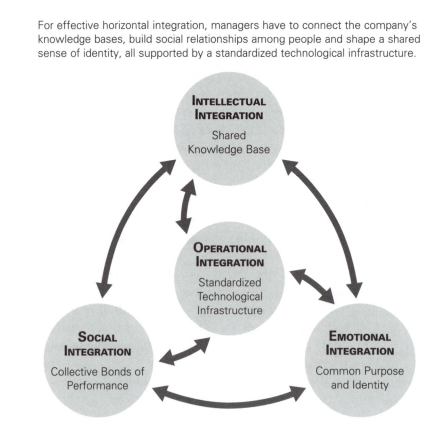

A Framework for Organizational Integration

to implement the global platforms, Oracle's operating margin improved from 14% to 35%. Ellison has now upped the ante from $1 billion in savings to $2 billion, and the company is going through the next round of rationalizing its operating infrastructure to meet the new goal. Having consolidated the technological infrastructure supporting internal operations, the company is now using the same philosophy in its relationships with suppliers and customers – and in its sales and marketing activities.

What have such drastic standardization and centralization done to front-line entrepreneurship? According to CFO Jeff Henley, they have enhanced the kinds of entrepreneurial activity that Oracle values most. "It would be goofy to let people do as they please in building and managing a local IT operation to support internal processes," says Henley. "By standardizing those, we have channelled that entrepreneurship where it adds value – in serving customers. We think it is a good idea if a salesperson spends time selling product benefits rather than negotiating prices and discounts."

Oracle has been successful in standardizing its technological infrastructure while most companies have made only incremental progress. What makes Oracle different? The most important factor has been the commitment of a powerful CEO who made the initiative his top priority. To overcome objections from country managers and to accommodate their needs and contributions, he had them participate in designing the standardized systems. Then he gave them a choice: They could either adopt the standardized and centrally operated systems completely free of cost or continue with their local systems (accepting full costs and no adjustment in the returns they were expected to generate). Without exception, the local managers chose the first option.

Standardizing operating processes has always been a powerful integrating device, but it wasn't possible to create centrally managed, standard IT systems until now. The biggest benefits flow at the extreme, not with half-measures. It may be that the business Oracle is in allows it to do more standardizing than, say, a Unilever, but most companies could still wring more advantage from technological infrastructure than they have so far.

Intellectual integration through shared knowledge base

With the goal of "knowledge management," many companies have developed IT-based systems that are essentially databases for sharing information on an organizationwide basis. Such systems, however, are only the first step in establishing a shared knowledge base that truly integrates a company's intellectual capital. Because user *pull* must supplement the technological *push*, effective integration of knowledge requires a clear strategic link and extensive communication.[12]

At Ogilvy and Mather's OgilvyOne, an increased need for integration became apparent in the early 1990s because of two large clients – American Express and IBM. Both demanded integrated services and business solutions that combined interactive media with traditional direct marketing. In the 1980s, advertising agencies used costly mass-media campaigns to attract customers, but in the 1990s, they targeted the "anarchic" customer, who had a choice of infinite channels. OgilvyOne's historically fragmented organization, with highly autonomous divisions such as Data Consult, Direct Mail and Ogilvy Interactive, simply could not respond effectively.

OgilvyOne decided to focus on customer ownership and 360-degree brand stewardship, building both strategies on proprietary tools designed to support trust and long-term relationships with clients and clients' end customers.

Customer-ownership tools such as QuickScan (a sophisticated, proprietary data-mining tool) enabled Ogilvy's creative professionals to question clients' assumptions about end customers. QuickScan revealed, for example, that only 16% of Nestlé Pet Foods' customers accounted for 90% of the customer value for Friskies, a major cat-food brand. So OgilvyOne helped Nestlé target the more valuable segment. In addition, the firm employed a complex mathematical model for understanding, developing and enhancing the relationship between a customer and a brand in order to preserve and reinforce every aspect of brand strength.

But to get the most from its tools, OgilvyOne first needed mechanisms for creating, sharing and exchanging knowledge across the company. It had to harness the brainpower of its marketing gurus, mathematicians, statisticians, strategy consultants and individual creative talent. So OgilvyOne developed an integrated system called Truffles. Truffles provided not only a database and a system for testing ideas and hypotheses, but also opportunities for people to generate new ideas together through a variety of chat rooms, bulletin boards and dedicated forums.

The Truffles name came from a statement of founder David Ogilvy: "I prefer the discipline of knowledge to the anarchy of ignorance, and we pursue knowledge the way a pig pursues truffles." Supported by 60 knowledge officers across the company, the Truffles initiative was the product of years of documenting the accumulated intellectual capital of the company. It was also a living forum for creating and sharing new ideas.

What made Truffles work was not only the world-class IT infrastructure nor the tremendous effort and investment that kept its information current, but also the link between the system and the company's strategy. With all tools, techniques and relevant data on Truffles, research and ideas were directly connected to action. That link overcame initial resistance and motivated both senior managers and the creative staff to use Truffles.

Also contributing to the system's success were company efforts to build interpersonal relationships, or "soft bonds," to promote knowledge sharing. OgilvyOne created many conversation forums – Friday morning breakfast meetings, top-level "Board Away" days and other functions. With the motto that "the most important role of managers is to create friendships," the senior leaders invested considerable personal time to develop the internal trust that sustains intellectual integration. Nigel Howlett, the chairman of OgilyyOne's London office, for example, spent months building a relationship with Tim Carrigan, the CEO of NoHo Digital, an interactive marketing company Howlett wanted to buy. The discussions were as much personal as they were strategic. The results of the friendship they built were manifest immediately after the acquisition was finalized. Within two weeks, NoHo's employees were not only using Truffles, but also were contributing new information and techniques to the database for use by all Ogilvy employees.

Social integration through collective bonds of performance

Although learning and sharing are usually achieved horizontally in peer-to-peer forums, performance management and resource allocation are still the preserve of boss-to-subordinate relationships. Our research revealed, however, that enormous advantages can result when peer-to-peer interactions are extended to traditionally vertical areas. As BP's CEO John Browne recounts, "One theme we observed was the very different interaction between people of equal standing, if you will, when they reviewed each other's work than there was when a superior reviewed the work of a subordinate. We concluded that the way to get the best answers would be to get peers to challenge and support each other rather than to have a hierarchical challenge process."

Peer assist, a BP process that uses peer groups of managers from similar businesses to drive learning and knowledge sharing, is already well documented.[13] But over the last two years, BP's new *peer challenge* has extended that approach to address the traditionally vertical performance-management and resource-allocation processes.

The managers of each autonomous business unit enter into an annual performance contract with top management and are then free to achieve the results however they wish. Peer challenge requires managers to get their plans, including investment plans, approved by their peers before finalizing the performance contract with top management. "The peers must be satisfied that you are carrying your fair share of the heavy water buckets," says deputy chief executive Rodney Chase. "The old issue of sandbagging management is gone. The challenge now comes from peers, not from management."[14]

According to BP business-unit head Polly Flinn, "The peer challenge is about convincing people in similar positions to support your investment proposal knowing that they could invest the same capital elsewhere, and going eyeball to eyeball with them, and then having to reaffirm whether you have made it or not over the coming months or quarters." The process works because half of the unit manager's bonus depends on the performance of the unit, and the other half depends on the perform-ance of the peer group.

In an added twist, BP has extended the peer process even further. The three top-performing business units in a peer group have been made responsible for improving the performance of the bottom three. "We had 'not invented here' raised to an art form," says Chase. With peer assist and peer challenge, he says, "What we have raised to an art form is that if I have a good idea, my first responsibility is to share it with my peers, and if I am performing poorly, I will get the peer group to help me."

BP has achieved a powerful force in integration and knowledge shar-ing. According to Browne, "People do not learn, at least in a corporate environment, without a target. You can implore people to learn, and they will to some extent. But if you say, 'Look, the learning is necessary in order to cut the cost of drilling a well by 10%,' then they will learn with purpose." What is special about BP's peer groups is their effectiveness in transferring, sharing and leveraging cumulative learning through a direct link with performance.

Emotional integration through shared identity and meaning

Ultimately, the acid test of organizational integration lies in collective action. A shared knowledge base must translate into coordinated and aligned action across the different parts of an organization, or it is only an expensive library. Unless peer relationships based on trust and friendship allow excellent collective execution, they create no value other than the comforts of an exclusive country club.[15]

It was the coordinating and aligning of actions that historically made hierarchy appear necessary. A common boss could align the activities of different company parts both through direct orders and through formal planning and control.[16] Yet for most companies, hierarchy is no longer as effective – not only because it destroys front-line initiative and entrepreneurship, but also because of its inability to cope with uncertainty and rapid change.[17] As they say at OgilvyOne, "While classical orchestras follow a conductor and a musical score in a rigid and formal manner, jazz bands – like Web marketeers – must be fluid, flexible, improvised and should always trust the requests and applause of their audience."

Fluid and flexible collective action requires not only standardized infrastructure, shared knowledge and mutual trust, but also emotional integration through a common purpose and identity. Emotional integration has been the primary driver of success for companies such as Goldman Sachs.

Teamwork has always been a core value of the premier investment bank because, in the words of Goldman Sachs CEO Hank Paulson, "Quite simply, none of us is as smart as all of us." The entrenched tradition of teamwork underlies the firm's reputation for excellence in execution. "Everywhere and in every country around the world, when a Goldman Sachs banker walks into the room, all of Goldman Sachs comes with him or her," says Robin Neustein, head of the firm's Private Equity Group. "That, in turn, is the outcome of constant work on maintaining the one-firm identity and the internal challenge to be the best and help each other be the best."

This emotional alignment among individuals – and between them and the firm – is the product of three distinct Goldman Sachs characteristics. First, the culture of success is built on a relentless focus on client relationships. Anyone who steps inside the firm can palpably feel this obsession with building and maintaining close and trusting relationships with clients. According to Neustein, "At Goldman Sachs, honor comes in the form of client service. . . . That is why if you try to make a lot of money without putting your client first, it is not a mark of success, it is a mark of shame."

Stories of how the firm's legendary leaders – Sidney Weinberg, Gus Levy, John Whitehead and others – went to extreme lengths, such as having six client dinners in one night, are told and retold. There is pride in being seen as a trusted adviser by the most influential politicians, industrialists and wealthy individuals around the world. However, rather than protecting individuals' ownership of clients, client focus promotes integration because it explicitly emphasizes long-term retention. "Clients are simply in your custody," John Weinberg, a second-generation leader of the firm, consistently reminded employees. "Someone before you established the relationship, and someone after you will carry it on."

Although client focus provides a force for emotional integration with outsiders, pride in the quality of colleagues is an equally powerful force for emotional integration with insiders. As an internal survey conducted in 2000 revealed, 99% of Goldman Sachs employees were proud to work for the firm. Extraordinary levels of investment in recruiting only the most talented people around the globe – and then in continuous training and development for excellence – have, over decades, created the mystique about the firm as a magnet for talent, a mystique that reinforces the pride of belonging.

Second, it is not just the salary that has allowed the firm to become a magnet for talent. Inherently linked to the identity-shaping pride of belonging is a broader sense of purpose that emotionally connects each individual to the ethos of the firm.

Says Goldman Sachs president and co-chief coordinating officer John Thornton, "Anyone with any depth and talent has to ask the question, 'What am I doing with my life?' The purpose of my life is to use my talent for some larger and better purpose." In Goldman Sachs, a broader purpose has historically been at the heart of that positive cycle of building emotional integration by linking purpose, talent and the pride of belonging.

The third contributor to emotional integration in Goldman Sachs is the one-firm mentality that is supported by, for example, doing the evaluation and selection of partners on a firmwide, rather than a divisional or product basis – and by a compensation system that until recently relied on the overall profit and loss to determine each partner's fortunes. Each partner was allotted a fixed proportion of whatever the income for the year might be, with no discretionary payment based on any aspect of the partner's or the unit's performance. "We all had a piece of the action," says Phil Murphy, co-head of investment management. "We didn't care where the action came from. There was no disincentive to take that call from Hong Kong to help me out. . . . You and I didn't care who got the credit for it; we knew we would both share the benefits." After Goldman Sachs became a public company, the link between overall firm performance and each partner's compensation was still important, although 60% rather than 100% of the rewards are now based on the common pool.

Entrepreneurial activity and horizontal integration co-evolve

Our research demonstrates that individual and subunit autonomy co-evolve with horizontal integration in a dynamic process. It is in this dynamic evolution that horizontal integration differs from vertical integration. Instead of smothering bottom-up initiatives, horizontal integration creates a reinforcing process through which both autonomy and integration can flourish. (See "The Co-Evolution of Autonomy and Horizontal Integration.") BP is typical of how the dynamic worked at all the companies we studied.

When John Browne was CEO of BP's North American subsidiary, Sohio, he conducted a careful experiment to test his growing belief that a spirit of entrepreneurship was possible in a big company if the organization were broken up into relatively small, empowered units. He created a separate

Managers need to trust that autonomy and horizontal integration will lead to a symbiotic process through which their joint outcomes – superior business performance and the deepening of a culture of collaboration – will reinforce each other over time.

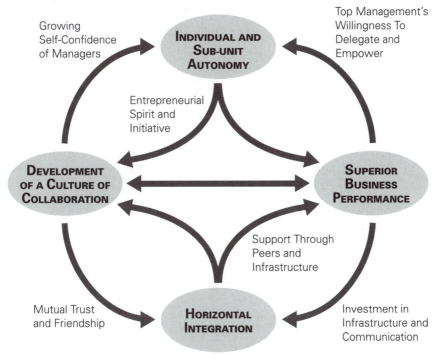

The Co-Evolution of Autonomy and Horizontal Integration

unit out of one operation that chronically lost money. To prevent any positive outcome from appearing purely a result of outstanding local leadership, he appointed managers of normal abilities. Allowed complete autonomy and freedom from the company's central controls, the unit dramatically improved performance, confirming Browne's theory.

When he became CEO in 1996, Browne acted on that lesson by restructuring BP into 150 business units and giving unit managers considerable freedom. The only conditions were that they respect certain "boundaries" – essentially, the core values of the company – and deliver on their performance contracts. Simultaneously, Browne downsized or completely eliminated much of the staff-supported, vertical, command-and-control infrastructure, abolishing the offices of country presidents and several functional departments in London.

To support the empowered and fully accountable business-unit leaders, he created the BP peer groups. Thus managers who ran similar businesses were assigned to help one another to improve both individual and collective performance.

The peer-assist process became effective in about two years as much of BP's business-performance improvement began to flow from combining the business units' entrepreneurial spirit with the peer groups' knowledge sharing and mutual support. For example, when Polly Flinn – then a young manager from Amoco with no experience working outside the United States – became the managing director of BP's retail business in Poland, she drew on active help from the marketing peer group and turned her business from a $20 million-per-year loss to a $6 million profit within 18 months.

The combination of empowerment and support improved business performance, producing two main results. First, top-level managers developed growing confidence in their strategy of delegating authority to the business-unit leaders. Second, the company had more resources to invest in developing the integration infrastructure, including IT systems, and in building conversation and communication mechanisms. Those investments further strengthened the mechanisms and the processes of horizontal integration.

As the symbiotic effects of autonomy and horizontal integration evolved, a culture of collaboration gradually emerged. Rodney Chase described the culture change thus: "In our personal lives – as fathers, mothers, brothers or sisters – we know how much we like to help someone close to us to succeed. Why didn't we believe that the same can happen in our business lives? That is the breakthrough, and you get there when people take enormous pride in helping their colleagues to succeed."

And as the culture evolved, managers' self-confidence grew. They set themselves increasingly tough targets and achieved them through their own initiatives and the support of their peers.[18] Their success strengthened their sense of autonomy and their spirit of entrepreneurship. Moreover, the culture led to the reinforcement of mutual trust and friendship – and the peer-group processes of horizontal integration.

A cautionary note: The symbiotic co-evolution of autonomy and horizontal integration takes time to mature. Vertical integration – bringing different units under a common boss and a common planning and control system – can be implemented relatively quickly. But to develop people's self-confidence and to build trust and friendship can be achieved only through persistent action and reinforcement over time. For senior executives, that is the greatest challenge in building horizontal integration: Although they have to be relentless in driving the process, they also have to be patient about results. For those who respond well to that challenge, the ultimate benefits are durable enhancement of organizational capability and sustainable improvement of business performance.

Lynda Gratton is an associate professor of organizational behavior at London Business School.

This paper appeared in *MIT Sloan Management Review*, Fall 2002.

REFERENCES

1. For a theory-grounded analysis of the tension, see R.P. Rumelt, "Inertia and Transformation," in "Resource-Based and Evolutionary Theories of the Firm," ed. C.M. Montgomery (Boston: Kluwer Academic Publishers, 1995), 101–132.

2. For a rich description and analysis of that tension in the context of large, diversified global companies, see C.K. Prahalad and Y. Doz, "The Multinational Mission: Balancing Local Demands and Global Vision" (New York: Free Press, 1987).

3. For a description of companies that followed the strategy of creating small units to rekindle front-line entrepreneurship, see S. Ghoshal and C.A. Bartlett, "The Individualized Corporation: A Fundamentally New Approach to Management" (New York: HarperCollins, 1997).

4. That sequential process of performance improvement – first building the strength of the units and then building integration mechanisms across them – was described in S. Ghoshal and C.A. Bartlett, "Rebuilding Behavioral Context: A Blueprint for Corporate Renewal." Sloan Management Review 37 (winter 1996): 23–36.

5. For a classic analysis of that need, see P.R. Lawrence and J.W. Lorsch, "Organization and Environment" (Cambridge, Massachusetts: Harvard University Press, 1967).

6. The impact of the Web on integration opportunities can be inferred from the analysis of R.L. Daft and R.H. Lengel, "Information Richness: A New Approach to Managerial Information Processing and Organizational Design," in vol. 6. "Research in Organizational

Behavior," eds. L.L. Cummings and B.M. Staw (Greenwich, Connecticut: JAI Press, 1984), 191–234. For a focused discussion on the role of IT in facilitating communication, see A.D. Shulman. "Putting Group Information Technology in Its Place: Communication and Good Work Group Performance," in "Handbook of Organization Studies," eds. S.R. Clegg, C. Hardy and W.R. Nord (London: Sage, 1996), 357–374.

7. See A. Edstrom and J.R. Galbraith, "Transfer of Managers as a Coordination and Control Strategy in Multinational Organizations," Administrative Science Quarterly 22 (June 1977); 248–263.

8. The important but often ignored role of middle managers in organizational integration has been described in R.M. Kanter, "The Change Masters: Innovation and Entrepreneurship in the American Corporation" (New York: Simon & Schuster, 1983).

9. Such vertical processes of organizational integration lay at the heart of the divisional organizational model. For one of the richest and best-known expositions, see A.D. Chandler, "Strategy and Structure: Chapters in the History of American Industrial Enterprise" (Cambridge, Massachusetts: MIT Press, 1962).

10. See J. Galbraith, "Designing Complex Organizations" (Reading, Massachusetts: Addison-Wesley, 1973); and for a discussion of horizontal mechanisms in large, global companies, see C.A. Bartlett and S. Ghoshal, "Managing Across Borders: The Transnational Solution" (Boston: Harvard Business School Press, 1988).

11. We focus on the challenges of internal integration across existing and established units within large, complex organizations. Clearly, there are other important integration contexts – such as integrating strategic alliances, joint ventures, upstream and downstream partners on the value chain and so on. We do not address those contexts here, but interested readers can find comprehensive discussions elsewhere: for example, in Y. Doz and G. Hamel, "Alliance Advantage: The Art of Creating Value Through Partnering" (Boston: Harvard Business School Press, 1998). Within the organization, integration of new ventures poses unique challenges. An outstanding analysis of the topic appears in C.M. Christensen, "The Innovator's Dilemma" (New York: HarperBusiness, 1997).

12. Several authors have highlighted the need of a social structure to support IT-based systems for effective knowledge management in distributed organizations. See, for example, the discussion on social ecology in V. Govindarajan and A. Gupta, "The Quest for Global Dominance; Transforming Global Presence Into Global Competitive Advantage" (San Francisco: Jossey-Bass, 2001).

13. See, for example, M.T. Hansen and B. Von Oetinger, "Introducing T-Shaped Managers: Knowledge Management's Next Generation," Harvard Business Review 79 (March 2001): 106–116.

14. This is essentially a sophisticated use of social control. See W.G. Ouchi, "A Conceptual Framework for the Design of Organizational Control Mechanisms," Management Science 25 (September 1979): 833–848.

15. See J. Pfeffer and R.I. Sutton, "The Knowing-Doing Gap: How Smart Companies Turn Knowledge Into Action" (Boston: Harvard Business School Press, 2000).

16. The benefits of hierarchy provide the theoretical basis for influential economic analysis of why companies exist, one of the most well-known being O.E. Williamson, "Markets and Hierarchies: Analysis and Antitrust Implications" (New York: Free Press, 1975).

17. For a discussion on the limitations of a hierarchical system in coping with uncertainty and rapid change, see S.L. Brown and K.M. Eisenhardt, "Competing on the Edge: Strategy as Structured Chaos" (Boston: Harvard Business School Press, 1998).

18. See A. Bandura, "Self-Efficacy: The Exercise of Control" (New York: Freeman, 1997).

CHAPTER 13

Beware the busy manager

Heike Bruch and Sumantra Ghoshal

This is the first of many papers co-authored by Sumantra and Heike Bruch. Here Heike and Sumantra ask, why do some managers exhibit "purposeful action-taking" while others do not? They show that purposeful action-taking is a combination of two traits – energy and focus. While 10% of the managers in their research had high energy and high focus, the remaining 90% suffered from a lack of one or the other, or both. And the most dangerous condition was busyness – high energy but low focus. Many managers suffer from low energy and lack of focus – Sumantra and Heike explain what firms can do to generate purposeful action-taking in all their managers.

If you listen to executives, they'll tell you that the resource they lack most is time. Every minute is spent grappling with strategic issues, focusing on cost reduction, devising creative approaches to new markets, beating new competitors. But if you watch them, here's what you'll see: They rush from meeting to meeting, check their e-mail constantly, extinguish fire after fire, and make countless phone calls. In short, you'll see an astonishing amount of fast-moving activity that allows almost no time for reflection.

No doubt, executives are under incredible pressure to perform, and they have far too much to do, even when they work 12-hour days. But the fact is, very few managers use their time as effectively as they could. They think they're attending to pressing matters, but they're really just spinning their wheels.

The awareness that unproductive busyness – what we call "active nonaction" – is a hazard for managers is not new. Managers themselves bemoan the problem, and researchers such as Jeffrey Pfeffer and Robert Sutton have examined it (see "The Smart-Talk Trap," HBR May–June 1999). But the underlying dynamics of the behavior are less well understood.

For the past ten years, we have studied the behavior of busy managers in nearly a dozen large companies, including Sony, LG Electronics, and Lufthansa. The managers at Lufthansa were especially interesting to us because in the last decade, the company underwent a complete transformation – from teetering on the brink of bankruptcy in the early 1990s to earning a record profit of DM 2.5 billion in 2000, thanks in part to the leadership of its managers. We interviewed and observed some 200 managers at Lufthansa, each of whom was involved in at least one of the 130 projects launched to restore the company's exalted status as one of Europe's business icons.

Our findings on managerial behavior should frighten you: Fully 90% of managers squander their time in all sorts of ineffective activities. In other words, a mere 10% of managers spend their time in a committed, purposeful, and reflective manner. This article will help you identify which managers in your organization are making a real difference and which just look or sound busy. Moreover, it will show you how to improve the effectiveness of all your managers – and maybe even your own.

Focus and energy

Managers are not paid to make the inevitable happen. In most organizations, the ordinary routines of business chug along without much managerial oversight The job of managers, therefore, is to make the business do more than chug – to move it forward in innovative, surprising ways. After observing scores of managers for many years, we came to the conclusion that managers who take effective action (those who make difficult – even seemingly impossible – things happen) rely on a combination of two traits: focus and energy.

Think of *focus* as concentrated attention – the ability to zero in on a goal and see the task through to completion. Focused managers aren't in reactive mode; they choose not to respond immediately to every issue that comes their way or get sidetracked from their goals by distractions like e-mail, meetings, setbacks, and unforeseen demands. Because they have a clear understanding of what they want to accomplish, they carefully weigh their options before selecting a course of action. Moreover, because they commit to only one or two key projects, they can devote their full attention to the projects they believe in.

Consider the steely focus of Thomas Sattelberger, currently Lufthansa's executive vice president, product and service. In the late 1980s, he was convinced that a corporate university would be an invaluable asset to a company. He believed managers would enroll to learn how to challenge old paradigms and to breathe new life into the company's operational practices, but his previous employer balked at the idea. After joining Lufthansa, Sattelberger again prepared a detailed business case that carefully aligned the goals of the university with the company's larger organizational agenda. When he made his proposal to the executive board, he was met with strong skepticism: Many believed Lufthansa would be better served by focusing on cutting costs and improving processes. But he kept at it for another four years, chipping away at the objections. In 1998, Lufthansa School of Business became the first corporate university in Germany – and a change engine for Lufthansa.

Think of the second characteristic – *energy* – as the vigor that is fueled by intense personal commitment. Energy is what pushes managers to go the extra mile when tackling heavy workloads and meeting tight deadlines. The team that created the Sony Vaio computer – the first PC to let users combine other Sony technologies, such as digital cameras, portable music players, and camcorders – showed a lot of energy. Responding to CEO Nobuyuki Idei's challenge to create an integrated technological playground for a burgeoning generation of "digital dream kids," Hiroshi Nakagawa and his team put in 100-hour weeks to create the kind of breakthrough product Idei hoped for. One manager, Kazumasa Sato, was so devoted to the project that he spent every weekend for three years conducting consumer reconnaissance in electronics shops. Sato's research into consumer buying patterns helped Sony develop a shop layout that enhanced traffic flow and, by extension, sales. In the end, the Vaio captured a significant share of the Japanese PC market.

While both focus and energy are positive traits, neither alone is sufficient to produce the kind of purposeful action organizations need most from their managers. Focus without energy devolves into listless execution or leads to burnout. Energy without focus dissipates into purposeless busyness or, in its most destructive form, a series of wasteful failures. We found that plotting the two characteristics in a matrix offered a useful framework for diagnosing the causes of nonproductive activity as well as the sources of purposeful action. The exhibit "The Focus–Energy Matrix" identifies four types of behavior: disengagement, procrastination, distraction, and purposefulness.

Before we look at each type more closely, we should note that these behaviors have both internal and external causes. Some people are born with high levels of energy, for example, and some, by nature, are more self-reflective. But it is important not to overlook the organizational context of these behaviors. Some companies foster fire-fighting cultures; others breed cynicism and, hence, low levels of commitment in their workers. To change the behaviors of your managers, it may be necessary to alter the organizational landscape.

The procrastinators

Of the managers we studied, some 30% suffered from low levels of both energy and focus; we call these managers the procrastinators. Although they dutifully perform routine tasks – attending meetings, writing memos, making phone calls, and so on – they fail to take initiative, raise the level of performance, or engage with strategy.

Some procrastinators hesitate, Hamlet-like, until the window of opportunity for a project has closed. At Lufthansa, for instance, the manager who was charged with developing an internal survey delayed beginning the project until the deadline passed. "I could have done [the work]," he admits, "but for some reason, I could not get started." The nearer the deadline loomed, the more he busied himself on other projects, rationalizing that he couldn't turn to this task until he cleared his desk of less important jobs.

People often procrastinate when they feel insecure or fear failure. One young lawyer, assigned a key role in an important merger project, was initially excited about the prospect of making a presentation to the executive board. But as time passed, he found the challenge of the task overwhelming. He began imagining horrible scenarios: losing his train of thought, saying the wrong thing, seeing the stifled yawns and suppressed smirks of his audience. He became so obsessed with the notion of failure that he was almost paralyzed.

Other procrastinators coast along in the chronically passive state that psychologist Martin Seligman called "learned helplessness." At some point in their lives, they were punished or suffered negative consequences when

A mere 10% of managers are purposeful – that is, both highly energetic and highly focused. They use their time effectively by carefully choosing goals and then taking deliberate actions to reach them. Managers that fall into the other groups, by contrast, are usually just spinning their wheels; some procrastinate, others feel no emotional connection to their work, and still others are easily distracted from the task at hand. Although they look busy, they lack either the focus or the energy required for making any sort of meaningful change.

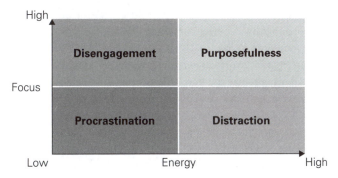

The Focus–Energy Matrix

they took initiative. Now, as managers, they believe that any effort they make will be shot down. They think they have no control over events, so they do nothing, which can ultimately debilitate their companies.

Surprisingly, in the early phases of Lufthansa's turnaround – when things were chaotic and managerial jobs were relatively unstructured – fewer managers than we expected were procrastinators. But when circumstances returned to normal and formal procedures were reestablished, many managers lost both focus and energy. They stopped setting goals for themselves and became passive. This reinforced our sense that procrastination doesn't wholly depend on personality; it can be influenced by organizational factors.

The disengaged

Roughly 20% of managers fall into the disengaged category; they exhibit high focus but have low levels of energy. Some of these managers are simply exhausted and lack the inner resources to reenergize themselves. Others feel unable to commit to tasks that hold little meaning for them. Disengaged managers have strong reservations about the jobs they are asked to do; as a result, they approach them halfheartedly.

From disengaged to purposeful: a convert's story

In 1995, Siemens Nixdorf Informationssysteme was in the midst of a crisis. Facing cumulative five-year losses of DM 2.1 billion and a progressive erosion of market, the company's survival was uncertain. Internally, the vastly different corporate cultures of two merger partners (Nixdorf computers and the computer division of Siemens) had created a politically vicious, unstable environment – a perfect breeding ground for procrastination, disengagement, and distraction.

Klaus Karl, a young software engineer in the relational database part of the business, had reached the end of his rope. Exhausted by the political battles, Karl grew apathetic and began looking for a new job. He received an excellent offer from software manufacturer Sybase and was less than a month away from his planned departure when he attended a meeting organized by the newly hired CEO, Gerhard Schulmeyer

That meeting was a call to arms: Schulmeyer reminded employees of the company's European roots, saying that it was destined to be a far better technology partner to companies on the Continent than any U.S. competitor could possibly be. Dubbing the company "the IT partner for change," Schulmeyer announced that he would give its technology-savvy young people an opportunity to take part in corporate strategic planning. Their common challenge was to help top management rethink SNI's approach to the market, to technology, and to change. Karl's name was on the list of bright young employees fingered to join the new team.

"I faced a real dilemma," says Karl. "I had an excellent offer, with higher pay and great prospects. My boss made it very clear that it was quite likely that the change effort would fail and that I might find myself looking for a job. On the other hand, if I was willing to join the change agent program, I would be sent for a special change management training program spanning three months at MIT – along with top managers, including Schulmeyer himself – and then could define my own change initiative." He weighed his options carefully, and the opportunity to make a difference proved too enticing. Karl committed to SNI.

During the training program in the United States, Karl learned to use strategy and change management tools. He formed close bonds with colleagues in the program. By the end, Karl and the other trainees – including Schulmeyer – were "committed to transforming the company."

Over the next two years, we saw Karl completely shake up the middleware development department. "We had to focus on a smaller portfolio of projects, so as to allocate our resources better," he says. "Initially, we tried to persuade people to use a new set of analytical tools. They would laugh at us. Some walked away from the meetings. Many senior people even refused to attend." But Karl stuck to his guns and continued his campaign of persuasion. "Gradually, they began to listen. They began to alter their ways of thinking about projects." As a result, a new product-portfolio analysis system was completed in a mere three months.

Karl's contribution had a powerful impact on the company's bottom line. Within three years, it successfully launched a variety of new projects that boosted the bottom line by DM 400 million. Without the contributions of Karl and other reenergized, refocused managers, SNI would never have achieved such a dramatic turnaround.

Many managers in this group practice a form of denial we call "defensive avoidance": Rather than acknowledging a problem and taking steps to correct it, they convince themselves that the problem doesn't exist. Plenty of denial was at play when Lufthansa stood at the brink of bankruptcy in 1992. Even though the entire industry faced a severe downturn and Lufthansa was losing revenue, these managers ignored or reinterpreted market signals, convincing themselves that the company's expansionist strategy was correct. Many of them continued to hire new employees in the face of massive operating losses.

By contrast, some disengaged managers refuse to take action – even when it's obviously needed. One manager responsible for ground services in a major airport, for example, fully understood the threat of bankruptcy and the need to make radical changes. He enthusiastically participated in all the change management meetings and offered ideas for improving operational productivity. Yet deep down, he believed his job was to protect his area and his people. He convinced himself that his department was a core group and should be spared from layoffs. Later, when it became clear that cuts in all areas were inevitable, he agreed to the layoffs in principle, but his personal discomfort kept him from truly committing to them. He delayed making the decision and invested little energy in making the right cuts. As a consequence, his results were less than stellar.

Disengaged managers tend to be extremely tense. That's hardly surprising, for they are often plagued by feelings of anxiety, uncertainty, anger, frustration, and alienation. They deal with those emotions by withdrawing and doing the bare minimum, which make the situations worse. Despite their low levels of energy, these managers suffer from burnout far more frequently than their colleagues do. And they are easily overwhelmed by unexpected events.

While some managers are inherently more likely than others to distance themselves from their work, disengagement is often a result of organizational processes. In a major U.S. oil company, for example, we witnessed a committed and enthusiastic manager gradually become apathetic. An IT specialist, he was assigned to an interdisciplinary strategy-development task force that was charged with creating a new business model for an up-stream division. The team came up with several radical proposals, but they were met with lukewarm responses from senior managers. After several months, the team's ideas were diluted to the point that not even the IT manager found them interesting. What had once been an exciting task became a farce, from his point of view. Believing that no one was interested in new ideas, he concluded that he was foolish to have been as engaged as he was. "I distanced myself," he says. "I knew that none of our innovative ideas would ever make it to implementation. So I continued working out concepts and ideas – but with no skin in the game."

To be fair, even the best organizations occasionally create cynics out of enthusiasts. But some organizations seem to make a practice of it by consistently sabotaging any flickers of creativity or initiative.

The distracted

By far the largest group of managers we studied – more than 40% – fall into the distracted quadrant: those well-intentioned, highly energetic but unfocused people who confuse frenetic motion with constructive action. When they're under pressure, distracted managers feel a desperate need to do something – anything. That makes them as dangerous as the proverbial bull in a china shop.

In 1992, for example, when Lufthansa's senior management made it clear that the company was going to have to reduce expenses, managers in this category shot first and aimed later. "Everybody knew that we had to do everything to reduce costs, and I was frantic," admits one. "I let go of people who were vital to our future. We had to re-recruit them and hire them back later at higher salaries." He had acted too quickly because he felt that something had to happen fast. He didn't take the time to consider what, exactly, that "something" should be.

Because they don't stop to reflect, distracted managers tend to have trouble developing strategies and adjusting their behaviors to new requirements. One manager on the task force charged with driving Lufthansa's change strategy assigned responsibilities according to functional categories instead of deliberately choosing the best person for each job. "We made the technical guy responsible for technical issues and the marketing guy for marketing issues," he says. "You do so many things just because you are used to doing them." He later realized that if he had been less bound by traditional functional silos, the work would have progressed much faster.

Moreover, because distracted managers tend to be shortsighted, they often find themselves overcommitted. They get involved in multiple projects with the best of intentions, but eventually their interest pales, and they wind up either constantly fighting fires or abandoning the projects altogether. In the space of two months, one HR executive we observed enthusiastically took on three enormous projects – redefining the role of the HR department, renewing the 360-degree feedback system, and creating a leadership development program – over and above his everyday job requirements. In the end, he abandoned one project, passed on responsibility for another, and did a poor job on the third.

Managers are more likely to feel distracted during a crisis, but the behavior is by no means limited to turbulent times. Even in stable business situations, many managers feel enormous pressure to be busy. Of course, some of this pressure is internal: Many insecure managers try to impress others with how much work they have. But the pressure to perform can be amplified by organizations themselves. Indeed, many companies encourage, and even reward, frantic activity. We have noticed, for example, that in organizations whose CEOs and senior executives exhibit aggressive, unreflective behavior, it's far more likely that other managers will be distracted.

The purposeful

The smallest proportion of managers we studied – around 10% – were both highly energetic and highly focused. Not only do such managers put in more effort than their counterparts, but they also achieve critical, long-term goals more often. Purposeful managers tend to be more self-aware than most people. Their clarity about their intentions, in combination with strong willpower, seems to help them make sound decisions about how to spend their time. They pick their goals – and their battles – with far more care than other managers do.

Making deliberate choices can be a hard and sometimes painful process. Consider the plight of one middle manager at Lufthansa. He had been offered the difficult job of assuring the implementation of 130 do-or-die operations projects that would be overseen by managers more senior than he was. If he failed, a board member told him, he'd probably have to leave the company because he would have upset so many people during the turnaround effort. "I really struggled for a couple of days," he says. Making this huge decision was this manager's personal Rubicon: "After I went through that process, I was sure I really wanted to do it." Lufthansa's successful turnaround was a testament to his conviction.

A sense of personal responsibility for the company's fate also contributes to purposefulness. Convinced that the organization needs them, purposeful managers feel accountable for making a meaningful contribution. "When nobody is responsible, I am responsible," one Lufthansa manager says. "I own an issue and do what I think is necessary – unless and until [CEO] Jürgen Weber pulls me back." Interestingly, many Lufthansa managers refer to their contributions to the turnaround in the stark vocabulary of life and death. Like warriors, they were "fighting for survival," "stanching the loss of blood," or providing "first aid" to the corporate body.

While one could infer that managers become purposeful only when faced with a crisis, the managers we studied did not lose their energy or focus once the turbulence had passed. Rather, they continued to welcome opportunities and pursue new goals. Even after the success of the turnaround was reported in the press and people were ready to celebrate Lufthansa's victory, one purposeful manager, for example, led a wide-ranging cost-management program. By watching costs, he believed, Lufthansa would not merely survive, but thrive.

One reason that purposeful managers are so effective is that they are adept at husbanding energy. Aware of the value of time, they manage it carefully. Some refuse to respond to e-mails, phone calls, or visitors outside certain periods of the day. Others build "think time" into their schedules. One executive, for example, frequently arrived at the office at 6:00 AM to ponder issues before his colleagues showed up. "In the busiest times, I slow down and take time off to reflect on what I actually want to achieve and sort what's important from irrelevant noise," he says. "Then I focus on doing what is most important."

Purposeful managers are also skilled at finding ways to reduce stress and refuel. They commonly draw on what we call a "personal well" – a defined source for positive energy. Some work out at the gym or get involved in sports. Others share their fears, frustrations, and thoughts about work with a partner, friend, or colleague. Still others refuel their inner reserves through hobbies like gardening.

Perhaps the biggest difference between purposeful managers and the other types is the way they approach work. Other managers feel constrained by outside forces: their bosses, their peers, their salaries, their job descriptions. They take all those factors into account when they're deciding what's feasible and what isn't. In other words, they work from the outside in. Purposeful managers do the opposite. They decide first what they must achieve and then work to manage the external environment – tapping into resources, building networks, honing skills, broadening their influence – so that, in the end, they meet their goals. A sense of personal volition – the refusal to let other people or organizational constraints set the agenda – is perhaps the subtlest and most important distinction between this group of managers and all the rest.

Indeed, this sense of volition allows purposeful managers to control the external environment. A major drain on most managers' energy is the perception that they have limited influence. Purposeful managers, by contrast, are acutely aware of the choices they can make – and they systematically extend their freedom to act. They manage their bosses' expectations, find ways to independently access required resources, develop relationships with influential people, and build specific competencies that broaden their choices and ability to act.

That's why purposeful managers can place long-term bets and follow through on them. Consider the accomplishments of one of Lufthansa's purposeful managers. During the turnaround, he was responsible for negotiating the tricky relationship between the corporation and the German airline industry's demanding labor unions. To develop the trust required to make the tough change agenda work, he initiated a series of meetings between board members and union leaders. Every two weeks, representatives from each wary camp met for three hours and discussed the critical turnaround steps. The board members had reservations because the meetings ate up their time – the one thing they didn't have during this phase. They complained that the meetings weren't producing immediate results – neither cost reductions nor revenue increases. But the executive convinced the board members that a focus on short-term performance would not get them very far in building trusting relationships with union members, which would be essential if they were to turn Lufthansa around. "I told them that we could not hope to transform [Lufthansa] without the help of the employees and that it made no sense to try to hurry trust building," he explains. Over time, the two sides came to trust each other and to reach an extraordinarily high level of consensus. Not only did the company avoid a strike, but the wage concessions achieved in agreement with the union were unique in German history.

Challenge and choice

We can imagine readers wincing as they ask themselves, "Are only 10% of the managers in my company truly effective?" The number may be higher in your company, but probably not by much. Senior managers can raise the energy and focus levels of their teams – of that we have no doubt. However, trying to prevent managers from losing energy or focus (or both) is an ambitious proposition. It involves paying far more attention to how individual managers perceive the broad meaning of their work, what challenges they face, and the degree of autonomy they enjoy. It can't be done by pulling small-scale HR levers; it can only happen with vision, oversight, and commitment from the top.

In a striking metaphor, the French World War II pilot and writer Antoine de Saint-Exupéry pointed executives in the right direction: "If you want to build a ship, don't drum up the men to go to the forest to gather wood, saw it, and nail the planks together. Instead, teach them the desire for the sea." In managers, a desire for the sea springs from two sources: meaningful challenge and personal choice. If you combine challenge and choice with a sense of profound urgency, you've gone a long way toward creating a recipe for success. Consider the starting point for Lufthansa's turnaround. On a weekend in June 1992, CEO Weber invited about 20 senior managers, as well as the entire executive board, to the company's training center. He wanted to create a network of managers who would drive the change process throughout the company. At the meeting, he revealed the unvarnished facts: Lufthansa was facing a massive shortfall. It was obvious that if things didn't change, the company would be in financial ruin. Weber made it very clear that he didn't have the solution. He gave the managers three days to develop ways to save Lufthansa. If they determined that it could not be saved, he would accept their conclusion, and bankruptcy was assured. Then he and the executive board left.

According to personal accounts of what followed, the place was in chaos for a short time. The managers were shocked at how dire the situation was, and they quickly experienced waves of paralysis, denial, and finger-pointing. But soon they settled down to the problem at hand, and it quickly became clear that they all thought Lufthansa was worth fighting for. Once that fact was established, a kind of excitement emerged. They committed themselves to ambitious goals. They eventually embraced 130 radical changes and implemented 70% of them during the transformation. By 2000, Lufthansa had not only recouped its DM 750 million loss, but it had also achieved a record profit of DM 2.5 billion. Many factors went into that success, but the combination of challenge and choice that the CEO handed his colleagues was extraordinarily important.

To be sure, the prospect of one's own hanging focuses the mind. But a crisis need not be a precondition for challenge and choice. Sony's Idei achieved precisely the same result with the image of a future community of Vaio users, the "digital dream kids." Convinced that they were building a creative tool for a whole generation, Sony's engineers charged ahead with amazing determination.

Note that neither Weber nor Idei used typical managerial tools to create energy and focus in their subordinates. "Motivating" people, or telling them what to do, has dismal results. In fact, such exhortations often lead to exactly the opposite of what's needed. When executives outline desired behaviors for middle managers and set goals for them, the managers aren't given the opportunity to decide for themselves. As a result, they don't fully commit to projects. They distance themselves from their work because they feel they have no control. To avoid that kind of reaction, top managers should present their people with meaningful challenges and real choices in how they might meet those challenges.

We are not suggesting that meaningful challenge and personal choice are guaranteed to turn around a failing company. Nor do we want to imply that individual managers will be able to overcome lifelong behavioral patterns simply because they're presented with challenge and choice. Nevertheless, we strongly believe it would be a mistake for a top manager to conclude about a subordinate, "John is never going to be a purposeful manager because he is just not built that way." Focus and energy are indeed personal characteristics, but organizations can do much to enhance those traits in their managers,

In fact, leaders can directly affect the type of behavior exhibited in their organizations by loosening formal procedures and purging deadening busywork. Presented with a challenge for which their contributions are essential, managers feel needed. Asked for their opinions and given choices, they feel emboldened. When corporate leaders make a sincere effort to give managers both challenge and choice, most managers can learn to direct their energy and improve their focus – and ultimately find their way to the sea.

To further explore the topic of this paper, go to www.hbr.org/explore.

Heike Bruch is a professor of leadership at the University of St. Gallen in St. Gallen, Switzerland.

This paper appeared in *Harvard Business Review*, February 2002.

Commentaries and reflections

Creating a legacy: the philosophies, processes, and person behind the ideas

Christopher A. Bartlett

Although the articles in this book represent only a small selection from a long list of Sumantra Ghoshal's publications, they are a testament to the intellectual impact of his contribution to management literature. But it is not just his prolific output that is remarkable; it is its consistent quality and its enormous range that make this such an impressive body of work.

How did he achieve so much and have such an impact in his relatively brief academic career? I believe the answer lies in how Sumantra approached his chosen profession. Over the next few pages, I would like to reflect not on the content of the written contribution – that is already well represented and reviewed in earlier chapters – but on the process of its creation.

In 20 years of research and writing together, I probably developed as good an understanding as anyone of the critical influences and core practices that shaped the way Sumantra worked. To understand his approach to research, I believe one has to recognize the foundation stones on which it was built: his strong research philosophy, his established working process, and his unique personal attributes.

The research philosophy: built on a respect for managers

Sumantra was such a conceptual thinker and so knowledgeable about theory that it was easy to forget that he began his career as a practicing manager. Before coming to the United States to earn his masters degree and the two doctorates, he spent eight years as an executive with Indian Oil, rising to become one of its youngest-ever division managers. That background remained a powerful influence that shaped the philosophy he brought to his research.

His great respect for the difficulty of the management task and his admiration for those who carried it out effectively were reflected in a belief that research had to begin in the field talking to those closest to practice. But data gathering was a continuous activity for him, and the field research that ended up as research notes or case studies was just the most structured and formal part of his constant observation of management practice. Classroom assignments became a means to collect students' experiences; consulting engagements turned into data-gathering opportunities; conversations with colleagues led to discussions of their latest field observations; even casual cocktail interactions with managers became an opportunity to test ideas and collect anecdotes.

Beyond his ability as a field researcher, Sumantra's understanding of a broad range of theory established him amongst the most knowledgeable of management academics. But unlike many of his peers, his motivation in accumulating that knowledge was to fulfill a second part of his research philosophy: to link theory and practice. In this pursuit, his approach was to always to start with his field data and test the theory against it, rather than vice-versa. More often than not, it was the theory that was found wanting.

Having identified a theory-practice gap, Sumantra's driving motivation was always to bridge it. The question was to decide which theoretical links to build on and reinforce and which to challenge or cut. His biases were clear: to him, the seminal insights of practitioner Chester Barnard rang truer than the agency theory-based economic models he saw driving strategy discussions in many MBA programs.

So he decided to do something about it. In the mid-1990s, he explicitly set out to develop a managerial theory of the firm, grounded in real field-based data rather than in the economists' dominant assumptions about human motivation and firm behavior. As he often said, "Nothing informs good theory like good practice." This was more than an old bromide to Sumantra; it was a philosophy he harnessed to drive his research.

A third strong belief in Sumantra's research philosophy was that its purpose was not to develop elegant ideas but to become the stimulus of change. He loudly lamented the oft-cited statistic that the average article in a scholarly journal was read by 2.5 academics. In his typically provocative way, he would ask, "What's the point if we do all this work to reach 2.5 people who, at best, will cite and recycle the ideas to another 2.5 people? We could add more value by sweeping the streets."

Early on, his publication objective became to write books and articles that would reach a large audience. More important, he wanted to challenge the readers to think and, if possible, provoke them to act.

The process: collaboration as an art form

Anyone browsing through the articles in this book must be struck by the fact that all of them are written with one or more co-authors. While this group of eight research and writing partners probably represents Sumantra's principal collaborators over the past 20 years, a complete listing of his work would identify at least 18 other co-authors – and dozens more if one included the many research associates, doctoral students, and other collaborators with whom he has written case studies or other classroom materials.

Over the years in a variety of settings, Sumantra and I gave several joint presentations to students and colleagues on the strengths and challenges of research partnerships. Having heard him express his views on the topic several times, I have some feeling on why he felt collaboration was such an important part of his research and writing process.

First, as a social being, Sumantra acknowledged that he simply enjoyed the opportunity to work with others around the development of ideas. Due to his enormous capacity to work, he rarely passed up an invitation to join in a project that intrigued him as long as it was with a person whom he found stimulating. And he engaged in each new venture not only as a scholarly pursuit, but also as a new opportunity for intellectual banter and social engagement.

More pragmatically, he believed that collaborative effort was the most efficient way to tackle big research agendas. Not only did a team approach allow the work to proceed on a broader front (doing in-depth field research in 20 companies for *The Individualized Corporation*, for example), but it also gave the researchers the opportunity to probe more deeply into each of those organizations.

But at the core of this preferred mode of working was a firm belief that effective partnerships could develop a stronger and richer set of conclusions, always his prime objective. His oft-repeated mantra, "Both of us together are smarter than either of us individually," did more than reflect the old saw of "Two heads are better than one." It captured his preferred way of developing ideas: using collaborators as intellectual sparring partners.

A gifted debater, Sumantra enjoyed nothing more than developing arguments literally face-to-face. He was, above all, a very verbal individual and the process of developing ideas through rational discussion and passionate debate was at the core of intellectual creation. In the process, he believed that both parties articulated ideas they did not know they had, and built arguments they had never made before. Behind each of his co-authored papers and books lies a myriad of intense, engaged, and often exhausting debates that forged the resulting argument and conclusions.

The only thing more surprising than the frequency of Sumantra's co-authored work is the diversity of the partnerships that produced it. He was equally at home writing with collaborators who were practice-oriented or theory-driven; trained in economics, sociology, or psychology; young doctoral students or renowned gurus. To him they were a means of broadening the scope of his inquiry and deepening his understanding of the phenomena.

This engagement with a diverse set of partnerships supported and reinforced another aspect of Sumantra's research process: his preference, even need, to pursue multiple research agendas simultaneously. He was a true master of intellectual multi-tasking, a capability that spoke not only to his intellectual capacity, but also to his enormous physical and mental energy. It was a level of vigor that few collaborators could match and could therefore be satisfied only by engaging in multiple projects and working with multiple partners simultaneously.

At the time of his death, Sumantra was committed to at least four major research and writing streams that were engaging his time and energy. He had just finished a book with Heike Bruch and was translating that into articles; with Peter Moran he was drafting a book manuscript that built on his "bad for practice" arguments; he and Lynda Gratton had finished some fieldwork and were developing on the ideas presented in their article, "Integrating the Enterprise"; and Sumantra and I had completed several pieces of the fieldwork and the first article that would be the building blocks for a new book focused on the managerial task of treating human capital rather than financial capital as the firm's constraining strategic resource. At least speaking for myself, I found the agenda we had set on our project to be stretching and demanding; for Sumantra, however, it was just one of four balls he kept in the air as he engaged across his broad spectrum of intellectual pursuits.

The person: intense, bold, compassionate

Sumantra had a brilliant mind, as anyone who encountered him in person or read his work would readily acknowledge. But to understand what allowed him to leave such a rich intellectual legacy, one needs to understand several other characteristics of this complex, multifaceted man.

If his incredible intellectual capacity was the vehicle that allowed him to take on such a huge research and teaching load, the engine powering it was his driving energy and relentless intensity. He pursued his work on close to a 24/7 basis, long before that phrase came into the common vernacular. From conversations over breakfast till the last arguments over a post dinner glass of port, Sumantra was constantly engaging managers, questioning students, and challenging collaborators to push their ideas. The light in his office burned deep into the night, and you could find him at work on any day of the week, including weekends and public holidays. (This enormous appetite for work was evident from his time as a PhD student when his professors, incredulous that one individual could carry such a huge course load and still generate such prolific output, dubbed him "the triplets.")

Beyond the drive and intensity that were the immediately obvious parts of his personality, Sumantra also exhibited a boldness and curiosity that fueled his ever-changing and often surprising pursuit of new research interests. It was this trait that inevitably led him to ask the big question, to opt for the bold research design, and in the end, to draw the most challenging and provocative conclusions.

His passionate curiosity is evident not only in the topics addressed in this book's individual chapters, but also in the fact that it is divided into three parts, each representing a major inflection point in Sumantra's 20-year research voyage. While many would have been content to build on the strong reputation he had established in his early international business research, he wanted to push into new territory. As he did so, he migrated from transnational strategy, to organizational transformation, to the study of management roles and responsibilities, and eventually to a focus on personal skills and competencies.

Sumantra's boldness extended beyond a relentless willingness to expand his research horizons. More than almost any other academic in his field, he was ready to question accepted practice and challenge conventional wisdom, even when it meant taking on the most established of theories. His favorite target was economists, and particularly those associated with agency theory and transaction cost economics. He boldly asserted that their pathological assumptions of human behavior – characterized by opportunism, shirking, and cheating – resulted in management norms and practices that were destructive of organizations. And he was willing to carry the battle to them on their terms and on their turf.

But there was another side to this man that trumped both his driving intensity and his passionate boldness. Sumantra had a personal warmth, generosity, and caring compassion that was never diminished by his many successes, nor dulled by the cynicism so often associated with academic research. It was this attribute that made him such a unique individual in our profession – someone who had as much time for the nervous student or the worried support staff member as for the CEOs, journalists, or leading academics who sought his views or advice.

Some time ago, when Sumantra and I were talking about where our research together might take us next, he presented his views simply. "We dedicated *Managing Across Borders* to our wives, and *The Individualized Corporation* to our mothers. Our next book should be for our children. Let's write something that gives our kids a sense of the force for good that well-run business enterprise can be. Maybe we can help a new generation see that the field of management can be an exciting, worthwhile, and honorable profession."

It was classically Sumantra: a big, idealistic, generous thought, at once noble and naïve, which reflected the positive view he held about the profession he had chosen and the work he was doing. Sumantra believed strongly that academic research, writing, and teaching was worth doing not for the elegance of the idea created but for the lasting and positive impact it could have. He wanted his work to shape the way students thought, affect the way managers acted, and perhaps even change the role of business in society at large. The work represented here suggests he was succeeding: that he did not have a chance to finish the work he had begun is the world's loss.

Sumantra Ghoshal:
the practical dreamweaver

Gita Piramal

By training I am a historian, by profession, a journalist. Sumantra started out as a manager, working for almost a decade in India's biggest oil company, Indian Oil Corporation, before becoming a teacher of managers. Our research styles reflected our very different backgrounds, leading to several early clashes when we began writing case studies together. I would always want to dig more, explore further around issues, request one more round of interviews. As a historian, every fact had to have a context; as a reporter, there was always another truth behind every truth. As someone who created frameworks and innovated management theory as he journeyed the research path, Sumantra's approach was very different. He would observe minutely every situation, and treat it as the truth at that specific point in time, just as a balance sheet records financial transactions at a point in time. All data was collected in one go, and once the data was in, he felt no need to revisit. I quickly learnt to appreciate his economical use of time.

This ability to instantaneously recognize truth from trivia, to swiftly drill down to core issues, combined with his energy and bias for action, accounts for Sumantra's prodigious output. In the world of management publishing, a billion dollar market overflowing with books (in 1995, $750m worth of books were sold in the USA alone), writers consider themselves lucky if they can come up with anything more than one book. Very few are like Peter Drucker, and barely a handful have more than half a dozen books to their credit. It's hard to come up with ideas with metronomic regularity.

In this context, Sumantra was prolific. From 1988 to 2004, a period of roughly 15 years, he produced 12 books, 18 chapters in other people's books, 70 major research articles, over 50 case studies, numerous teaching videos for the BBS, the Harvard Business School and the London Business School, besides a popular TV series for India. His productivity is comparable only to fiction writers. In the 52 years of his life, William Shakespeare wrote 14 comedies, ten historical plays, ten tragedies and five romances besides a diverse assortment of sonnets and poems. John Grisham, perhaps the highest selling contemporary author (over 60 million copies), has written 17 books in 15 years since 1989.

Sumantra worked with over 30 coauthors on his articles published in leading academic journals. (There is no list of articles for newspapers and magazines for which he wrote condensed versions based on key ideas.) On the case studies, he worked with an awesome number of students and faculty from business schools as well as managers from companies. This diversity of collaborators was a distinctive feature of Sumantra's work. People who write together generally decide to work together because they share certain ideas and beliefs, as well as perceptions of the future, or what ought to be the future. As Sumantra often said, "Collaboration should not be $1 + 1 = 2$. Collaboration is worthwhile only when the equation is $1 + 1 = 3$." Inclusiveness was inherent in his character and in his philosophy.

Working with Sumantra, perhaps one of the biggest lessons I learnt was to stop thinking in terms of simple options. "We tend to begin our thinking in 'either-or' terms. If you take an 'and-and' approach, so many more solutions to a problem become evident," he would advise. He practiced as he preached: the double PhD, the double shifts working days and nights. Yet there is a "but" in this philosophy. It requires energy, both physical and mental. All of us possess high energy but we frequently dissipate it by not spending enough time asking ourselves what we really want. "Look into the future, let the future guide the present. Then focus. Every effort will release more energy," he would chide.

If there is one core, one fountainhead as it were, from which Sumantra drew his beliefs and ideas, it would be his faith in the goodness of people. We are not programmed to be selfish; selfishness comes to the fore as a self defense mechanism only when we are threatened. Normally we are programmed to be good. Hence, because companies are today so powerful, they can, if they want to, be a force for good, capable of creating a world worth living in. This belief perhaps originated in his Indian background. Christianity expounds the concept of original sin, in Hinduism there is no such negativity. Every person has a "Divine Nature" and enters this world to fulfill his or her destiny. Along the way, every good deed will take one closer to Nirvana (enlightenment), while every "sin" or evil deed will set us back a step. Both Christianity and Hinduism recognize desire as the source of evil, but while Christianity blames Eve in the Garden of Eden, Hinduism says people stumble on desire when they arrive on earth.

Sumantra's bias for action, mentioned earlier here and elsewhere in this volume, also has strong Indian roots. "Action is superior to inaction," says Krishna in the central text of the Bhagvad Gita, the Hindu equivalent of the Bible, which deals with action and at least three forms of nonaction, including the passive nonaction pathology that Sumantra and Heike describe in the article "Beware the busy manager" (see Chapter 13), and in their book, *A Bias for Action*. And once again, Sumantra practiced what he preached.

Sumantra's life was extraordinary by any standards. Yet it was extraordinary not because he was a gifted person and he used his talents wisely; it was extraordinary because he chose to make it so through his volition and actions. Elsewhere in this book, you will have read about how Sumantra urged managers to create a growth environment by enabling "stretch" within the organization. "You alone are responsible for your future, take charge of yourself" was another key lesson he taught. Born in Kolkata the son of an All India Radio employee, paying his own way through the best education the US offers, working his way up the academic ladder in Europe, Sumantra continuously stretched himself through self-education, observation and dedication.

What made Sumantra such a great teacher was the passionate expression of his beliefs, and his ability to make people believe in themselves. Those who came into his orbit always left feeling energized, confident, privileged. And it can be argued that Sumantra's biggest contribution to management and managers lay not just in the realm of pure theory but equally in the lyrical phrases he created.

These phrases inspire courage, especially in managers who are weary of work, who are tired of the relentless pressures on them. "Cooking sweet and sour," "the valley of death," "the smell of the place," "crossing the Rubicon," "killing the dragon," and "winning the princess": underneath each of these memorable phrases lie profound insights into managerial behavior backed by clinical research and empirical data gathering across companies, industries, cultures and companies. Once heard or read and understood, these compelling and evocative phrases etch themselves in managers' minds, helping them to make sense of their working lives and themselves. As the lessons are internalized, managers find themselves renewed. Surely the best outcome for a guru. "I never met Professor

Ghoshal, but his work inspired me, I don't know why I am writing to you but I want you to know that he helped me," a reader wrote to me. His tribute was just one of hundreds we received at *The Smart Manager*, the journal I edit.

In India, Sumantra's work impacted managers enormously. Serendipitously, *Managing Radical Change* appeared on bookshelves at a watershed in the history of the Indian corporate sector. India began a major reform of its economic policies in 1991. Initially managers went into a state of shock. By the mid-1990s, they began sprucing up their companies, cutting cost and pruning flab, yet mentally they remained unprepared for the competitive onslaught which they faced by the beginning of the new millennium. In this crisis of confidence, many turned to Sumantra's work, accepting his home truth of satisfactory under-performance, and began cooking sweet and sour. While there is a long way to go yet, there is no doubt in my mind of the critical role Sumantra played, and will continue to play, in the revitalization of Indian business.

Perhaps the most important message Sumantra wanted to deliver was the exhortation to be always world class. Several centuries of poverty and almost 150 years of colonial rule are a heavy burden. Indians are tip-toeing towards self respect. Through the case studies of Indian companies, we tried to show that nuggets of world class management exist at various levels in many Indian firms, both large and small, and in diverse businesses. As he said, "If they can do it, so can you." In the end, the talented storyteller taught through the dictum that managers are the best teachers of managers. That is why managers listened to him, that is why his work will endure. Authenticity is irresistible.

The role of creative dialogue

Lynda Gratton

Scholars create and describe their world in many ways. They think and build theoretical frameworks, they analyze the empirical data they have collected from the phenomena they are interested in, and they empirically test propositions. There are many paths to scholarship and each scholar chooses the path they will tread.

For Sumantra Ghoshal the path of scholarship he trod had two profoundly important features. Perhaps most importantly, the path he chose for himself was essentially a path bounded by his deeply held personal values and beliefs, and in particular by his beliefs about human nature and human intentionality. Secondly, in treading his own scholarly path, Sumantra's methodology of scholarship was essentially a process of creative dialogue that he entered both with himself and with others.

To understand the scholarship of Sumantra Ghoshal, one needs to understand his personal values. These personal values became over time increasingly at the core of his insights and arguments. Many people who worked with Sumantra have spoken about the essentially positive approach he took to others. This was a core value. His starting assumption in his relationships with others and in his work as a scholar was that people are basically good and could be trusted to behave in a positive and cooperative way. The role of the company, then, becomes one of creating the container for this good.

Given this predisposition, he steadfastly took a broad view of the role of the organization. I heard this at first hand in the conversation he and I had with Lord John Browne on what the role of the enterprise could and should be. Our case research had highlighted Browne's initiative termed "A Force For Good" and Sumantra was fascinated to hear more. Moving rapidly beyond the researcher role he engaged Browne in a long conversation about how the modern industrial enterprise could make a difference to the lives of employees and consumers. In this conversation with Browne he was continuing on a trail of thought which had become increasingly important to him. His work with Peter Moran culminating in the article "Bad for practice" had laid out the foundation for what he hoped would be a coherent and fully formed theory of the role of the company. Poignantly, in the months before his death, Sumantra was actively writing the book he hoped would be his most ambitious to date. His ambition was to provide a clear and articulate counter point to what he saw as the overly market led and economically driven foundation of contemporary management theory. We have fragments of his work in this area, and although this book was not to be, the ideas he articulated have created the platform for other scholars.

Personal and deeply held values about human nature bounded the path of scholarship along which Sumantra trod. The energy that propelled him along the path of his scholarly work was the energy of creative dialogue. Sumantra was a wonderful conversationalist. Many people who entered his room at London Business School would be greeted by a question that began a conversation that could go on for many hours. In 2002 Sumantra gathered his thoughts together about the power of conversation when we wrote an article on the subject. In it we argued that much of what we observed as passing for conversation in organizations could more accurately be described as "dehydrated talk."

> In these conversations, there was neither analytical rigor nor emotional authenticity. Listening to these conversations, we heard no doubt, no curiosity, no puzzling. Sometimes they seemed to be simply a string of trivial and unrelated fragments. (Gratton and Ghoshal, 2002)

In our own relationship, conversations had played a pivotal role and we believed that they played a pivotal role in great companies. This is how we described creative dialogue later in the same article:

> Rationality is essentially about structure, emotions are largely about meaning. Rationality is an exercise in disaggregation. It is deductive, and it focuses attention on tangible data and their inter-relationships. Emotions, on the other hand, are holistic, less amenable to such disaggregation. They deal with feelings and ideas. As a result, the two are always hard to combine. Yet, like the yin and the yang of Chinese philosophy, the most creative, insightful and energizing conversations occur when the two are combined: one hard, the other soft; one rooted in the categories of

structure, the other in the images of meaning. Bringing thinking and feeling together is difficult, but to do so is to move from fragmentation to unity (p. 216).

Sumantra conversed with others much of his waking life. And if he was not conversing with others, he was conversing with himself. I recall watching him at times when he was deep into his own thoughts. I asked him what this inner process was and he described that at such times he had set up two sides of an argument and was going through the argument, arguing for both sides in sequence. This thought skill had been honed during his early years as a student at Delhi University's debating society. It was during this time that he had learnt to argue at will for a point of view. He found this going back and forward with both rational data and emotional images to be crucial to his own life as a scholar, and was able to practice this skill with others or in his own inner world of thoughts.

Sumantra had created a life with many opportunities for conversation. Teaching provided a possibility for conversing, as did his own preferred method of research, case writing. It is interesting to reflect that the teaching process Sumantra most enjoyed was that which enabled him to actively engage with students and executives in the creation of new knowledge and learning. This was clear to me when we first worked with each other in 1996 designing a program that we called "The Global Business Consortium" or GBC as it was always known. In it, we took 36 senior executives from six companies around the world to learn from each other by conversing and visiting the factories and offices of these companies. On the journeys to ABB's factories in Germany, LG's research labs in Seoul or Lufthansa's joint venture in Brazil, we encouraged executives to engage in creative dialogue with Sumantra often playing the pivotal role in these conversations.

Teaching created a forum for conversation, and so did case writing. At the heart of Sumantra's work as a scholar was his love of, and delight in, the practice and process of case writing. Although trained as an empiricist, and with a strong mathematical mind, his preference was always for qualitative methodology. Perhaps it was the Bengali love of conversation which drove him to spend a considerable amount of time with practicing managers, talking with them about their perceptions of their company and their views of the foundations of its success. Sumantra approached the process of writing a case with enormous pleasure and joy. In these conversations he was interested in the unusual, or what he termed "the sizzle". The "sizzle" was crucial; he had little interest in the mundane, the predictable, or the obvious. He wanted to surprise, to intrigue, to question.

His co-conspirators on this journey of surprise were the executives with whom he conversed. In the last paper we co-authored in the spring of 2004, we described the approach we adopted for our case interviews as "collaborative and participative research." In the methodology section we described our approach in this way:

> We believed that the members of the organization we studied should actively participate in the research process, rather than just be subjects. The "thing" that our data represent is not a concrete object or experience . . . instead, it is a human conception. We attempted to establish a two-way relationship in which the researcher and the practitioner jointly engage in the sensemaking process to establish "fidelity" of data. In effect, the interview became an open conversation through which the practitioner's experiences and knowledge of the organization's processes and practices are combined with the on-going interpretation and evolving theories so as to refine and improve those theories in the course of the interview itself.

In doing so Sumantra made some assumptions about executives: (i) that they are willing to respond truthfully; (ii) that they are intelligent and smart and can understand the questions as the researcher intends them to be understood; (iii) that they are reflective about their own practice and can make the judgment that the questions require; and (iv) that they can effectively communicate their judgments in a manner that enables the researcher to fully comprehend their contents. Sumantra saw the case writing methodology as a two-way conversation. In doing so he neither suspended a-priori theoretical inclinations, nor indeed did he take the more positivistic approach of having a clear a-priori specification of the constructs of the relationships. Instead he believed his role with executives to be similar to the discussions he would have with a competent and trusted co-researcher from a related but different discipline attempting to arrive at a shared interpretation of data provided by the research partner.

In our article entitled "Integrating the enterprise" Sumantra returned again to a set of beliefs that he had articulated for over 20 years: The power of conversation, the importance of a purpose, and the benefit of relationships. These recurring themes in his work could be traced back to the earliest writings in *Managing Across Borders* and fleshed out in *The Individualized Corporation*.

What can we learn from the life of Sumantra Ghoshal? I believe that his view of the humane organization will form one important tributary in a growing realization that simply using the creation of shareholder value as a measure of organizational worth, will no longer be sufficient. We can also learn from him the enormous energy that can come when, like him, we are engaged in an activity aligned to our personal values and to our preferred way of working. On the path of scholarship which Sumantra trod, he kept his values intact and engaged in the process he found most energizing, the process of creative dialogue.

Creating a desire for the sea

Heike Bruch

Between 1998 and 2004, I worked very closely with Sumantra – more closely than I ever had with anyone before in my life. We developed research findings as well as concepts and ideas which probably could not have emerged as they did with anyone else. The research process – and the outcome of it – are closely linked with his unique nature. I would like to illustrate some of my personal views toward this end by using key milestones from our joint work.

Beware the busy manager[1]

Sumantra felt that management was the art of doing and getting done. But he fought against the mentality of managers who felt that their job was to make the inevitable happen, i.e. managers who lived in routines, were satisfied with mere obedience, and had forgotten how to believe in dreams.

The starting point for our research was the question: why do some managers take action while others do not? This question came as a result of the conviction that purposeful action-taking lies at the heart of relentless execution – the most critical challenge for companies today. In this respect we wrote in one of our articles, "Behind every significant improvement in productivity, every successful new product, and every strategic or organizational change, lies persistent, disciplined, and purposeful action-taking by some people in the company."[2]

Our research shows that purposeful action, as we use the term, is based on two traits – energy and focus. However, our studies also show that only 10% of all managers actually engage in such purposeful action-taking. Fully 90% suffer from a lack of energy, a lack of focus, or both. The most dangerous hazard to managers' effectiveness is busyness – high energy with low focus.

I see Sumantra's connection with purposeful action-taking in above all two respects. First, Sumantra used his research to improve the management of companies and to personally encourage managers to devote their energy and focus toward the right things. Secondly, he was, in my opinion, a person who, like almost no one else, exhibited great energy and focus in everything he did. High energy, as we found in our research, entails enthusiasm, momentum, persistence, and extraordinary effort in driving certain intentions. Focus constitutes the ability to concentrate on selected things which are of central importance and which really make a difference. Sumantra concentrated on his major goals with remarkable discipline. He channeled his attention and energy almost completely toward whatever he believed was right, and his works have influenced and shaped both the study and practice of business as few others. He numbers among those whose actions – whose purposeful action-taking – have made, and continue to make, a true difference.

Reclaim your job[3]

Sumantra was convinced that nothing in one's environment could ever be held responsible for one's inability to realize one's dreams. This belief is reflected in our research, which maintains that the reason why many managers spin their wheels without much progress is very rarely a matter of context but rather – in most cases – a matter of how managers deal with their jobs. Most managers who fail to take purposeful action do so because they fall victim to one or more of the three traps of non-action: overwhelming demands, unbearable constraints, and unexplored choices.

Sumantra himself was a living example of how to avoid these traps and always encouraged people around him to do so. He counseled them to not be shackled by others' expectations; to emancipate themselves from the narrow corset of constraints, rules, and regulations holding them back; and to let go of their tunnel vision so that they would have the freedom to take action on key challenges. He established for himself great degrees of freedom in his own life; he was never a victim of the traps of non-action.

Going beyond motivation to the power of volition[4]

During the course of our research, Sumantra became enthusiastic about volition, a new construct which fascinated him. As we asked ourselves what it was that distinguished a small minority of managers with the high energy and focus for making things happen, we first assumed that these individuals were motivated in some unique way. Our research does indeed indicate that motivation is important in that it enables managers to perform routine tasks well, but motivation is not sufficient for making significant, innovative, or complex things happen. Managers who make challenging things happen rely on a different force: Their volition, i.e. the power of their will.

Willpower goes a decisive step further than motivation. It implies the commitment that comes only from a deep, personal attachment to a certain intention.[5] Willpower springs from a conscious choice to make a concrete thing happen. This commitment to a certain goal – to achieve rather than to simply do something – represents the engagement of the human will.

Willpower enables managers to execute disciplined action even when they lack motivation and the desire to do something. Their will gives them the power to overcome barriers, to deal with setbacks, to persevere through the long, high-energy journey from the development of a vision to its realization. With willpower, abandoning an intention is not an option; subjectively, there is no way back. Willful managers are determined to achieve their intention, no matter what.

Sumantra's will was unshakeable in many respects. Giving up, resigning oneself to setbacks, and failing to persist with increased energy were not options to him. It was with invulnerable confidence and goal-orientation that he pledged his commitment to difficult and seemingly impossible things which he wanted to make happen. He gave off a unique assurance that things would go right and gave others the courage and strength also to make particularly difficult challenges happen.

However, in other respects, Sumantra lacked will, and it was here that he often openly, almost jestingly, admitted through his winning smile, "I simply don't have the self-discipline." Among other things, this combination of his almost infinite strength of will and the blunt honesty with which he stood by his weaknesses made him such an impressive and at the same time so approachable human being.

Unleashing organizational energy[6]

As we worked together, Sumantra became increasingly interested in emotions in companies and leadership tasks such as emotion management. Our research revealed that few managers pay explicit attention to the emotional aspects of their organizations, although the most important driver of collective action is organizational energy, which is a manifestation of an organization's emotional state. To build the capacity for determined, persistent, and collective action, a key leadership task is to create strong, constructive energy as a force in the company.

Many have seen the symptoms of a lack of organizational energy: Apathy and inertia, exhaustion, inflexibility, and cynicism. They know that highly energetic organizations can be ineffective if their energy turns corrosive: Their force is invested in selfish or destructive actions. By contrast, some have experienced the momentum of positively energized organizations which have fully activated their potential in the pursuit of their business goals.

In our research, we found that leaders have two critical tasks in managing the energy of their companies. First, they must mobilize organizational energy and focus it on key strategic initiatives. We discovered three different ways in which leaders can unleash and leverage the energy of their companies. The first, which we labeled the "killing the dragon" strategy, focuses an organization on a clear, unambiguous threat and channels the energy created as a result into the highly disciplined process of executing concrete projects to overcome that threat. The second way, which we describe as the "winning the princess" strategy, creates energy by drawing an organization's attention to an exciting vision and enabling people to take self-initiated action to pursue the dream. The third strategy combines these two approaches, thereby essentially creating a vision whose pursuit resolves short-term problems or challenges.

Nevertheless, we have also observed the fallacies of trying continuously to drive a company to higher and higher levels of energy. No organization can exist in a state of permanent acceleration. The second leadership task in managing organizational energy, therefore, is to sustain corporate vitality and momentum over long periods of time.

I would like to make two points about Sumantra regarding organizational energy. First of all, it was possible with him to create, use, and introduce incredibly beautiful metaphors. "Killing the dragon" and "winning the princess" are so on-the-mark, expressive, and at the same time practical as telling images which nevertheless only a handful of individuals aside from him would have developed and established as he did. Second, the use of these strategies is in part closely connected with a leader's personality. Sumantra was a great leader and was strongly inclined toward the "princess" strategy. He focused people's attention on opportunities, options, and the bigger things that could be achieved in life. He knew how to turn the things which were possible into an enchanting picture and how to generate incredibly strong energy for it through enthusiasm and excitement.

A bias for action

In our book, which was published in May 2004, we present a summary of the main findings from our research. Sumantra loved this book, but he never actually saw it in print. He looked forward to this publication with the enthusiasm of a child because he was so convinced of the power of the ideas in it – purposeful action-taking, willpower, and human dreams. Our book has so much to say about this conviction of his and ends with the words, "Ultimately, what distinguishes human beings from almost all other species are two things – dreaming and willpower. These two wonderful capacities have allowed the enormous progress that human society has forged over time. Corporate leaders have many resources at their disposal – money, technology, equipment – but none as valuable as their ability to take purposeful action. Leaders must harness that same willpower in their people and instill a bias for action in their organizations. As we move forward into the future, this is *the task* of the purposeful leader."[7]

A desire for the sea

Relatively early on in our collaboration, I showed Sumantra a quotation which I like. He was enthusiastic about it and, at first, used it for all possible occasions.

It is the quote by the French World War II pilot and writer, Antoine de Saint-Exupéry, which says: "If you want to build a ship, don't drum up the men to go to the forest to gather wood, saw it, and nail the planks together. Instead, teach them the desire for the sea."

This quotation reflects in an indescribably telling way Sumantra's most fundamental beliefs about leadership. And it describes in a wonderfully romantic way the effect which Sumantra himself had on and instilled in others. In the acknowledgements for my book on leaders' action, I wrote in 2003, "Energy and focus also came from a particularly special individual: my teacher, adviser, and research partner, Prof. Sumantra Ghoshal at the London Business School. It is impossible to describe what he has given me – the time and work with him have been a precious gift. (. . .) He taught me the desire for the sea."[8] Sumantra has enriched my life, and continues to do so, both personally and professionally. I miss him every day, but I am also thankful every day for the things he gave me, and if I had to say which of these things had enriched me the most, it wouldn't take me long before I said, "The desire for the sea."

NOTES

1. Bruch, H./Ghoshal, S. Beware the Busy Manager, in: Harvard Business Review, February 2002, 62–69.

2. Bruch, H./Ghoshal, S. Management is the Art of Doing and Getting Done, in: Business Strategy Review, 2004, Vol. 15, 4–13; (p. 6).

3. Ghoshal, S./Bruch, H. Reclaim Your Job, in: Harvard Business Review, March 2004, 41–45.

4. Ghoshal, S./Bruch, H. Going Beyond Motivation, in: Sloan Management Review, Spring 2003, Vol. 44, No. 3, 51–57.

5. Bruch, H./Ghoshal, S. The Bold, Decisive Manager: Cultivating A Company of Action-Takers, in: Ivey Business Journal, Ivey Management Services, July/August 2004, 1–6.

6. Bruch, H./Ghoshal, S. Unleashing Organizational Energy, in: Sloan Management Review, Fall 2003, Vol. 45, No. 1, 45–51.

7. Bruch, H. and Ghoshal, S. A Bias for Action: How Effective Managers Harness Their Willpower, Achieve Results, and Stop Wasting Time. Boston, MA: Harvard Business School Press, 2004 (p. 178).

8. Bruch, H. Leader's Action. Model Development and Testing, Rainer Hampp Verlag, München and Mering, 2003.

A final word

Henry Mintzberg

Sumantra's passing is one of personal sadness for me, not only or even especially because he was such a thoughtful, and profound scholar. He was a great human being and a cherished friend. I never knew anyone quite like him – no-one who could challenge so directly, so energetically, so playfully. We all have a certain human energy inside of us, but no-one more than Sumantra.

I was asked here to comment on work we did together. I can't do that. Working with Sumantra was never work! It was pleasure. And doing other things with Sumantra was always work: he was so full of ideas about everything that I never stopped learning in his presence.

Shall I write about his leadership program that I joined one year at Insead? He had crazy ideas. Like flying managers all over Europe to each other's companies for a day. What could they learn in a day? So much, in fact, that when we designed our International Masters Program for Practicing Managers, we incorporated such "field studies" in every module. In this world of so many "Why?" people, Sumantra was the quintessential "Why not?" person. Nothing fazed him, least of all failing or being embarrassed. The former was just a learning experience, the latter didn't exist, so far as I could ascertain.

Sumantra was a major reason that drew me to and kept me at Insead. I have always had plenty of people to speak with everywhere I went, but I think it fair to say that with no-one did I exchange ideas, on a personal and professional basis all blended together, in a more stimulating manner. I missed him when he left Insead, and I miss him now. But I cherish what he left behind.

Index